PLAYBOY
COMPLETE GUIDE TO
CASINO
GAMBLING

PLAYBOY COMPLETE GUIDE TO CASINO GAMBLING

BASIL NESTOR

ILLUSTRATIONS BY LEROY NEIMAN

BARNES & NOBLE

NEW YORK

ISBN-13: 978-0-7607-6679-8
ISBN-10: 0-7607-6679-7

Designed by Jeffrey Rutzky

Femlin illustrations by LeRoy Neiman
Additional illustrations by Jeffrey Rutzky

Slot machine images courtesy of the IGT Media Center

Printed and bound in the United States of America

10 9 8 7 6 5 4 3 2 1

This book is dedicated to Miracle.

Acknowledgments

Thanks to my editor Nathaniel Marunas. He is exceptionally talented, and he understands the spirit of gaming. He also has the patience of Job.

Thanks to my editor Betsy Beier for reviewing every single page of this book with me. If there is a comma missing or an apostrophe out of place, she and I jointly bear the responsibility.

Thanks to Jeff Rutzky for his beautiful illustrations and designs. And of course, deep appreciation to Hugh Hefner and LeRoy Neiman.

Thanks to Fay Nestor for her love and support.

Thanks to Freddy Koenig who is still (after all these years) a source of inspiration for me.

Special thanks to Merv Griffin, Ed Fishman, and Hope Murray. They taught me the beauty of strategy and how to win the big games.

Special thanks and kudos to Sharyn Rosart. Her positive energy has influenced me (and my readers) in so many wonderful ways.

CONTENTS

PART TWO Slots and Video Poker

Stuff for Winners

This book is about winning. Do you like to win? How much do you like it? Be honest. You love it, don't you?

Playboy Complete Guide to Casino Gambling is packed with all sorts of valuable tools to help you win at gambling games. This book analyzes every major gambling contest and provides you optimal strategies that are easy to understand and to follow. These strategies are "professional quality," meaning that experts use these techniques when they play for a living.

By the way, you'll be happy to know that you do *not* have to be a math genius to play like an expert. This book does the heavy lifting when it comes to numbers. I do the calculations, then you apply them in your unique situations.

But if you *do* enjoy math, that works, too. I give you the numbers and you can use them for your own calculations.

Winning with Style

Of course, there is more to winning than just collecting a big pile o' chips. Half the fun is doing it with style and livin' large. That is why major sections of this book are dedicated to gambling etiquette, customs, comps, safe procedures for handling large amounts of money, and other gambling knowledge.

The more you know as a casino insider, the easier it is to play the "big game," which is getting the most for every dollar you risk. That means more entertainment, more luxury, more of the perks that make playing such a treat. Indeed, this is the very essence of the Playboy experience, and it reflects a tradition in gaming and entertainment going all the way back to 1966 when the first Playboy Club and Casino opened in "swingin'" London.

These days, the Playboy tradition raves on in Las Vegas at the Palms Casino. The Playboy Club is three levels of awesome fun at the top of the Palms' Fantasy Tower.

Wow!

But before we dash off to the sizzling party (however tempting), let's return to the matters at hand, optimal strategies. We want to beat our honorable opponents (even at the Palms) and wallow in the booty of our winnings.

The old saying is, "You can't win 'em all." This is true. But you certainly can win more. And you can play well. This applies to any game from slots to blackjack, baccarat, craps, video poker, and every other gambling contest.

So how about it? Are you in the mood for winning?

If the answer is yes, then let's get started.

Opposite: 'Round and 'round she goes... The original Playboy Club in London.

PART ONE
Casinos: the Big Picture

CHAPTER 1

The Science of Winning

 Why do coins flip the way they do? Why do cards fall a certain way? What combination of symbols will appear on the reels of a slot machine?

This chapter is about probability and how probability works in gambling.

As I mentioned in the introduction, if you're not mathematically inclined, don't panic. We won't wade through complicated formulas or graphs.

But learning about randomness, probability, and what to expect from dice, cards, and wheels is important because an effective gambling strategy depends on you being able to reasonably predict certain outcomes. It might seem like magic to the uninitiated, but eventually you will be able to just look at a game and in most cases know how to beat it (if it can be beaten). All this before you risk the first dollar. Cool, huh?

Yes, but to get to that ninja-like state of expertise we need to go through probability, and also game theory.

A Brief History of Probability and Game Theory

If you want "just the facts" skip ahead to page 12, but I promise you that this is an interesting story.

Once upon a time (in 1654 to be exact), there was a Parisian gambler named Antoine Gombaud, the Chevalier de Méré, and he had a problem.

The Chevalier was losing his cloak night after night playing dice games. Specifically, he was betting on double sixes.

How many rolls does it take to give a player a *greater* than 50 percent chance of rolling double sixes? The Chevalier calculated twenty-four rolls, but the dice weren't cooperating. Oddly enough, nobody in the history

of the world up to that time had correctly and comprehensively answered this basic question (as it applies to dice, cards, or anything else). For the poor Chevalier, it was a bit like needing directions to Marseilles, and nobody on earth had a map.

So the Chevalier contacted one of his gambling pals, an odd little man named Blaise Pascal.

THE FACT IS...

Slot machines, spacecraft heat shields, global positioning satellites, weather forecasting, life insurance, and a multitude of other things in our modern world are made possible through the science of probability.

Pascal's Math Appeal

It is an understatement to say that Blaise was a genius. He was born in 1623. His father (a mathematician and tax collector) schooled his son at home and intentionally *didn't* teach him math, reportedly because he didn't want to overwork the boy. Indeed, all books about math were removed from the house. Nevertheless, the youngster somehow taught himself geometry, including Euclid's Proposition 32, by analyzing tiles on the floor of his playroom.

The father eventually gave up and allowed math into the curriculum when Blaise was twelve.

At sixteen Blaise presented his first research paper; at seventeen his work on geometry was published; at eighteen he invented a mechanical calculator (similar to adding machines popular in the twentieth century). By the age of twenty-four he was experimenting with vacuums, postulating that a vacuum existed above the earth's atmosphere, and arguing about this conclusion with another great mind of his age, René Descartes. In fact, Descartes once wrote, "He [Pascal] has too much vacuum in his head."

To Do This Correctly, You Need the Right Fermat

Believe it or not, the Chevalier's dice problem had Blaise stumped at first. He wanted to bounce his ideas around, so he asked friends to suggest a collaborator. Eventually, Blaise was put in touch with a lawyer in Toulouse, Pierre de Fermat.

Remember that this was literally the age of the Renaissance man. Nobody specialized in one branch of science or the arts. Everyone studied everything and wrote about everything. Having dozens of areas of expertise was a good thing in those days (where as now it causes people to cluck their tongues and wonder if you are "unfocused").

In his spare time, when not lawyering, Pierre had discovered differential calculus, independently developed analytic geometry, and he had determined many of the basic properties of light and optics. Yup, in his spare time. During the summer of 1654, Blaise and Pierre wrote a series of letters to each other that became the foundation for the science of probability.

Blaise and Pierre on a Roll

I won't cross your eyes with an in-depth explanation of Blaise's solution to the Chevalier's dice problem, but I will tell you that double sixes have a 50.6 percent chance of appearing after *twenty-five rolls* (not twenty-four). And of course, this is true for any double number.

The two mathematicians then went on to solve the "problem of points." Imagine that you're watching a best-of-seven series in baseball. Both teams are evenly matched (as in a coin flip), but one team is up three games to two. What's the probability for each team to win the series? Obviously, Blaise and Pierre didn't use baseball as a model, since it hadn't yet been invented, but they developed methods to determine the answer.

The science of probability had been born. And it was all for the purpose of solving questions about gambling!

The Invention of Game Theory

Fast forward to the middle of the twentieth century. World powers were struggling for domination. Civilization was in danger of being exterminated by a cataclysmic showdown. How should the United States play this global "game"? The answer was provided by John von Neumann. He was a nuclear scientist and Cold War strategist who also happened to be an avid gambler.

THE FACT IS...

In one of his letters to Pierre de Fermat, Blaise Pascal wrote, "M. [Chevalier] de Méré has a good intelligence, but he isn't a geometer and this, as you realize, is a bad fault." In other words, the dude is reasonably smart, but he's no Euclid.

Von Neumann helped save the world for democracy (no kidding) by co-writing a book called *Theory of Games and Economic Behavior.* Essentially, he used poker and other gambling games to develop a system for making decisions in competitive situations. These days his invention is called **game theory**. Diplomats, economists, generals, and presidents study game theory, and they use it to prevent the world from blowing itself up.

But in spite of these high-minded applications, at its heart, game theory is still simply a gambling strategy. It's the best way (indeed, the only way besides dumb luck) that players can win more at blackjack, video poker, craps, roulette, and other gambling games. We use probability to calculate the **odds**, and game theory to make the decisions.

Thank you Blaise Pascal, Pierre de Fermat, and John von Neumann!

Now that you know the history and the science behind gambling strategies, let's look at some practical applications.

Heads vs. Tails

Take a quarter and flip it. Will George Washington be on top when the coin stops moving? There's no way to know. That's why they call it a "toss up." Neither side has an advantage. Neither side can expect to win one decision or the majority of decisions. A lucky streak could favor George, or the streak could go the other way. A streak may never appear, or there may be many streaks. Anything is possible.

Tip

Payoffs in gambling are usually stated as money paid for money risked, so 1:1 would mean that one unit is paid for every unit risked. A double payment would be 2:1, and 6:5 would mean six units paid for five risked. But note that some payoffs are stated differently. For instance, 5 for 1 means they take your bet and pay you 5 (a net profit of only 4).

If the payoff on a heads-or-tails wager is 1:1 (one unit paid for every unit risked), then both players have an equal probability of earning a profit or suffering a loss. Remember that a bet requires two opposing persons or entities.

But let's say the payoff goes higher or lower (1:2, 2:1, etc.). The **true odds** are still 1:1, but the **payoff odds**, or **house odds**, have been shifted. The player who is getting the extra money has a long-term positive advantage. This is called a **positive expectation**. The person who is giving the extra money has a disadvantage, a **negative expectation**.

The difference could be as little as one penny on a dollar wager, but that alone would do it. There is still no way to predict who will win most of the decisions, but one side will inevitably, inexorably, and permanently win more money as the flips continue.

It's a mathematic fact, a rule of the universe. The person wagering the positive side could quit her job and retire if the other guy would just consistently and rapidly keep flipping and betting. This is how casinos earn a profit. They don't have to win all the time. They don't even have to win most of the time; they just need to have a positive expectation. This advantage is commonly known as the **house edge**, and it's usually measured as a percent of the wager.

In the above example a one-penny difference in the payoff ($0.99 paid instead of $1) translates into a 0.5 percent house edge and a payback to the bettor of 99.5 percent. In other words, a typical bettor would lose once, win once, and be down an average one cent after two decisions or one-half cent after one decision.

Of course, it's impossible to lose one-half cent in our flipping contest; a player either wins $0.99 or loses $1. And the flips are random, so there are streaks. A player might win twenty flips out of thirty, or lose thirty of fifty. Anything could happen in a few hundred or a few thousand flips, but over time the side with the negative expectation eventually will lose about one-half percent of all the money that is wagered. It doesn't sound like a lot, but those giant palaces in Las Vegas and Atlantic City were built on similar minuscule advantages.

Does that mean everyone who plays against a casino is "doomed" to lose? Not necessarily. Luck plays a role, and so does strategy. But the positive effects of luck and strategy are diminished as the house edge grows. That's why casinos work hard to entice you with games that have a big house edge.

THE FACT IS...

A slot machine keeps your original wager regardless of whether you win or lose, so a two-credit win is actually only one credit of profit. And a one-credit win is actually a **push** (a tie with no winner or loser). In contrast, a 1:1 payoff in table games means you keep the original bet and win an equal amount.

Inventing a Slot Game: Hot Dollars!

Let's say you're betting on George Washington, but now the wager is $4, and we're flipping dollar bills on a video screen, two bills simultaneously. You get $15 every time that George appears on both bills. Yay! How often does that happen? About one in four flips.

Does that sound like a good bet?

Fifteen dollars is enticing, especially if George hits a streak, but the other bettor (the casino) has a 6.25 percent edge in this contest. Number-wonks like me figure it this way:

$$4 \text{ trials} \times \$4 \text{ per trial} = \$16 \text{ invested}$$
$$\$16 \text{ invested} - \$15 \text{ returned} = \$1 \text{ of casino profit}$$
$$\$1 \div \$16 = 6.25 \text{ percent house edge}$$

Wow! Compare this to the original contest. I increased the payout from $0.99 to $15, and I still managed to balloon the house edge from 0.5 percent to 6.25 percent.

Tip

There are two ways to change the house edge: adjust the payoff or adjust the odds of winning. But remember that both of these figures work together. So a bigger payoff isn't necessarily good if the odds of winning the payoff are considerably worse. For example, your chance of winning $1 million is actually better when playing blackjack than when playing a typical state lottery.

But what if you win once when playing Hot Dollars, lose once, and then win once more? It's hardly a streak, but that particular combination would put you ahead by $27. Should the casino be worried? Nope. You or someone else will continue playing the game. Hot and cold streaks will come and go, but the casino will get about a 6.25 percent return on all the **action** (money wagered) as the number of trials stretches into the thousands and then millions.

Measuring the House Edge

The following table, "Good and Bad Casino Bets," gives examples of the house edge on various popular contests.

Good and Bad Casino Bets

Game	Bet	Casino Advantage
Blackjack	Using basic strategy with counting	−1.00%
Slots: Video Poker	Deuces wild played with optimal strategy	−0.76%
Slots: Video Poker	Jacks-or-Better 9/6 played with optimal strategy	0.46%
Blackjack	Using basic strategy with no counting	0.50%
Baccarat	Banker	1.06%
Craps	Pass line	1.41%
Roulette	European wheel with no surrender	2.70%
Slots: Video Poker	Jacks-or-Better 8/5 played with optimal strategy	2.70%
Roulette	American wheel with no surrender	5.26%
Slots: Reels	Flat-top dollar machine (Las Vegas)	6.00%
Slots: Reels	Flat-top quarter machine (Atlantic City)	8.00%
Slots: Reels	Progressive	10.0%
Slots: Reels	Nickel machine (Las Vegas)	10.0%
Baccarat	Tie	14.4%
Craps	Any seven	16.7%
Keno	Most "big board" bets	30.0%

Blackjack, slots, and keno figures are averages for typical games.

Notice that most games are negative expectation for players. It's possible to shift some contests from negative to positive by using an **optimal strategy** (essentially, using game theory), but doing that requires a bit of effort and patience.

Keep in mind that the typical advantage remains around one percent or less when it's pushed to the player's side. The house gets more when they have the edge, but most games still earn 10 percent or less. There is no money spigot in a casino. In fact, an often-used phrase from late-night television absolutely applies here; casinos earn money with volume, volume, volume! That's also how optimal strategy players do it.

But why would a casino offer games that don't give the house a huge advantage. Why would they play any contests with an edge that could be shifted against them? The answer is somewhat complex and involves public relations and marketing considerations (which we'll cover in Chapter 22), but it boils down to this; most players *don't* use optimal strategy. They either don't know that a strategy exists, or they think it's too much trouble to learn. Some people want to be "spontaneous." They prefer to choose whatever game strikes their fancy. Others rely on hunches and superstitions. Whatever the reasons, the result is that typical players win less and lose more on average than players who use optimal strategies. Casinos get the PR boost of offering "certified games that pay back 100 percent" or "the best blackjack in town." But the games still earn money.

Incredible but true.

The table below shows the average expected loss of a regular player compared to that of an average optimal-strategy player.

Cumulative Effects of the House Edge

Number of Decisions	Average Loss for a Regular Player: 8% casino edge, $5 bets	Average Loss for an Optimal Strategy Player: 1% casino edge, $5 bets
100	$40	$5
200	$80	$10
300	$120	$15
400	$160	$20
500	$200	$25
600	$240	$30

One hour of typical slot machine play is about 500 to 600 decisions.
One hour of table play is usually about 50 to 100 decisions.

Of course, anything can happen. The regular player might smack a big jackpot or catch a winning streak, but consider how much less luck is required for the optimal-strategy player to turn a profit. And it's easy to see which player will last longer if the tables and machines turn cold. Bad luck, good luck, or no luck, the optimal-strategy player will always lose less or win more in the long run.

Deconstructing the "Gambler's Fallacy"

Let's return to our humble quarter and flip it some more. Forget the payouts. Now we're just interested in heads or tails. The coin is "designed" to deliver heads in about half of the contests. Right? Okay, let's flip. It's tails. Will the coin now "force" heads on the next flip to even the score? No, the probability of seeing heads is still only 50 percent.

What if George hits a bad streak and loses five consecutive times. What's the probability that the streak will extend to six? Should you bet for or against our former commander-in-chief?

Some folks would say that George is "due." Is that right? Others would say that the eagle (or state symbol) is "on a rush," and betting the trend is the way to go. Which choice is correct?

They're both wrong. It's still a coin toss. The odds are exactly the same for every flip, always 50/50. History doesn't matter.

There *are* situations when history will affect the future, but in most casino games this is not the case. Here's why:

Deal yourself one card from a deck of cards. You have a 1 in 52 chance of receiving any particular card. Let's say you draw the jack of diamonds. The chance of someone else drawing the jack of diamonds has dropped to zero. In addition, the chance of drawing another diamond has dropped to 12 in 51. In this situation the first decision (history) will affect subsequent decisions (the future).

Now put the card back and shuffle the deck. The chance of drawing the jack of diamonds is back to 1 in 52. The deck doesn't remember your previous draw.

Spin a roulette ball. Let's say red wins seven consecutive times. Is red now less likely to hit? No. The wheel has no memory. Dice are the same. Gambling devices are not sentient. They do not say to themselves, "Hey, it's time to average things out and end the trend." And they cannot think, "Whoa, let's keep this streak alive." They are inanimate and do not respond to history.

So your next spin of the reels is no more or less likely to win than the last spin. Your next hand of video poker is no more or less likely to be a royal flush than the last hand.

Misunderstanding this one truth has cost gamblers more money than all the unfavorable games and poor odds in the entire history of gambling. The error is known as **gambler's fallacy**. Gambling systems based on this fallacy are doomed to fail. Why? Because they don't accurately predict the probability of a win. Bets are increased or decreased for no valid reason.

We'll talk more about faulty gambling systems in Chapter 26, but right now just remember that a pattern of

THE FACT IS...
There's no mathematic law that says both sides in a gambling game must eventually be exactly even at some particular point. On a 50/50 proposition, one side could get lucky and stay ahead practically forever.

wins or losses generally tells you nothing about what will happen on the next decision. The only thing that matters are the actual odds. Nobody is ever "due" for a win or a loss.

But if nobody is ever "due," how can probability work?

Zen You Very Much

Luck in its purest form is absolutely random, entirely capricious, and maddeningly fickle. The very definition of the word indicates that you're not supposed to know when and how it will affect you.

Short-term luck and long-term results are tied together in a mathematic system that often seems to be a Zen-like conundrum. This is how it works. Strictly speaking, none of us can ever reach the long term. It's a mirage always receding in the distance. We live in the present.

In the short term, luck is swinging wildly back and forth like an unlatched door in a hurricane. All sorts of weird and seemingly unlikely things can happen in the short term. But luck must ultimately bend to the odds (because 10 billion games will be played by someone eventually, even if we're not around to play them). So luck becomes predictable in gradual stages as the number of trials increase. Another way to say it is that the overall effect of luck diminishes over time.

Where does the long term begin? Is it ten trials, one hundred trials, one thousand, one million? Nobody can say definitively. The journey there is like a sunrise. Everyone knows the difference between night and day, but the transition from one to the other is gradual and nobody can exactly pinpoint the moment when a definitive switch occurs.

But if you keep playing, you will reach the long term, as surely as the morning, even though you will still be playing in the short term.

That's the Zen of gambling.

If you're scratching your head, take heart. Mathematicians and scientists have to deal with these bizarre yin-yang truths every day (indeed, quantum mechanics vs. relativity was always a problem for Einstein).

In any case, you *will* reach the long term. So you might as well plan for it now.

Essentially

- Game theory is the science of analyzing contests to develop optimal strategies. Players who use optimal strategies can win more at blackjack, video poker, craps, roulette, and other gambling games.

- Positive-expectation games are long-term money earners for the person (or entity) playing the positive side. The opposite side of the game has a negative expectation. People who bet the negative side will be long-term net losers.

- Positive expectation is typically referred to as an edge, and it's measured as a percent of the wager. A larger edge is synonymous with having a bigger advantage. The casino's advantage is called the house edge.

- Optimal strategies can reduce and in some cases eliminate the house edge.

- Having the edge doesn't necessarily mean you'll win the next bet, or even the majority of the next few bets. But it does guarantee that you have an advantage every time you play the game.

- Past results do not affect the current contest except in circumstances when there has been an actual physical change in the game. Inanimate objects are not sentient. They do not remember previous contests.

- Nobody can say definitively when the "long term" begins. Nevertheless, the effects of luck inevitably diminish as the number of trials increase.

CHAPTER 2

Your Bankroll

 True story: Molly and Bill go on a cruise, their first. They like to gamble, and they both hit the casino soon after the boat leaves port. After a couple of hours, Molly takes a break and walks out on the deck. There she finds Bill, sitting in a deck chair staring out at the ocean. He doesn't look happy.

"What's wrong?" Molly asks.

"I can't play anymore," says Bill.

"Why not?"

"I'm broke."

"How can you be broke? You brought $1,000 just for playing, and we've only been cruising for a few hours."

Bill doesn't reply. He just looks up at Molly with a sad smile and shakes his head. Then he lays back on the deck chair. Molly sits down next to him.

This vacation is in trouble.

What happened? Was it bad luck? Perhaps, but Bill's downfall mostly involved bad bankroll management.

What is a **bankroll**? It is money reserved specifically for wagering.

Even extremely good luck is of little value when a bankroll is poorly handled. On the other hand, a bankroll that is well managed can minimize the effects of bad luck, and it can give you a chance to capitalize on good luck (I'll show you how this works in the next few pages). All professional gamblers, and even casinos, use **money management** to safeguard their bankrolls and maximize their profits. You can, too.

Size Matters

The basic premise of money management is simple. You want to bet big enough to maximize profit, but you also want to bet small enough to minimize risk and keep yourself in the game.

For example, let's say we're betting on coin flips. If the coin comes up heads, you win $20. Tails costs you only $10. Who would give you such awesome odds? Nobody probably, but here's the point; that's a sweet bet. You could quit your job and flip a coin for a living with 2:1 payoffs like that.

But what if we take the same odds and make the base bet $10 million. Clearly, that changes things. Even with 2:1 odds in your favor, $10 million is an outrageous risk on a single coin flip. A smidgen of bad luck, just one loss, would leave you super-bankrupt, unless you're a billionaire.

Now imagine that the stakes are only one penny. Even with favorable odds, it will take a while to earn substantial money. In fact, the game is hardly worth playing. But on the bright side, even the worst luck will have little effect when the stakes are so low. So you can play forever.

Here's a real-world example of the same principle:

Imagine that you own a casino. When would be the best time to "quit while you're ahead?" Of course, the answer is never. Usually, a casino has an advantage. The more it plays, the more money it earns.

On the other hand, there is luck to consider. Let's say you build a casino, but you have only $1,000 to cover all the bets on opening night. Yes, you have an advantage, but the average swings of luck could bankrupt you anyway. That's one of the reasons why casinos have **jackpot-reserve** requirements, **table limits**, and a specific range of denominations on their slot machines. Nobody, not even a casino, can risk an unlimited amount of money.

And here's the kicker… You and the casino are playing in the same "mathematic universe." The basic math is the same for everyone, even though the edge in various games may be different (sometimes the casino has an edge, other times it's you who has an advantage). Either way, everyone is playing the balancing game.

So you should use professional money management techniques to maximize profit and minimize risk. After all, your opponent is using them.

THE FACT IS...

It Begins With a Bankroll

Everyone needs a bankroll for gambling. This keeps us from accidentally spending our grocery money. Typically, the bankroll is treated as a simple **stop-loss**, that is, the gambling stops when the money is gone. This approach is fine, but of course, it doesn't solve problems of the sort Bill had on his cruise. Indeed, here are some better and more sophisticated ways to use a bankroll.

Session Bankroll: One popular method used by many professional gamblers is to divide a bankroll into portions that are risked during **sessions**. Typically, these are two to three hours of play, once or twice a day. Some people have sessions that are four or six hours. The particular length doesn't matter, but the important thing is that the session ends immediately if the session bankroll dips to zero. Thus one bad session cannot nuke a whole gambling trip.

Rolling Stop-Loss: A rolling stop-loss is a more sophisticated method of handling a stop-loss. It works better than the typical "stop when you lose it all" rule. It also prevents the disappointment of being significantly up and then losing it all.

A rolling stop-loss can be any amount you choose and there are various ways of calculating it, but the "sliding window" is pretty typical. Let's say you start a session with 100 bets.If you win 50 bets then the window slips forward by that amount.

The original stop-loss was zero (a net loss of 100 bets); the new stop-loss has moved forward to 50. You always exit the session if you lose 100 bets from the highest point of the bankroll. That means you're permanently in a profit zone after a net win of more than 100 bets.

Some people have a rolling stop-loss of three. That's right, three. For example, I have a buddy who is a craps player. He bets one unit per pass and slowly increases if he's winning. His rule is "three lost bets and I'm out of there."

Tip

A stop-loss is effective because it limits action. It's a practical way of managing your money when playing a negative-expectation contest, but it doesn't change the house edge. Wager-for-wager you won't win any more or less on average than someone who never stops playing until the bankroll is exhausted. But if losing is in your future, you'll go there slowly.

Setting a Stop-Loss and a Win-Limit

The downside to having a narrow stop-loss window is that a session can end abruptly. That's not necessarily a bad thing, but it's not automatically good either. Keep in mind that there is a direct relationship between the size of your stop-loss and the total amount you can lose or win. In other words, limiting your losses also limits potential profits because you cannot predict when the dice, cards, or wheels will turn your way.

The ideal stop-loss is one that matches your temperament and betting style.

Ditto for a **win-limit**. This is a win amount that would cause you to exit a session. Many people use a static win-limit of double the **buy in** or double the session bankroll. Some people have a rolling win-limit.

Like a stop-loss, a win-limit doesn't change the house edge, but it does lock up profits for a particular session. After all, you must leave the casino at *some* point. You might as well leave when you're up.

Bet Size and Bankroll Size

How much should you bet? And how big should your bankroll be in relation to the size of your bets?

Professional gamblers use a system called the Kelly Criterion to determine optimum bet size and/or bankroll size. The way it works is that a player arbitrarily chooses either a bankroll amount or a bet size, and the Kelly formula produces the optimum size of the other variable. The resulting bet-to-bankroll ratio gives the player the greatest probability of winning and the lowest probability of losing everything.

Unfortunately, Kelly tells us to bet zero dollars when the casino has an advantage. That doesn't help much when we're playing slots. There's a calculation similar to Kelly that estimates **risk of ruin** (the probability that your bankroll will dip to zero), but I won't cross your eyes with either of these formulas.

Instead, I'll just tell you that a bankroll for a two-to-three-hour session should be at least 250 times the size of your average bet when you're playing penny and nickel slots. This doesn't necessarily mean you should buy in for that amount, but having that money available will keep you playing for up to three hours in most circumstances, sometimes longer.

If you're playing quarters, then your session bankroll should be at least 200 times the size of your average bet. When playing dollar slots and above, 150 bets should keep you going up to three hours.

Note that the number of bets needed for your session bankroll goes down as the denomination increases. That's because quarter slots are generally **looser** (have a higher overall **payback**) than penny and nickel slots, dollars are looser than quarters, and so forth. I'll tell you more about slot paybacks in Chapter 4.

Video poker machines don't get looser at higher denominations (though sometimes the pay tables do get better). In any case, all denominations of video poker require at least 150 bets for a three-hour session bankroll.

You should have at least 50 bets for table games such as blackjack and baccarat.

Session Bankroll

Game	Decisions per Hour	Recommended Minimum Session Bankroll
Penny Slots	500–600	250 bets
Nickel Slots	500–600	250 bets
Quarter Slots	500–600	200 bets
Dollar Slots	500–600	150 bets
Five-Dollar Slots	500–600	150 bets
Video Poker	400	150 bets
Table Games	50–100	50 bets

Bankroll amounts in this table are calculated for three-hour sessions.

Why can a table-game bankroll be smaller? First, let's remember that table-game bets are usually bigger in actual dollars. So the total amount required for a blackjack game may be more than the amount for a video poker game, even when a blackjack bankroll contains fewer bets.

On a *per bet basis*, table games require smaller bankrolls because they tend to have lower **volatility** compared to slots and video poker. In other words, there are fewer extreme swings between winning and losing. Most table bets pay 1:1, or sometimes 3:2. Roulette's top payout is 35:1. In contrast, slot games have jackpots that pay

1,000:1, 10,000:1, and even more. The money for those big jackpots has to come from somewhere. Games with big payoffs tend to have fewer small wins and longer stretches of losing.

When calculating the size of your bankroll, also keep in mind that an average bet is not necessarily the lowest bet. For example, if you're betting max credits on a $0.25 video poker machine, and you're playing single hands, then each bet is $1.25. Multiply that by 150, and your session bankroll should be at least $187. But if you're playing ten hands per game, then each bet is $12.50, and the session bankroll should be at least $1,875. Similar caveats apply if you're covering a lot of numbers in roulette and craps, or playing two or three spots in blackjack.

If all this math makes your head spin, don't fret. Just take your base bet and tack two zeros on the end. Double that amount. That's 200 bets. You'll rarely go wrong with a session bankroll of 200 bets for slots, or 50 bets for table games.

What if...

What if you can afford only 100 bets for slots, or 25 bets for table games? Ideally, you should lower the amount of your base bet to fit the size of your session bankroll. If you don't want to do that, then just accept the fact that you may go bust in an hour or less, unless you hit a lucky streak.

What if you can afford 250 bets for one session, but not 1,000 bets for four sessions (or whatever you need for the length of your trip)? Happily, you *will* win sometimes, especially if you use optimal strategy and a rolling stop-loss. Let's say you begin with a trip bankroll of 750 bets. You may find that it's enough to cover four or even five sessions. But if you want to be sure that you can play the entire time, then play fewer sessions, or lower the amount of your base bet.

Tip

Some people use numbered envelopes to manage their bankroll. They put the equivalent of one session bankroll in each envelope, and take only that envelope to the casino. The net win (or loss) goes back into the envelope, and the money stays there until the end of the gambling trip.

What if you want to play longer than two to three hours? That's okay, but take a break and begin a new session (with a new bankroll) when you return.

What happens if your session bankrolls consistently disappear too quickly? Stop playing, and start thinking about your game. You're either not using optimal strategy correctly, or you're not funding the bankrolls correctly. Think things through before you take more money from your main bankroll to fund another session. We'll talk more about your main bankroll in the next section.

What if you hit a big jackpot? What do you do with the windfall? Same advice as above. Stop playing, and start thinking about your game. Set aside some of the money (for spending and such), and use the balance to fund your main bankroll. Now you can increase the size of your bets and shoot for bigger wins. However, before you bet bigger, you've got to think about the vig.

What is the Vig?

Vig is short for **vigorish**. It's a fee that a casino charges for providing betting services (the venue, machines, drinks, and so forth), and it's synonymous with the house edge. The vig for most gambling games is subtracted from the payback. For example, slots pay back only a portion of the money put into them. But in some games, such as craps and baccarat, the vig is a separate fee.

Either way, the vig eats into your bankroll, unless your luck is consistently above average, or you eliminate the house edge.

If you're playing against a vig, then you *are* depending on luck to some degree, and nobody has good luck forever. The amounts I suggest for session bankrolls are meant to keep you comfortably ahead of the vig, and to give you a good chance to hit some wins. But when it comes time to calculate the size of your main bankroll, then you must accept the fact that you usually will be putting money in and rarely pulling money out, unless you erase the vig with optimal strategy.

Main Bankroll

You should have a main bankroll of at least 3,000 bets to play video poker indefinitely with no vig. And you'll need at least 300 bets to play table games indefinitely with no vig. If you're playing against a vig, then you'll need to replenish your main bankroll at approximately the following rates:

Penny and nickel slots ....10 percent of your action
Quarter slots...8 percent of your action
Dollar slots and above ....5 percent percent of your action
Video poker and table games
    (without optimal strategy)........................5 percent of your action
Video poker and table games
    (with optimal strategy) ....1 percent or less of your action

So let's say you have a main bankroll of 3,000 bets, and you're playing nickel slots. Typically, you'll wager about 500 bets per hour or 3,000 bets every six hours. You'll win some; you'll lose some. But overall, you'll be cycling through your main bankroll about once every six hours (even if you don't physically risk all the money). Usually, you'll need to recapitalize your main bankroll by about 10 percent of 3,000, or 300 bets, for every six hours that you play.

On the other hand, if you're playing video poker or table games with optimal strategy, you'll need to recapitalize your main bankroll by only 1 percent per cycle, or maybe not at all.

And of course, all these figures are averages. You'll see a lot of variance in the short run. If you hit a lucky streak, or the cards go dead, you might think the edge isn't working at all, or that the rules of the universe have ceased to function. But rest assured, everything is still working. When you're gambling, it's easy to see only the "tallest trees," and miss the larger forest.

THE FACT IS...

Slots and video poker require bigger bankrolls mostly because of the volatility of the games. Large jackpots tend to create long stretches when you can be losing. In contrast, a game such as blackjack pays 3:2 at most, so losing streaks tend to be shorter, thus requiring fewer bets in the bankroll.

The Fuzz

An edge that shrinks to less than 0.5 percent isn't much of an edge anymore. I call it "the fuzz." By that point it is nearly a coin flip. Yes, the edge is still working, but you usually won't see its effect in a typical session. At 0.25 percent or 0.1 percent it takes thousands of trials for the edge to appear, and a run of luck can push the inevitable imbalance even farther into the future.

On the other hand, 1 or 2 percent is definitely not in the fuzz range. And a combination of small advantages (or disadvantages) that are individually worth 0.1 percent or 0.2 percent can add up to numbers that push well out of the fuzz.

This concept is important because some people doubt the importance of edge calculations when they get into the tenths of a percent, and this sometimes leads to a general disregard for the edge. It's kind of like giving an inch and then surrendering a mile. First they give away one-half percent, then a whole percent, then 2 percent, and pretty soon they're playing keno.

So remember that the fuzz is only good for about one-half percent at best.

Why Bother?

From time to time you may tempted to say, "Why should I hassle with all these calculations? Main bankroll, session bankroll, rolling stop-loss, edge calculations… Why not just go down to the ATM, get $300, and go play? The worst that can happen is I lose $300. Right?"

Well, yes. But without money management the $300 might be gone in twenty minutes. And then you'll be tempted to go back to the ATM. Bad scene.

In contrast, a good bankroll strategy gives you something that is valued in the gambling world. You're financed. You're set. You get to play as much as you want, for as long as you want.

The only limits are the limits that you impose upon yourself. And if you run out of money in a session, it's because you deliberately played a long shot. You were in control. No accidents. No regrets. No pile of ATM or credit-card slips as a silent testament to a wild night gone awry.

Bill's Bankroll Adjustment

Bill accidentally vaporized his bankroll because he bet too big. He played the wrong games and made some bad bets. He didn't divide his bankroll into sessions, and he didn't use a rolling stop-loss. Fortunately, Molly was a better gambler. She saved the vacation.

First, she helped Bill rework their vacation budget, and they shifted some money from other incidentals to his "new bankroll." Then she insisted that he follow her rules for bankroll management. They both stopped playing for a day. He cooled off, and was in a more disciplined frame of mind when they returned to the casino. By the end of the trip, Bill had whacked a few big wins and his net losses were nearly erased.

Another important thing Molly did was that she convinced Bill to give up the notion that he was "due" for a big win to cancel out his big loss. Molly explained that wins come when they come.

There's no way to predict when a big win will arrive. Money management won't make a windfall come sooner. It doesn't change the odds or beat the vig. It simply keeps you in the game. After that, the luck is up to you.

Dangerous Gambling

While we're on the subject of bankrolls and staying in the game, this is a good place to discuss mental mistakes. Here are some things that will bust your bankroll faster than the worst house odds.

Going "On Tilt"

It's easy to slip into a bad mood or get tired without realizing it, especially in the heat of a game. Pros use the term **on tilt** to describe a mood that adversely affects judgment. Strategy is meaningless without good judgment. Going on tilt is a fast way to bust a bankroll.

You should stop playing when you're tired. Stop when you're hungry. Stop when you're frustrated. Stop if you get the feeling that you "can't win."

Games should be fun. If you're not having fun, go do something else.

Drinking Alcohol While Gambling

Drinks are "free" in many casinos when playing at the tables and machines. Gee, aren't those casino guys nice? Toast them with a complimentary coffee or a soda, and stay away from the alcohol. Inebriating drinks cloud a player's judgment and inevitably earn the casino many times more than the value of the beverage. Don't surrender that edge. Stick to your strategy, win some money, and buy your drink later.

Going Beyond Your Limits

We've already talked about setting bankroll limits. The important thing to remember here is that limits are established in advance when your mind is clear precisely because casinos can be confusing. You will be constantly tempted to bet more, play more, or wager in ways that are unwise. Never give in to the temptation. Always follow your optimal stop-loss and win-limit strategies.

And of course, never play with **scared money**. If you can't comfortably afford the loss, then don't make the bet.

Playing for Comps

Fifteen-dollar bets will get you free drinks and friendly service in a typical casino. Twenty-five dollar bets usually will result in a discounted room. One hundred dollar bets usually garner free meals and discounted or free rooms. By the time you're handling multiple black chips ($100 units) gregarious casino hosts in stylish suits will be treating you as a respected and dear friend. You'll be addressed warmly by your last initial, "Mr. P, it's great to see you again!"

Yes, **comps** (complimentary rewards and incentives) are a nice perk if you were already planning to risk forty or fifty Ben Franklins, but it's financially foolish to bet more money for the sole purpose of getting more comps.

Tip

The value of a comp is typically one-third or less of your expected loss. Don't get caught up in a ridiculous system of faux status. You should establish betting levels and session lengths that suit your bankroll, and treat comps like optional icing on the cake.

Taking the Game Personally

The purpose of the game is to generate excitement. Shout, cheer, cry if you must, but remember it's just a game. Revel in your winnings, lament your losses, but don't take either situation personally. Streaks happen. Luck will sometimes kiss you sweetly, and other nights it will slap you down with a vengeance. Remember, it's not about you.

Of course, there is one big exception to this last rule. If you play poorly and cost yourself money as a result, then you should take it personally! Luck is one thing; bad play is something entirely different. Learn from each mistake and resolve to never do that again.

The Big Game

When you're gambling in a casino, it's a good idea to think *beyond* the immediate game (slots, blackjack, or whatever), and look at the bigger contest. Who is playing whom, and for what?

The casino industry is very much like the movie business, theme parks, cruising, and other leisure industries; it's all about selling entertainment. Casino managers measure everything by long-term profit.

They don't care very much about winning or losing individual decisions. In fact, they absolutely love to give away huge jackpots and big piles of cash. And they certainly don't want to "take all your money." That would be horrible because it would make you unhappy, and you might not come back next week, next month, or next year.

Casino managers would prefer that you visit frequently and play for a while, win some, and lose a bit more than you win. Meanwhile, you're eating in the restaurants, seeing the

shows, and generally enjoying the casino's party atmosphere. Of course, the idea of smacking a big win never entirely leaves your mind, so you find yourself drifting back to the machines and tables. And if you don't hit big this trip, maybe next time. See? You're already planning another visit.

That is the game the casinos are playing. What is your game?

THE FACT IS...

The gaming industry generates more revenue than the combined income from movies, the music business, theme parks, and organized sports: over $70 billion every year. And that's gaming only. The figure doesn't include income from restaurants, shows, shops, and other peripheral businesses.

Inevitably, someone *will pay* for the casino's dealers, cards, chips, electricity, carpet, exploding volcano, and so forth. But that someone doesn't have to be you.

Your game should be to get the most for the least. It's like using a frequent flyer coupon, or a two-for-one ticket to the movies. Maybe you'll pay something. Maybe you'll pay nothing, or you might even earn a profit. But one way or another, you should *never* pay full price. You should get the goodies for less, or for free. Let the other guy pay your bills. He's the one who is in too much of a hurry to learn the right strategies. Let him pay for his convenience...and your entertainment.

If you do that, then he's happy, you're happy, and the casino is happy. Everyone wins. That's the big game.

Essentially

- Everyone needs a bankroll for gambling. A bankroll is money that is specifically designated for wagering, and nothing else.

- One popular bankroll strategy used by professional gamblers is to divide a bankroll into portions that are risked during sessions. Typically, a session is two to three hours of play, once or twice a day. Whatever the length, the session ends immediately if the session bankroll dips to zero.

- A rolling stop-loss is a practical way of managing your money to prevent a big loss after a big win. The system works by limiting action and bankroll volatility, but it doesn't change the edge.

- There are various ways to calculate the optimal size of a session bankroll, but a good shortcut is to always begin a session with at least 200 bets for slots or 50 bets for table games.

- You should have a main bankroll of 3,000 bets or more to play video poker indefinitely with no vig. And you'll need at least 300 bets to play table games indefinitely with no vig.

- You shouldn't gamble when you're tired, hungry, or in a bad mood. It's best to avoid alcohol when playing. Stick to your budget, and don't play for comps.

PART TWO
Slots and Video Poker

CHAPTER 3

Simply Slots

 Slot games have an aura of simplicity. Slide a few dollars into the machine, pull the handle or push a button, reels spin, music plays, and you win or lose. Wheeee! The whole process takes just a few seconds.

But this simplicity is only a façade. A typical slot machine has billions of variables, and its internal functions are infinitely more complex than poker, blackjack, craps, or any other supposedly "complicated" casino contest. Most of this internal complexity is designed to create random results and prevent you from influencing the game, but happily, not everything is beyond your control. Your choices *can* significantly affect the outcome of the contest.

In other words, there *are* slot strategies that work, and you don't need to be a rocket scientist to use them. I'll explain more about that as we go along, but first let's briefly review basic slot machine functions. If you've spent much time in a casino, then the next few paragraphs may be old news, but just in case…

Buttons, Paylines, and Jackpots

When you look past the flashing lights, bells, music, video screens, and other modern paraphernalia, the basic slot game (on the outside) is pretty much the same today as it was a century ago. A typical machine has three or more reels. Each reel has sections that are called **stops**, and every stop is covered with a symbol. It might be cherries, a pot of gold, a Sizzling 7, or something else (sometimes just a blank space). A player puts money into the machine, pulls a handle or pushes a button, and the reels spin. A few seconds later the spinning stops; the combination of symbols displayed on the reels directly under the **payline** determines how much (if anything) the player has won.

The prizes associated with various reel combinations are displayed on a **pay table** that is on a panel above and/or below the reels. Credits are scored on a meter, and the machine dispenses printed vouchers that can be cashed or played in other games (older slots use coins and drop their jackpots into a tray at the bottom of the machine).

Standard Slot Machine

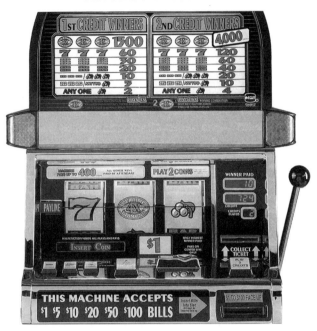

Slot games have different designs, but they all have layouts similar to this. Note the pay table on the upper portion of the machine.

Some slots still come with an old-fashioned handle. Pulling it will deliver a wonderfully visceral drag that approximates some designer's idea of how moving gears should feel, but it's just an illusion. The handle performs the same function as the **Spin** button; it activates a separate mechanism that makes the game go.

The **Service** button is used to summon a slot attendant (when the machine malfunctions). **Cash Out** is used to cash out.

Bet One wagers credits in single increments. **Bet Max** wagers multiple credits (whatever the machine allows as maximum per spin). Bet Max also activates the spin mechanism.

THE FACT IS...

Have you ever wondered why some slots have "bar" symbols on the reels? They're a holdover from the early twentieth century when slot machines delivered chewing gum in their jackpots. Look at an old-style pad of Bazooka bubble gum, and you'll see the resemblance.

There's a slot for your **players club** card (more on players clubs in Chapter 22), and there's usually a comfy seat where the casino would like you to settle for the next few hours. But don't get too comfortable; the strategies in this book soon will have you moving to a better machine.

Game Types

Slot machines come in various types with many sub-classifications. These distinctions are important because in most cases they indicate how a game should be played for maximum return. I'm going to list them briefly here, and then cover them later in detail.

The casino-industry term "slots" includes **reel-spinners** (often called traditional reels) and video slots. The latter is subdivided into video reels, video poker, video keno, and other video-machine games.

Contests that pay a fixed amount for the top prize are known as **flat-top** or **non-progressive** machines. In contrast, **progressive** games have a top jackpot that grows incrementally each time the game is played.

Many reel games these days have multiple paylines, but you can still find some that have single paylines. Video poker games come in single-hand and multiple-hand versions.

The latest whiz-bang slots have a basic game and a bonus game. One or more of the reel combinations in the basic game will bounce you into a bonus level, and you get to choose something, spin something, and so on.

And finally, some video machines contain multiple games. Youcan play five different slot games, six different video poker games, blackjack, or keno at one terminal.

Yes, it's a breathtaking cornucopia of options and types. And it's even more amazing when you consider how similar these machines are on the inside.

The Reel Story of Slot Machines

Once upon a time the handle on the side of a slot machine actually made the game go. The reels actually decided the outcome of the contest. A player could determine the probability of winning by simply counting the symbols on the reels and doing some basic multiplication.

It was all very straightforward. Unfortunately, it was also very susceptible to fraud. A player could jiggle the handle and control the spin of the reels. Slot manufacturers temporarily solved this problem by separating the handle from the spin mechanism, but thieves simply learned to open the machines and set the reels manually. Other methods of cheating involved drilling holes into a machine to fool it into thinking coins had been deposited, wedging objects into the chute under the coin hopper, or spraying chemicals into the coin slot.

And as the twentieth century progressed, another problem developed. Players wanted big jackpots, but big jackpots required longer odds (fewer possibilities of winning the top prize) and that meant more reel stops. Bigger reels needed bigger machines, and that created even more opportunities for cheating. Physical reels were becoming a major liability. Something had to change.

The fundamental shift occurred on May 15, 1984, when Inge Telnaes (a Norwegian scientist working for Bally) received U.S. Patent 4,448,419 for an "Electronic Gaming Device Utilizing a Random Number Generator for Selecting the Reel Stop Positions." It was a simple yet stunning leap; put the game on a computer chip. Reel size was no longer an issue. Cheaters setting reels was no longer a problem. Mega-jackpots were possible, and the modern era of slot games had arrived.

RNG: The Heart of the Machine

You want to beat a slot machine in the twenty-first century? Then you need to know how a **random number generator** (RNG) works. All slot strategy is based on evaluating these tricky little mechanisms that are at the heart of every modern slot.

By the way, for you tech-heads out there, RNG (the function) and EPROM (the chip) are synonymous in this book.

Zero to a Billion

An RNG is a computer chip that randomly selects numbers in a particular range, usually zero to a few billion. Each number is divided using a predetermined formula, and the remainder (the amount left after the division) corresponds to a particular stop on one of the machine's reels.

Yeow! Does that sound complicated? Think of it this way. When you put money in the slot and push the spin button, the number that happens to be on the RNG at that particular moment is delivered to a mechanism that controls the reels. The reels spin and give the impression that the contest has yet to be decided, but in fact it's all over. The symbols that appear simply reflect the numbers selected by the RNG. The handle, buttons, and everything else are just for show.

Not very romantic, huh?

Yes, but an RNG can do amazing things that were never possible with the old reels. Bigger jackpots are just one example. Bonus games are another. And while an RNG is random, it's also designed to operate within certain parameters. This is good news for players who use strategy because manufacturers build machines with different *predictable* rates of return. Casinos use these **loose** and **tight** games in complex placement strategies to maximize profits, and you can take advantage of those strategies to win more money. It's like buying a cheap airline seat that was sold as a promotion. Meanwhile, the poor schmuck next to you is paying full price.

The Game Inside the Game

An RNG never stops working. The game is played internally even when the machine is idle. Every millisecond a new number is selected, one after another, forever. That means thousands of losing combinations and hundreds of jackpots are generated in the time it takes you to sit down and push a bill into the machine. Pause for a sneeze or a yawn, and countless decisions will disappear forever into the electronic ether.

Tip

Loose slots pay back more on average than tight slots, but remember that short-term payback tends to be more volatile than long-term payback. So a game may at first appear to be tight, but may actually be loose (and vice versa). For more on volatility, see page 47.

Hesitate for one-tenth of a second, and you will receive an entirely different game.

This is a very good thing because you never have to worry about missing a jackpot. Just scratch your ear and you've missed a dozen. Thus *the results of physical play are not sequential.* They're random. That means a slot machine is never "due" for a hit, and it's never "getting ready to pay off."

In fact, the RNG isn't even aware that money is involved in the contest. RNG operations are entirely indifferent to the number of credits in play or the size of the payoffs. They're also not affected by the presence of a slot club card. The chip is simply oblivious. Nothing you legally can do to a machine will affect the function of an RNG.

RNGs and the Law

Speaking of legal, every RNG in every slot machine is thoroughly tested and licensed in all *regulated* North American gambling jurisdictions. State laws require that every RNG perform to a certain standard and produce a minimum (or greater) frequency of wins over time. Nevada law requires slots to pay back a minimum of 75 percent of the money that cycles through the machine. New Jersey requires a minimum 83 percent payback. Most states (and Canada) are at least as tough as Nevada or tougher. And these regulations are vigorously enforced. For example, every RNG in Atlantic City is individually certified and sealed by the New Jersey Division of Gaming Enforcement. A casino cannot alter or replace an RNG except with the following procedure:

- The casino makes an application to the DGE.

- The machine is opened under DGE supervision.

- The DGE breaks the processor's seal and supervises the program/chip replacement.

- The DGE creates a new seal, and re-certifies the machine.

New Jersey Division of Gaming Enforcement maintains a database of every slot machine in the state. The specific payback percentage of every machine is part of that database. Every RNG is numbered and tracked.

Other states have similar regulations and databases. In Nevada a casino can change an RNG without notifying the state, but it can use only state-approved chips, and the switch must include a paper trail. Inspectors randomly check machines for compliance.

Why should all this matter to you? Because if you find a loose machine tomorrow, it will probably still be loose next month or next year. And you can track that machine by number even if it's moved from one end of the casino to the other. Ditto for avoiding tight machines.

We'll get into the nitty-gritty of finding and tracking loose machines in the next chapter, but first let's take a closer look at…

THE FACT IS...

The average payback of a slot machine in Atlantic City is about 92 percent. The average payback of a slot machine on the Las Vegas Strip is about 93 percent. The loosest slots in the world can usually be found in North Las Vegas. Machines there typically pay back about 96 percent.

What Makes This Game Different?

It's easy to get caught up in the theme of a slot game (Munsters, Tabasco, Three Stooges, or whatever). Watching Luke Skywalker slay Darth Vadar in the Star Wars game is very entertaining. But frankly, the battle on the RNG is more important to your bankroll than the battle on the video screen.

The RNG plays a game according to a particular set of rules. Those rules are what we study to develop a strategy for beating the game. It takes some practice, but once you become familiar with the various rules of the game, you can pretty much look at a machine and immediately know your chances of beating it, and how it will pay over time.

In the next few pages we'll review those rules, and then I'll tell you how they affect strategy.

The first step is to identify the denomination of base units/credits that a game accepts. Pennies, nickels, quarters, dollars, and five-dollars are most common, though some machines use other units (such as half-dollars).

Here are some other important things to notice.

Reels and Paylines

Reel-spinners are typically three-reel games with one or more paylines. Each payline requires a wager for the line to be active, so playing three lines is essentially the same as playing three games simultaneously (see the illustration below). Games with one, three, five, and nine paylines are common, and a game with multiple paylines can be played with fewer lines than the maximum.

Video reels typically have four or more virtual reels with multiple paylines, but aside from the ability to display animation and bonus games, the practical operation of video slots is identical to reel-spinners.

Multiple Paylines

Each payline requires a separate bet. The game can be played with bets on fewer than all the lines.

Buy-a-Pay, Multipliers, and Progressives

One conceptual variation of multiple paylines is the **buy-a-pay** game. In this situation you're not purchasing additional paylines, but you're buying the opportunity to hit additional winning combinations. In other words, three bars are worth 50 credits and three sevens are worth nothing if you wager one dollar, but two dollars will "activate" the sevens, and they'll be worth 100 credits if they hit.

Yet another variation is a **bonus multiplier**. It's one of those industry terms that often confuses more than it explains. A standard **multiplier** game pays exact multiples of whatever amount is wagered. Smack the top prize with one credit and you win 500 credits. Whack it with two credits and you win 1,000 credits. It's simple multiplication. A bonus multiplier adds a bonus to the top prize when a player wagers maximum credits.

Buy-a-pay and bonus multipliers are taken to an extreme with progressive machines. A portion of every dollar you wager builds the top prize, and it's often worth millions. The pay table has a meter showing the current value of the big jackpot, and there's usually another large display meter above the machine. A player must wager the maximum per spin to be eligible for the top prize. Imagine the horror of playing one credit, hitting the magic combination, and missing a multi-million-dollar payoff. Sadly, this happens from time to time.

Hit Frequency and Volatility

Hit frequency is a measure of how often a machine pays out. Volatility measures the relative value of those payouts over time. A machine with high volatility will hold a lot for a while, and then pay out a lot very quickly (or vice versa). A low-volatility game will return its payback percentage in less time. High hit frequency and high volatility are not necessarily mutually exclusive, but they do tend to occupy opposite ends of the spectrum.

Bonus Games, Wild Pay, and Other Gimmicks

Every game has a gimmick, something to separate it from the crowd. A typical gimmick is one or more bonus levels. A player hits a particular reel combination and the game goes into bonus

Tip

On March 14, 2001, Kirk Tolman put two coins into a Megabucks slot machine. He pushed the button. The Megabucks symbols lined up and delivered a $10,000 jackpot. Nice, but Tolman missed the top jackpot of $7.9 million because he didn't play a third coin. Lesson: If you're going to play a progressive machine, always go for the top payoff.

mode. It can be as simple as a spinning wheel for Wheel of Fortune, or as complex as a round of Yahtzee.

Another common gimmick is wild symbols that double, triple, quintuple, or otherwise increase the payout of any reel combination. Wild symbols also sometimes **nudge**; they hit just above or below the payline, and then they click into position. Hurrah! But of course, this cliffhanger is just for show. The winning combination was predetermined when you pressed the button.

Some machines have wild symbols that make them go bonkers; the game spins and hits many times without requiring extra credits.

Video Poker, Video Blackjack, and Video Keno

Strictly speaking, video poker, video blackjack, and video keno are slot games. But from a strategic point of view, video poker and video blackjack are virtual card games that have the same odds and strategies as real card games. We cover video poker in Chapter 5, and blackjack in Chapters 7–9.

Video keno odds are identical to "big board" keno odds. We cover keno in Chapter 18.

The important thing to remember here is that video poker, video blackjack, and video keno have an edge that can be calculated precisely because we know the payback and the exact odds of winning. For example, a standard deck (video or actual) has exactly fifty-two cards, and a keno game has exactly eighty spots.

In contrast, the exact odds on reel-spinners and video reels are *not* standard. It is possible to map the stops on virtual reels (the theoretical reels spinning in an RNG), but there are so many variations and so many thousands of different slot games, you'd need an encyclopedia to record all of them.

Imagine walking into a typical casino, with your encyclopedia set on a cart, confronted with a few

THE FACT IS...

Hit frequency for slot machines is typically between 10 and 50 percent. Reel-spinners usually hit less often than video slots, but it depends on the game and the number of lines in play. A game that hits frequently is not necessarily loose, especially if most wins are less than the value of the wager.

thousands machines. There is no practical way for a typical slot player to know the exact odds of winning every reel game.

But happily, there is an effective shortcut, a strategy to help you find loose machines.

I'll tell you about that in the next chapter.

Essentially

- An RNG (random number generator) is at the heart of all modern slot machines. These include traditional reels, video reels, video poker machines, video blackjack, and video keno.

- Every RNG in every slot machine is tested and licensed in all regulated gambling jurisdictions in North America. Laws require that slot machines perform to a particular standard and have a minimum payback.

- An RNG never stops working. The game is played internally even when the machine is idle. A new number is selected every millisecond, one after another, forever.

- RNG operations are not affected by the number of credits in play or the size of the payoffs. They're also unaffected by the presence of a slot club card, or any other outside influence.

- An RNG is random in the short-term, but consistent over time. This gives a slot machine a particular long-term character. Loose machines are more generous than tight machines.

- An RNG plays a game according to a particular set of rules. Those rules are what we study to develop a strategy for beating the game.

CHAPTER 4

How to Find Loose Slots

 Playing a slot machine is like starring in your own television show. Each spin is a five-second episode. There's tension, excitement, resolution, a few laughs, some tears, plenty of cliffhangers, and then the episode ends. What will happen next? The machine is just one big never-ending "must-see" promotion until you start the next game. Of course, winning is the obvious goal, but anticipation keeps people coming back. Everyone loves that delicious feeling when the show is starting and anything can happen. That's why players sit and spin for hours. That's also why so many of the newest slots are based on TV shows and movies. In fact, all modern slots have a theme and "story" that plays out in the sequence of wins and losses.

You should know this for two reasons. First, all stories are not alike (and I don't mean Wheel of Fortune is different from Hollywood Squares). Rather, a particular game has a unique character, and it will produce wins with frequencies and in amounts different from other games. Your enjoyment of the contest will be enhanced when you choose a game with payouts that fit your taste.

Second, a game that you choose for enjoyment may not necessarily be the easiest game to beat. For example, Game A is fun and it has payouts to fit your taste. But Game B pays back more over time. You have a decision. Should you play the game that is more fun, or the one that gives you a better shot at finishing with a net win? Should you choose the fun of entertainment or the fun of profit?

This question frequently arises in all types of gambling, but it's particularly common for slots. Sometimes the decision is easy, but other times it requires the wisdom of Solomon. Keep this mind as we explore strategies for finding loose games.

Paying the Most
from Coast to Coast

A nickel machine requires the same amount of electricity, maintenance, and floor space as a machine that takes dollars. Even though nickel games are designed to attract players with smaller budgets, the machines still must earn a profit. Lower-denomination games do this by being tighter than higher-denomination games.

Thus nickel slots typically pay back less than quarter slots. Quarters are tighter than dollars. Dollars are tighter than five-dollar games, and so on (see the chart below). There are exceptions to this rule, but not many.

Typical Slot Machine Payouts (by percent)

Jurisdiction	5¢	25¢	50¢	$1	$5
Atlantic City	89.7	91.8	91.8	92.3	94.1
Connecticut	89.2	90.7	90.7	92.2	94.1
Las Vegas Strip	89.7	92.0	NA	94.5	95.0
Las Vegas Downtown	90.9	94.6	NA	95.7	95.0
North Las Vegas	92.9	96.3	NA	97.2	96.0
Mississippi North River	90.7	92.8	93.3	95.5	96.3
Mississippi Coast	92.0	94.1	95.0	95.1	96.0
Reno	91.8	93.8	NA	95.9	96.8

The above figures are percent payback averages from totals reported in the summer of 2005. They include slots and video poker. Notice that machines are generally looser at higher denominations.

Size Matters

Big jackpots are created by reducing the size or frequency of smaller payoffs, so the tightest machines are usually million-dollar progressives. Similar math applies to flat-top machines with large top jackpots. Generally, your chance of hitting the big prize goes up when the size of that prize goes down, and mid-size jackpots become easier to hit, too.

Location, Location, Location

The title of this section isn't a repeat of the old real estate maxim. Location actually applies in three different ways.

First, slots are looser in some jurisdictions. For example, slots are typically 2 to 4 percent looser in Las Vegas than in Atlantic City.

Slots are tighter on the Las Vegas Strip than in downtown Las Vegas. Slots in Reno are generally looser than those in Connecticut. Competition and the character of the local market cause these variances. When you consider that the entire population of the northeast U.S. is served by slightly more than one dozen "local" casinos, and that all of them could fit into a couple miles of the Las Vegas Strip with room left over, it's easy to understand why Las Vegas slots are loose.

Second, slots tend to be tighter at upscale properties, particularly those frequented by tourists. Games are generally looser when a property is older or when it caters to a local crowd. Thus Bellagio is generally tighter than Sam's Town in Las Vegas.

Third, a game's placement in the casino is a big indicator of how it will play. In fact, it's such a big indicator that the information deserves its own section.

Evaluating the Casino Layout

Slot machines are not positioned willy-nilly in a casino. There's a definite structure, and a thought process that governs their arrangement. In the old days loose machines were near entrances, and the sound of falling coins would lure players in. Since those machines were occupied, new players would move further into the casino and play tighter machines. It was an effective strategy for its time, but more sophisticated and improved placement strategies have been developed in the last decade.

Here's an overview of what a casino executive is thinking when the layout plan is developed:

Slots and Tables

Table players don't like ringing bells and other distracting noise because it tends to slow the game and it creates confusion. Also, table players

who pass by or through a row of slots sometimes play a few credits just for kicks. But they rarely spend more. Table players prefer tables. On the other hand, a slot-playing spouse or friend of a table player will often play a nearby machine if the person at the table is at the end of a session (they're waiting to go to a show or dinner).

So slots near tables are generally tight to cut down on noise and because most people who play those games will be doing it spontaneously without any big expectation of winning. The machines are there to suck up loose bills, not necessarily to draw someone in for a long session.

Tip

Two games can be identical on the outside but set to pay back differently on the inside. This is especially true when the two games are in different casinos. Don't assume that Double Diamond in Casino A will necessarily pay the same as Double Diamond in Casino B. But if you see identical games together in a bank, then it's likely that they're all set with the same payback.

Slot Player Psychology

In contrast to table players, slot players love to see and hear people winning on the machines. Ringing bells and bonus rounds are absolute "proof" that the games can be beaten, so a typical slot player is more likely to play faster and stay longer when people are hitting nearby.

Slot layouts take advantage of this by putting the loosest machines in highly visible areas that are deep inside the layout (rather than on the edges). Crosswalks, elevated sections, and places at or near the end of rows are where the most liberal machines are placed. But beware…loose machines are invariably surrounded by tighter games (though not necessarily the tightest). It's typical to have one or two 96 percent machines that are easily visible, and they'll be surrounded by *different* games that pay back somewhere in the range of 88 percent to 94 percent.

On the other hand, if you see a bank of *identical* progressive games, all of them will have the same payback, usually less than 90 percent, regardless of the game's denomination. So a one-dollar Wheel of Fortune will be tighter than a one-dollar Double Diamond.

And position does not trump denomination. Nickel and penny machines tend to be tight wherever they are placed, even in areas with high visibility.

Tight, Tighter, Tightest

Tight machines are mostly squeezed back into corners and areas where players are pushed when the casino is full. Consider the typical person who arrives on a busy Friday or Saturday night. It's like a parking lot: the convenient spaces are taken, so the player heads deeper into corners of the layout to find an available machine. That game is invariably tight.

Slots near a hotel's front desk, a line for a show, a restaurant, or any other waiting area are similar to the machines near tables. The audience is essentially captive, so the games are usually not generous.

Big Bertha machines (the giant games with the oversized reels) will be played regardless of their payoff, so they're notoriously tight. Ditto for any novelty game that people will play just to see the reels spin.

The tightest of the tight slots can be found in non-casino venues like airports, gas stations, and convenience stores. The Brake-n-Buy is not competing with a casino, and it doesn't care about generating slot excitement. A few occasional dollars from bored patrons is the lone goal.

A similar situation applies to a riverboat or Native American casino that doesn't have competition nearby. Tight games are more common when customers cannot easily go elsewhere.

Of course, tight doesn't mean impossible. Any game that operates within legal specifications will occasionally provide a nice jackpot, but remember that the difference between 83 percent and 98 percent isn't just 15 percent more for the casino. It's also a 750 percent increase in a player's long-term loss.

Now you know the basics of where to find loose slots. In the next section we're going to put it all together in a unified strategy.

Choose the Right Casino

Licensed casinos in North America are required to report the *actual* payback percentages of their slot machines to regulators. That information is available to the public in most states and in Canada. Thankfully, you don't have to call a dozen

THE FACT IS...

Slot machine optimal strategy differs from video poker optimal strategy because the latter is absolute; there is only one way to correctly play a video-poker hand (the cards and the pay table determine the strategy). In contrast, reel games have unknown variables, so optimal strategy requires some informed guesses.

different agencies to get those numbers. They're collected, organized, and published in the magazines *Casino Player* and *Strictly Slots*.

For example, October 2005 numbers show that Trump Taj Mahal had the loosest dollar slots in Atlantic City. They returned an average of 93.9 percent. The tightest dollar slots were at Harrah's; they paid a stingy 91.5 percent. The absolute tightest slots in Atlantic City were Showboat's nickel slots. They paid 88.1 percent.

The figures are published monthly and they vary a bit over time, so you shouldn't judge a casino by only one chart. But I can tell you that Showboat's nickels were tightest in September and August, too. Read the charts for a few months and it's easy to see which casinos and machines are consistently looser.

Casino Player and *Strictly Slots* are published by Casino Publishing Group. You can subscribe via the web at casinocenter.com or by telephone: (800) 969-0711. Both magazines are also available at major newsstands and bookstores.

Define Your Game

Slot charts are an important first step, but they have limitations. They don't tell you where the best games are in a particular casino, and in some jurisdictions the numbers are published by region rather than property. For example, the charts show that North Las Vegas is looser than the Strip, but they don't say how Texas Station stacks up against the Flamingo.

Another limitation of the charts is that video poker is included in the numbers. As you know, video poker (played with optimal strategy) has a significantly higher payback, and that tends to skew the figures upward.

So the next step in slots optimal strategy is a personal choice. Where do you want to play? What games do you like? You already know the variables. But how will you apply them? Here are some options to consider.

Nickels and Pennies vs. Higher Denominations

Many of the hottest new games take nickels or pennies. Nine lines multiplied by five nickels per-line is forty-five nickel-credits per spin or $2.25. Most people play about 500 spins per hour. That's $1,125 of action (money cycled through the machine). With 90 percent payback on average, the action will result in a loss of about $112 unless a player hits one or more good jackpots.

Tip

Compare this to playing max credits on a three-line dollar machine that pays back 94 percent. The action is $3 per spin, $1,500 per hour, but the casino keeps only $90 on average. Fewer jackpots are needed to break even or pull ahead. This advantage is even more pronounced if you play a one-dollar game that takes two credits max.

IGT has a toll-free hotline that provides the current progressive jackpot amounts of all their Megajackpot games. Are you wondering if Megabucks is currently over $15 million? Find out by calling (888) 448-2946, or visit IGT.com on the web.

Of course, you could always play single credits in a nickel machine. That would be $25 of action in an hour at a total cost of $2.50. Very cheap, but also kind of boring. Most of the wins would be less than one dollar.

Shoot for the Moon?

Do you love pulling for millions? Then by all means, shoot for the moon. But remember that a typical progressive game of any denomination is comparable in tightness to a nickel or penny machine, usually 90 percent payback or worse. And the probability of hitting the top prize on a million-dollar progressive is microscopically small.

While we're on the subject of big versus little, let's talk about the allure of tight mega-casinos versus the frugal advantages of smaller properties. Do you want chandeliers and tapestries hanging overhead while you pull for a seven-digit jackpot, or will standard track-lights and chain-restaurant-style decorations suffice? What if a casino has loose slots but lousy restaurants? What if the games are good but the drink service is slow? What if your friends want to go to the fancy place?

As you can see, there's no absolutely correct answer to any of these questions. It's all a matter of taste, preference, and your budget.

But remember that optimal strategy for slot machines is only as optimal as you make it. With that caveat, here's the pure strategy. You can choose what works best for you.

Prep for the Session

First, all things being equal, you should always opt to play video poker. Take another look at the chart on page 15. Almost any video poker game will pay back more over time than a typical slot machine. So unless your heart is set on reels, go with video poker.

Still want to spin for gold? Fine. The next step is to determine the size of your bankroll.

Base-Unit Wager and Session Bankroll

Choose an amount that you feel comfortable wagering per spin. It can be a quarter, a dollar, five dollars, whatever. Keep in mind that this isn't about the denomination of games you'll play. This is an internal choice. How much to bet per spin? Let's use one dollar as an example. We'll call that your **base-unit wager**.

As we discussed in Chapter 2, your session bankroll should be at least 150 times the one dollar per-spin bet or $150, and it may need to be as high as $250 if you'll be playing nickel or penny machines. Remember, this is gambling, so you should be prepared to lose it all.

Tip

Increase your session bankroll to 200 times the base-unit wager if the game takes quarters, and 250 times the base-unit wager if the machine takes nickels or pennies. This gives you more chances to win on tighter games. Remember, your base-unit wager is the amount you bet per spin, not the denomination of machine credits.

Frankly, it would be unlikely that you could nuke the whole amount in one session unless you seriously deviate from optimal strategy, but jackpots happen, and so do losing streaks. Keep in mind that slots are a negative-expectation game; you're *supposed* to lose in the long run. Optimal strategy is designed to reduce those losses and give you more chances to hit a big jackpot.

Each session will be about two hours. Two sessions a day is typical for most players. If you prefer to calculate your bankroll on a per-day basis, set aside at least 250 bets per day for dollar games and higher denominations, 400 bets per day for quarters, nickels, and pennies (notice that the variance goes down gradually as the time and trials increase).

Optimal Strategy in Action

Okay, it's time to hit the machines.

Choose a casino and a loose area of that casino as described on pages 53–56. This is important. The following system won't work if you play tight machines. Well, actually, it will work because it will quickly stop you from playing. But the point of this system is to increase your chance of winning, so you should choose the right area.

Progressive games are out. Just walk right past them. You'll have plenty of time to dump a few dollars into Wheel of Fortune or Megabucks later (if your current session goes well).

Stick to flat tops. The exact game types are entirely up to you. Video or physical reels are fine. Ditto for single or multiple paylines. Try to find games with a top jackpot lower than 10,000 credits. Less than 5,000 is even better.

You're looking for games that pay a bonus for max credits, and a max-credits bet that matches your base unit. Choose the highest denomination that fits the math.

Using a one-dollar bet as an example, that would be a quarter machine that pays a bonus when you play four credits. A half-dollar machine that pays a bonus for playing two credits would be even better.

If you can't find a game in the right denomination that pays a bonus, then choose a game in an *even higher* denomination and play single credits.

You won't be able to exactly match your ideal bet size all the time, but try to stay in a reasonable range. A $1 per-spin bet can shrink to $0.75 or expand to $1.25, but $2 is too high, and $0.50 is too low.

Here We Go!

Pick a machine that looks juicy and load it with ten bets (your base units, not machine credits). Spin ten times. If you don't get a hit, move

to another machine. Repeat the process. When you do get one or more hits (and you soon will if you've chosen the right section of the casino to play), continue playing until the meter hits zero or it goes over twenty bets. If it goes over twenty, cash out and reload with ten bets.

Always exit the machine when you hit zero or when the amount on the meter is less than your base bet. Don't hesitate, just cash out and move on.

THE FACT IS...

Every machine has a multiple-digit identification number somewhere on its exterior. The number is unique to that machine, so having the number will help you find it again if it's moved to another section of the layout.

If the machine keeps you going for a while, then you've probably found a loose one. Record the machine's number and write a detailed description of the machine's denomination, game, and location so you can find it again. Did I mention that you should be carrying paper and a pen?

The purpose of this system is to get you off tight machines, and off machines that are bleeding you dry with small wins and a high hit frequency. You'll either stay with a machine and earn money, or walk away with a loss of ten units or less.

This system will make some casinos and/or areas of casinos unplayable. Good! You shouldn't be feeding money into tight machines.

Stop after an hour or two. You should have a profit or a small loss (part of your bankroll should still be intact). If you lost most of your money, or you finished the bankroll in less than an hour, then you were playing in the wrong casino or the wrong section of the casino. Don't play there again.

You'll eventually build a list of loose machines, and a picture will emerge of the loose/tight layout like a connect-the-dots puzzle. Soon you'll be walking straight to the loose slots.

Modifying the System

The money management system in the previous section can be modified to accommodate your personal style and the games you like to play. For example, low hit-frequency games are more playable when you increase the spin cycles from ten units to twenty and you double the buy-in. But of course, that puts more money at risk on one machine. It's a personal choice.

Similarly, if you would rather play nickel or penny contests, don't fret. Play what you want, but stay away from the progressive games, and be sure to play max credits if the game offers a bonus for a max bet.

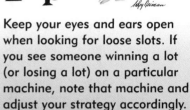

When in Doubt, Cash Out

Keep your eyes and ears open when looking for loose slots. If you see someone winning a lot (or losing a lot) on a particular machine, note that machine and adjust your strategy accordingly.

Remember that cashing out is not a bad thing. It's perfectly okay to load the machine, play one spin, and then decide you don't want to be there anymore. Just hit the cash button, collect your money, and move on. Let's say a machine has been stringing you along for ten minutes, and it never quite reaches an upper limit or zero. Stay with it if you're having fun, but cash out if you're tired of the stalemate. Yes, one spin more might nail you a big jackpot, but saving that spin for another better machine might give you an even bigger win. Let your instincts guide you at these borderline moments.

By the way, you probably noticed that this strategy has you moving around the casino a lot. That's a good thing. You shouldn't get too "invested" (emotionally or otherwise) in one machine unless it's generous. Also, walking around will give you a better sense of the layout.

Searching for a Needle

There are some places where you simply won't find any loose slots because a lack of competition and restrictive regulations keep the machines tight. For example, the law in West Virginia requires all machines to pay back no more than 95 percent, and games in that state usually pay back less than

THE FACT IS...

The best time to play slots is when a casino is relatively empty. Fewer people will be competing for the loosest machines, and it will be easier to move from machine to machine. Avoid weekends, holidays, and major conventions. Mornings and afternoons are typically better than evenings.

92 percent. So evaluating the layout at Charles Town Races is a waste of time. Ditto for a Native American casino or a riverboat that has a lock on the local gambling business. And you won't find a loose nickel machine at Mandalay Bay or Venetian. These are just a few examples of venues where the games are tighter than average.

The RNG and Minimum Payback

What about this concept of "minimum payback" (required by law) for a slot game? Couldn't the slot be monitored and played only when the RNG is "due" for a hit?

Unfortunately, no. Even if you could read numbers as fast as the Flash, and you had X-ray vision like Superman to monitor every RNG game, it wouldn't help.

Imagine a flipping coin. As I mentioned in Chapter 1, the coin is "designed" to deliver heads in about half of the contests. Right? Okay, let's flip. It's tails. Will the coin now "force" heads on the next flip to even the score? No, the probability of seeing heads is still only 50 percent.

An RNG is designed the same way, except it has a few billion variables instead of just two.

Why Bother?

Occasionally, you may tempted to say… "Reading payback charts, calculating bet sizes, searching for loose machines… Why should I hassle with these slot strategies? Why not just go down to the ATM, get $300, and go play whatever machine strikes my fancy? The worst that can happen is I lose $300. Right?"

Well, yes. But without money management the session might be thirty minutes of action followed by two hours of standing around watching your friends play. And then you might be tempted to make another trip to the ATM.

As I mentioned at the beginning of the chapter, sometimes it's tough to balance the fun of entertainment vs. the fun of profit. But one way or another, you should be sure that you *are* having fun.

For example, let's say you *prefer* nickel games. And let's say you *want* to park yourself in front of one machine for four hours. There's nothing "wrong" with that. Indeed, you should play what you want to play.

But even in those situations, the strategies we've covered can help you properly fund your bankroll. That will keep you in the game, and give you a better chance of smacking a win while you're having fun.

Slot Machine Nirvana

Wouldn't it be cool if you could play slots for free? Imagine if it would cost you nothing to spin, but if you hit a jackpot then you could win money. And the machine would hit jackpots at ten times the normal rate. Wouldn't that be awesome?

It's not a fantasy. It's called a slot tournament, and most casinos have them. I'll tell you about that in Chapter 23.

But in the next chapter, we're going to talk about a game that consistently beats "traditional" slots in payback. It's video poker. If you want to be a winner in a casino, video poker is one of the best games to play.

Essentially

- Denomination is one of the biggest indicators of how a slot machine will pay. Lower-denomination games tend to be tighter than higher-denomination games.

- The loosest slots are placed in highly visible areas near the center of a slot layout. But visibility does not trump denomination. Nickel and penny machines tend to be tight wherever they are placed, even in areas with high visibility.

- Tight machines are usually found at the edges of the slot layout in corners and other low-visibility areas. These are places where people will play when the casino is crowded.

- Machines tend to be tight near table games, show lines, check-in lines, and restaurant waiting areas. The tightest slots can be found in airports, convenience stores, and other non-casino venues.

- Slots are looser in jurisdictions where many casinos compete for customers. The games also tend to be looser in older properties, and casinos that cater to locals.

- Slot paybacks for most casinos in North America are published monthly in the magazines *Casino Player* and *Strictly Slots.*

- The purpose of optimal strategy and money management is to get you off tight machines, and off machines that are bleeding you dry with small wins and a high hit frequency.

- All things being equal, you should play video poker instead of reel games.

CHAPTER 5

Video Poker

If you like to gamble, and you like to win, then video poker is a better game than slots. Simply, it's easier to beat. There is no hidden house edge, no secretly tight machines. Each draw is from a freshly shuffled (virtual) deck.

Best of all, video poker is one of the few casino games that has a positive expectation. That's right. Play the right machine, long enough, in the right way, and video poker is mathematically guaranteed to pay back more than it takes in.

But that doesn't mean you should quit your job to go play video poker. The effort required to earn a steady income as a gambler is a full-time job itself. On the other hand, it's fairly easy to play a near-neutral game (pushing the edge to just above or below zero). Add the value of comps, and video poker can be a ticket to a free or nearly free vacation.

It's a brainpower contest that pays.

Before we get into that (especially if you're skipping around in this book), please be sure to read Chapters 1 and 2 because the information there is the basis for the strategies presented here.

Basic Video Poker

If you know poker, then the fundamentals of video poker will be familiar. There is a hierarchy of hand ranks (see the next section) and a draw, but beyond that you should forget everything you know about the table game when playing the video version. You can't bluff the machine, raise, or call. There's no pot. The game deals you five cards. You can keep all of them, some, or none. Replacements are dealt as necessary. The revised combination is your final hand. Winners are paid according to a pay table posted on the machine.

The most basic game is jacks or better; any hand with a pair of jacks or better is a winner. Other versions make deuces or jokers **wild** (they count as any card the player requires). Wild-card games typically raise the minimum winning hand to kings or better, two pairs, or three

Tip

Some players become excited and forget to hold cards when they're dealt a royal flush or another perfect hand before the draw. One more press of the deal button does not bring a big payout, but five more cards. Ouch! Be sure to press the hold button for every card you intend to keep. The screen should acknowledge your choice.

of a kind. Multiple-hand games allow you to repeat the same starting cards three, five, ten, fifty times, or more. Each time the draw is different.

Whatever the game, the play remains essentially the same; receive five cards, draw, the result is your hand (or hands).

Buttons on a video poker machine are similar to those on a slot machine except that "Spin" is replaced by "Deal," and each card has a "hold" button. In addition, most video poker machines use touch screens; just touch the cards to hold them.

Ranking the Hands

Poker hands are ranked as follows:

Royal Flush: Ace, king, queen, jack, and ten of the same suit.

Straight Flush: Five cards of the same suit in exactly adjacent ranks.

Four of a Kind: Four cards of the same rank and a fifth card of any rank and suit.

Full House: Three cards of the same rank and a pair of another rank.

Flush: Five cards of the same suit that are not exactly adjacent ranks.

Straight: Five cards not of the same suit in exactly adjacent ranks. An ace can be used to make both the highest and the lowest straight.

Three of a Kind: Three cards of the same rank and two cards of different ranks.

Two pairs: Two cards of one rank, two cards of another rank, and a fifth card of a third rank.

One Pair: Two cards of one rank and three cards of different ranks.

No Pair: Five cards that don't make any combination.

The Pay Table IS the Game

The RNG in a typical slot machine is a mysterious mechanism. What's the payback? Who knows? It's all a big head-game. But video poker is different because the range of choices is fixed. The RNG simulates dealing from a shuffled deck of cards. No loose or tight machines. No mysterious house edge. The likelihood of receiving any particular hand from a real deck is identical to a video poker deck.

That makes the pay table the most important element of every video poker game. Here's why. A casino can't tighten or loosen a machine by changing how the cards are dealt, so the only way the house can get an edge is to change the payouts. Thus you can simply look at a pay table and (with a little practice) instantly know the casino's edge.

Consider the pay table for the venerable original version of video poker (see below). It's called 9/6 jacks or better because a full house pays nine credits and a flush pays six credits per credit wagered. This particular pay table returns 99.5 percent when the game is played with optimal strategy.

Jacks or Better 9/6 Pay Table

Credits	1	2	3	4	5	Frequency	Return
Royal Flush	250	500	750	1000	4000	0.0025%	1.98%
Straight Flush	50	100	150	200	250	0.01%	0.55%
Four of a Kind	25	50	75	100	125	0.24%	5.9%
Full House	9	18	27	36	45	1.15%	10.3%
Flush	6	12	18	24	30	1.10%	6.6%
Straight	4	8	12	16	20	1.12%	4.5%
Three of a Kind	3	6	9	12	15	7.44%	22.3%
Two Pairs	2	4	6	8	10	12.9%	25.9%
Jacks or Better	1	2	3	4	5	21.46%	21.5%
Tens or Worse						54.54%	0%
Total						100%	99.5%

A typical pay table includes the figures in black above. The figures shown in red are provided here to show you what happens when the game is played with optimal strategy. Note that each credit increases payments proportionally except for the fifth credit. The fifth credit quadruples the payment for a royal flush. Percentages are rounded.

Some casinos think that 9/6 is too generous, so they reduce the payout for a full house from nine credits to eight and a flush goes to five credits. Thus the game is called 8/5. That drops the overall payback to 97.3 percent. Lounges, convenience stores, and less competitive locations often have 6/5 machines. Those pay back only 95 percent.

Experienced players have learned to avoid the lower-paying machines, so casinos jigger pay tables in other ways to attract customers (see "Comparison of Pay Tables" on the next page). A typical ploy is to offer a bonus for four of a kind, and then to reduce the payout somewhere else on the table where the player doesn't notice. Double Bonus (B) looks like a 9/6 machine, but it's not. The payout for two pairs is only one credit.

Another gimmick is to make deuces or jokers wild, and then entirely delete the payment for a high pair or two pairs. Whoops! And then there are copycat versions. Look closely at the two columns on the far right of the chart below. They're nearly identical except for the payout for four of a kind. The one-credit difference drops the return by nearly six percent.

Similarly, at first glance, deuces wild NSU looks like it has better payouts than full-pay deuces. But actually, NSU's net payback is about one percent lower. By the way, NSU is short for "not so ugly." Players have given it this moniker because it's close enough to 100 percent to be a good gamble.

Comparison of Pay Tables

	J-O-B 9/6	J-O-B 8/5	Bonus Poker (LV)	Bonus Poker (AC)	Double Bonus (A)	Double Bonus (B)	Deuces Wild (NSU)	Deuces Wild (full)	Deuces Wild (low)
Royal Flush	800	800	800	800	800	800	800	800	800
Four Deuces	–	–	–	–	–	–	200	200	200
Wild Royal	–	–	–	–	–	–	25	25	25
Five of a Kind	–	–	–	–	–	–	16	15	15
Straight Flush	50	50	50	100	50	50	10	9	9
Four Aces	–	–	80	50	160	160	–	–	–
Four 2s, 3s, 4s	–	–	40	40	80	80	–	–	–
Four of a Kind	25	25	25	20	50	50	4	5	4
Full House	9	8	8	8	10	9	4	3	3
Flush	6	5	5	5	7	6	3	2	2
Straight	4	4	4	4	5	5	2	2	2
Three of a Kind	3	3	3	3	3	3	1	1	1
Two Pairs	2	2	2	2	1	1	–	–	–
Jacks or Better	1	1	1	1	1	1	–	–	–
Payback	99.5%	97.3%	99.2%	98.3%	100.1%	97.8%	99.7%	100.6%	94.3%

Payments and percentages are calculated per single credit wagered, but they reflect the bonus that is paid for max credits. Example: Royal flush is 4,000 ÷ 5 = 800.

There are dozens of different video poker versions, each with its own pay table, and each pay table requires a unique strategy. Yikes! Wait, don't go flipping back to the slots section. Video poker optimal strategy is easy to learn when you avoid machines with stingy pay tables and learn to play just a few games that pay near 100 percent. I'll show you how to do that in the next few pages.

For now just remember that VP optimal strategy is all about finding good pay tables. Video poker pros usually don't play anything that pays back less than 99.5 percent, but I recommend 97 percent as a low limit for casual players. In other words, stay away from 7/5 and 6/5 J-O-B. Scrutinize bonus games carefully (using the chart on page 69) to be sure all the hands are full-pay.

You Gotta Know When To Hold 'Em

Get ready; I'm going to cross your eyes in the next paragraph. But don't worry, this is only an example.

Did you know that a double-inside three-card straight flush has a different expected value if it has no high cards vs. one high card? And did you know that those hands are different from a single-inside three-card straight flush with zero, one, or two high cards? They're all worth less than a sequential three-card straight flush with one high card. And of course, that affects the draw strategy if a five-card combination includes one of the above and two high cards of another suit.

You probably didn't know that, and I don't blame you. Video poker purists revel in these subtle nuances that increase the return by fractions of a percent, but I'm guessing that you'd like the game to be a bit easier. So strictly speaking, the strategies in this chapter are less than optimal. They're very close but intentionally *not* perfect because twenty lines are easier to memorize than thirty-six lines. A shorter strategy generally sacrifices a portion of a percent for the sake of convenience, but simply using the strategy (rather than guessing) will improve your overall game by 5 percent or more.

Jacks or Better

The following strategy works for "plain vanilla" (no bonus) jacks-or-better games with 9/6 and 8/5 pay tables. You can also use it on 7/5, 6/5, 10/6, 9/7, and most bonus contests that pay 1-2-3-4 or 1-1-3-5 at the bottom end of the table. Examples of these games can be found in the chart on page 69. The way to use the strategy is to match your hand to the highest one in the list and then play as directed. So if your hand is 2♦ 7♦ 8♦ J♦ J♥, you hold the two jacks instead of the four-card flush or three-card straight flush because a high pair is highest on the list.

Jacks or Better Strategy

Hand	Discard
Royal or straight flush	0
Four of a kind	1
Four-card royal	1
Full house, flush, or straight	0
Three of a kind	2
Four-card straight flush (open-ended or with a gap)	1
Two pairs	1
High pair (jacks or better)	3
Three-card royal	2
Four-card flush	1
Low pair (tens or lower)	3
Four-card straight (open-ended)	1
Two-card royal (two suited cards jacks or higher)	3
Three-card straight flush (open-ended or with gaps)	2
Ace, king, queen, and jack unsuited	1
King, queen, and jack unsuited	2
Two high cards (drop an ace if necessary)	3
Suited high card and ten	3
One high card	4
Toss everything	5

The above strategy works for "plain vanilla" no-bonus jacks-or-better games that pay 9/6, 8/5, 7/5, 6/5, 10/6, and 9/7. This strategy also can be used with most jacks-or-better bonus games that pay 1-2-3-4 or 1-1-3-5 at the bottom end of the table.

Here are some more examples:

This hand should be played as a low pair (hold the **10**s) rather than as a four-card straight or three-card straight flush.

Yes, you should bust a perfectly good straight for the chance of hitting a royal flush. Discard the **K**.

Hold the low pair. Resist the temptation to also hold the **Q** or the **A**. Keeping extra high cards (known as **kickers**) dramatically *reduces* the chance of improving to quads, trips, two pairs, and such.

Hold the two high cards. By the way, you should never draw to an inside straight (a straight requiring one rank) in jacks or better except **A-K-Q-J**. Outside straights can be made with two ranks, so an outside draw is twice as likely to succeed.

Hold the **Q** and **J**. Do *not* hold an unsuited **A** with two other unsuited high cards. Of course, if the **A** in this example were diamonds, you would keep the two-card royal and drop the unsuited **Q**.

Deuces Wild

Deuces wild strategy is radically different from jacks or better. In deuces wild, two pairs and worse (97 percent of all starting hands) are worthless without a deuce or a good draw. Of course, the wild cards make paying hands easier to construct, but those hands aren't worth as much, so the game tends to be more volatile even though it often has a greater long-term return. The "full pay" version of deuces wild (see page 73) is more than one percent better than 9/6 J-O-B, but you may not notice it unless you stick around for the royals.

The following strategy works on full-pay deuces wild, and it also works reasonably well on most other versions, notably the popular and generally available almost-full-pay NSU 800/200/25/16/10/4/4/3/2/1 that returns over 99 percent.

Deuces Wild Strategy

Hand	Discard
Hands With Four Deuces	
Four deuces	1
Hands With Three Deuces	
Royal flush	0
Five of a kind	0
Three deuces	2
Hands With Two Deuces	
Royal flush	0
Five of a kind	0
Straight flush	0
Four of a kind	1
Four-card royal	1
Four-card straight flush (open-ended)	1
Two deuces	3
Hands With One Deuce	
Royal flush	0
Five of a kind	0
Straight flush	0
Four of a kind	1
Four-card royal	1
Full house	0
Four-card straight flush (open-ended)	1
Flush or straight	0
Three of a kind	2
Three-card royal	2
Three-card straight flush (open-ended)	2
One deuce	4
Hands With No Deuces	
Royal flush	0
Four-card royal	1
Straight flush	0
Four of a kind	1
Full house, flush, or straight	0
Three of a kind	2
Four-card straight flush (open-ended or gapped)	1
Three-card royal	2
Pair	3
Four-card flush	1
Four-card straight (open-ended or gapped)	1
Three-card straight flush (open-ended or gapped)	1
Two-card royal	3
Toss everything	5

The above strategy works for full-pay deuces wild and most other versions. Note that a pat straight flush is not held when it's made with three deuces, and a pat full house, flush, and straight are not held when they're made with two deuces.

Here's a closer look at the strategy:

Two pairs are worthless, so drop one of the pairs (it doesn't matter which one) and the extra card.

Don't be tempted by the three-card royal or the four-card straight. Keep the two deuces and discard the rest.

Yes, a four-card flush is staring you in the face, but it's not very valuable when made with one deuce (which is why it's not on the list). Go for the three-card royal.

It looks promising, and then you realize this is deuces wild. Toss all five cards.

Hold the queens and deuce (making three of a kind). That ranks higher than the three-card royal.

Optimal Strategies in Action

Take another look at the J-O-B pay table on page 68. You'll notice that the royal flush is worth roughly 2 percent of the payback, and that *includes* the bonus for maximum credits. Thus if you play less than the maximum, you're giving up a tremendous edge. *Always* bet the max per hand when you're playing a 99 percent or better payback game. If that's too expensive, drop down to a lower denomination.

Once you've chosen a denomination, the next step is finding a favorable pay table. You may be tempted to play machines simply because they're colorful or artistically inviting, but take your time and stroll through the casino. Beginners often see a confusing swirl of numbers, so it might help to carry a slip of paper with four or five pay tables written on it. Then you can compare the machines to known payouts. You can also write down unfamiliar pay tables and study them later.

As I mentioned in Chapter 2, you should begin a session with at least 150 bets. And remember that a "hand" in this situation isn't necessarily a lone five-card combination because you might be playing multiple five-card hands simultaneously.

Volatility Comparisons

Jacks-or-better games come in three primary types. The traditional games

THE FACT IS...

Video poker optimal strategy does not change when multiple hands are played simultaneously. One hand should be played the same way as four, ten, or fifty hands. However, the overall volatility goes down with multiple hands because losers are combined with winners. That makes jackpots smaller (in relation to bet size) but increases the frequency of net wins.

(9/6, 8/5, and such) change the payouts only on the lines for full house and flush. Bonus games change those two lines and also offer a bonus for quads. Double-bonus games do all that and they also typically lower the payout on two pairs from two credits to one.

Deuces wild games entirely drop the bottom payouts, and they push the wins even further up into the higher hands.

As you know, bigger jackpots toward the top mean less is available in the middle or bottom. Thus jacks or better is the least volatile video poker version. Bonus poker is more volatile, and double bonus and deuces wild are the most volatile.

Why would people want to play volatile games? They do it for excitement. You can expect to see quads about once an hour when playing jacks or better. That's $125 on a 9/6 $1 machine, but bonus or double-bonus games will pay $200, $400, $800, or even more in some circumstances (depending on the rank of the cards). You can look forward to one or two of those in a typical half-day session. Oh yeah!

Of course, those mini-jackpots don't affect the long term payback, but some people like the extra short-term action.

By the way, volatility is the reason why I recommend you look first for standard jacks-or-better or bonus poker over double-bonus games. The full strategy for double bonus is about fifty lines, and you'll need it to get the most out of that contest. On the other hand, the sky won't fall if you play a double bonus game with standard J-O-B strategy (it's much better than slots). But don't blow your bankroll.

Also, I didn't include a strategy for joker poker in this book, partly because of its volatility and mostly because there are too few full-pay versions out there and too many copycat low-paying versions.

Here We Go!

Choose your game and settle in. Machine-hopping is entirely unnecessary once you've found the right pay table. There is no such thing as a "tight" video poker machine. There is only good luck and bad luck. Of course, I always encourage people to wander and poke around just for fun. Move if it pleases you. You may find an even better pay table across the aisle, but staying put is perfectly okay when playing video poker.

Another thing that's perfectly okay is carrying your strategy on a small card or slip of paper (or taking this book with you). There's no rule that says you have to play only from memory. Even pros occasionally get stumped. The more you practice, the more you'll remember, and pretty soon you'll be zooming through the hands.

While you're zooming, keep in mind that optimal strategy identifies the combination with the greatest long-term expected value, but it doesn't guarantee that any particular draw will be successful. Look at the chart on page 68. More than half of J-O-B hands are losers. About 21 percent return the original wager, and only about 24 percent actually return a profit. In other words, sometimes you're going to lose even when you play a perfect strategy.

Tip

All video poker games tend to be volatile compared to table games. About 55 percent of VP hands are losers, and another 21 percent are a push. The rest, about 24 percent of hands, are profitable. So you'll finish most sessions near even or with a net loss. Only about one in four sessions will be winners. But those sessions sometimes will be very profitable.

Smart Machines

Speaking of perfect strategy… Some video poker machines are programmed to play optimal strategy (or a reasonable approximation of it); the game automatically marks cards to be held for the draw. You can accept what the machine recommends or choose your own cards.

Should you follow the machine's recommendations? Yes, if it matches the strategy you are using. But you should evaluate each hand. Resist the temptation to hit the deal button until you're sure that the correct cards are marked.

Similarly, some "smart" machines allow you to choose your wild cards (something other than deuces). It doesn't matter what you choose as long as you avoid cards that can make a royal flush. This gives you more chances to hit a wild royal. For example, let's say you're drawing to a four-card royal and you need the ten of spades. You want something other than tens to be wild because if you miss the natural royal draw, you would prefer four chances to hit a wild royal rather than three.

A Progressive Look at Progressives

Remember how I told you to stay away from progressives in the slots section? Well, all that changes when you're playing video poker. Progressives are a good thing when they reach a certain value (this takes a bit of calculating, but it's definitely worth the effort).

A 4,000-credit royal flush is worth about 2 percent of a total payback (see the chart on page 68). That's $1,000 on a single-hand quarter machine. Let's say you're looking at an 8/5 quarter machine with a $3,000 progressive jackpot. You know an 8/5 game typically returns 97.3 percent, and this *includes* the normal value of a royal. But the progressive royal is three times larger (2 percent + 2 percent + 2 percent). It is 4 percent more payback than normal. Add 97.3 and 4; the total is over 101 percent. Should you play this game? Absolutely! It's a positive-expectation contest.

But wait a second! What if you don't hit the royal today, tomorrow, or whenever? What if someone else hits the top prize? That may happen, but it's okay because your gambling life is one long session. Ditto for the casino's gambling life. Just make good bets every day, and the long-run will take care of itself.

Essentially

- Video poker uses regular poker-hand ranks to determine winners. The most basic game is jacks or better. Deuces or jokers are wild in other versions. Whatever the game, the play remains the same; receive five cards, discard and draw, the result is your hand.

- The RNG in a video poker machine simulates dealing from a shuffled deck of cards. The likelihood of receiving any particular hand from a real deck is identical to a video poker deck.

- The pay table is the most important element of a video poker game. A casino can't tighten or loosen a video poker game by changing how the cards are dealt, so the only way the house can get an edge is to change the pay table. Thus you can simply look at a machine and instantly know the casino's edge.

- Some machines pay slightly fewer credits on selected hands. The difference may seem small, but it can dramatically increase the house edge.

- Always play maximum credits per hand on games that pay 99 percent or better. If that's too expensive, drop down to a lower denomination.

- Traditional jacks or better (no bonus) is the least volatile video poker version. Bonus poker is more volatile, and double bonus and wild-card games are the most volatile.

- Machine-hopping is entirely unnecessary once you've found the right pay table. There is no such thing as a "tight" video poker machine.

- It is a good idea to carry a slip of paper with pay tables and a strategy (or bring this book) when you go to the casino. That will help you find the best games and play them correctly.

CHAPTER 6

An Interview with Mr. Casino

 Casino executives are notoriously tight-lipped about how they set paybacks on their slot machines. And they're absolutely Sphinx-like when it comes to talking about strategies for slot layouts.

For example, the payback and strategy info in Chapter 4 (and elsewhere in this book) was culled from documents that casinos are legally required to file, also from direct analysis of the contests, and from dozens of *off-the-record* interviews that I've done over the years with various casino executives. But on-the-record interviews about slot paybacks and placement? Fughetaboutit!

That's why the following interview is so rare. It's a conversation with a person who I will call "Mr. Casino." He (or maybe she) is a highly placed executive with a major gaming company, and he has first-hand experience with operations at multiple properties.

Getting to Know Mr. Casino

Mr. Casino doesn't mince words. He's not toeing a PR line. Why does he talk with me? I think he is as interested in hearing my questions (understanding what is important to players) as I am in hearing his answers.

You'll notice that Mr. Casino's philosophies of game selection and slot placement match closely, but not exactly, with the information I gave you in Chapter 4. That's because the casino industry is not a monolithic business. There are a lot of people with various views jostling for supremacy. Mr. Casino is one of them, and he freely admits that not everybody sees it the way he does. Mr. Casino is a proponent of what I would call a "tight philosophy." He and like-minded executives represent a major trend in the gaming industry. During our conversation, I challenge him on this subject, and I ask him to justify his policies from a standpoint of profitability. His answers are very revealing.

As you read this conversation, remember that Mr. Casino is speaking from his own perspective. Other executives may do some things differently.

My only requirement of Mr. Casino was that he tell me the truth (and I checked his statements against other sources just to be sure).

His requirements of me are that I keep his identity a secret, and that I write nothing to directly identify his company.

Tip

Mr. Casino often refers to "hold." This is the mirror opposite of payback. Thus if a machine holds 8 percent, that means it has a 92 percent payback.

Mr. Casino and I spoke in multiple interviews. What follows are excerpts from our conversations.

The Interview

BN: Let's begin with game settings, specifically $5 machines. In your casinos, how tight would they be on average?

Mr. Casino: Five dollars would range anywhere from 3 to 6 percent [hold]. And this isn't to say that this is all that they're available in. There are absolutely going to be exceptions. But this is how you would typically have them.

BN: Okay, dollars. What is the range loose to tight?

Mr. Casino: It does vary by state because of market factors and stuff like that, but for the most part the tightest dollar would be 7 or 8 percent. The loosest dollar machine might be at 4 or 5 percent.

BN: You never would have a dollar game that is paying back 98 percent or 99 percent?

Mr. Casino: Never say never, but you'd need a really good reason.

BN: What would that really good reason be?

Mr. Casino: I don't know. I can't even imagine.

BN: So you wouldn't normally ever have a 98 or 99 percent $5 machine?

Mr. Casino: Right. You would need to have some strategy, and there is not one I can think of that fits in my company's culture, where you would say, "Let's make a big loud deal with this machine." Why you would do that with a dollar I can't imagine.

BN: What is your standard payback for quarters?

Mr. Casino: Quarters probably range from 6 to 10 percent hold.

BN: Nickels?

Mr. Casino: Now you're getting up there. Now your hold is somewhere between 9 and 15 percent.

BN: In an average bank of dollar machines, what would be the mix in your casino, loose to tight?

Mr. Casino: It's probably five and five. They're probably different by two points.

BN: Would the range ever be eight points in the same denomination in the same bank?

Mr. Casino: No. We're not talking about big ranges. There are other factors that decide what games go next to each other, what games go in the same section. We're never making a decision that the game holds this, so it can't go next to that game. [For dollars] it's somewhere between 4 and 8 percent, and then the games are put into banks and sections based on other factors. The holds end up where the holds end up as far as what is next to what.

BN: Are progressive games of the same type all set at the same payback? If you have ten Wheel of Fortunes, they are all set the same. Yes?

Mr. Casino: That is true.

BN: And if it's a dollar progressive, it's going to pay back in the range of 88 to 91 percent. Yes? Whereas if it was not a progressive game, it would go back up to the range we were discussing, in the range of 95 percent payback. Is this correct?

Mr. Casino: Yes.

Where are the Tightest Slots?

BN: Are slots near tables tighter?

Mr. Casino: Probably, yes. Nobody is seeking those games out.

> "Video poker is a discipline unto itself. Video poker is priced lower [holds less] because it's visible to the player how it is going to play. You can look at the pay table and say, 'Why would I play this, when I can play this?'"
>
> —Mr. Casino, Casino Executive

It's something that a table player is going to play because he is waiting for a seat to open or something like that. It may be at a blackjack table where they are playing $5 a hand, so we would typically put dollars and sometimes $5 games, something that has a comparable average bet to the mindset they're in. And they're probably priced [hold] a little higher because we know it's an audience that is going to play it because it's there. They may never become a slot player, and they're not going to come back the next day because they loved playing that machine, so at that point it is not our priority to give them a great slot experience. We just want them to have something to do while they're standing there.

BN: What about restaurant lines, check in-lines, and other places where people are waiting?

Mr. Casino: For the same reasons they may be priced [hold] a bit higher, but depending on the operator, it might also be a place where they choose to debut new slots or new technology. You have people stuck there. Why not give them a little bit of entertainment while they're standing there, and have them play something that they typically wouldn't. Maybe we'll put something there that is really a poor performer because it would make it get some play because it has a captive audience. Maybe we bring something in there that is a brand new concept in bonusing, so people play it and say, "Oh, that's cool. Never saw that before."

As far as lines go, or people standing around the table game, it's all kind of the same. Are people standing there for some reason? If so, let's give them something special or something priced a little higher.

BN: Where would you put loose machines?

Mr. Casino: There are a couple of schools of thought here. You cannot make a rule because you want people to see people winning. You also want to see machines busy. What we try to do is that anywhere there is an entrance, any major entrance to the casino floor, you want to have a lot of noise and every seat full. Those should be the first places to fill up so that as people enter they get a sense of excitement and anticipation. Other people are playing and having fun, so it might be about having the newest machines, the most popular themes. On a macro level, when you look at the popularity in the last few years of penny and nickel slots, primarily video, these are significantly higher priced than the quarter and dollar reels of yesterday, but that is what people love to play. That is what they are playing. So it's not necessarily that people are always going with the game that has a lower hold. We have penny machines at every entrance because that is where all the butts are in seats.

BN: I don't understand. Are you saying loose machines are near the door?

Mr. Casino: No. I'm saying our tightest machines are near the door because they are most popular. The important thing is to just get the crowd, and the important place is a very visible area, a cross-walk, a major pathway through the casino, an entrance to the casino. Attractive and loose are kind of two different things.

BN: You're saying the tightest machines are the most popular machines. This is a major shift from the traditional paradigm that loose machines are more popular. Does that mean the strategy of having *any* loose machines on the floor is fading away?

Mr. Casino: I don't know if it's gone forever, but my thought is if I have a game out there that is really fun to play, people are clamoring to play it, even though it is holding 16 percent… You know what I mean? You put the popular games where you want crowds. It's a separate issue from hold. Right now these penny machines hold like 12 to 16 percent. They are really up there, but people can't get enough of them. You don't hold back on how you are pricing them because it's supply and demand. It's like anything else. If everyone in the world tomorrow wanted a Ford Taurus, Ford would raise the price. These penny machines, they're so much fun to play. It is constant action, and the bonus rounds are so much fun, people are willing to pay that price. They [penny games] are dribblers. You're constantly winning something, and you're constantly losing something, so over the long haul it's holding more, but you're having a much better time than a boring old quarter reel that is only holding 6 percent.

BN: Why don't you just rip out all your loose machines and make them all tighter nickels and pennies?

Mr. Casino: Well, most floors at this point are 50 percent nickels and pennies, or more. That has happened over the last couple of years.

> *"We have as much trouble with it [hold] as I can tell you do... There is always someone who is like, 'Let's try it at nine and see if it makes a difference.' And I'm like, 'Okay, we'll move it to thirteen later on.' There's always a question. This is fairly new research. It's only been a couple of years. You're kind of like, 'Well, what if...?'"*
>
> **—Mr. Casino, Casino Executive**

BN: Will penny and nickel games become so popular that in five or six years all games will be pennies and nickels and pay back only 90 percent?

Mr. Casino: It's hard to imagine there wouldn't be a floor with a three-reel quarter on it.

BN: But regardless of denomination, you said that your tightest machines are your most popular machines. Why not make all your $5 machines multi-line and set them at 90 percent?

Mr. Casino: For the same reason that a $5 game isn't set at 90 percent today... A player can tell the difference between a 10 percent hold and a 3 percent hold, and traditionally we've given a $5 player a better experience by having it only hold 3 percent or 4 percent.

BN: Okay. But I'm seeing a contradiction. Even though penny machines with high holds are extremely popular, you're saying $5 machines with low holds are a "better experience." Here's what I think. In spite of the current popularity of high-hold penny and nickel machines, I think savvy players prefer games with a lower hold. They see the effect on their bankroll. Do you agree?

Mr. Casino: Between three and ten? I agree with you. You'd absolutely have a better chance of feeling it, if you're playing a lot. It's a seven-point difference.

BN: So in the end, there is never going to be a floor that is all 90 percent because casino operators will want to offer a looser game to better customers, and give them more chances for winning. Yes?

Mr. Casino: Yes. I would think so. I think there is always going to be variation, and you're always going to see the hold creep up as the denomination goes down.

The Strategy of Slot Layouts

BN: Okay. Let's talk about machine placement. In the floor of the future, five or ten years from now, will machines still be arranged according to denomination and hold?

Mr. Casino: That's a very interesting question. Things are changing so fast. Now that multi-denomination games are a regular availability on most casino floors, that kind of changes everything right there. Now you can sit down at a game, and you choose if you're going to play a penny, a quarter, or a dollar. And there are multi-games. In the future that all comes together, and you can sit down at any unit and play any game in any denomination. So the placement of machines by their hold, that kind of disappears.

BN: When do you think that is going to happen?

Mr. Casino: I don't know, maybe six or seven years down the road.

BN: You're saying that six years from now the whole concept of positioning loose and tight machines won't exist anymore.

Mr. Casino: Yes, because every bank address on your floor will be so much more flexible. You will no longer be able to say, in this location, this is what I'm going to offer. Because in that location, that game will offer any one of three denoms and any one of seven games. So it's up to them [the players]. They can sit where they want and play what they want. Now, you'll always have some control. Like in a certain area the games are multi-denom with a lowest denom of $1. In another part of the casino, the lowest denom on a multi-denom game will be a penny. So you'll still have some control. But it's much more flexible than it was in the past.

BN: Okay. Let's get back to the way it is today. At one point you said that hold was not a factor in positioning games, but you also said that games were tighter in some areas. Please explain that. By what criteria do you position games?

Mr. Casino: The way they play, the kind of game, the average bet, the kind of player who will play it.

BN: You're not thinking about hold when you're positioning games?

Mr. Casino: That's right. Except what we talked about where you're putting stuff that holds a little higher in places where you have a captive audience, next to table games, or next to the lines at the buffet, where no one needs to like the game. They don't need to like the way that it plays. They just play it.

BN: And when you're designing a slot layout, you have no thought as to a machine's hold? You're just thinking I want to put Reel 'Em In next to I Dream of Jeannie?

Mr. Casino: Right. What does the average bet tend to be? Is this a progressive game that will influence a player to play max bet? There are nickel games where the average bet will be $0.45, and other nickel games where the average bet will be $3.95. So which one makes more sense in a bank next to a bank of dollars? You're not going to put a game where most people play $0.45 a spin next to a game where most people play $2.50 a spin. There are all kinds of things you're lining up, but hold is not one of them.

You tend to group manufacturers because Aristocrat plays differently than Williams, and if you like this Aristocrat, you might like that Aristocrat. So you're grouping by denom, definitely by manufacturer, definitely by max bets.

BN: What will you put in a high-profile area where everyone can see the machine?

Mr. Casino: You may want to use that to debut brand new product before it gets moved somewhere else. You may want to put a really hot "link" with a great progressive payout there. Some people say put your worst game in your best location, but after years of going back and forth we've kind of arrived at put your best game in your best location and peak the peak.

BN: And your best game is your most popular game, not necessarily one that will pay back the most?

Mr. Casino: Right. Put your most popular game in your highest traffic location and whoa, look how high it goes.

BN: So you're never thinking loose when you're thinking high profile?

Mr. Casino: That's right because coin-in is the judge of popularity. At whatever end of the casino I started at [when designing a layout], I had a reason for each next bank of games. So it's not that I go out and say, "Now we're at the table games. We have to surround this with the higher hold games." It's not my primary motivation, but if you're redoing a table area, and you're going to disrupt a bunch of slots around it, you say to yourself, "We have to put them [tight slots] somewhere." It's not that you say, "Oh these are a point or two higher, they need to be next to a captive audience." I would think about it more in terms of the math profile and the volatility. If this is a game that doesn't pay often, that doesn't play fun, we'll put it somewhere where you have people standing. They can enjoy it because it is something to do.

BN: Why would you ever have a game like that on your slot floor?

Mr. Casino: You never would on purpose, but I never have enough capital to replace everything this year that I don't like. If one game that sucks is only a year old, and we didn't know it when we bought it, I have to wait until it is fully depreciated, and I have other bigger fish to fry. I have to find somewhere to put it.

Buying slot machines is very difficult. You would be shocked at how little information and how little market testing data manufacturers give you to buy slot machines. Every year you buy stuff that six months later is a dud. You have to live with it. Slot machines depreciate over five years.

BN: If what you're telling me is correct, then why are some casinos still positioning machines with a greater emphasis on their payback?

Mr. Casino: Because there are so many casino operators, you'll never get them all to agree.

BN: So some casino operators *do* believe that loose machines can be perceived by the player, and those loose machines attract players?

Mr. Casino: Absolutely. I am sure that I am in the minority, and I'm sure my company is in the minority.

> **"You're always going to push the envelope if you're an aggressive operator. You're always going to say, 'How high can I price this before it starts to negatively affect my business?' But maybe I want to be able to say, for perception, 'loosest quarters.' I think it's just a balance."**
>
> —Mr. Casino, Casino Executive

Setting the Payback on a Game

BN: How do you decide the payback of a particular game?

Mr. Casino: You do it based on what else is on your floor, what has been accepted, whatever the market will bear. It's like you price any other product in America.

BN: How long do you let a machine sit on your floor before you evaluate its hold?

Mr. Casino: We would start evaluating performance after maybe six weeks.

BN: Would you ever move the payback up, say that a machine is too tight?

Mr. Casino: No. We do not tend to react to machine performance by hold changes. We don't say this machine isn't doing very well, let's loosen it or tighten it.

BN: You just pull the machine off the floor?

Mr. Casino: Yes. We think of that as a theme-based thing. Because if you were to try to manage hold that way, you've really got the interest of the casino and the player at odds. If a machine is not doing well, I would probably want to make it tighter so I could get more money out of it. If you're arguing that the customer could perceive it, then the right action would be to make it looser, so more people would play it. So if it's not cutting it, then that's because it's not a good theme. It doesn't play in a fun way.

BN: So machines rarely are made looser?

Mr. Casino: That's right.

BN: Let's say you have a casino with 2,000 slots. How many of those slots after a year or two years will have had their paybacks changed?

Mr. Casino: Maybe 20 or 25 percent.

BN: So once a machine is placed on a casino floor, there is at least a 75 percent chance that it will never have its payback changed?

Mr. Casino: Oh, yes. For the reels, you have to go out and buy the chips. That adds up really fast.

THE FACT IS...

Harrah's in Iowa has 1,218 slots. The Hilton in Atlantic City has 2,034 slots. Borgata has 3,572. Trump Taj Mahal has 4,383, and Foxwoods in Connecticut has 7,278. There are about 60,000 slots on the Las Vegas Strip.

You want to get it right the first time. We don't do a lot of changing unless there is some specific reason that it ought to be changed.

BN: When you're evaluating, more often than not, you might just evaluate to pull that machine off the floor rather than change the payback. Yes?

Mr. Casino: Yes. In a perfect world, the first thing I'm worried about is the popularity of the game. I don't want to manage a game by its hold. I don't want to have it make enough money by changing how much it is holding. I want it to be a game that people love to play, and then I want to keep my fair share of that.

BN: Why are slots in Las Vegas and Mississippi looser than slots in Connecticut and Atlantic City?

Mr. Casino: The biggest factor is probably the variation you find in tax rates. As the operator, you want to hit a certain operating margin. If you're paying 4 percent tax or 20 percent tax, that makes a difference.

BN: When taxes are lower, the games tend to be looser?

Mr. Casino: Absolutely.

BN: Thank you for the interview. Is there anything else you want to say?

Mr. Casino: I think people should play slots for fun… You could stack all the circumstances in your favor and still lose $20 in twenty minutes.

BN: I agree.

Analysis of the Interview

On the broader issues, Mr. Casino confirms what we already know. Games near tables and waiting areas tend to be tight. Progressive games pay back less than non-progressive contests. Games are looser in higher denominations. Popular games are placed in areas of high visibility.

But it's on this last point that Mr. Casino and his company go a unique way. For them, popular means tight. His company is competitive on looseness when it's necessary, but Mr. Casino and his associates mostly see looseness as something to be remedied rather than celebrated or promoted. Essentially, Mr. Casino feels that if he gives you a good enough gaming experience, you'll gladly risk more money and tolerate spending more.

Many casinos follow this "tight" model. There's nothing wrong with playing in those casinos, but remember that your long-term prospects for winning go down dramatically as the casino's hold goes up. Even if you prefer penny and nickel games, it makes sense (from a bankroll perspective) to choose properties with looser games, or at least be aware that you're playing in a tight casino, and adjust your strategy accordingly.

Specifically, be extra careful when playing penny and nickel machines. You may be getting only 85 percent payback rather than the 90 percent payback that is standard for games in these denominations.

Also, in tight casinos, expect less payback spread between loose and tight games.

Whatever you play, remember to follow Mr. Casino's advice... Be sure you have fun!

Essentially

- The casino industry is not a monolithic business, so all slot layouts are not designed the same way. Some casinos focus more on promoting loose games; others prefer to have tighter games.

- The loosest games usually will be $1 and $5 contests, even in casinos that are overall tight.

- Progressive games usually pay back 90 percent or less. Progressive games that are identical and in a bank are all set at the same payback (one machine will not be looser than the others).

- Casinos rarely change the payback on games. If a game is a poor performer, a casino is more likely to pull it off the floor rather than dicker with the payback.

- Mr. Casino confirms basic principles of slots optimal strategy outlined in Chapter 4.

PART THREE
Cards and Dice

CHAPTER 7

Blackjack: Basic Strategies

 Are you brand new to blackjack? Then this chapter is for you. It's an overview of how blackjack is played.

If you've played blackjack before, this chapter is probably for you, too (so don't go skipping ahead just yet). Blackjack has some rule variations that are often unknown to casual players, and these rules can have a tremendous impact on your long-term profitability. If you're at all unfamiliar with blackjack terms such as "basic strategy," "natural," "surrender," "hole card," "soft hand," or "insurance," then you should stick around because we cover all of that and much more in the next few pages.

But first the essentials.

Blackjack is About 21

Blackjack is all about the number 21.

The game uses one or more decks of standard playing cards. The suits of the cards have no significance; only their rank is of importance. Cards ranked 2 through 10 are counted at their number value. Jacks, queens, and kings are counted as 10. Aces can be 1 or 11, as the player requires.

Each player competes with the dealer to build a hand that has a point total closer to 21 but not over that amount. The initial hand is two cards. If it's a combination of 10 and an ace, 21, it's called blackjack or a **natural**; the hand will either win or be tied, but it cannot lose.

Obviously, a hand with a lower total does not have this status, so a player can ask for additional cards in an attempt to get closer to 21. Receiving an additional card is called a **hit**. Refusing an additional card is a **stand**. Players who exceed 21 automatically lose. This is called a **bust** or a **break**. When all the players have finished hitting, standing, and sometimes busting, it's the dealer's turn to complete her hand. The rules of the game require her to hit a 16 or less and stand on 17 or more (there is one minor exception to this involving an ace and 6 that we'll cover later).

And finally, the dealer compares her hand with each player's hand.

● **If neither hand busts, the highest total wins.**

● **If neither hand busts, and they are tied, then it's a push. There is no winner and no money changes hands.**

● **If the player busts, then that's it. The player loses and the dealer's hand is of no consequence.**

● **If the dealer busts and the player has not busted, the player wins.**

A player's natural earns 3:2. That means a $10 bet wins fifteen additional dollars. All other winning bets are paid 1:1 (except insurance, an option we'll cover in the next section).

It all sounds fairly equitable, but it's not. The casino has an advantage because players must complete their hands first. Thus a player will lose with a bust even when the dealer busts, too. The casino's entire profit in the game depends on this order of play. But happily for us, there are strategies to reduce and eliminate the casino's built-in edge.

The Flow of the Game

Now that we've covered the basic rules of blackjack, let's take a closer look at how the game is actually played. Keep in mind that in almost every case a rule variation (such as multiple decks rather than a single deck) has an effect on the casino's advantage. There are dozens of these variations, so I'll just mention them here, and we'll review them later in depth.

Here's the Deal

Blackjack is played at a table like the one on the next page. Note that important rules are always printed on the table cover. Additional rules will be on an upright plastic or Plexiglas card next to the dealer. Some casinos offer single-deck games in which the dealer actually holds the deck as she distributes the cards, but most casinos have multiple-deck games. Four to eight decks are stored in a box called a **shoe**. The dealer pulls cards from a slot at the front of the shoe (we'll discuss dealing and shuffling on page 134).

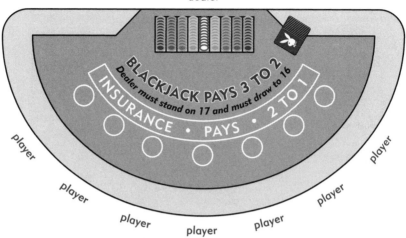

dealer

BLACKJACK PAYS 3 TO 2
Dealer must stand on 17 and must draw to 16
INSURANCE · PAYS · 2 TO 1

player
player
player
player
player
player
player
player

This is a standard blackjack table. Note the house rules printed at the center of the table.

Players' cards are usually dealt face-down in a single-deck game. Multiple-deck games are usually dealt face-up. Your chances of winning are the same either way, though there are some practical differences between the two methods. Players handle cards when they're dealt face-down, but they're usually not allowed to touch cards when they're dealt face-up. Some people enjoy holding cards, but it's strictly a personal preference. Concealed faces offer no advantage.

Getting into a game is easy. Just choose a table and sit in an available seat. Any seat is fine. You have an equal chance of winning at all of them. Lay some money on the felt, and the dealer will take the money and give you chips (see Chapter 20 for more on handling cash and chips). Then put a wager in the circle in front of you and don't touch the chips again. You'll either lose them at the end of the hand, or you'll win and be given more chips by the dealer.

Starting on her left, the dealer gives one card to each player and then one card face-up to herself. A second card is dealt to each player and the

THE FACT IS...

The seat to the dealer's far left (player's right) is commonly called "first base." The seat at the other end of the table is "third base." The terminology is of no consequence in the game, but knowing it may help you in a conversation with an experienced blackjack player.

dealer receives another card called the **hole card**. This time it's face-down.

Thus you can see only one of the dealer's cards. Let's say it's a **9**. Does the dealer have an ace in the hole, giving her 20? Does the dealer have 18? Does the dealer have 13? If you have 21 or 20 it doesn't matter; you'll stand and probably win or push. But what if you have 16? Should you hit? What's that other card?

Insurance

The question of the hole card becomes an even greater issue when the upcard is an ace because, of course, you lose if the dealer has a natural and you don't.

The solution (for some players) is to take **insurance** against a dealer blackjack when the dealer is showing an ace. Insurance is an additional bet of typically one-half the value of the original bet, and it pays 2:1. In most casinos the dealer will then check the hole card for a 10 before continuing the hand. Let's say you have a $10 original bet and a $5 insurance bet; you don't have a natural but it turns out that the dealer does. She will take $10 and pay $10. The net effect is that zero dollars change hands. It's a push. The hand is over.

If the dealer doesn't have blackjack, you lose the insurance bet and the hand continues.

Insurance sounds like a wonderful thing, but it's usually a bad bet. I'll explain why in a later section.

Tip

It's very important for you to give the dealer clear visual cues such as tapping the table or waving your hand rather than saying "hit" or "stand" because the casino's overhead cameras must be able to see the action. This is a security precaution that insures a visual record will be available in the event of a dispute.

Hit, Stand, Double, or Split

Most dealers' hands aren't naturals, so players have an opportunity to either request additional cards or refuse them. The dealer works from her left to her right.

Tapping or scratching the table with your index finger indicates your desire for an additional card. A small wave with one hand as if to say "stop" or "go away" indicates that you are standing. Another way to show a stand when cards are dealt face down is to push the edge of your cards a bit under the wager and move your hands away. Conversely, scratching the cards lightly on the felt signals a hit.

Tip

Most casinos that deal cards face-up require that you never touch the cards. This includes splitting. In this case, simply put an additional wager next to the original bet (not on top of it). The dealer will separate the cards and hit or stand as you request.

One variation of a hit is called a **double down**. It requires an additional bet, usually an amount equal to your original wager. You put the extra chips next to your original chips. The dealer gives you exactly one more card and that is your hand. No additional hits are allowed. Doubling is usually restricted to first action on an original hand.

If your original hand has cards with an equal point value (**A,A**; **8,8**; **9,9**; and so on) you can **split** them for an additional wager equal to the first wager. You then have two hands. A second card is dealt to each hand, and you play the hands separately (hitting, doubling, splitting, or standing, as necessary). Some casinos restrict resplitting and doubling on splits. Most require that split aces get only one extra card per ace.

The Dealer's Hand

If you don't bust, it's up to the dealer to beat you. She turns over her hole card and draws according to the rules mentioned earlier. The only variation to this is that some casinos require a dealer to hit a **soft 17** (**A** and **6**).

By the way, any hand with an ace counted as 11 is called a **soft hand** (because it cannot bust with a hit). A **hard hand** does not contain an ace, or the ace is counted as one. Hard hands between 12 and 16 are also sometimes called **stiff hands**.

The dealer completes her hand as required. Losing bets are taken, winners are paid, the cards are collected, and the process begins again.

Rule Variations

If your initial hand seems hopeless, some casinos will allow you to take back half your bet and forfeit the rest. This is called **surrender**. It's usually restricted to situations when the dealer doesn't have a natural, and in these circumstances it's called **late surrender**. If the move is also allowed against an ace that turns out to be blackjack, then it's called **early surrender**.

Other rule variations include different payouts on naturals, not checking the hole card on insurance bets, restrictions on splitting and doubling, and a cornucopia of side bets that usually offer worse odds than the basic game. Every casino has its own unique combination of rules, so you should always check the upright card on the table or ask the dealer before playing.

Bad Play vs. Strategy

Let's say a player has a hand that totals 9, and the dealer's upcard is a **6**. What should the player do? Most people hit, and that's a mistake. What about a soft 18 against a dealer's **4**? Most people stand. That's a mistake, too (the correct plays are on page 103–104).

Multiply those mistakes by all the possible card combinations and you'll find that the majority of blackjack players unintentionally put themselves at a tremendous disadvantage. It's a self-imposed burden that is usually many times larger than any disadvantage actually built into the game.

This is ironic because even though blackjack is "beatable," the game can be far worse than slots or roulette when it's played incorrectly. Indeed, casinos earn the bulk of their blackjack profits from three types of non-strategy players.

One huge source of revenue comes from beginners and casual players who don't know that strategy exists. These people usually play short sessions and lose all their money quickly.

THE FACT IS...

Why does the dealer win so much? The casino's "secret" advantage in blackjack is the order of play. The dealer completes her hand last, so a player can bust and lose even when the dealer also busts. If the order of play were reversed, casinos would cease to exist because players would bankrupt the industry.

Another cash cow is players who *don't believe* that blackjack can be beaten because they've bought into the myth that "the casino always wins in the end." Nevertheless, these folks still want to play blackjack (because gambling is fun). So they do play, but with absolutely no plan for winning. They treat it like the lottery. Their only goal is to not lose too much. And that's how it usually goes. Their aggregate losses fill casino coffers.

The third group is folks who know that strategy works, but they prefer an unpredictable gamble. Players in this mindset enjoy following hunches and trends; they bet with intuition, and revel in surfing the whims of luck. Strategy is a total buzz-kill for them. Losing an extra $500, $1,000, or more is what they consider to be a reasonable price for a wild and crazy shot at the big money. Double down on a stiff hand? Yeah, baby!

Of course, it's perfectly okay to be a novice, be spontaneous, or to play with no expectation of winning. Strategy is not for everyone, and winning isn't everything. People should spend their leisure money in whatever way makes them happy. After all, blackjack is only a game. What's the point of playing if you're not having fun?

On the other hand, if your idea of fun does *not* include losing a wad of cash, then you'll be pleased to know that the strategies on the following pages are much more effective than hunches and guessing. And the casino doesn't "always win." On the contrary, the advanced strategies in Chapter 9 are so powerful that players who use them are sometimes ejected for winning too much (but we'll get to that later).

Right now just remember: there is luck and there is skill. Luck comes and goes, but skill is forever.

Basic Strategy

Basic strategy is actually a blackjack-specific term that refers to a strategy that was developed back in 1956 by four mathematicians, Roger Baldwin, Wilbert E. Cantey, Herbert Maisel, and James P. McDermott. These four men were the first people to thoroughly analyze blackjack, and they subsequently published their results as "The Optimum Strategy in Blackjack" in the *Journal of the American Statistical Association*.

Since then, the strategy has been refined and tested over countless trillions of hands played in real casinos and computer simulations. All professional blackjack players use basic strategy, and it's the starting point of every optimal game.

THE FACT IS...

You can expect to see a natural about once in every twenty-one hands. Pairs appear about once in every seventeen hands (when playing a single-deck game). Double aces occur about once in every 221 hands.

The Strategy Charts

The next few paragraphs may seem unusually complicated. But don't worry, this is only an off-the-wall example.

Let's say you have a hard 13 and the dealer's upcard is **6**. What should you do?

If you were a math genius, you might instantly calculate that 62 percent of the cards in a deck have a rank of **6** through **10**. So there's a 62 percent chance the dealer has a stiff hand, and it's very likely the hand is 15 or 16 because 38 percent of the cards in a deck have a rank of **9** or **10**.

Then you'd do additional calculations in your head and conclude that the dealer has an overall 42 percent chance of busting when she's showing a **6**. Meanwhile your chance of busting with a hit on hard 13 is about 38 percent. You'd add the possibility of hitting and getting an **A** through **3**, and realize the overall chance of busting or remaining stiff would be about 62 percent. Finally, you'd compare those two figures with a few others I haven't mentioned and come to the conclusion that a hit would do more harm than good. So you'd stand and the dealer would bust four times out of ten.

Brilliant!

But frankly, even a math genius might have problems doing the above calculations on the fly. So this particular combination and all the rest have been pre-calculated and organized into basic strategy. The only thing you need to remember is to stand on hard 13 against a **6**.

Basic strategy is easy to use. Just find your card combination on the left side of the chart and the dealer's upcard at the top (see below and page 104). Follow the column down until it intersects with the row for your card combination. That's how you should play the hand. If some of the strategy choices seem odd, then you'll find the chart on page 104 helpful. It shows the probable outcome of a dealer's hand based on the upcard.

Basic Strategy for Splitting Pairs

Player's Hand	Dealer's Upcard									
	2	3	4	5	6	7	8	9	10	A
A,A	sp	sp	sp	sp	sp	sp	sp	sp	sp	sp
10,10	NC	NC	NC	NC	NC	NC	NC	NC	NC	NC
9,9	sp	sp	sp	sp	sp	NC	sp	sp	NC	NC
8,8	sp	sp	sp	sp	sp	sp	sp	sp	sp	sp
7,7	sp	sp	sp	sp	sp	sp	h	h	h	h
6,6	sp	sp	sp	sp	sp	h	h	h	h	h
5,5	db	db	db	db	db	db	db	db	h	h
4,4	h	h	h	sp	sp	h	h	h	h	h
3,3	sp	sp	sp	sp	sp	sp	h	h	h	h
2,2	sp	sp	sp	sp	sp	sp	h	h	h	h

sp=split, NC=stand, h=hit, db=double

This is basic strategy for splitting pairs in a multiple-deck game. See the chart on page 104 for additional game rules.

Basic Strategy for Soft Hands

Player's Hand	Dealer's Upcard									
	2	3	4	5	6	7	8	9	10	A
Soft 19–21	NC	NC	NC	NC	NC	NC	NC	NC	NC	NC
Soft 18	NC	dbN	dbN	dbN	dbN	NC	NC	h	h	h
Soft 17	h	db	db	db	db	h	h	h	h	h
Soft 16	h	h	db	db	db	h	h	h	h	h
Soft 15	h	h	db	db	db	h	h	h	h	h
Soft 14	h	h	h	db	db	h	h	h	h	h
Soft 13	h	h	h	db	db	h	h	h	h	h

NC=stand, h=hit, db=double (hit if a double is not possible), dbN=double (stand if a double is not possible)

This is basic strategy for soft hands in a multiple-deck game. See the chart on page 104 for additional game rules.

Basic Strategy for Hard Hands

Player's Hand	Dealer's Upcard									
	2	3	4	5	6	7	8	9	10	A
Hard 17–21	NC	NC	NC	NC	NC	NC	NC	NC	NC	NC
Hard 16	NC	NC	NC	NC	NC	h	h	sr	sr	sr
Hard 15	NC	NC	NC	NC	NC	h	h	h	sr	h
Hard 14	NC	NC	NC	NC	NC	h	h	h	h	h
Hard 13	NC	NC	NC	NC	NC	h	h	h	h	h
Hard 12	h	h	NC	NC	NC	h	h	h	h	h
11	db	db	db	db	db	db	db	db	db	h
10	db	db	db	db	db	db	db	db	h	h
9	h	db	db	db	db	h	h	h	h	h
5–8	h	h	h	h	h	h	h	h	h	h

NC=stand, h=hit, db=double (hit if a double is not possible), sr=surrender (hit if surrender is not allowed)

This is basic strategy for a multiple-deck game, when the dealer stands on soft 17 and late surrender, doubling after splits, and doubling on any two cards is allowed. These game conditions also apply to the charts on page 103.

Dealer's Bust Probabilities

Dealer's Upcard	Final Total						
	17+	18+	19+	20+	21	BJ	Bust
2	65%	51%	37%	24%	12%	0	35%
3	63	49	36	24	12	0	37
4	60	47	35	23	11	0	40
5	58	46	34	22	11	0	42
6	58	41	31	20	10	0	42
7	74	37	23	15	7	0	26
8	76	63	27	14	7	0	24
9	77	65	53	18	6	0	23
10	71	60	49	38	4	8	21
A	58	45	32	19	5	31	11

This chart shows how the upcard affects the probability of a dealer bust. Numbers are rounded and reflect multiple decks when the dealer stands on soft 17. Hitting soft 17 will produce slightly different numbers.

At first glance, basic strategy may seem complicated, but it's actually quite simple. Nearly half of the hands should always be played the same way, regardless of what the dealer is showing. The rest, with a few exceptions, should be played one of two ways. This is determined by the dealer's upcard.

The strategy in these particular charts is optimized for multiple-deck games (four or more decks) when the dealer stands on soft 17, and the rules allow late surrender, doubling after splits, and doubling on any two cards.

Games with one or two decks, restricted doubling, or soft 17 hits by the dealer have slightly different strategies. We'll cover those in a later section.

Strategy Shortcuts

Basic strategy is easy to memorize when you use a few shortcuts. First you look for a pat hand (a total that requires no action), then a low hand (an automatic hit), then situations for splits and doubles. Finally, you evaluate soft and stiff hands and take action based on the dealer's upcard. For simplicity, let's label a dealer's upcard of **2** through **6** as "vulnerable," and **7** through **A** as "strong."

Pat Hands—Always stand on 19 or higher. Always stand on hard 17 and hard 18 (except for a pair of nines as noted below).

Low Hands—Always hit any hand of 8 or less except for pairs (discussed below).

Pairs—A hand of **A,A** or **8,8** should *always* be split. A hand of **10,10** or **5,5** should *never* be split.

The remaining pairs are mostly split against a dealer's vulnerable cards and hit against his stronger cards, but there are some exceptions.

9,9—Split them against vulnerable cards and also against **8** or **9**. Stand against **7**, **10**, and **A**.

7,7—Split them against vulnerable cards, and also against **7**. Hit against **8** and above.

6,6—Split against vulnerable cards. Hit against strong cards.

4,4—Split against **5** and **6**. Hit against everything else.

2,2 and **3,3**—Split against all the vulnerable cards as well as **7**. Hit against everything higher.

Double Down—There are two types of doubling situations, hands that total 9, 10, or 11, and soft hands that aren't pat. The dealer's upcard determines if your hand should be doubled or hit.

11—Double against everything except an **A**. Hit against the **A**.

10—Double against everything except **10** and **A**. Hit against **10** and **A**.

9—Double against all the vulnerable hands except for **2**. Hit against **2** and all strong cards.

Soft Hands—Here's the strategy for soft hands that aren't pat (totals lower than 19). If the strategy calls for a double down but the rules don't allow it, then the hand should be hit, except for soft 18 as noted below.

A,7—Double a soft 18 against vulnerable cards except for **2**.

If a double is not possible then stand. Stand against **2**, **7**, or **8**. Hit against **9** or higher.

A,6—Double against vulnerable cards except for **2**. Hit against **2** and against strong cards.

A,5 and **A,4**—Double against **4**, **5**, and **6**. Hit against **2**, **3**, and against strong cards.

A,2 and **A,3**—Double against **5** and **6** only, and hit against everything else.

Stiff Hands—*Always* hit a stiff hand against a dealer's **7** through **A**. Never hit a stiff hand against a dealer's **2** through **6** except as noted below.

16—Surrender against **9**, **10**, or **A**; hit if surrender isn't allowed.

15—Surrender against **10**; hit if surrender isn't allowed.

12—Hit against a **2** or **3**.

From 5 Percent to Fuzz

Remember the "fuzz" that I mentioned back in Chapter 2? It's the hazy area where negative expectation blends into positive expectation. People who play blackjack *without* using basic strategy are nowhere near the fuzz. They usually lose somewhere between 2 percent and 5 percent of all the money that they bet over time (depending on how much a player deviates from optimal choices). And this is cumulative, so it's at least 2 percent plus 2 percent and so on until all of the player's money is gone.

In contrast, basic strategy lowers the house edge usually to somewhere less than 0.5 percent (well into the fuzz), and it occasionally pushes the edge into the positive range depending on the game's exact combination of rules. But you have to use the *entire* strategy to get the full benefit. Here are some examples.

The Importance of Doubling and Splitting

Some people try to "save money" by doubling only on 11 or 10 and splitting only **A**s, But in fact, this variance from strategy actually costs money. That's because all doubling situations are *positive-expectation wagers*. You could earn a living making double-down bets if blackjack rules allowed you to wager them exclusively.

Ditto for splitting, though splitting also includes the factor of losing less on hands like **8,8** (16 being a consistent loser). Splitting **8,8** gives you a good chance to catch a **10**, **9**, or **A** to make a pat hand, and you might catch a **2** or **3** for a double-down opportunity.

Remember, a positive-expectation game absolutely requires doubling and splitting in all appropriate situations.

Hitting Stiff Hands

Busting with a stiff hand is a drag, especially when the dealer's hand turns out to be stiff, too. But your overall chance of losing is much greater when you stand on stiffs against **7** through **A**.

This is a situation of losing less rather than winning more because, frankly, stiff hands against strong cards are consistent money-losers. So you're simply trying to squeeze the most out of a bad situation.

Conversely, the situation isn't so bad that you should surrender a hand unless basic strategy actually indicates a surrender. Consider this: surrender costs two full bets after four hands (one-half bet per surrender). A stiff hand would have to lose three times out of four to equal that cost (1 win − 3 losses = −2). Most stiff hands have a greater value than that.

Tip

Third-base players are sometimes harassed by other players for not playing basic strategy correctly. Drawing a **10** that would otherwise bust the dealer is particularly unpopular. If you don't want the attention, don't play third base.

So you should surrender only hands that total 15 and 16, and only in specific circumstances. A hand of 15 should be surrendered against 10, and 16 should be surrendered against **9**, **10**, or **A**.

The Insurance Gamble

Insurance is a bad bet. The probability of finding a **10** under the dealer's **A** is less than 1 in 3 (about 31 percent), but insurance pays only 2 to 1. It works out to a house edge of about 7 percent. That's worse than roulette and about the same as slot machines.

Nevertheless, some people insure their naturals when the dealer is showing an **A** because it guarantees a 1:1 payout. Insurance in this situation is still a bad bet, but here's how the wager works:

- If the player insures and the dealer has a natural, the two naturals push and insurance wins. 0 + 1 = 1

- If the dealer doesn't have a natural, the player's natural wins and the insurance loses. 1.5 − 0.5 = 1

So either way the player receives the same amount of money. It sounds nifty, but the payout on a natural cannot "heal" the bad bet on insurance. They're still two separate bets. Over time, when the wins and pushes are combined, you'll earn nearly 4 percent more on naturals when you don't insure.

There are only two situations when insurance is correct. The first occurs when a player is **counting cards** (see Chapter 9), and he knows that the deck contains enough 10s to raise the probability of a dealer natural above 33.3 percent.

The second situation is entirely personal, but it's one of the few instances when deviating from basic strategy makes sense. If you have an enormous bet on the table, and you would be sorely disappointed if the hand resulted in a push (the kind of disappointment that might ruin your evening), then go ahead and

THE FACT IS...

The casino usually wins **48 percent** of blackjack hands on average, players win **43 percent**, and **9 percent** of hands are a push. A player's 5 percent disadvantage in win frequency is offset by payouts for naturals, and extra profit on splits and doubles. That's why it's important for you to double and split according to basic strategy and avoid taking insurance.

insure. It's not good math, but it might be correct from a psychological point of view. Remember, you do want to have fun.

Probably is not Definitely

Keep in mind that basic strategy doesn't absolutely predict the outcome of a hand; it simply tells us the most profitable choice if that hand were to be played repeatedly forever. So in some situations you will lose when following basic strategy, but that doesn't mean the strategy has failed, it just means that the casino was lucky. Nobody owns the edge, and nobody owns luck either.

Also, the casino has an overall advantage in win frequency (see the sidebar on page 108), but that advantage is offset by the extra payouts you receive for naturals, doubling, and splitting. What this means is that you generally lose a bit more than you win for a while, and then you jump ahead (or vice versa).

And finally, there is standard deviation to consider. The fact that you're playing with a near-zero edge doesn't guarantee that you and the casino will be absolutely even at the end of a session. On the contrary, it's highly likely that one side will be ahead of the other. After all, it is a game. But basic strategy gives both sides a nearly equal chance of being ahead.

Casinos don't like that, so some of them are constantly jiggering the rules to push basic-strategy players out of the fuzz and solidly onto the negative side. Meanwhile, other casinos are improving the rules to attract players who are turned off by the jiggered game across the street. As a result, all blackjack games are not identical. You have to shop around to find the most favorable rules.

We'll talk about that in the next chapter.

Essentially

- Blackjack is all about the number 21. Each player competes with the dealer to build a hand that has a point total closer to 21 but not over that amount.

- When playing blackjack in a casino, you must give the dealer clear visual cues (tapping the table for a hit, or holding up your hand for a stand) rather than saying "hit" or "stand."

- Blackjack basic strategy reduces the casino's edge to less than one percent, but this reduction occurs only if you use the entire strategy. You must double down and split as recommended to get the full positive effect.

- You should stand on all hands of 19 and higher when playing standard basic strategy, and you should hit all hands of **8** or less (except for pairs in some situations). A hand of **A,A** or **8,8** should always be split. A hand of **10,10** or **5,5** should never be split.

- Don't take insurance. It's a bad bet unless you're counting cards.

CHAPTER 8

Blackjack: Favorable and Unfavorable Games

 Some blackjack games are played with a single deck. Others use multiple decks. Some dealers hit soft 17, some don't. Naturals traditionally pay 3:2, but a lot of games these days pay only 1:1, or 6:5 for naturals.

For every rule there is usually a variation. Even the "bust-over-21" rule is sometimes bent.

All these variations change the house edge. And while one change by itself isn't necessarily dramatic, the effects of multiple changes can accumulate and drag a player well into the negative side, especially when basic strategy is not adjusted to compensate. An overall 2 percent jump in the house edge is not uncommon when an incorrect strategy is applied to a mediocre or extremely unfavorable game.

You certainly don't want to be playing under those conditions, so in the next few pages I'll show you how to quickly identify favorable and unfavorable games.

The Good, the Bad, and the Sneaky

Once upon a time (in the middle decades of the twentieth century) blackjack was played mostly one way. It was a single-deck game, and dealers always stood on soft 17. Doubling was allowed on any two cards, and doubling was also allowed after splits. Naturals paid 3:2.

Blackjack with these rules was extremely profitable for casinos because people used to do all sorts of nutty things like splitting **10,10**, standing on **8,8**, or hitting 12 regardless of the dealer's upcard. Nobody knew any better. But all that changed in 1962 when casino managers noticed that some blackjack players were winning enormous amounts of money. The managers did some research and learned that these particular players were using strategies from a book called

Beat the Dealer written by Edward O. Thorp, a mathematics professor. The book explained and expanded on the original basic strategy developed back in 1956, and it introduced the advanced strategy of counting cards.

This was traumatic for the casino industry. Blackjack was suddenly beatable. Since then, casinos have been endlessly experimenting with **countermeasures** such as multiple decks and hitting soft 17 to mitigate the effects of the various blackjack strategies. But it's a tricky balance for them because they don't want to make blackjack too tough for novice players. Whenever a casino introduces rules that completely kill the effects of strategy, it also essentially ruins the game, and many players (including the novices) move to other casinos. Casino vice presidents are then summarily fired, and the blackjack rules are relaxed. The crowds return, along with the **advantage players** (people who use advanced strategies), and the cycle repeats itself. Managers fume as they watch a few really good players skewer the house. And when managers aren't fuming, they're jiggering rules to make games seem beatable when they're really not.

It's a sneaky system of bait and switch, as you'll soon see.

THE FACT IS...

Multiple decks increase the house edge. Part of the reason for this is that extra decks lower the overall probability of receiving a natural. Also, multiple decks reduce the chance that a double down will beat the dealer.

Rule Variations and Their Costs

The good old single-deck game of yesteryear is pretty much gone forever, but it's still useful as a standard to measure the effects of various rule changes. And since the truly classic old Las Vegas blackjack game was actually a positive-expectation contest (when using basic strategy), we need to restate the rules a bit to bring it down to zero.

This is our standard zero-advantage contest; it's a single-deck game, dealer stands on soft 17, doubling is allowed on any two cards, but doubling is *not* allowed after splits. Naturals pay 3:2.

The following chart shows the relative advantages and disadvantages of the most common rule variations.

Rules and Their Effect on the Edge

Unfavorable Rules

Two decks	–0.35%
Four decks	–0.52%
Six decks	–0.58%
Eight decks	–0.61%
Dealer hits soft 17	–0.20%
Double only on 9, 10, or 11	–0.10%
Double only on 10 or 11	–0.20%
No splitting of As	–0.17%
Tied hands lose (per rank)	–1.78%
Naturals pay 1:1	–2.29%
Naturals pay 6:5	–1.37%

Favorable Rules

Resplit As	+0.08%
Draw to split As	+0.19%
Double after split	+0.12%
Late surrender	+0.07%
Early surrender	+0.62%
Surrender after doubling	+0.10%
Double on more than two cards	+0.21%
Five-card automatic winner	+1.49%
Six-card automatic winner	+0.15%
Tied naturals always win 3:2	+0.32%
Suited naturals pay 2:1 (per suit)	+0.30%
Naturals pay 2:1	+2.29%

This table shows the effects of various rules on the house edge. The baseline is a zero percent house edge in a single-deck game when the dealer stands on soft 17 and doubling is allowed, but not after splitting. Some figures are adjusted for multiple decks.

Calculating the edge for a game is easy. Simply start at zero and then add or subtract the amounts that correspond to the various rules. For example, a six-deck game (–0.58), with the dealer hitting soft 17 (–0.20), double on any two cards (0), double after splits (+0.12), and late surrender (+0.07), adds up to –0.59 percent.

Here's a game I've seen on the Las Vegas Strip. It's played with a single deck (0), dealer hits soft 17 (–0.20), doubling is allowed on 10 or 11 only (–0.20), no doubles after splits (0), and naturals pay 6:5 (–1.37). That game has a whopping edge of 1.77 percent!

Now compare the above game to one I found in downtown Las Vegas: It's a single deck (0), dealer hits soft 17 (–0.20), doubling

is allowed on any two cards (0), no doubles after splits (0), and naturals pay 3:2 (0). This game has an edge of only 0.20 percent.

Tip

Occasionally a casino will offer a promotion of 2:1 payouts on naturals. This will push almost any blackjack game solidly into positive expectation. If you see such a promotion, play it soon because it won't last long. But be careful. Some casinos advertise 2:1 payouts for one kind of suited natural, and 1:1 for all others. This is much worse than the standard 3:2 payout.

Clearly, many casinos hope you'll see a single-deck game and instantly sit down without investigating all the rules.

Other casinos try a different approach; they vigorously promote favorable rules with slick brochures and bold advertisements, but the unfavorable rules such as low-paying 1:1 naturals get less type and hype.

Whatever the marketing strategy, it's always a good idea to read the upright card and ask some questions before putting your money on the table.

Variations of Basic Strategy

Realistically, you could use the basic strategy on pages 103–104 for almost any blackjack game, and in most situations it would serve you reasonably well. But if you exclusively play games that hit soft 17, prohibit doubles after splits, or use less than six decks, then you should learn the exact strategy for your favorite contest (because those fractions of a percent add up). And with a little a practice it's actually pretty easy to switch back and forth between strategy variations.

Rather than reprinting the entire strategy for every variation, I'll simply list the differences compared to the standard strategy.

Dealer Hits Soft 17

A dealer hitting soft 17 (often abbreviated as H17) may seem at first to be an advantage to the player because it increases the probability of a stiff and then a bust, but it's actually a long-term disadvantage because the bust probability is more than offset by the value of a possibly higher total (that's why basic strategy always tells you to hit or double down on soft 17).

Here are the strategy variations when the dealer hits soft 17:

8,8—Surrender against an **A**. Split as usual if surrender is not allowed.

A,8—Double down on soft 19 against a **6**. Stand as usual if a double is not allowed.

A,7—Double down on soft 18 against a **2**. Stand as usual if a double is not allowed.

11—Double down on an 11 against an **A**.

17—Surrender against an **A**. Stand as usual if surrender is not allowed.

15—Surrender against an **A**. Hit as usual if surrender is not allowed.

No Doubles After Splits

Some of the value of splitting comes from the possibility that you might double down on a split hand. If this option is not allowed, then some splits become less valuable, and you should hit instead of split. By the way, NDAS is a common abbreviation for no doubling after splits (see the sidebar below for more abbreviations).

6,6—Hit against a dealer's **2**.

4,4—Hit against a dealer's **5** or **6**.

2,2 and **3,3**—Hit against a dealer's **2** or **3**.

One and Two Decks

One- and two-deck games typically hit soft 17 and prohibit doubling after splits, so use the modifications to basic strategy in the previous sections as necessary and include the following for two decks:

Two Decks

6,6—Split against a dealer's **2** (yes, this is a reversal of the strategy for NDAS)

9—Double down against a dealer's **2**.

Single Deck

All of the above and…

THE FACT IS...

Professional blackjack players often use abbreviations to describe game conditions. Some of these abbreviations include H17 (dealer hits soft 17), DA2 (doubling is allowed on any two cards), NDAS (no doubles after splits), and LS (late surrender).

7,7—Stand against a dealer's **10**.

2,2—Split against a dealer's **3** (this reverses the strategy for NDAS).

A,7—Stand on soft 18 against a dealer's **2** (this reverses the strategy for H17).

A,6—Double down on soft 17 against a dealer's **2**.

A,2 and **A,3**—Double down on soft 13 and soft 14 against a dealer's **4**.

8—Double down on **8** against a dealer's **5** and **6**.

Remember, the sky won't fall if you use the multiple-deck strategy from the previous chapter in a single-deck game, but you will be giving away some of your edge. For example, doubling down on a **9** against a dealer's **2** is a positive-expectation wager when playing one or two decks. As the saying goes, this is money sitting on the table waiting to be taken.

Single-Deck Strategy on a Chart

Okay, let's put it all together. The following pages have the unified basic strategy for a single-deck game when the dealer hits soft 17, no surrender, doubling is allowed on any two cards, but doubling is not allowed after splits.

You'll see that basic strategy changes in some important ways as the rules change, but overall the main points are consistent. Always split **A,A** and **8,8**. Never split **5,5** and **10,10**. Always stand on 19 or above (with one H17 exception). Generally you're hitting against stronger dealer's cards and standing or doubling down against vulnerable ones.

The one seemingly oddball single-deck play is **7,7** against **10**. You stand on this hand in a single-deck game because there are only two **7**s left in the deck to give you a one-hit 21.

Single-Deck Strategy for Splitting Pairs

Player's Hand	Dealer's Upcard									
	2	3	4	5	6	7	8	9	10	A
A,A	sp	sp	sp	sp	sp	sp	sp	sp	sp	sp
10,10	NC	NC	NC	NC	NC	NC	NC	NC	NC	NC
9,9	sp	sp	sp	sp	sp	NC	sp	sp	NC	N
8,8	sp	sp	sp	sp	sp	sp	sp	sp	sp	sp
7,7	sp	sp	sp	sp	sp	sp	h	h	NC	h
6,6	sp	sp	sp	sp	sp	h	h	h	h	h
5,5	db	db	db	db	db	db	db	db	h	h
4,4	h	h	h	h	h	h	h	h	h	h
3,3	h	h	sp	sp	sp	sp	h	h	h	h
2,2	h	sp	sp	sp	sp	sp	h	h	h	h

sp=split, NC=stand, h=hit, db=double

This is basic strategy for splitting pairs in a single-deck game.
See the chart on page 118 for additional game rules.

Single-Deck Strategy for Soft Hands

Players Hand	Dealer's Upcard									
	2	3	4	5	6	7	8	9	10	A
Soft 20–21	NC	NC	NC	NC	NC	NC	NC	NC	NC	NC
Soft 19	NC	NC	NC	NC	dbN	NC	NC	NC	NC	NC
Soft 18	NC	dbN	dbN	dbN	dbN	NC	NC	h	h	h
Soft 17	db	db	db	db	db	h	h	h	h	h
Soft 16	h	h	db	db	db	h	h	h	h	h
Soft 15	h	h	db	db	db	h	h	h	h	h
Soft 14	h	h	db	db	db	h	h	h	h	h
Soft 13	h	h	db	db	db	h	h	h	h	h

NC=stand, h=hit, db=double (hit if a double is not possible), dbN=double (stand if a double is not possible)

This is basic strategy for soft hands in a single-deck game.
See the chart on page 118 for additional game rules.

Single-Deck Strategy for Hard Hands

Player's Hand	Dealer's Upcard									
	2	3	4	5	6	7	8	9	10	A
Hard 17–21	NC	NC	NC	NC	NC	NC	NC	NC	NC	NC
Hard 16	NC	NC	NC	NC	NC	h	h	h	h	h
Hard 15	NC	NC	NC	NC	NC	h	h	h	h	h
Hard 14	NC	NC	NC	NC	NC	h	h	h	h	h
Hard 13	NC	NC	NC	NC	NC	h	h	h	h	h
Hard 12	h	h	NC	NC	NC	h	h	h	h	h
11	db	db	db	db	db	db	db	db	db	db
10	db	db	db	db	db	db	db	db	h	h
9	db	db	db	db	db	h	h	h	h	h
8	h	h	h	db	db	h	h	h	h	h
5–7	h	h	h	h	h	h	h	h	h	h

NC=stand, h=hit, db=double (hit if a double is not possible)

This is basic strategy for a single-deck game when the dealer hits soft 17 and there is no surrender and no doubling on splits. Doubling on any two cards is allowed. These game rules also apply to the charts on page 117.

Learning Basic Strategy

The best way to learn basic strategy is to play a lot of blackjack, but the worst place to learn while playing is in a casino. That's because there are too many distractions in a casino. The dealer and other players want to keep the game moving, and there is always the pressure of betting. It's tough to concentrate on strategy when chips are appearing and disappearing.

Of course, you'll eventually need to thrive in that busy atmosphere, but in the beginning it's better to learn basic strategy at home where you can give the game your full attention. Some people play blackjack on a computer, and that's a good way to go, but an even better way to learn is by dealing a real deck of cards (or multiple decks).

Tip

One good way to learn basic strategy is to write each hand from the strategy chart individually onto an index card, and write the correct move on the back of the card. Then shuffle the index cards and review them one by one.

It's easy to play blackjack alone, and in many ways it's more fun than solitaire.

Simply deal the hand as a casino dealer would: one card for you, one face up for the dealer, one more for you, and the last card face down. Follow basic strategy and then complete the dealer's hand according to the rules.

Pretty soon you'll be speeding through hands and doubling, splitting, standing, or hitting like a pro. You can track wins and losses with coins, poker chips, or use a notepad.

Keep in mind that your home game is identical in its results to games that you would play in a casino; the act of wagering doesn't magically change how cards fall. So if you lose fifty coins, that would have been $250 dollars in $5 chips. Likewise, winning fifty coins means you would have earned $250 in a casino.

This realization can be sobering when you quickly toast a pile of coins. On the other hand, it can make you giddy when you're consistently ahead because you know this represents real money that you could have won (and you likely will win some day).

Practice until you're entirely comfortable and you make no mistakes. This may take a few hours, a few days, or a few weeks. Everyone is different. Take your time, and don't rush to play for real money. Blackjack is not like a Broadway musical that will leave the theater next month. It will be there forever.

You'll know that you're ready when you can play without looking at the charts. Ditto if you can make it through the entire strategy on flashcards and not make a mistake (see the sidebar on page 118).

The Perils of Guessing

It's a drag to double down, get a small card, and have the dealer beat you with a 17. And it's even a bigger drag when that happens three times in a row.

Bad streaks like that cause some people to lose confidence. They abandon basic strategy and play

THE FACT IS...

You and the dealer have an equal probability of receiving any particular two-card hand, so it's just a coincidence if it seems as if the dealer is getting all face cards and you're getting all stiffs.

any old way, or they try to dissect luck and predict the future by studying trends and other non-mathematic strategies.

All that crystal ball stuff is fine, but playing blackjack without basic strategy is essentially a giant leap into the "guessing pool." It works for people who are psychic, but regular folks don't fare so well over time. In non-psychic circumstances, the best way to influence the outcome of a hand and play with an actual (though imperfect) knowledge of the future is to follow basic strategy.

But what if your ears start burning, and you have a spooky feeling that you should hit that hard 14 against a 6? It's your money. Do what feels right. Just realize that you are paying for the pleasure of bucking the odds and making a guess.

Spanish 21

The handbill shouts "More Ways to Win!" Player blackjack beats dealer blackjack. Player 21 beats dealer 21. Naturals pay 3:2. Surrender is allowed. Split aces can be hit and doubled. Double down is allowed on any number of cards. A double down that produces a small card can be surrendered. Wow!

In very small print the handbill says, "Played with six Spanish packs **2–9, J, Q, K, A**."

What's a Spanish pack? What happened to the **10**s?

Obviously, eliminating the **10**s reduces the chance of seeing a natural. Also, the dealer is less likely to bust, and you're less likely to finish with a strong hand after a double down.

As Homer Simpson would say, "Doh!"

In all fairness, Spanish 21 isn't a bad game, but it requires a special strategy that is substantially different from standard blackjack basic strategy.

THE FACT IS...

Spanish cards (decks without **10**s) are not the invention of a marketing wizard. Decks of this type have been around for centuries. They're still sold in Spain and elsewhere in Europe. However, genuine Spanish cards usually have Latin suits: coins, cups, swords, and batons.

The following pages contain a strategy for Spanish 21 that has been designed for simplicity and ease-of-use. It is intentionally *not* optimal, but it's very close and much easier to memorize. This strategy will lower the house edge on Spanish 21 to around 0.8 percent, just a fraction of a percent higher than perfect strategy, depending on the exact combination of rules (it works with both S17 and H17).

Spanish 21 Strategy for Splitting Pairs

Player's Hand	2	3	4	5	6	7	8	9	10	A
A,A	sp	sp	sp	sp	sp	sp	sp	sp	sp	sp
10,10	NC	NC	NC	NC	NC	NC	NC	NC	NC	NC
9,9	NC	sp	sp	sp	sp	NC	sp	sp	NC	NC
8,8	sp	sp	sp	sp	sp	sp	sp	sp	sp	sr
7,7	sp	sp	sp	sp	sp	hsp	h	h	h	h
6,6	h	h	sp	sp	sp	h	h	h	h	h
5,5	db	db	db	db	db	db	db	h	h	h
4,4	h	h	h	h	h	h	h	h	h	h
3,3	sp	sp	sp	sp	sp	sp	sp	h	h	h
2,2	sp	sp	sp	sp	sp	sp	h	h	h	h

sp=split, NC=stand, h=hit, db=double, sr=surrender hsp=hit when suited, otherwise split

This is Spanish 21 strategy for splitting pairs. See the chart on page 122 for additional game rules.

Spanish 21 Strategy for Soft Hands

Player's Hand	2	3	4	5	6	7	8	9	10	A
Soft 19–21	NC	NC	NC	NC	NC	NC	NC	NC	NC	NC
Soft 18	NC	NC	db	db	db	NC	NC	h	h	h
Soft 17	h	h	db	db	db	h	h	h	h	h
Soft 16	h	h	h	db	db	h	h	h	h	h
Soft 15	h	h	h	h	db	h	h	h	h	h
Soft 14	h	h	h	h	h	H	h	h	h	h
Soft 13	h	h	h	h	h	H	h	h	h	h

NC=stand, h=hit, db=double

This is Spanish 21 strategy for soft hands. See the chart on page 122 for additional game rules.

Spanish 21 Strategy for Hard Hands

Player's Hand	2	3	4	5	6	7	8	9	10	A
Hard 17–21	NC	NC	NC	NC	NC	NC	NC	NC	NC	NC
Hard 16	NC	NC	NC	NC	NC	h	h	h	h	sr
Hard 15	NC	NC	NC	NC	NC	h	h	h	h	h
Hard 14	h	h	NC	NC	NC	h	h	h	h	h
Hard 13	h	h	h	h	NC	h	h	h	h	h
Hard 12	h	h	h	h	h	h	h	h	h	h
11	db	db	db	db	db	db	db	db	db	db
10	db	db	db	db	db	db	db	h	h	h
9	h	h	h	h	db	h	h	h	h	h
5–8	h	h	h	h	h	h	h	h	h	h

Dealer's Upcard

NC=stand, h=hit, sr=surrender db=double

This is Spanish 21 strategy for hard hands. Spanish 21 is played with six or eight decks that contain forty-eight cards each (standard decks with 10s removed).

The first thing you'll notice about the strategy for Spanish 21 is that it doesn't have as much doubling or standing compared to standard blackjack basic strategy; there is a lot more hitting. Also keep in mind the following strategy variations involving bonuses:

- A hand composed of a **6, 7,** and **8** (in any order) wins 3:2 when it's mixed suits; it wins 2:1 when suited and 3:1 when it's all spades. So you should hit rather than stand against a dealer's **2** through **5** when it's possible for you to win the bonus.

- A five-card 21 pays 3:2, a six-card 21 pays 2:1, and 21 made with seven or more cards pays 3:1. But the bonus is not paid when the hand has been doubled. Thus you should hit rather than double down on hands of four or more cards (when doubling would otherwise be the standard strategy).

- Three suited 7s against a dealer's upcard of **7** pays a $1,000 bonus for bets up to $25, and it pays $5,000 for $25 bets and above. So you should hit rather than split when you have two suited 7s against a dealer's **7**.

- If the dealer doesn't have an upcard of **7**, three unsuited 7s pay 3:2, three suited 7s pay 2:1, and three 7s in spades pay 3:1. Nevertheless, you should hit or split two 7s as per the chart on page 121. Don't chase this particular bonus.

Some things in Spanish 21 strategy mirror regular basic strategy. A hand of **A,A** or **8,8** is always split (except **8,8** is surrendered against an **A**). A hand of **5,5** or **10,10** is never split. Soft 17 or lower is always hit or doubled. Hands of 19 and higher always stand. Nevertheless, there are important differences between the two strategies, and the house edge on Spanish 21 jumps to well over one percent when the game is played with standard blackjack basic strategy. That's not as bad as roulette, but you could do better.

Double Exposure

Would blackjack be easier to beat if both the dealer's cards were exposed? Surprisingly, no. Double Exposure was developed and introduced in 1979 by Bob Stupak (the casino entrepreneur who created the Stratosphere in Las Vegas). Since then, variations of the game have been offered at other casinos under monikers such as Show & Tell, Peek-a-Boo, and Face-Up.

All the incarnations have similar rules:

- Both dealer's cards are face up.

- Naturals pay 1:1.

- Dealer wins all ties except for 21. Player natural always wins.

When you consider that ties occur about 9 percent of the time, the last rule is a major hit. And any remaining advantage from seeing both of the dealer's cards is pretty much wiped out by the 1:1 naturals.

As with Spanish 21, Double Exposure isn't a bad game, but it's not necessarily better than standard blackjack, and the strategy is so radically different that you might find it difficult to switch back and forth between the two games. In fact, that's what the casino is hoping. The house is trying to make it easy for you to play badly.

The strategy charts for Double Exposure are much larger than standard charts (by about three times), so I've chosen not to include them in this book. Instead, I'll use a simplified list that is near-optimal, and much easier to remember.

Double Exposure Strategy List

Regular blackjack strategy always starts with your hand (from a decision-making point of view), and it modifies some decisions based on the dealer's upcard. Double Exposure strategy works in reverse. First you look at the dealer's hand, and then you make choices based on your own hand.

A dealer's hand in Double Exposure comes in five types (the following designations are my own). A dealer's hand of 17 and above is pat, 12 through 16 without an **A** is stiff, 12 through 16 with an **A** is soft-drawing, 7 through 11 is strong, 6 and below is small.

Against a dealer's pat hands (17 and above): Always stand against a dealer's pat hand when your total is higher. Always hit (or in some cases split) against a pat hand that is beating you. Never double down against a pat hand. We'll cover splits in a later section.

Against a dealer's stiff hands (12 through 16): Stand with hard totals of 12 or above. Split pairs, *including* **10,10**, but not **5,5** (see pairs below). Double down on *everything else,* including any soft hand lower than a natural.

Against a dealer's strong hands (7 through 11): Stand on hard totals of 16 or above and soft totals of 19 or higher. Hit everything else (except for pairs as noted).

Against a dealer's other hands (soft 12 through soft 16, and 6 or lower): Stand on any hard totals of 12 or above. Stand on soft totals of 19 or higher. Hit everything else (except for pairs as noted).

Splitting Pairs

A,A—Hit against pat hands and against an 11. Split against everything else.

10,10—Split against a dealer's stiff hands. Stand on everything else (except, of course, hit when the dealer has 20).

9,9—Hit against 19 or above. Split against 18. Stand against everything lower.

8,8—Hit against 18 or above. Split against everything lower.

5,5—Treat it like a standard (non pair) 10.

The rest of your pairs should be split against stiffs and hit against everything else.

Learning Double Exposure

The standard blackjack strategy from Chapter 7 has 360 choices, and many of them are duplicates (such as always splitting **A,A** or **8,8**). In contrast, Double Exposure has 792 separate decisions. I simplified them considerably in the previous list, but you

can see that Double Exposure is a game unto itself. It's nearly impossible to "wing it" by playing regular blackjack strategy. Your best bet is to thoroughly learn this separate strategy or avoid the game altogether.

With perfect play, Double Exposure has an edge of usually about 0.7 percent, similar to Spanish 21 and not much worse than regular blackjack. Beware of versions that push tied naturals. That bumps the edge well above one percent.

21st Century Blackjack

21st Century Blackjack has two features that makes it significantly different from regular blackjack. First, the bust-over-21 rule is bent somewhat. Players who bust don't automatically lose; the bet is a push if the dealer later busts with a higher total. Second, the game is played with multiple decks that include jokers, and a hand with a joker is an automatic 21. Two jokers is the top hand, and that pays 2:1. All other winning hands pay 1:1.

The nice thing about 21st Century Blackjack is that you don't need a radically different strategy to play the game, and the off-beat rules add an interesting twist. The downside is that regular blackjack is still a better contest.

Two jokers appear about once in every 3,300 hands, so the 2:1 payoff on those combinations is a relatively rare event. Meanwhile, the lowered 1:1 payoff on "traditional" naturals adds more than 2 percent to the house edge.

The joker-as-21 adds an interesting boost of volatility, but it has nearly zero long-term effect because everyone, including the dealer, has an equal probability of drawing a joker.

And finally, the no-bust rule isn't as useful as you might imagine because you're most likely to bust hitting stiffs against strong cards (dealer hands with a low probability of a busting). Conversely, you probably will be standing when the dealer busts.

Side Bets and Bonuses

Side bets and bonuses are designed to jazz up traditional blackjack and increase the casino's profit on the contest. A side bet is an extra wager that conveniently soaks up dollars won on the basic low-edge game. In contrast, bonuses are free, but they act as enticements to a higher-edge game. Remember, a casino is like any business. Nothing is really free, the money has to come from somewhere.

Your goal is to make sure the money is coming from someone else's pocket.

Sideshow Side Bets

A good general rule to follow is that side bets are nearly always bad bets. Save your money for doubling and splitting. But if you're still curious, here are some typical propositions on the side.

Royal Match: Will your first two cards be suited? Some casinos allow you to bet on this possibility. Two suited cards

typically pay 5:2 and a royal match—king and queen of the same suit—pays 25:1. The actual probability of drawing a suited match is about 24 percent or slightly less than 1 in 4. The chance of smacking a royal match is about 0.3 percent or about 1 in 335 hands (depending on the number of decks

THE FACT IS...

Casino side bets almost always have a negative expectation. Conversely, all double-down bets (when properly executed) have a positive expectation, so it's always a better idea to save your money and double down rather than wager on a blackjack side bet.

in the game). That works out to a house edge of around 7 percent. Ouch! Did someone say royal?

By the way, if you ever see this bet paying 6:2 (3:1) instead of 5:2 for a regular match, and the game is played with four or more decks, then it's a positive-expectation wager. Someone in casino management will have made a mistake (it's been known to happen), and you'll want to capitalize on these odds before they're changed.

Super 7s: What's the chance that your first card will be a **7**? How about two **7**s in two cards, or maybe three **7**s if you take a hit? Some casinos will pay you 5,000:1 for three suited **7**s in a multiple-deck game. Unfortunately the odds of drawing the big one are closer to one in 60,000. Even with extra payoffs for one and two **7**s, the overall edge for this bet is typically about 12 percent.

Red/Black: This bet pays 1:1 when you guess the color of the next dealer's upcard. Deuces of the color you choose are a push, so there are twenty-six ways to lose and only twenty-five ways to win. The house edge is about 2 percent.

Over/Under: Will your next two cards be over 13 or under 13? Did I mention that 13 was a loser? The over bet has an edge of about 7 percent and under is more than 10 percent. Make this bet too often, and you'll definitely go under.

Bonus Onus

Bonuses are enticements, off-beat favorable rules designed as promotions. One example is giving an automatic win to players with five cards in their hand, or paying more for hands with triple numbers. One particularly cute variation is the **envy bonus**. If one person at the table wins a big prize, everyone at the table gets something extra.

Bonuses cost you nothing unless you deviate from basic strategy to pursue them. While it's technically correct in some situations to change basic strategy for a bonus, those changes don't necessarily add much long-term value. You're better off sticking with basic strategy unless you play a particular bonus game exclusively. Then you should learn a strategy that optimizes for the specific bonus (as in Spanish 21).

Essentially

- Seemingly minor changes in the rules of blackjack can have an extreme effect on the house edge. An overall 2 percent jump in the house edge can occur when an incorrect strategy is applied to a game with unfavorable rules. Your overall performance will improve when you use the correct strategy for a particular game.

- Single-deck games are better than multiple-deck games when all the other rules are the same, but the advantage of a single-deck game is more than wiped out when doubling is restricted and naturals pay less than 3:2.

- A good way to learn basic strategy is to play with real cards and deal the game yourself. The act of wagering doesn't change how cards fall. Your home game is identical in its results to games that you would play in a casino.

- Playing hunches is okay, but it will eventually cost you money.

- Spanish 21 is a variation of blackjack played with forty-eight-card Spanish packs (decks with 10s removed). Eliminating the 10s reduces the chance of naturals. Also, the dealer is less likely to bust, and you're less likely to finish with a strong hand after a double down.

- The disadvantage of removing the 10s in Spanish 21 is partially offset by favorable rules such as doubling on any two cards and 3:2 naturals that automatically win.

- The casino has an edge of more than 1 percent when Spanish 21 is played with regular blackjack basic strategy, so it's best to learn the strategy for Spanish 21 if you're going to play that game.

- Double Exposure is a version of blackjack in which both of the dealer's cards are exposed. Naturals pay 1:1 in this game, and the dealer wins all ties except for 21.

- The strategy for Double Exposure is radically different from standard blackjack basic strategy. As with Spanish 21, your best bet is to learn the special strategy or avoid Double Exposure altogether.

- A good general rule to follow is that side bets are nearly always bad bets. Save your money for doubling and splitting.

CHAPTER 9

Blackjack: Etiquette and Advanced Strategies

 A few years ago a major beer company sponsored an advertising campaign that used the slogan, "Can your beer do this?" One of the television commercials in the campaign was a comedy spot called "Full-contact Golf." It was a mock sport in which a golfer attempts to play his golf game against a football team. At one point the play-by-play announcer whispers, "Here's the putt." And then he shouts, "There's the blitz!" Meanwhile, the entire football team tackles the golfer.

Funny stuff, but it's sad to say that using advanced strategies when playing blackjack is sometimes a real-life version of full-contact golf.

Advanced strategies (primarily these are methods of **counting cards**) are legal, but they're not welcome in casinos. It's no surprise that casinos don't want you to beat them. They'll tolerate basic strategy, but players who are too good, who are consistently too "lucky," or otherwise very profitable, may be ejected or harassed by casino security. I'll explain these unpleasant specifics later in this chapter, but first, let's focus on this basic truth:

The key to winning a lot of money at blackjack is to not be noticed.

It's best to be unmemorable. You should want to be perceived as just any regular player. And this perception begins when you follow blackjack etiquette properly.

Blackjack is like any organized activity; it works best when everyone follows the rules. A well-played blackjack game has a pleasant rhythm; there's no confusion about who gets what or who has won. But players who lose the rhythm or break the rules can turn the whole thing into lumbering chaos.

Miscommunication can cause hands to be improperly hit (or not hit). Mishandling of chips or cards can delay the game and create confusion about payoffs or the results of a hand. And in some instances a mistake can cause *other* players at the table to lose their bets. This misfortune is not anyone's fault from a strictly statistical point of view (every player competes independently with the dealer), but from a practical point of view it is easy to blame the guy at third base who incorrectly took the dealer's bust card.

And you don't want that attention.

So our journey into the intricacies of advanced blackjack strategies begins with a closer look at the customs and procedures of the game.

Thou Shalt Not

Every game has some strict rules, like pass interference or roughing the kicker in football. These standards are sometimes inconvenient, but they're necessary or the game cannot be played safely. The following rules involve casino security, game integrity, or financial transactions. Bending or violating these standards will bring a warning from a dealer. Repeated violations (in extreme situations) may cause a player to be barred from the game or ejected from the casino.

Money transactions must be observable. Never hand money directly to a dealer. Instead, you should put it flat on the felt. A dealer will count the bills so that cameras above the table can see the transaction, then she'll exchange the cash for chips.

When you decide to leave the table (hopefully with more chips than at the buy-in), you can ask the dealer for a **color up**. She will exchange your lower-denomination chips for fewer chips with a higher value. You can exchange chips for cash at the **cage** (the bank-like area of the casino where money transactions are conducted), or you can take them to another table and buy in there.

By the way, these procedures for handling chips and cash are standard for all table games. We'll talk more about them in Chapter 20.

Cards must be handled correctly. A hand that is dealt face-up should not be touched. A hand that is dealt face-down should never be removed from the table or placed out of view at any time. Cards should not be scratched, bent, or marked in any way.

Chips in the circle must not be touched during play.
Scammers sometimes try to add or remove chips after seeing their hand (adding chips is called **past-posting**). Casinos prevent this by prohibiting players from touching their bets after a hand begins. Also remember that this rule affects doubles and splits. You should never stack the extra bet on top of the chips already in the circle. Instead, place the extra chips next to the original bet.

Hand signals must be clear and observable. Verbal instructions don't count. You must tap the table clearly or scratch your cards for a hit, and lift up one hand (as if to say "stop") or push the cards under the bet for a stand. For example, let's say you're in a splitting situation, and you're trying to remember the strategy. Don't tap the table while thinking or you may receive a hit.

Mechanical assistance is forbidden. Assistance from a computer or other mechanical device is prohibited by law when playing blackjack in a casino. The exact prohibitions vary in various states and provinces, but if you hear about someone playing blackjack with a computer in his shoe, there's no doubt he's breaking the law. On the other hand, there is no law prohibiting a mental process or strategy that can be implemented without mechanical assistance.

Superstitions and Customs

Blackjack is essentially a game of skill. Luck ultimately has zero long-term effect, but the path to the long term goes through thousands of individual decisions in which luck plays a significant role, and this inevitably creates myths and superstitions. Rituals and customs have developed around blackjack to help players mentally cope with the ups and downs. These various beliefs and customs are not necessarily based in fact, but for the sake of harmony it's usually a good idea to respect and follow these tenets whenever possible.

Preserving the Order of the Cards

It's obvious that hitting, standing, or splitting will change the cards going to later hands, but of course, there is no way for anyone to know if that change will be good or bad. In other words, there is absolutely *nothing* you can do in normal play that can predictably cause another person to lose at blackjack. Unfortunately, the rest of the table may not see it that way.

A classic example is when the third-base player "takes the dealer's bust card." Let's say the dealer is showing **4** and you have 13. Basic strategy tells you to stand, but you decide to play a hunch and hit. The next card is **9**; you bust. And here's where it gets ugly... The dealer's downcard is a **10**, giving her 14. She takes a hit, gets **7**, and wins with 21. Four other players at the table stood on 19 or 20, and they've just lost because you didn't play basic strategy correctly.

Ouch!

Now in all fairness, that loss would not be your fault. The two cards could have just as easily come in reverse order. Nevertheless, it's hard to make that argument to a group of unhappy strangers as the dealer is scooping up $1,000 of their chips. Obviously, the casino prohibits physical attacks or loud verbal abuse, but it is not uncommon for an "unconventional" third-base player to be on the receiving end of under-the-breath negative comments and nasty epithets from others at his table. Indeed, the goal of the other players is to sour the mood sufficiently enough to make the offender go away.

Of course, such boorish behavior is extremely inappropriate, but it sometimes happens. Thus it's best to play near-perfect basic strategy when you're sitting at or near third base, unless you enjoy a tense table.

Tip

Dealers sometimes make mistakes. You should speak up and correct mistakes when they cost you money. But what should you do when a dealer makes an error in your favor? That is a question for your conscience. However, you should *never* correct any payment made to another player. Payoffs are the casino's responsibility, and the parties involved are best left to their own resolutions.

Giving Other Players Advice

On the flip side of the above issue, you may see someone playing like a total boob. He may hit 16 against a dealer's **6,** or stand on 12 when the dealer shows a **10.** Whatever he's doing, it doesn't matter. You'll likely get more grief than satisfaction if you give him unsolicited advice. And even when someone requests advice, it's usually a bad idea to instruct that person at the table because your words invariably will be judged by the results of the next decision. Remember, most hands that require advice are often already on their way to being losers.

Tokes

A **toke** is a tip in casino-industry parlance. You might be surprised to know that casino dealers typically earn half or more of their money from tokes. For example, dealers at MGM Grand in Las Vegas had a total average income of $63,728 and a base pay of $5.35 per hour in 2000. The difference was tokes. And remember, MGM is the largest hotel property in North America (5,005 rooms). Dealers at smaller casinos earn much less, and they depend heavily on the kindness of their customers.

Nobody expects a toke when you're losing, and you should definitely not toke if a game is poorly dealt, but if you're having a winning session and the dealers are making it fun then it's always nice to give something. There are a couple of ways to toke. You can put chips out on the felt and simply say, "This is for you." Another way is to bet something for the dealer. Put some extra chips next to your bet just outside the circle, and ask her if she'd like the toke straight or if she'd like to see it played. Most dealers will want the extra action.

Of course, it's a drag when a toke bet loses, so I recommend yet another option that gives you more control. Increase your standard bet by one-half of the intended toke amount, and then simply toke when a hand wins.

Tip

Many casinos require dealers to pool and share their tips so that dealers at lower-limit tables won't earn less per shift than their higher-limit counterparts. Keep that in mind if you're tempted to over-tip. Tokes of $1 to $10 per hour are customary for a player betting $10 to $100 per hand.

Cutting the Cards and Shuffling Procedures

Every so often you may be asked to cut the cards. It's no big deal. In a single-deck game, just lift a top portion of the deck and lay it next to the bottom portion. In multiple-deck games you will use a plastic card-sized stop. Put it somewhere near the middle of the stack. The dealer will complete the cut and **burn** (discard) one or more of the new top cards.

By the way, casinos use various shuffling procedures, and they can affect the advanced strategies that we'll cover later in this chapter.

- Single and multiple decks are sometimes shuffled by hand and then dealt handheld or out of a shoe.

- Some casinos use shuffling machines to mix the cards, and then they're dealt by hand or out of a shoe.

- The latest mechanical "innovation" is the **continuous-shuffling machine** (often called **CSM**). Cards from recent hands are returned to the machine and immediately shuffled back into the deck. So it's possible that you could see a **5 of diamonds** in one hand, and get that same card three hands later.

Blackjack experts spend a great deal of time analyzing and discussing the merits and disadvantages of these various shuffling methods. Entire books have been written about these subjects, but it's important to note that all of these issues involve advanced strategies (such as counting cards). A person who uses only basic strategy will find that all shuffling methods are about equal in overall results.

Counting Cards

And now we come to it...counting cards. This is the strategy that goes beyond the basic stuff. This is the way you erase the casino's edge and make blackjack a positive-expectation contest.

It's all about big and small cards.

There are many counting methods. Contrary to popular myths, none of them require you to remember hands that have been played previously. Instead, a counting method tracks the ratio of **10**s to smaller cards in the deck.

Tens are very helpful to players and not so helpful to dealers for a number of reasons:

First, players can choose to hit or stand on a stiff hand, but dealers always must hit their stiffs. So a deck with a lot of **10**s will likely bust the dealer more than it will bust players.

Second, a player who doubles or splits is either hoping to draw a **10** to make a high pat hand, or (in the case of some soft doubling and splits) hoping for a **10** that will bust the dealer. Thus small cards lower the probability of winning with a double or a split.

Third, small cards tend to create stiff hands, and they also save them. If both you and the dealer are stiff, and you stand as per basic strategy, the dealer can beat you by drawing a small card (which takes us right back to the first item).

Of course, there is no way to know exactly how the cards will fall, but generally, players win more when the ratio of **10**s is high, and they lose more when small cards dominate.

A card counter simply bets more when the deck has a lot of **10**s, and he bets less or leaves the table when the **10**s are mostly consumed. The result is about a 1 percent edge for the player. As I said in Chapter 1, 1 percent may not sound like a lot, but it's all of the casino's profit and more.

The Hi-Lo System

One of the most popular and easy-to-learn counting systems is called Hi-Lo. Here's how it works:

The player watches the cards as they are revealed during play. Cards with a rank of **2**, **3**, **4**, **5**, and **6** are counted as +1. Cards with a rank of **7**, **8**, and **9** are zero. **10**s and **A** are −1. The player adds the numbers and the result is an exact measure of how many **10**s and **A**s are left in the deck compared to smaller cards.

Simple, isn't it?

THE FACT IS...

Counting cards doesn't work on most video blackjack games because the deck is shuffled after every hand. Also, video blackjack games usually pay only 1:1 for naturals, and they restrict doubling to hands that total 10 or 11. The house edge on video blackjack with these rules is typically about 2.5 percent.

Let's say it's only you and the dealer playing with a freshly shuffled deck. During the first hand you receive two **10**s. You stand. The dealer has a **10** and a **3**. She hits the 13, draws another **10** and busts. Great for you, but the count is now –3. The cards remaining in the deck favor the dealer. You might win the next hand and the next one after that, but those three little cards eventually will appear. Conversely, if the count is positive you can expect big fat **10**s to come out of the deck at some point.

Card counters increase their bets when the count is positive. The table below shows a typical 5:1 bet spread.

5:1 Bet Spread for Card Counting

True Count	Bet	Player Advantage
0 or negative	$10	–1.0% or worse
+1	$10	0
+2	$20	0.5%
+3	$30	1.0%
+4	$40	1.5%
+5 or more	$50	2.0% or more

The top bet is five times larger than the base bet. Player advantage is for multiple decks and is an average.

Running Count and True Count

Tip

Here's a good way to practice card counting: Shuffle one or more standard decks of cards and then deal the cards face up in pairs while counting. The final count should always be zero when the last cards are dealt. A good counter can accurately count down a single deck in about thirty seconds.

Three **10**s missing from a single deck is a big deal, but three **10**s from a six-deck shoe is barely a blip. Card counters adjust for this by doing some division when playing against multiple decks. The raw count or **running count** is the pure number of extra **10**s and **A**s or extra small cards. A counter divides the running count by the number of decks that have not yet been played. This produces a **true count**, which is a better general measure of advantage per deck.

For example, +3 is both the running count and the true count for a single deck. A running count of +3 is only +1.5 when two decks are left, and it's only +0.5 when six decks remain in the shoe.

Let's say you're in the middle of a six-deck shoe (three decks left). In this case, a +3 running count would be +1 true count. If all this is a little confusing, the chart below will help to explain it. Keep in mind that this calculation is only necessary for positive counts. Negative counts are simply negative and they don't need to be converted (in this particular counting system).

By the way, if you feel comfortable with half-deck calculations, then go ahead and do the extra math dividing the running count by fractions. The results are worth it. But if that's just too much bother, and you prefer to work with whole numbers, then it's perfectly okay.

Running Count to True Count Conversions

Running Count	Decks Left	True Count
+12	7	1.7
+3	6	0.5
+15	5	3
+14	4	3.5
+4	4	1
+15	3	5
+12	2	6
+9	2	4.5
+4	1	4

The running count is the actual number of extra big cards or small cards remaining in the deck. It is divided by the number of decks left, and that produces the true count.

Developing Speed as a Counter

Blackjack proceeds at its own pace; it's not as if you can say to a dealer, "Please go slower, I'm counting these cards." So it takes some practice to learn how to count quickly enough to keep up with the game. Most people begin by counting cards in pairs, and they learn predictable patterns. For example:

Q♠ J♦ = −2		K♣ 8♥ = −1
9♦ 8♣ = 0		7♠ 7♥ = 0
6♣ 9♠ = +1		8♦ 2♠ = +1
5♦ 5♥ = +2		A♥ 9♣ = −1

Obviously, it's easier to count games that are dealt face-up, but face-down contests are also countable. You just have to be quick enough to read the card ranks as the hands are revealed and resolved. The real trick is to do the necessary calculation quickly and put a bet out in a reasonable amount of time without looking like a counter.

How Casinos Fight Counters

As I mentioned previously, card counting is legal in the United States, but it's extremely unwelcome in casinos. Since the courts won't put counters in jail, the gaming industry has developed elaborate safeguards to discourage counting, and they've created their own internal systems to identify and persecute (if not prosecute) people who they suspect of counting. Some of their tactics are really unpleasant. I don't mean to frighten or discourage you from counting, but it's a lot like that analogy I made earlier. You must play like a golfer in the middle of a football game.

The Tame Stuff

Multiple decks are the casino's first line of defense against counters. Six or eight decks are tougher to count than one or two decks, and the positive/negative swings are generally not so extreme with multiple decks. Frequent shuffling is another tactic; counters call it **poor penetration**. The deeper you go into a deck (or decks), the greater the power of the count. Penetration of less than 60 percent reduces the chance of profiting from a high count. It's a major drag when the true count goes to +10 and the dealer promptly shuffles.

Continuous-shuffle machines are yet another way of preventing players from counting. Cards go right back into the deck so there is essentially no penetration.

Unfortunately, all of these tactics have an adverse effect on the game. These complicated procedures and devices are not only hated by counters, they're unpopular with typical players who don't count. It's no surprise that most people prefer a hand-shuffled single-deck contest; it just seems more honest. People don't like their cards coming out of a big machine, and they don't like too many long delays for frequent shuffling.

Thus casinos that use these tactics find themselves saving pennies but losing dollars when everyone moves to a better game at the property across the street.

Casino managers aren't dummies. They do their research, and they read the bottom line. That's why single- and double-deck games can still be found in competitive markets (such as Las Vegas). It's also why continuous-shuffle machines have not yet taken over, and why games with multiple decks sometimes still have good penetration.

Tip

Some optimal decisions in basic strategy change as the count changes. There are dozens of these adjustments. Here are two of the easiest and most important to remember: Stand on 16 vs. 10 when the true count is 0 or greater. Take insurance if the count is +3 or greater.

Most casino managers have given up on making the games entirely uncountable (it's an impossible goal), and now they're focusing on identifying and stopping counters one by one.

The Rough Stuff

It starts with a tap on the shoulder. The player turns around and sees a big burly man in a suit. Muscle-boy looks like he might have once been a wrestler, or maybe a Marine drill sergeant. He is accompanied by two equally burly security guards.

"Excuse me, sir. Could you come with us?"

"What's the problem?" the player asks.

The man in the suit ignores the question as he turns to the dealer and says, "Color up the gentleman's chips. He'll be leaving the table."

If the player doesn't immediately stand up, one of the guards will firmly take him by the upper arm and lift him to his feet. The trio will cash him out, walk him to the front door, and tell him that he is prohibited by law from returning to that casino…ever. That's what happens if the player is lucky.

If the player is unlucky, the security team will **backroom** him. This will be a humiliating trip to a behind-the-scenes security area where they will treat the player like a criminal. They will ask for identification (that he's not legally required to provide); they will photograph and question him; then he will be ejected without his bankroll. He wants his money? He can go to court to get it.

Is the player staying in the casino's hotel? Then it's even worse. The security team will inspect his possessions and put them out on the sidewalk. The player's spouse, parents, children, whoever is staying with him will be ejected in the same manner.

Why did all this happen? The casino suspected that he was counting cards.

This treatment is commonly referred to by counters as **heat**, and it comes in varying degrees. Sometimes a casino will tell a suspected counter that he cannot play blackjack, but he's welcome to play other games. Sometimes the counter is watched and the dealer shuffles more frequently. Some of this depends on if the player is winning or losing and how much he's betting.

Ejection is prohibited in Atlantic City, so counters there are **backed off** with zero table service, ultra-poor penetration, and their players club cards are revoked.

You might wonder how a casino knows that a person is counting (besides the fact that he's winning). Actually, when a casino has enough computers and cameras it's pretty easy to spot counters.

The High-Tech Stuff

Heat from the pit begins when a floorperson or the pit boss sees a player exhibiting counting behaviors.

One obvious giveaway is bets that go up and down for no apparent reason (no consistent system of pressing or regression), and bets that always go to the minimum after a shuffle. Other clues include intense concentration, a preoccupation with seeing all the cards, and constantly glancing at the discard tray (estimating the number of decks left). All of this just gets the heat going. Then the

THE FACT IS...

Casinos in Nevada are legally allowed to eject anyone at any time for any reason (except for discrimination), and the ejected person has no legal recourse. If he returns he may be arrested for trespassing. Casinos in Atlantic City cannot eject players for counting, but the house is allowed to shuffle the deck at any time.

pit calls upstairs and gets the cameras looking at the player. Someone in a surveillance room begins counting the game and looking for a correlation between the player's bets and the true count. Meanwhile, a video image of the player is fed into a computer that uses face recognition software to match the player's face to those of known counters.

> *"Casinos have house rules. They don't like to lose. So you never show that you're counting cards. That is the cardinal sin, Ray."*
>
> —Charlie Babbitt, as played by Tom Cruise in *Rain Man* (1988)

Casinos subscribe to various database services that provide pictures and information about gamblers who cheat. Suspected card counters comprise a large portion of these databases (in spite of the fact that counting is legal). So if a counter was identified two years ago in Atlantic City, and he reappears in Las Vegas just once after all that time, he'll be nailed in a matter of minutes. Once a player is in a major database, he's cooked for life. The most notorious card counters don't even bother to play in casinos anymore; they earn a living training other people to count cards.

And here's the amazing part…it's like Prohibition and bootleggers in the early twentieth century. Nothing stops the counters, they just get more sophisticated. These days many successful counters work in teams. Part of the team counts and bets without a spread (essentially, they're invisible to the casino). Those players signal others who jump in with bets when the count is high. It's an elaborate camouflage system. So casinos are looking for individuals *and* groups of people.

The latest high-tech innovation designed to stop teams and individual counters is a computer system that uses chips/cheques embedded with radio frequency identification tags. Hardware in the table reads the cards and tracks the bets. Essentially, the table counts the game for every player.

Card-Counting Camouflage

So where does all this hullabaloo leave you, an average player who just wants to play blackjack with a legal edge?

The good news is that you can count and not receive heat if you take some simple precautions.

- Avoid high-tech tables that automatically count the game. Generally, they're easy to spot. The dealer's chip tray will have some sort of computer log-in display or there will be other computer-like contraptions (such as a card swiper) attached to the table.

- Learn to count without looking like a counter. You should be able to order a drink, talk to your pals, tell the dealer a joke, tip the waitress, push out a bet, and do it all while handling the arithmetic. You should achieve that level of expertise first before you begin to raise or lower your bets according to the count.

- Don't spread your bets beyond 6:1. In fact, 4:1 or 3:1 is safer when you're playing against a single or double deck. For example, don't jump from $10 to $100 and then back to $10 on three consecutive hands.

- Stick to betting red chips ($5 units) or green chips ($25 units) when counting. Casinos won't hassle you much for what they consider to be nickel-and-dime stuff. Black-chip play ($100 units) and above is when they go bananas.

- Don't lower your bet when the deck is shuffled unless the previous hand was a loss.

- Don't change your bet after a push.

- Don't watch a table and then enter mid-shoe with a big bet.

- Don't look nervous or act as if you're thinking too hard. Be friendly. Banter with the dealer.

- Do tip occasionally. A well-timed toke will get the dealer on your side. He may give you better penetration, and he'll be less likely to rat you out to a floorperson or the pit boss.

Frankly, some dealers and pit bosses are more vigilant than others; some are zealous and some don't care. If you do feel heat developing, don't panic. Just take your chips and calmly exit before you get the tap on the shoulder. You can cash in later.

Profitable Card Counting

A person who wagers $500 per hand on average with a 1 percent edge will earn $600,000 per year working forty hours a week. That's why casinos are so fanatical in their detection of card counters.

On the other hand, $25 average bets will net only about $30,000 per year or $15 per hour, not such a big deal to a casino. So profitable counting is possible, but it's tough to get rich playing blackjack without taking major heat.

And keep in mind that these average figures don't reflect volatility. In other words, profit does not come in a steady stream. It comes in chunks, and it's entirely possible (though not probable) for a counter to play twenty-five, fifty, one-hundred hours or more and still be in the red. On the other hand, playing those exact hands without counting and without basic strategy would likely produce an even *bigger* loss. From a strictly financial point of view, there's no downside to counting. It's the statistical equivalent of swapping places with the casino. That's a very good thing, but in the short run (a few thousand decisions) it's still gambling. Anything can happen, though a positive outcome is definitely more likely than a net loss.

So should you count cards? Is it worth the hassle? That depends on you. If counting sounds like fun and you'd enjoy the cat-and-mouse challenge, then go ahead and do it. But if counting makes your head hurt, then don't sweat it. Just accept the fact that you're giving up some profit for the sake of convenience. That's okay. Remember, you're doing this for pleasure.

Essentially

- Casino rules require that money transactions be observable. Cards must be handled correctly and never marked or concealed. Chips in the circle must not be touched during play. Hand signals must be clear and understood by the dealer.

- Assistance from a computer or other mechanical device is prohibited by law when playing blackjack in a casino.

- If you sit at or near third base, others at the table may blame you unfairly if you deviate from basic strategy and they lose. This is less likely to happen if you sit at or near first base.

- Every so often you may be asked to cut the cards. In a single-deck game just lift a top portion of the deck and lay it next to the bottom portion. In multiple-deck games you will use a plastic card-sized stop. Put it somewhere near the middle of the stack.

- All card-counting systems track the ratio of 10s to smaller cards left in the deck. This ratio is important because 10s tend to bust the dealer, and small cards often create stiff hands for players.

- The Hi-Lo counting system assigns a value of +1 to cards with a rank of 2, 3, 4, 5, and 6. Cards with a rank of 7, 8, and 9 are valued as zero. 10s and As are –1. The player adds the numbers and the result is an exact measure of how many 10s and As are left in the deck compared to smaller cards.

- Card counters increase their bet to correspond with a positive count. A typical bet spread for a multiple-deck game is 5:1 (if the base bet is $10 then the highest bet is $50).

- Card counting is legal in the United States, but it's extremely unwelcome in casinos. Nevada casinos eject people who they suspect of counting. Casinos everywhere go to great lengths to identify and discourage card counting.

CHAPTER 10

Craps:
Basic Strategies

Craps is by far the most exciting and fast-moving of all the casino table games. It's a communal experience. You and a bunch of other people toss a pair of dice and bet on the results. Players win and lose en masse. If the dice are hot, everyone is shouting. Craps is the sort of contest that appeals to gregarious gamblers and those who love fast action and mercurial ups and downs. Indeed, it's a contest that has bewitched players for centuries.

The origin of craps is quite remarkable. The game of hazard (the forerunner of craps) was developed in Palestine way back in the time of the Crusades, around AD 1100. In fact, the English word "hazard" comes from the Arabic phrase for dice, "al-zahr." Clearly, medieval players thought the contest was dangerous, even though they loved playing it.

Crusaders brought the game back to Europe, and it flourished as the centuries passed, all the while maintaining its volatile reputation.

Geoffrey Chaucer wrote about hazard in his *Canterbury Tales* around the year 1390. One of Chaucer's characters is a kind of priest called a pardoner. The pardoner describes hazard as the "mother of leasings (lies), and of deceit, and cursed forswearings." He includes the following gambler's oath: "Seven is my chance, and thine is cinque and trey. By Godde's armes, if thou falsely play, this dagger shall throughout thine hearte go."

Ouch!

Violence aside, Europeans were hooked on the contest. Charles Cotton, an English author, wrote in 1674, "Certainly Hazzard is the most bewitching game that is played on the Dice; for when a man begins to play he knows not when to leave off; and having once accustomed himself to play at Hazzard he hardly ever after minds anything else."

French sailors brought hazard to the New World via New Orleans some time after 1718. By that point, the contest had morphed into a variation called crabs (which was the nickname for a roll of two).

When the French said "crabs" it sounded like "craps" to the Americans, and the name stuck.

Hazard is still around (mostly played in Europe), but these days craps is the definitive dice game. In the last two centuries it has contributed many ubiquitous phrases to the English language. Examples include "no dice," "on a roll," "crapshoot," and "crap out" to name just a few.

Best of all, even after 1,000 years, the contest has retained its mercurial nature. That's good news for you because the contest wasn't invented for casinos. The house edge was grafted onto the game in the modern casino era. So if you study craps strategies and play well, you have a good chance to win.

THE FACT IS...

French sailors shouted "Crabs!" while playing hazard on the wharves of New Orleans in the early nineteenth century, and the Americans heard "Craps!" Thus craps became the name of the world's most famous dice game. Coincidentally, the English lexicon already had a similar-sounding word, "crap," meaning garbage or excrement. Then along came Thomas Crapper and his patented toilets. The resulting linguistic confusion has caused problems for polite society ever since. But rest assured, *craps* comes from the word *crabs*.

Craps is about Dice

When people think about craps, they often think of a modern invention, the craps table. It's a monstrously large contraption covered with lines, numbers, and seemingly incomprehensible phrases.

But ironically, the contest does not require a table. All you need are dice. That's one of the reasons why craps has such a long history; it's a physically convenient game to play. You can carry the dice in your pocket and play anywhere: on a curb, in the dirt, in a palace, in a foxhole, in a tank, in a submarine...anywhere.

So, let's forget the table for now. We'll use it later to help organize the bets. In this section, we'll talk about the dice.

How Will the Dice Roll?

A standard pair of dice can make thirty-six combinations that total eleven numbers (2 to 12). The table below shows the various possible sequences.

Possible Dice Combinations

Number	Ways to Roll		Combinations					True Odds	Percent Probability
2	1	1–1						35:1	2.8%
3	2	1–2	2–1					17:1	5.6%
4	3	2–2	1–3	3–1				11:1	8.3%
5	4	1–4	4–1	2–3	3–2			8:1	11.1%
6	5	3–3	2–4	4–2	1–5	5–1		6.2:1	13.9%
7	6	1–6	6–1	2–5	5–2	3–4	4–3	5:1	16.7%
8	5	4–4	2–6	6–2	5–3	3–5		6.2:1	13.9%
9	4	3–6	6–3	4–5	5–4			8:1	11.1%
10	3	5–5	4–6	6–4				11:1	8.3%
11	2	5–6	6–5					17:1	5.6%
12	1	6–6						35:1	2.8%

A pair of dice can create thirty-six possible combinations. Each cube has six sides and 6 × 6 = 36. Percent probabilities in the far right column are rounded.

Let's say you're the **craps shooter** (the person throwing the dice). On your first roll, called the **come-out roll**, there are two numbers that can win and three that can lose. The winners are 7 and 11. If you roll 7 or 11, the contest is over. You rolled a **natural** and **passed**.

If you roll 2, 3, or 12, it's **craps**—you don't pass—you lose, and the contest is over.

Most of the time you won't roll a natural or craps; the come-out roll will be 4, 5, 6, 8, 9, or 10. When that happens the number becomes your **point**. You must roll the same number again to pass. There is no limit to the attempts allowed for a pass. You can pass in one roll or one hundred. After a point is established the only way to lose is to roll a 7. Yes, it was good for the come-out, but now it's bad. All the other numbers (including 11 and craps) have no importance at this stage. Roll the point and you win; roll 7 and you lose. End of contest; the next roll is a come-out.

That's it. That's basic craps. Very simple. A winning wager pays 1:1 (even money). The table below shows the various rolls required for a pass and the odds for each outcome.

Note that a come-out roll is *twice as likely* to pass with a natural than lose with craps. The most likely outcome is establishing a point. Rolling 7 after the come-out (losing) is called a **seven-out**.

Winning and Losing Rolls for the Shooter

Come-Out Roll	Numbers	Probability of Rolling
Pass (Win) with Natural	7,11	22.2%
Don't Pass (Lose) with Craps	2,3,12	11.1%
Point	4,5,6,8,9,10	66.7%
Rolling to Repeat the Point		
Pass (Win) with Point	Point	8.3% to 13.9%
Don't Pass (Lose) with Seven	7	16.7%
No Effect	All other numbers	69.4% to 75%

A come-out roll is twice as likely to pass with a natural than lose with craps. The most likely outcome is establishing a point. If a point is established, the shooter must roll the point again to pass. The shooter loses if he rolls 7 before repeating the point.

Of course, there is much more to craps than pass and don't pass, but it's mostly about the shooter and this contest. If you understand how to pass, you understand craps.

Wagers on pass have a house edge of 1.41 percent. In other words, the casino will earn an average of $14 for every $1,000 you bet. That's not bad when you consider that the casino provides the table, the crew, and a palatial atmosphere. Just the smallest amount of luck can easily push you into the plus column.

Pass vs. Don't Pass

Strict regulations these days ensure that craps games are honest, no loaded dice and no hanky-panky. But in the old days when you had to knock on a door and whisper a password to play craps, the integrity of the game wasn't always so absolute. What could you do if you didn't trust the shooter's dice? The obvious solution was to bet against the shooter. That option is still available to this day.

A wager on **don't pass** is essentially the reverse of betting on pass; naturals (7 or 11) lose on the come-out. Craps wins (with one exception). Making the point loses. Seven-out wins.

The one exception is 12 on the come-out. It's a push. No money changes hands. That's the casino's entire advantage. If 12 wasn't a push, then you could earn 1.41 percent just like the house. A push on the 12 shifts the edge to the opposite side, and it gives the casino an advantage of 1.36 percent on the don't pass (from here forward we'll round this number to the nearest tenth, 1.4 percent).

This yin-yang do-don't structure is repeated throughout the game of craps. Most of the bets can be played on both sides. Some people use the terms "right" or "wrong" when describing these wagers. Others say that "do bettors" are "against the house" and "don't bettors" are "with the house." Such phrases aren't quite accurate, but you will hear them from time to time. Just remember that the house has an edge both ways. It might be psychologically upsetting for some people to see other players betting "against" them, but it's really no worse than betting red when someone else bets black at roulette. The house covers both wagers.

Playing the Basic Game

There are dozens of interesting craps bets that we'll cover in later sections and in the next chapter, but right now let's talk about the practical aspects of playing the game.

Craps is played on a table like the one pictured below. It's big, typically about five feet wide and ten feet long. The sides are high to prevent dice from coming off the layout. The top edge has a rail with grooves to hold your chips, and below that is a ledge for drinks. It's everything necessary to shoot craps like a member of the Rat Pack.

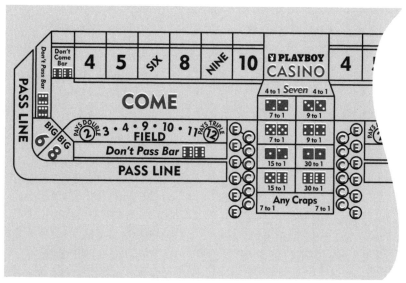

Standard craps layout. The section on the right is the same as the section on the left.

Notice that the layout has boxes that correspond to the various points, and a long strip called the pass line that runs nearly the length of the table. Above that is an area labeled "don't pass."

The dealer at the center of the table holding the long curved stick is the stickperson (or "stickman" for the old-timers). She retrieves dice after a throw, returns them to the shooter, and is responsible for all other issues concerning the cubes.

Across from the stickperson is the boxperson. He keeps an eye on the bank of casino chips, supervises the game, and settles disputes. On either side of the boxperson are dealers who pay bets, take wagers, position bets for players, and generally run the game.

Buying In

Buying in to craps is a little different from some other games because the table may be busy and you may have to get the dealer's attention. Put your money on the layout (when the dice aren't rolling) and say "change" in a clear voice. As in blackjack and all other table games, don't hand anything to the dealer. Security procedures require that money and chips be displayed on the table before being converted. The bills will be counted, and a dealer will give you chips in whatever denomination you request.

Betting

For obvious reasons, pass and don't-pass wagers are made only when a shooter is coming out (there's an oddball exception to this rule, but for now let's stick to the typical wagers). You'll know when a shooter is coming out by finding the puck. It's a large disk that's black on one side and white on the other.

Tip

Some casinos "bar the two" instead of the 12 on don't-pass wagers. Changing the push from 12 to 2 has no effect on the house edge or the overall probability of winning.

"ON" or "POINT" is printed on the white side; "OFF" or "COME-OUT" is printed on the black side.

The puck will be in or near the section of the layout marked "don't come" with the

OFF side up when the shooter is coming out. It will be moved to a corresponding number box and turned to the ON side after a point has been established. When the puck is OFF, just lay your wager on the pass line or the don't-pass bar.

Puck Positions

OFF or COME-OUT =
Shooter is coming out

ON or POINT =
Shooter is trying to roll a point

A dealer will double your chips or take them away depending on the results of the rolls. Be sure to remove your winnings from the layout promptly. Too many high-fives and cheers may cause you to miss the next roll, and the rule is "If it lays, it plays." Your money could be gone before the celebration has concluded.

THE FACT IS...

"Don't-pass bar" is a misnomer. On most layouts it's labeled "Don't Pass Bar 12," meaning "This is the don't pass section and we bar the 12." But people have a way of mangling meanings. Some players drop the number and simply call the don't-pass section a "bar."

Throwing the Dice

Shooting isn't mandatory, but it's a lot of fun.

When the stickperson offers you dice, simply choose two from the selection or decline. If you decline, the person next to you will be offered the dice. If you decide to throw, you'll hear the stickperson say, "Shooter coming out!"

Throw the dice hard enough to hit the wall at the other end of the table. This is very important. A throw in which the dice don't take a bounce at the end may be considered a **no roll**. This will make you very unpopular with the crew and the other players, especially if the invalid numbers would have paid someone big money.

Tip

Always throw dice hard enough to hit the end of the table, but don't throw them so wildly that they come off the table. The game will be delayed until the dice are found and checked for tampering. Some superstitious shooters request "same dice" if the cubes escape because they believe changing dice will cause a seven-out.

Time-consuming rituals before throwing are equally unloved. It's okay to rattle the dice for a few moments or whisper a mantra, but elaborate performances are not appreciated. Keep your throwing hand in sight at all times when holding the cubes. Don't hold or touch them with both hands. Don't smack the cubes on the surface of the table. Don't grind or rub the cubes together. Why all the rules? You'd be amazed at the sneaky things people do to cheat. The craps crew has seen it all, so they're extra cautious when dice are handled in an irregular way. It's best to simply take the cubes, set them as necessary (we'll talk later about setting dice), and throw them.

You're allowed to shoot indefinitely, as long as you continue to pass with a natural on the come-out, roll craps, pass with a point, or roll numbers other than 7 after a come-out. If you seven-out, it's over. You lose, and the dice are offered to the person standing next to you.

Everyone gets a chance to shoot, but players betting the don't pass often decline the dice. If they do take the dice, the stickperson will announce that the player is shooting from the don't. Other players may refuse to bet until the dice have passed. There is no practical or mathematical reason for any of this. It's just custom and superstition, but remember that craps is a social game. If you're playing alone, or it's just you and friends, then it really doesn't matter. On the other hand, shooting from the don't is a judgment call when the table is crammed with strangers. Are you feeling like a maverick? Then go ahead, shoot from the don't.

More Craps Bets

The average pass attempt takes about four or five rolls, though boomerang rolls (point-point) are quite common, as are point followed by an immediate seven-out. Naturals and craps on the come-out are also pretty frequent. But even though there are plenty of quick decisions that can occur for pass and don't pass, the reverse is also true. It can take twenty minutes or longer for a shooter to hit her point or seven-out. Craps lore is filled with amazing stories of people who have held the dice for an hour or more. A feat like that would be extraordinarily boring if the only wagers at stake were the pass and don't pass. Craps is exciting because every roll can be a winner. The extra action comes from bets like these…

Come and Don't Come

Come is the largest area of the layout on most tables. It's the first thing most people see (or at least the first thing that registers) when they peer over the rail. What the heck does it mean?

The origin of the phrase is lost in the mists of history, but you'll find it helpful to consider "come" as a hearty welcome to players who have arrived at the game during the shooter's attempt to pass.

It's simple. A come bet works like a pass-line bet except that a come bet is made after the shooter establishes a point. Nevertheless, the wager has a full opportunity for a natural win on the first roll.

How does that work? The key to understanding come (and its opposite, don't come) is to forget about the shooter's attempt to pass and simply focus on the numbers as the shooter rolls them. Think of the numbers as a series. Remember, the rules for winning and losing are exactly the same for pass and for come.

For example, a come wager will win on the first roll when the dice produce 7 or 11, and it will lose with craps. A winning 7 for a come bet might be a seven-out for the shooter, but the shooter's contest doesn't involve the come bet. A come bet has its own come-out and its own point. Come is entirely independent of the shooter's attempt to pass except that both wagers use the same sequence of numbers.

"Do and Don't Betting Examples" shows how this works. Imagine that four players simultaneously arrive at the table. Each player bets only one way and waits for a win or loss before placing another bet. The various wagers are shown side by side. They all occur during the same random rolls of the dice. Empty spaces indicate no effect from the roll.

Do and Don't Betting Examples

Roll	Dice Results	Pass	Don't Pass	Come	Don't Come
1	7	win come-out	lose come-out	no action	no action
2	6	point est.	point est.	no action	no action
3	3			lose craps	win craps
4	4			point est.	point est.
5	12				
6	5				
7	10				
8	4			win point	lose point
9	2			lose craps	win craps
10	3			lose craps	win craps
11	2			lose craps	win craps
12	6	win point	lose point	point est.	point est.
13	8	point est.	point est.		
14	6			win point	lose point
15	7	lose (7-out)	win (7-out)	win come-out	lose come-out
16	11	win come-out	lose come-out	no action	no action
17	5	point est.	point est.	no action	no action
18	9			point est.	point est.
19	7	lose (7-out)	win (7-out)	lose (7-out)	win (7-out)
	Total	3 wins	2 wins	3 wins	5 wins
		2 losses	3 losses	5 losses	3 losses

Pass and don't-pass bets are made when the shooter is coming out. Come and don't-come bets are made after a shooter's point has been established. Wins and losses in this table reflect these particular random dice rolls.

Notice that the first roll in the sequence is the shooter's come-out. It has no effect on the come and don't come because action is not allowed for those wagers. The next 7 (fifteenth roll in the sequence) is a win for the come but a loss for the shooter. The final 7 (final roll in the sequence) is a loss for both do bettors and a win for both don't bettors.

Tip

When a come or don't-come bet wins, it is promptly paid and returned. Don't delay retrieving the chips or the entire amount will be in play for the next roll.

There is no limit to the number of come and don't-come wagers a player can make alone or in tandem with other bets. Betting on multiple successive rolls is common, though it can get expensive. If a shooter throws 7, the current come bet will win, but the others that are waiting for a point will be lost. On the other hand, if the shooter is throwing a lot of numbers and 7 is nowhere to be seen, multiple come bets will earn a lot of money. And of course, the opposite is true for multiple don't-come bets; one 7 brings rich rewards, but a hot shooter will knock off multiple don't-come bets like a kung fu master in a martial arts movie.

Pass Line vs. Come: Practical Differences

A bet on come has the exact same house edge (1.4 percent) and overall probability of winning or losing as a bet on the pass line. Ditto for don't come and don't pass. But there are some practical differences beyond the issue of when the bets are allowed.

Come and don't come belong to a category of craps wagers that are handled in whole or in part by a dealer. Points are not designated with a puck. Instead, the chips are moved into the numbered squares, an area that is off-limits to the players. Here's how it works for come.

As with line wagers, you begin by noting whether the shooter is coming out or trying to roll a point. You can make a come bet if the puck is ON.

Just reach across the layout and put your chips on the come. Come bets that win or lose on the first roll are handled like any bet; they're either paid or taken. If a point is rolled, a dealer moves the come bet to the corresponding number box on the layout. The exact placement of the chips in the box will reflect where you're standing at the table. The chips will stay there until a 7 or the point is rolled. A roll of 7 makes them disappear, but a point will bring them back to the come box with a matching pile of chips.

If you're making multiple come bets of equal value and a previous one happens to win while the current one has just established a point, the dealer won't bother switching multiple stacks of chips. He will pay the bet on the come, and then move chips from one number to another if necessary. This is called **off and on**.

Wagers on the don't come are placed and handled similarly to come bets. Simply put your chips on the don't come. They're moved to a corresponding number box if a point is rolled. A roll of 7 brings the wager back with matching funds; a point makes it disappear.

Odds: The Best Bet on the Table

The best bet you can make at a craps table is called **odds.** When you bet odds, house odds are identical to true odds.

Got that?

To put it another way, the casino has zero advantage on an odds bet. Here's how it works.

Odds is technically a stand-alone bet, a separate wager, but it is always linked to an original flat bet on pass or come, don't pass or don't come. Odds for a do bet is called **taking odds;** it's an extra wager (made after the come-out) that the shooter will successfully roll the point. **Laying odds** is the opposite of taking odds. It's a bet that is hoping for a seven-out. The table below shows the various payoffs.

Taking and Laying Odds

Point	True Odds	Taking Odds (Do) $30 Bet Returns	Laying Odds (Don't) $30 Bet Returns
4	2:1	$60	$15
5	3:2	$45	$20
6	6:5	$36	$25
8	6:5	$36	$25
9	3:2	$45	$20
10	2:1	$60	$15

Odds bets are paid at true odds and have no house edge.

Odds bets don't earn the casino any money; they're a premium. So the house has lots of rules restricting the wagers (sort of like fine print on a discount coupon).

The first and most important rule is that odds are allowed in multiples of the original flat bet, and there is always a limit. For example, if the flat bet is $10 and the odds allowed are 3×, you can take odds in any amount up to $30, and you can lay odds up to a $30 payoff.

Let's say the point is 10. The following table shows the various amounts and possible payoffs for a flat bet and odds when the base bet is $10 and odds are 3×. You'll notice that laying odds (winning with a seven-out) doesn't pay as much as taking odds (winning with a point). That's because it's easier to win with a lay bet.

Do vs. Don't Odds Comparison

	Base Bet	3× Odds Bet (point is 10)	Bet Total	Win Total	Win Probability (against)
DO	$10	$30 (3 × $10 base bet)	$40	$70	2:1
DON'T	$10	$60 (3 × $20 bet payoff)	$70	$40	1:2

Laying odds (winning with a 7) doesn't pay as much as taking odds (winning with a 10) because the lay bet has a greater chance of winning. There are six ways to roll 7 and only three ways to roll 10.

Keep in mind that the base bet is paid 1:1, and the odds bet is always paid at the true odds of winning. Also, odds must be taken or laid on the same side as the flat bet.

How much in odds can you take or lay at your favorite casino? The limits are posted along with the other table limits on a plastic card attached to the inside wall of the craps table. 3× for points 4/10, 4× for points 5/9, and 5× for points 6/8 is pretty standard these days, though 10× for all the points can be found at some properties. Occasionally you'll find a house that offers 20× or 100×, and casinos with a monopoly on the market often allow only 1× or 2× for all the points.

Odds Secrets

The tricky thing about odds is that there is no place for the bets on the layout. It's a bit like an "off the menu" special; odds are available only to people who know enough to ask.

Taking odds on the pass line is easy. Put your chips directly behind the original bet (on the blank space next to the wall) after the point is made. Your bet will be paid or swept away as the dice warrant.

Laying odds on the don't pass is a little weird. You place the chips next to the original bet, but you heel the stack. That means the bottom chip is off center and the stack slants to one side. The dealer will show you how to do it. Odds bets are **heeled** when the payoff will be a *different amount* than the payoff for the flat bet. If the payoff will be

THE FACT IS...

If you're betting the don't and the point is 4 or 10, you may be tempted to load up on odds to get a bigger payoff (you'll win $1 for every $2 risked). What is the probability that you will win? It is 2:1 in your favor, but the other ⅓ of the time the dealer will sweep away your chips. Keep that in mind, and lay odds in reasonable amounts.

Tip

One way to avoid misunderstand-ings when making bets that require dealer assistance is to put wagers on a line that separates betting areas. That way your odds on the 10 won't accidentally become a brand-new come bet.

the same, then the stack should be bridged instead of heeled. A **bridged stack** is two stacks with a third perched on top. The dealer will show you how it's done.

Yes, it's arcane, but for a house edge of zero percent the hassle is worth it.

Taking and laying odds on the come and don't come require a dealer's assistance. You do this by putting chips on the layout (preferably on a line that separates betting spaces). Tell the dealer that you want "odds on the four" or whatever. She will pick up the chips and place the wager accordingly.

One of the most important things to remember about taking odds is to do it in multiples that the casino can pay. If the point is 6 and you take $8 odds, the payoff would be $9.60. The casino will only give you $9. To get the full payout you must take odds in multiples of $5 when the point is 6 or 8, $2 for points 5 and 9. And any whole-dollar amount is fine for points 4 and 10.

Do it in reverse when laying odds (see the "Taking and Laying Odds" chart on page 156). Odds on 4/10 should be divisible by two, 5/9 by three, and 6/8 by six.

Working Bets and Taking Wagers Down

Most casino games trap a bet once it's made. The reels spin or the cards snap and your money is trapped until a decision is rendered. Win, lose, or push, you're stuck until the contest is over. Craps is different. Multiple rolls can occur before the dice deliver a decision. A bet in this situation is said to be **working**. This is an important distinction because many craps bets can be turned on, turned off, or taken down (removed entirely) as a player wishes.

Odds is an excellent example of this. Let's say a shooter is giving you a bad feeling. You can temporarily turn off your odds on the come or don't come, or even have the bet removed from the layout.

It's perfectly okay. Just tell the dealer to "take the odds down." Pass and don't pass are even easier: just reach over and remove the odds bet.

Unfortunately, basic pass or come wagers cannot be turned off or taken down. Remember, they have their best chance of winning (2:1) on the first roll, but they're at a big disadvantage after that. The casino takes the upfront risk, so it wants a shot at the reward. Those bets are trapped on the layout until a point or seven-out.

The reverse is true for don't-pass and don't-come wagers. You take the early risk, so you have the advantage after a point is rolled (between 2:1 and 6:5). Thus you can remove or reduce a don't bet at any time. Indeed, this would be a huge favor for the casino. But you can't put the bet back up once it's been taken down.

Another example of a working bet occurs when a "do" player is betting the pass line. If he has working come bets, he usually wants come odds off during a come-out because a 7 is good for the pass but bad for the working come. Retrieving the odds wagers and replacing them on the next roll would be time consuming, so the casino shortens the process by considering come odds automatically off during a come-out unless a player requests otherwise. If you don't care about what happens on the pass line, tell the dealer you want odds always on.

In contrast, don't-come odds are *not* automatically off when the shooter is coming out because don't-come bettors are rooting with the pass line (only on that roll) and hoping for a 7.

Did you follow that? If it seems convoluted, don't worry. The procedures are standard unless you request a change. Here are the basic rules: come odds are automatically off when a shooter is coming out, unless you request otherwise. Don't-come odds are always on, unless you request otherwise.

Even More Craps Bets

It's amazing, but pass, don't pass, come, don't come, and odds (sometimes referred to as "free odds") make up just a fraction of the bets available on a craps table. There are more than two dozen others!

None of them are as good as the wagers we've previously covered. You won't miss any bargains if you skip the next few pages and go directly to Chapter 11—Craps: Advanced Strategies, but you will miss learning about some of the sneaky ways that a casino extracts a monster edge. Knowledge will also eliminate temptation, so you should read the next few sections to avoid being lured by whiz-bang payoffs and bets that are oh-so-tempting to make.

Place Bets

Let's say a shooter throws the following sequence: 6,5,8,10,4,7. That's death to a do bettor; it's a bunch of points and then seven-out, a real drag. One alternative is to bet the don't, but there's no guarantee that the next sequence won't be 6,5,8,8,6,5. What can be done? Some players prefer to bet numbers directly so they'll pay off each time the shooter rolls those numbers.

A **place bet** is simply a wager that a number will appear before 7. The table below shows the various place bets, the odds, and how they pay.

Place Bets

Number	True Odds (against)	House Odds Pay	$60 Bet Pays	Place House Edge
4	2:1	9:5	$108	6.7%
5	3:2	7:5	$84	4.0%
6	6:5	7:6	$70	1.5%
8	6:5	7:6	$70	1.5%
9	3:2	7:5	$84	4.0%
10	2:1	9:5	$108	6.7%

Notice that the 6 and 8 have an edge that's just 0.1 percent worse than a bet on the line or come, but the edge nearly triples or quadruples on the rest of the numbers. A $60 bet on 4/10 pays $108, but odds would return $120. A bettor may not notice the $12 difference if the dice produce a lot of points, but in the long run the winning won't keep pace with the losing. A roll of 7 will appear frequently enough to wipe out the profits. When will that happen? It might take hours, days, years, or it could happen on the next roll. Remember, the house edge works. That's how casinos pay for the plush carpets and chandeliers.

A place bet is handled in a similar way to odds. Just put money down and say "Sixty dollars on the eight" or "Place it on the five." A dealer will move the chips to the appropriate box. Also note that

6 and 8 should be wagered in multiples of six. If you bet $25 you'll only be paid for a win on $24.

Place bets are automatically off during a come-out. And of course, you can take them down at any time.

Buy Bets

Buy bets are similar to place bets, but they're paid at true odds. Sounds great! Did I mention the vig? What's a vig? We covered that in Chapter 2, but here's a quick refresher: Vig is short for vigorish, and it's basically a fee for making a bet. Strictly speaking, vigorish is synonymous with any casino house edge, but the word is mostly used in situations that involve a betting fee.

> **THE FACT IS...**
>
> Craps is a very balanced game with the do and the don't almost everywhere. So where is the mirror-opposite of the place bet? Place was originally called place to win, and there is a bet called place to lose, but most casinos don't offer it.

Buy bets have a vig of 5 percent on the wager. Aside from that, they're handled like place bets. Tell the dealer which number you want to buy, and he'll take the vig and move the chips to the appropriate box.

Buy Bets

Number	True Odds (against)	$60 Bet Pays	5% Vig	Buy House Edge (standard)	Buy House Edge (vig on win only)
4	2:1	$120	3	4.8%	1.6%
5	3:2	$90	3	4.8%	1.9%
6	6:5	$72	3	4.8%	2.2%
8	6:5	$72	3	4.8%	2.2%
9	3:2	$90	3	4.8%	1.9%
10	2:1	$120	3	4.8%	1.6%

Note that the total bet is actually $63 even though the payoff is based on $60.

The vig is returned if the bet is taken down. An additional vig is charged every time the dice deliver a decision. Some casinos only charge a vig on winning wagers and that drops the edge considerably, particularly on the outside numbers (4/10).

As with place bets, buy bets are automatically off during a come-out, and you can take them down at any time.

Lay Bets

Lay bets (sometimes called no bets) are the mirror opposite of buy bets. They pay true odds when the shooter rolls a 7 before the number. That makes a lay bet essentially the same as laying odds, except a 5 percent vig is charged on the *amount to be won*.

Lay Bets

Number	True Odds (against)	$120 Bet Pays	5% Vig	Lay House Edge (standard)	Lay House Edge (vig on win only)
4	1:2	$60	3	2.4%	1.6%
5	2:3	$80	4	3.2%	1.9%
6	5:6	$100	5	4.0%	2.2%
8	5:6	$100	5	4.0%	2.2%
9	2:3	$80	4	3.2%	1.9%
10	1:2	$60	3	2.4%	1.6%

Note that the total bet is actually $120 plus the vig even though the payoff is based on $120.

As with buy bets, the vig is returned if the bet is taken down. An additional vig is charged every time the dice produce a decision. Also note that some casinos charge a vig only on winning wagers.

Lay bets are always on unless you request them to be turned off.

Squeezing the House

Some players squeeze a little extra value from their buy and lay bets when they wager an amount that cannot be conveniently charged in whole dollars equal to 5 percent. Casinos typically round down on vig amounts less than fifty cents and round up otherwise, so a $25 buy bet (one green chip) would be charged only $1. That drops the house edge by about one percent. The exact amount depends on how much you squeeze.

Of course, if a player really wants to squeeze the house, then the best strategy is to avoid place, buy, and lay bets altogether. Some craps enthusiasts would argue that they're not "bad" bets when compared to slots and roulette. That's true. The world won't end if you play them. But your

Tip

Most casinos charge a minimum $1 vig for buy and lay bets, so a bet for any amount less than $20 effectively increases the 5 percent vig.

bankroll may die prematurely. If you make these bets, just be aware that you're paying for the pleasure.

From Bad to Worse

These are the sucker bets that your mother warned you not to make. These are the legendary wagers that have broken millionaires and laid waste to fat bankrolls. Much of craps' bad reputation rests on these extremely disadvantageous gambles.

The one thing that most of them have in common is that they pay handsomely when luck is your lover. But when luck leads you with teasing kisses and sweet promises into a dark corner and then mugs you, it's usually these bets that come crashing down on your head.

Playing the Field

Just below the area for come and above the don't pass is a section on the layout known as the **field**. A bet here can be made at any time without dealer assistance. It's an even-money wager that the next roll of the dice will be 3, 4, 9, 10, or 11; if the dice roll 2 or 12, the casino pays double the wager (some casinos pay triple). Rolls of 5, 6, 7, and 8 are losers. Eight winning numbers and only four losers may seem like a good bet but the true odds are 20:16 against the field. The house edge on a field bet is 5.6 percent when 2 and 12 pay double. It drops to 2.8 percent if either 2 *or* 12 pay triple. That's worse than roulette, though it's still better than most slot games. Of course, a slot machine might give you a big jackpot. The best you'll do on the field is 3:1.

People who play the field do it because it allows them to simultaneously cover many numbers without putting up a lot of money. Forty-four percent of all the number combinations including craps and 11 can win with one bet. That means the dealer is frequently pushing chips to players who bet the field. Unfortunately, he takes chips away at an even greater frequency.

THE FACT IS...

A **put bet** is a pass-line or come wager that is made or increased after a point has been established. In other words, no come-out. Why would anyone do that? It's a thoroughly rotten bet unless the player takes odds. A put bet with 10X odds has a lower house edge than a buy or place bet.

Big Six and Big Eight

Big six and **big eight** are found in the corners of some layouts, and they are the ultimate sucker bets. Each is a wager on one number, either 6 or 8, to roll before the 7. Big six or big eight works exactly like a place bet except the payoff is even money. That's right. $30 on the big six wins $30. The same money "place the six" will bring $35.

Why would anyone play the big six/eight? It's usually a favorite of minimum-bet players who don't want to put up the few extra dollars it takes to properly place the six/eight. Others bet big six/eight out of ignorance or because they don't like to work with dealers (the bets can be made without dealer assistance).

The house edge on big six/eight is a nasty 9.1 percent. That's comparable to a progressive slot machine, but without the one-in-a-few-million chance of winning a fortune. Big six/eight simply bleeds its suckers dry. The bet is so bad that it's not allowed in Atlantic City.

Hardways

A roll of 4, 6, 8, or 10 thrown as a double is called a **hard number** because it is produced the hard way. Betting the **hardway** is a wager that a particular number will be thrown hard before a 7, and before it is thrown the easy way. Hard four and hard ten pay 7:1. Hard six and hard eight pay 9:1. The area for these bets is at the center of the table, and they're sometimes called all-day bets because they can stay out there for quite a while if the shooter doesn't throw the number or 7. The bet can be made at any time and withdrawn at any time; it requires dealer assistance.

Tip

A payoff of "5 for 1" is not the same as "5 to 1." Some casinos play this cute little trick with the words on the felt in the center of the table. They pretend that they're paying one more because they take your original wager. The actual payout on 5 for 1 is 4:1; 10 for 1 is actually 9:1.

Just put your chips on the table and tell the dealer what you want...if you dare. The house edge for hard six and hard eight is a painful 9.1 percent. It's an excruciating 11.1 percent for hard four and hard ten.

The Rest of the Worst

The rest of the bets in the center of the table aren't better than the hardways, and they're frequently worse.

They're all one-roll propositions, and they're handled by the stickperson. The table below shows the various bets, true odds, house odds, and the house edge. I've also included the hardways and big six/eight so you can see and compare all of craps' worst bets in one place. It's a real rogues' gallery.

Craps' Worst Bets

Bet	True Odds	House Odds	House Edge
Any 7 (big red)	5:1	4:1	16.7%
2 (snake eyes)	35:1	30:1	13.9%
12 (boxcars)	35:1	30:1	13.9%
Hop (1 way)	35:1	30:1	13.9%
Whirl	10:5	8:5	13.3%
Horn	20:4	17:4	12.5%
Hop (2 ways)	17:1	15:1	11.1%
Three (ace-deuce)	17:1	15:1	11.1%
Eleven (yo-leven)	17:1	15:1	11.1%
Any craps	8:1	7:1	11.1%
Hard four	8:1	7:1	11.1%
Hard ten	8:1	7:1	11.1%
Hard six	10:1	9:1	9.1%
Hard eight	10:1	9:1	9.1%
Big six/eight	6:5	1:1	9.1%

Odds and payoffs for horn and whirl are an average (individual wins pay differently).

This is where the craps jargon really explodes. For example, **horn** is a combined bet on 2, 3, 11, and 12. The payoff is calculated as if you had bet each number separately. Your wager is divided into quarters, so if you make this long-shot bet it's a good idea to put money down in multiples of four or request a **horn high** and indicate on which of the four you want the extra money: "Horn high 12!"

Whirl is a horn bet with the 7 added. The bet is divided into five parts. **C&E** is craps plus 11. **Buffalo** is a combination of the four hardways plus a 7 or sometimes a "yo" 11. **Box cars** is a bet on 12. A **hop bet** is a wager that a single number will be thrown in a particular way on the very next roll. Technically, 2, 3, 11, and 12 are hop bets, but you can do it with any number (assuming that you'd be willing to make such a bad wager).

It's a cornucopia of colorful names and slang for basically rotten gambling. There isn't a single bet in the center of the table that has a house edge of less than 9 percent. Betting the 7 (big red) is a whopping 16.7 percent. That's the worst bet available in many casinos.

Now that you've seen the worst (hopefully) you won't be tempted to make these wagers. It's best to stay with the craps basics: pass, don't pass, come, don't come, and odds.

In the next chapter, I'll tell you about strategies for using these basic bets to lower the house edge.

Essentially

- The shooter's attempt to pass is the basic contest in craps. Players can wager with the shooter on the pass line or against the shooter on the don't-pass bar. These do and don't bets have a house edge of 1.4 percent.

- You can tell if a shooter is coming out or throwing for a point by finding the puck on the layout. It will show "OFF" or "COME-OUT" when the shooter is starting a new pass, and "ON" or "POINT" when the shooter is trying to throw a point.

- You should throw the dice with one hand, and be sure they bounce off the wall at the far end of the table. But don't throw them so hard that they fly off the table.

- Come and don't-come bets are made after a point has been established. They are independent of the shooter's contest, but otherwise they operate by the same rules as pass and don't-pass. Come and don't-come have a 1.4 percent house edge.

- Odds is an additional bet made in conjunction with a pass, don't pass, come or don't come wager. Odds wagers have a zero percent house edge; this makes them the best bet in craps.

- Come, don't come, and their related odds bets are handled by dealers. The chips are moved into the numbered squares on the table to signify the working point. Chips in the numbered squares (and the center portion of the table) are handled solely by the dealer, and they are off-limits to the players.

- Odds bets can be turned on, off, or taken down as the player prefers. Don't bets can be reduced or removed from the layout at any time. Do bets (pass and come) are trapped on the layout once a point is rolled.

- Odds on the come are automatically off when a shooter is coming out.

- Place bets and buy bets are similar to taking odds, but they don't require a previous wager on the line or come. Unfortunately, the casino pays less than true odds for winning place bets, and the casino charges a 5 percent vig (fee) for buy bets.

- Lay bets are similar to laying odds on the don't, but a bet on the bar or don't come is not required. The casino charges a 5 percent vig on the amount to be won.

- The field is a one-roll bet that pays 1:1 when the dice produce 3, 4, 9, 10, or 11; it pays double (or in some casinos triple) for 2 and 12. Nevertheless, the field is not a good wager. It has a house edge of 5.6 percent.

- Big six, big eight, hardways, and propositions (one-roll bets) are all extremely unfavorable wagers with house edges of 9.1 percent to 16.7 percent.

Craps: Basic Strategies

CHAPTER 11

Craps:
Advanced Strategies

 Here's where we get into the nitty gritty of beating the casino at the craps table.

Obviously, the first step is to stay away from the fancy bets in the center of the table. In case you're still temped, here's something to consider. It's an equation you learned as a child.

$$1 + 2 = 3$$

And, of course, switching the order of the numbers doesn't change the sum.

$$2 + 1 = 3$$

No matter how we divide or merge three units, the result will always be three, and never four.

$$1 + 1 + 1 = 3$$

Yes, it's simple enough, but craps' cornucopia of betting options tends to obscure this basic truth:

**A combination of bets will never outperform
the combination's individual components.**

And yet some people can't resist the challenge of trying to pull four out of three. For example...

Trimming the Hedges

The worst craps betting strategies usually involve hedge bets. These are tricky systems that combine bets to supposedly reduce risk. They actually do work to the extent that they protect against one particular result, but the alternative is usually even more expensive. For example, some bettors "insure" the pass line by also betting any craps. That supposedly turns the first roll into a can't-lose bet. Right? Wrong! Let's do the arithmetic. The table titled "Craps Insurance" shows why insuring the pass line is usually an expensive mistake.

Craps Insurance

	Ways to Win	Ways to Lose	No Effect (point)	Total Average Dollars Won
Line bet $20	8	4	24	$80
Line bet $20 and any craps $5	12	24	0	$60

The above numbers represent average results after thirty-six come-out rolls.

In this example $20 is wagered on the pass line and $5 is wagered on any craps. The combination guarantees that the first roll will always win $15 or establish a point at a cost of $5. Unfortunately those points come frequently enough to wipe out the advantage of winning on craps. The line bet does much better by itself.

Keep in mind that a bet on the pass-line has its greatest probability of winning on the come out. The above system hedges the bet precisely when it needs it the least.

Okay, so how about betting any 7 (often referred to as **big red**) once a point has been made? That would avoid a loss on seven-out, right? Yes, but only if a 7 or the point appears immediately. Those pesky dice are generally not so cooperative.

Seven-Out Insurance

	Point	Ways to Win	Ways to Lose	No Effect	Total Average Dollars Won
Line bet $20	6/8	5	6	25	−$20
Line bet $20 and any seven $10	6/8	11	25	0	−$80

The above numbers represent average results after thirty-six rolls.

The table titled "Seven-Out Insurance" shows that big red costs much more than it earns (on average) after thirty-six rolls. In this example it quadruples the expense of rolling 6/8. Any 7 with 5/9 or 4/10 is even worse.

That realization causes hedge bettors to search for new ways to protect their money against loss. Betting the field? Betting the hardways? Buying the numbers? It can't be done. The smart way to play craps is to pick a wager with a low house edge and make it even lower.

Flat Bets with Odds

Pass, don't pass, come, and don't come have a house edge of 1.4 percent. That's pretty low, but the table below shows what happens when odds are added to the equation.

> *"Lat not this wrecched wo thin herte gnawe, but manly set the world on six and seven."* (In other words, have courage in the face of adversity, and bet the best numbers.)
>
> —Geoffrey Chaucer, from his poem "Troilus and Criseyde," published in 1385.

Flat Bets Combined With Odds

Pass Line/Come	1.41%
With 1× odds	0.85%
With 2× odds	0.61%
With 3× odds	0.47%
With 5× odds	0.33%
With 10× odds	0.19%
With 20× odds	0.10%
With 100× odds	0.02%
Don't Pass/Don't Come	1.36%
With 1× odds	0.69%
With 2× odds	0.46%
With 3× odds	0.34%
With 5× odds	0.23%
With 10× odds	0.12%
With 20× odds	0.07%
With 100× odds	0.01%

The house edge on odds is always zero percent. The figures in the right column show the overall house edge when odds are combined with a flat bet.

Remember, the actual house edge on the flat bet doesn't change. If you put $120 on the pass line, it will always be fighting against a

1.4 percent house edge regardless of the odds allowed. But what if you don't put $120 on the pass line? If you wager $60 on the line and take $60 in odds (1×), then the average house edge on the combined bet drops to 0.85 percent. $20 on the line and $100 in odds (5×) will bring the house edge down to 0.33 percent.

Putting less on the line and more in odds always lowers the overall house edge. Of course, luck is luck. Don't confuse a lower house edge with an altered probability of any number appearing on the dice. A 7 is always the favorite.

This leads to an interesting objection from some players because odds is a separate wager. If you bet a reduced amount on the line or come, it means you'll win less money if the dice tumble the right way on the come-out.

It's a valid observation. The biggest opportunity for pass/come is on the come-out. Having less money on the line means a smaller win if a natural appears. On the other hand, would you rather get 1:1 on a flat bet with a 1.4 percent disadvantage, or 6:5, 3:2, or 2:1 on a bet at true odds?

Placing the Six and Eight

Place six and place eight have a house edge of 1.5 percent, just a smidgen more than a line wager and still a pretty good bet. Players who bet don't pass and don't come sometimes place the six and eight as a short-term hedge. It's not a bad bet, and it's the only hedge I recommend (if you are inclined to play a hedge strategy).

The best way to make this hedge bet is to be sure the combined total of the place six and eight is not greater than the don't wager. Let's say $30 is on the don't and the point is 5. You would place $12 on 6 and $12 on 8. If the shooter suddenly rolls 7, then the net win (after losses) will be $6. It's not ideal, but, hey, that's gambling and you're ahead. If the shooter rolls the point it won't affect the place bets and you would have lost the don't wager anyway. If the shooter rolls 6 or 8 a few times, the dealer will be giving you money. Just remember that the 7 is more likely than the point. Don't be greedy. Take the place bets down after they win once or twice. The wager on the don't will usually win in the end and then you can savor multiple victories.

Place bets on 6/8 are also fine by themselves or in conjunction with pass and come wagers.

Craps Optimal Strategy

This is it, the Holy Grail for craps. It's the culmination of all the material we've covered to this point. Follow this optimal strategy, and the casino will never have an advantage that exceeds 1.5 percent.

Tip

Buying the 6 or 8 is a waste of money. You can place the same numbers and get a higher net payoff. On the flip side, buying the 4 and the 10 is cheaper than placing them. Of course, the best deal is odds. That has no vig. So you're always better off taking or laying odds rather than buying or placing numbers.

- Bet the pass, come, don't pass, or don't come.

- Take or lay odds.

- Occasionally bet the place six or place eight (if you are so inclined).

- Don't waste time or money on place four, five, nine, ten, or buy and lay bets for the remaining numbers because odds wagers are better.

- Avoid proposition bets (hop bets, big red, and similar wagers). Stay away from the field.

A typical pass/come line of play using this strategy would be to bet pass, take odds if a point is rolled and place the six/eight (unless the point is 6 or 8). Aggressive bettors might follow up with one, two, or three additional come bets and odds.

A typical don't-pass/don't-come line of play would be to bet don't pass; take odds if a point is rolled and possibly hedge with the 6/8. Aggressive bettors might follow up with one or two additional don't-come bets and odds.

There is no "wrong" way to combine your bets when you stick to optimal strategy. The only real mistake would be putting too much money on the table (we'll cover that in the next section).

Craps Bankroll Management

Back in Chapter 2, I mentioned that you need at least 50 bets to play a table game for a full three-hour session. And I wrote, "When calculating the size of your bankroll, also keep in mind that an average bet is not necessarily the lowest bet."

This absolutely applies to craps. If the minimum bet is $10, then a pass-line bet with triple odds and two come bets with triple odds will require $120 on the table. All that money can disappear with one roll of 7. So a bankroll of $500 ($10 × 50 bets) can be overwhelmed quickly if the dice turn cold. To stay in the game with $120 on the table you must increase your session bankroll to at least $6,000, or lower the amount of money you're risking on one shooter.

If you choose the latter option, you should decrease odds and decrease the number of bets, or find a table that allows $5 bets.

Setting Dice

I have a friend who has an adage about craps systems. He says, "You tell me what you're going to roll, and I'll tell you how to bet."

In fact there are some shooters who can do that. They come in two types. First, there are "dice mechanics," who are professional cheats (we'll cover them in a later section). The rest do it the legal way. They're known as golden shooters, rhythmic rollers, hot shooters, golden arms, and other similarly descriptive names. They operate in the same realm of credibility as football coaches and psychics. Some people swear by their talents, but others aren't so sure. Most of these players use a technique that you can use yourself.

"My dear Tiberius, We had the same company for supper, except that Vinicius and the elder Silius also came. We gambled like old men all through the meal, both yesterday and today. Anyone who threw the 'dog' [a one] or a six, put a silver piece in the pot, one denarius for each of the dice, and anyone who threw Venus won it all."

—Augustus Caesar, Roman emperor, in a letter to his adopted son Tiberius.

The Science of Dice

Opposite ends of dice always total 7. Hold a pair between your thumb and forefinger with the 6s on the outside and the 1s facing each other. Notice that 2, 3, 4, and 5 are the exposed faces. If you were to toss those dice and they didn't turn sideways, the probability of rolling craps would be zero. The odds of seeing 7 would be 1:3 instead of 1:5. That would be a heck of an advantage on a come-out! Now hold the dice with a 6 on the outside of one cube and a 5 on the outside of the other. If the dice don't turn then 7 can be made only two ways, but 6 and 8 can be made three ways. That's an astounding advantage when you're rolling for an inside point.

A setup with 6 on the outside of one cube and 4 on the outside of the other gives all the points an equal chance against 7 (assuming the dice don't turn).

Dice Setups

Numbers											
2	3	4	5	6	7	8	9	10	11	12
Ways to Roll											
No setup	1	2	3	4	5	6	5	4	3	2	1
6–1, 1–6	0	0	1	2	3	4	3	2	1	0	0
6–1, 2–5	0	1	1	2	3	2	3	2	1	1	0
6–1, 3–4	0	1	2	2	2	2	2	2	2	1	0

Of course, casinos know all about this. That's why dice are constructed the way they are. The sharp edges are designed to make them catch on surfaces and tumble. The ends of the table are dimpled to make the dice turn when they bounce. And a bounce is required or the results may be declared a no-roll.

And then there's that long toss. Can you loft dice the length of the table without turning them? It can be done, but it takes some practice.

Casinos don't seem to be too concerned about people setting dice because most let you do it. It's no big deal as long as you use one hand and you don't delay the game. It should take about three seconds. Don't make a big show, just flip the dice, pick them up, and then pitch them in a way that will reduce a sideways turn. You want to just graze the back of the table.

Does it work? Sometimes yes, sometimes no. Setting dice certainly can't hurt your chances. Betting on someone who sets dice will never be worse than betting on a random shooter.

Tip

Setting dice with the 3s angled like a pyramid creates a 6–1 and 2–5 setup. That reduces the possibility of rolling a 7 and increases your chances of rolling a point (assuming the cubes don't turn sideways during the throw).

Craps Etiquette

Imagine a three-legged race with a dozen contestants tied together. That's craps. The game cannot function unless everyone cooperates. Dealers, stickman, players, and shooter have to be in a rhythm or the whole thing is absolute chaos.

Miscommunication can cause bets to be incorrectly handled or improperly paid. A shooter who doesn't hit the wall can cause a no-roll and delay the game. Ditto for dice that fly off the table. If you ever want to stop a craps game cold, just put one or both hands flat on the layout. A dozen people or more will turn their eyes to you. And you'd better have something important to say.

You shouldn't be intimidated by this need for cooperation, but you should understand that it's an important part of the game. Also understand that some rules are absolute, and others are more like customs or superstitions. The latter may not have a practical basis, but they're rarely broken without some sort of admonishment or minor incident.

Thou Shalt Not

Here are the inviolable rules. These involve the integrity of the game.

Dealers' areas must never be touched. The numbers, the center of the table, and the bank in front of the boxperson are inviolate. Players must never touch them. If a dealer makes a mistake placing a bet, say what you must to call attention to the problem, but don't reach for the chips.

Dice must be thrown correctly. I mentioned this previously, but it bears repeating here. Use one hand to throw the dice. Do not hold anything else in that hand when you grab the cubes. Do not conceal them from view at any time. Make sure they bounce off the far wall.

Do not slam them on the table or grind them in your hand. Aim for the end of the table and try not to knock over stacks of chips.

Money transactions must be secure and observable. This rule is the same one mentioned in Chapter 9, and it applies to all table games. In the case of craps, you should get chips onto the layout within a reasonable amount of time after the dice have been called. Promptly remove bets from the layout if you don't want them to play. Don't touch bets on the pass line when the puck is on. Never hand money to a dealer. Put it on the layout in a neutral space and ask for change.

A dealer must understand your bet or it is void. Tell dealers exactly what you want, and be sure they understand. If you want an odds bet on the come, mention the number and make sure you say it's odds, as in, "Odds on my four."

All players must have an equal opportunity to shoot. Moving around the table in an attempt to shoot the dice out of sequence is not allowed.

Other craps no-nos include hanging your hands over the edge of the rail, resting drinks on the rail, and betting cash (rather than chips) without approval from the boxperson.

Superstitions and Customs

Craps survived for 1,000 years from Palestine, through Europe, across the Atlantic, and up the Mississippi to reach your favorite casino. As a result, the game has developed a multitude of solemn customs and superstitions. Here are the most important traditions. Heed them or not; the choice is yours. Just be aware that other players really believe this stuff.

A don't bettor increases the chance of a seven-out. Betting against the shooter is tolerated by do players because it's allowed by the rules, but the negative energy is believed to cause a choppy table or a long string of losses. Don't bettors are not popular at crowded tables.

In fact, the stickperson will announce when a don't player is shooting so that do bettors can remove their bets from the layout.

Taking bets down during a pass attempt will cause a shooter to seven-out. This is related to the previous negative-energy superstition. If you lose faith in the shooter, then his magic may stop working.

Breaking the shooter's rhythm will cause a seven-out. Speaking to the shooter, touching him, or mentioning the word seven during a pass attempt is an extreme faux pas. The person is in a zone and must not be disturbed. Here's just one example. Let's say your best friend starts a monster roll while you're away from the table. You approach and realize a hot streak is in progress. The polite thing to do is to stay out of your friend's line of site and come no closer. The psychic elements that are causing the streak must not be disturbed.

Dice leaving the table will cause a seven-out, unless the shooter continues with the same dice. If one or both of the dice fly off the table, be sure to ask for "same dice" or you'll hear a groan from all the players.

Dice hitting a person's hand will cause a seven-out. Keep your hands off the layout when the dice are flying or the dealers and players will be yelling at you.

A woman who is shooting craps for the first time will always pass, and will likely pass a number of times after that. This is a big one. It may seem sexist, but it is a *huge* factor in the game. Women who have never played craps are called **craps virgins**, and everyone is looking for the next one. Here's a typical craps-virgin story:

"I was at the table once with a honeymoon couple. When the dice came to the woman she didn't want to roll, but every old-timer at the table begged her. Finally, the stickman talked her into it. As her pretty young hand reached for the dice I doubled my pass line and bet a YO (11)! Sure enough, she rolled a YO! Her next roll was an easy 6. I bet all the boxes, covered all the hard guys, and bet a 12. She rolled a 12. By this time the table

Tip

If you have a lot of chips on the rail, put the higher denomination chips in the center and the lower denomination chips on the outside. That way a thief will have to work extra hard to snatch the juiciest pickings.

was going nuts with bets. She hit a lot of box numbers and then the point number with a hard six. The stick called it the honeymoon special. She blushed when he said it. This went on for about fifteen minutes before she rolled the bad number. Everybody was happy! Chips for the players, tips for the crew, drinks for the shooter and her hubby."—Sam Shooter, craps player.

In contrast, male craps virgins are often believed to be bad luck. Sorry, guys.

Yes, these are just superstitions. But if you're wondering why a chip fill is delaying the game, and the dice are being s-l-o-w-l-y inspected, it's because the boxperson or floor supervisors see the table is hemorrhaging cash, and they're trying to break the shooter's rhythm. That's right. Even some casino bosses believe the superstitions!

Of course, most crews and managers don't believe this nonsense. They accept that streaks are a part of the game, and they congratulate players on their good fortune.

But if you find yourself in an establishment that is not so enlightened, don't hesitate to ask for a supervisor or manager and register a complaint. If the situation isn't corrected, you shouldn't play there. Find another place to toss the dice.

Unless of course you believe the superstitions. In that case, I suggest you switch to the don't because the shooter's rhythm has been interrupted.

Craps Thieves

A hot craps table usually involves a lot of shouting and a throng of people who are elbow to elbow. It's a lot of fun, but it's also a situation that a thief loves, confusion and noise.

When the table gets crowded, you should keep an eye (or a hand) on your chips to prevent any light-fingered larceny. One popular scam is to squeeze into a tight table and simply scoop off chips when a player is leaning over and not watching.

Another scam involves confusing the dealers and claiming someone else's winning bet. You might think this would be difficult, but remember that a hot table will have many players and dozens of bets working. That's a lot of chips changing hands. Keep an eye on your bets in the heat of the action.

Dice Mechanics

This is a more of a problem for the craps crew than for you, but I'm mentioning it because people who cheat the game are the reason why rules regarding dice and money are so stringent. **Dice mechanics** will switch dice, slide dice, fix dice, or do any number of other things to unfairly affect the outcome of the throw. The craps crew is always on the lookout for these criminals.

So the next time you grab the cubes, then lean below the table to put your drink on the ledge, and find yourself surrendering the dice for inspection…well, now you know what it's all about.

Have Fun!

You don't have to make a bazillion bets to enjoy craps, and the world won't end if you skip odds. Simple bets are okay. A bet on the pass line or one come bet can be just as much fun as throwing chips around. It all depends on your mood.

Likewise, if you decide to buy a few numbers, or if you decide to get fancy with some hardways or propositions, that's okay, too. I don't recommend high-edge bets, but the sky won't fall if you throw a few chips into the center of the table.

Craps is an amazing game because it offers all of these options. Some bets are more expensive than others, but in the end the choice is yours. Play how you want. Have fun!

Essentially

- Hedge bets that use propositions, hardways, or other high-edge wagers are unprofitable and a waste of money.

- The best way to lower the house edge is to make basic do and don't bets and take odds. Craps optimal strategy guarantees that the house edge will always be 1.5 percent or less.

- Setting the dice a particular way may help you roll naturals or points more often, assuming you can throw the dice without turning them.

- Many craps superstitions involve actions that will supposedly cause a shooter to seven-out. Speaking to the shooter, touching him, or mentioning the word "seven" during a pass attempt is extremely bad form.

- Keep an eye on your chips when the craps table gets busy. Thieves use confusion as a cover to steal from unwary players.

- Play how you want. Have fun!

CHAPTER 12

Poker: Basic Strategies

 Once upon a time (in December 1829 to be exact), an Englishman named Joseph Cowell took a trip down the Mississippi on a riverboat. Cowell was an actor touring the United States. The job made him a decent living, but frankly, his career on the stage was entirely forgettable. Hardly anyone remembers Joseph Cowell as a thespian. Rather, he is remembered for what he saw on the riverboat.

Cowell watched four passengers playing a card game. Later, he wrote an account of the contest. His report is the earliest record we have of a poker game.

The dealer in this game was the sort of person who would later be the archetype for a thousand Hollywood villains. He wore green spectacles and a diamond stickpin. Cardsharps in those days were known as blacklegs. And this particular blackleg was planning to scam the table for a tidy sum.

At one point during the journey, the riverboat was enveloped in a thick fog, and it hit an embankment. Everyone rushed to the windows to see what was happening, but the blackleg stayed behind (to stack the deck it seems). Soon after the confusion, "Green Spectacles" dealt an amazing hand. Though as you'll see, it didn't turn out the way the blackleg expected.

Cowell writes, "He did not lift his cards, but sat quietly watching the countenances of the others. The man on his left bet ten dollars. A young lawyer (son to the then mayor of Pittsburgh, who little dreamed of what his boy was about), who had hardly recovered from his shock, bet ten more." The third player raised the pot $500.

"'I must see that,' said Green Spectacles, who now took up his hand with 'I am sure to win,' trembling at his fingers' ends; for you could not see his eyes through his glasses. He paused a moment in disappointed astonishment, sighed 'I pass,' and threw his cards upon the table. The left-hand man bet 'that five hundred dollars and one thousand dollars better!'

"The young lawyer had time to calculate the power of his hand—four kings with an ace—it could not be beat! [Straight flushes and royal flushes had not yet been invented.] But still he hesitated at the impossibility, as if he thought it could [be beat]—looked at the money staked and then at his hand again, and, lingeringly, put his wallet on the table and called. The left-hand man had four queens with an ace, and the next four jacks and an ace.

"'Did you ever see the like on't?' said he [the blackleg] good-humoredly as he pushed the money toward the lawyer, who very agreeably astonished, pocketed his two thousand and twenty-three dollars clear!"

It seems that Green Spectacles intended the four kings for himself, and he accidentally gave them to the young lawyer. Cowell wraps up his report of the game with an observation that could apply to any modern game of poker. He writes, "All moral and social restraint was placed in the shade; there Jack was as good as his master."

These days poker games are more likely to be honest (when they're played in regulated venues), but the atmosphere at the table is pretty much the same. In poker, anything can happen. It is you against everyone else. And everyone, even a scoundrel, is equal when the cards are dealt. Jack is as good as his master.

Luck vs. Skill

Before we get into the details of how poker is played, let's take a quick (but important) detour into game theory as it applies to poker strategy.

Poker is fundamentally different from most casino gambling games. Here's why.

In most gambling games you have one opponent, the casino. And your opponent has a finite edge, usually less than 10 percent. Sometimes you win. More times the casino wins. It's a relatively safe arrangement. Everyone has a reasonable chance to beat the casino in the short run, even people who play badly. Dumb luck counts for a lot in most casino games because both sides are contesting a somewhat narrow edge.

Poker is entirely different. In poker you usually have multiple opponents, not just one. They're all trying to pick your pocket, and there is no limit to anyone's edge. In fact, it's possible in poker for someone to have a 100 percent edge, a lock on a winning hand. In a game like blackjack or craps that means the hand is over. But in poker a guaranteed winner can bleed money from losers over multiple rounds. The result is that dumb luck plays a roll in poker, but luck is usually trumped by skill.

> *"If you can't spot the sucker in your first half-hour at the table, then you're the sucker."*
>
> **—Mike McDermott, as played by Matt Damon in *Rounders* (1998)**

Thus your money is potentially at *greater* risk when playing poker than it is when playing most gambling games. On the other hand, your profit potential is higher, too.

Winners beat losers in poker with "relative" knowledge. In other words, you don't have to be the best player in the world; you don't even have to be the best player in the casino; you just have to be better than most of the people at the table. A big part of poker strategy is about choosing inferior opponents, or maneuvering superior players into making mistakes.

Keep this in mind as we cover the basics of the game.

Players, Pot, and Showdown

All genuine poker games have multiple players, typically six to nine people, competing to win a single pot (the combined bets of all the players). The pile of money increases as cards are dealt and players with strong poker hands (or bluffers representing strong hands) bet into the pot. Other players must match the bets or give up, thus losing whatever money they have invested. The contest ends when everyone concedes to one player, or when two or more players match bets in the final round and there is a showdown. The remaining players reveal their hands and compare them. The person with the best poker hand wins the pot.

Note that poker-based contests such as video poker, Caribbean Stud Poker, Let It Ride, Three Card Poker, and pai gow poker, don't have all three of the basic poker elements (multiple players, a pot, and a showdown). These poker-based games are closer in function to craps and blackjack than traditional poker, so we cover them elsewhere in this book. In this chapter and the next two chapters we cover pot games including Texas hold 'em, seven-card stud, and Omaha hi/lo.

Ranking the Hands

Poker hands are ranked in winning order as follows:

Royal Flush: Ace, king, queen, jack, and ten of the same suit. A royal flush can be made four different ways, but you'll be lucky if you see one in a lifetime.

Straight Flush: Five cards of the same suit in exactly adjacent ranks. Another example would be **5♦ 4♦ 3♦ 2♦ A♦**. Note that an ace is used to make the lowest straight flush.

Four of a Kind: Four cards of the same rank and a fifth card of any rank and suit.

Full House: Three cards of the same rank and a pair of another rank.

Flush: Five cards of the same suit that are not exactly adjacent ranks.

Straight: Five cards not of the same suit in exactly adjacent ranks. An ace is used to make both the highest and the lowest straight.

Three of a Kind: Three cards of the same rank and two cards of different ranks.

Two Pairs: Two cards of one rank, two cards of another rank, and a fifth card of a third rank.

One Pair: Two cards of one rank and three cards of different ranks.

No Pair: Five cards that don't make any combination.

Exactly five cards are used to determine a winner, no less and no more. Even though a five-card hand may be built from seven or more cards (depending on the game), those extra cards don't count in a showdown.

When two or more hands of the same rank (two straights, two flushes, etc.) are in a showdown, the high cards in each hand determine the winner. For example, a queen-high straight flush beats a jack-high straight flush. Three kings beat three jacks. A pair of aces beat a pair of queens. An ace-high flush beats a flush that has a high card of ten. If both players have identical combinations (both have two kings and two aces), then the highest fifth card in the hand determines the winner. This lone card is known as a **kicker**.

Full houses are judged first by the three matching cards and then by the pair, so kings full of jacks (three kings and two jacks) beats queens full of aces.

If neither hand makes a pair, then the hand with the highest single cards wins. If that card is matched, then the next card is used to decide, and so on. The pot is split when all five cards match in rank. Suit is never used to determine a winner. The order of the cards has no importance.

What are the chances that your **trips** (three of a kind) will be beaten by a straight? The following table shows the total number of possible five-card card combinations that can be dealt from a fifty-two-card deck. The column on the far right shows the probability of receiving any particular hand when exactly five cards are dealt.

Frequency of Poker Hands

Hand	Number of Occurrences	Percent Probability
Royal flush	4	0.00015%
Straight flush	36	0.0014%
Four of a kind	624	0.02%
Full house	3,744	0.14%
Flush	5,108	0.20%
Straight	10,200	0.39%
Three of a kind	54,912	2.11%
Two pairs	123,552	4.75%
One pair	1,098,240	42.26%
Everything else	1,302,540	50.12%
Total	2,598,960	

The column on the far right shows the probability of receiving any particular hand when exactly five cards are dealt. It's somewhat easier to make a hand with seven cards (as in seven-card stud or hold 'em), but two pairs or better still constitute less than 39 percent of seven-card hands.

Remember, the actual probability of getting any hand changes as the cards are revealed. For example, if you already have four cards to a flush, then the chance of finishing with a flush is significantly higher. And it's easier to make a hand when using more than five cards (as in hold 'em and seven-card stud). Nevertheless, you may go a lifetime without seeing a "natural" royal flush.

THE FACT IS...

Some versions of poker (like Omaha hi-lo and razz) are played for low, meaning that the worst hand wins. It sounds easy, but it's tougher than you might think. You have an equal probability of being dealt the best hand or the worst hand. For more on Omaha hi/lo and razz, see pages 237–239.

Choosing a Game and Buying In

Not every casino has poker, but if one does, it's usually in a space set apart from the hubbub of slots and other games. Some casinos (often called card clubs) primarily offer poker, and in these situations it's the hubbub that is set apart while poker dominates the layout.

Either way, you'll find a reception desk at or near the entrance to the poker area. A host there will be organizing games. If a seat is not immediately available, the host will put your name on a list and call you when something opens up. Games are identified by the type of poker (hold 'em, seven-card stud, etc.) and by betting limits, 3-6, 6-12, 20-40, or some other combination of numbers. In a **fixed-limit** game the first number is the dollar amount that can be bet or raised in the early rounds (usually round one and two); the second number is the amount that can be bet or raised in later rounds. A **spread-limit** game allows any bet between two amounts at any time. **No-limit** means just what it says; any amount can be bet at any time. **Pot-limit** means any amount up to the current value of the pot can be bet at any time. We'll begin with fixed-limit strategy examples and then cover strategies for other betting limits.

Important! If you watch a lot of tournament poker on television you may be eager to skip ahead to the sections on no-limit, but you should resist that temptation. Basic poker strategy is best learned with fixed-limit examples. Strategies for no-limit tend to be more complex.

The first order of business once you're seated will be your buy-in. It's somewhat different for poker than for other casino games (see Chapter 20 for more on handling chips and cash).

Fixed-limit poker games have a *minimum* required buy-in that is usually about ten times the minimum bet of that particular game ($40 for a 4-8 game). You're better off buying in for at least three to five times that amount. I'll explain why in a later section.

No-limit games generally have a *maximum* buy-in; something between $100 to $500 is typical.

Either way, a chip attendant or the dealer will take your money and give

Tip

Fixed-limit and spread-limit games are identified by minimum/maximum per bet limits (3-6, 15-30, and so forth). No-limit and pot-limit games are identified by the upper limit of the buy-in ($100, $500, and so forth). You should stick to low-limit or low-buy-in games until you're proficient at poker. Start with 2-4, 3-6, or 4-8 fixed-limit, or $100 no-limit.

you chips. Unlike most casino games, in poker this process can take a while. It's not uncommon for you to give an attendant $200; you get $40 in chips from the dealer, and the attendant brings the balance five minutes later.

Once you're settled, look around the table. All those people want your money. Get ready to swim with the sharks.

Texas Hold 'Em

You've probably seen Texas hold 'em played on television. It's the game that determines the champion in the World Series of Poker and the World Poker Tour. Hold 'em is also the basis for other popular variations such as Omaha hi/lo and pineapple. That makes it a good poker "starter" version. So we'll begin with hold 'em, but keep in mind that many of the strategies in the hold 'em sections apply to all genuine poker versions. You'll be four-fifths of the way to knowing every poker version on earth by the time we cover seven-card stud and other variations.

Community Cards

Hold 'em is played with a standard fifty-two-card deck. Each player receives only two cards. They are face down. During the course of play, five additional cards are dealt face up on the **board** (the table) as **community cards**; these are shared by all the players. We'll cover betting and raising in a later section; for right now just remember that players use the community cards and their two **pocket cards** or **hole cards** to build a five-card poker hand. A final hand can include one, both, or in some circumstances none of the pocket cards.

Let's say you have:

Your opponent has:

> *"I'd equate it [poker] with chess or other games of skill that require multilevel strategic, mathematical, or psychological skills. For the people who play it seriously, there's no luck involved at all."*
>
> —**Edward Norton, on his role in the film *Rounders* (1998)**

And the board shows:

You have a queen-high flush Q♦ J♦ 10♦ 8♦ 4♦, and your opponent has an ace-high straight A♣ K♣ Q♦ J♥ 10♠. You would win this hand in a showdown.

Note that your hand also can make two pairs J♦ J♥ 10♦ 10♠ Q♦, but in a showdown the highest hand is the only hand that matters.

If you hold:

Your opponent has:

And the board shows:

You have a full house, queens full of kings, but your opponent has a higher full house, kings full of jacks.

Here is a **bad beat** example from a hand I once played. I was holding:

My opponent was holding:

The board was:

My ace-high flush was beaten by a jack-high straight flush, and my opponent only used one card from his hand to do it.

If you grew up playing home-style poker games like five-card draw, the concept of community cards may seem odd at first, but as you can see it's a strong advantage for experienced players because reading your opponents' hands is much easier in an **open game** (some cards dealt face up) than in a **closed game** (no cards revealed).

For example, a full house is not possible in hold 'em unless there is a pair on the board. A flush is not possible unless the board has three suited cards. A straight is not possible unless three cards are within five ranks of each other.

Holding the Nuts

The straight flush in the previous section is an unbeatable hand. In other words, a higher hand is not possible with that particular combination of cards on the board. The person who holds an unbeatable combination is said to be holding the **nuts**.

Recognizing when you have the nuts (or when you don't) is an important part of profitable poker. Going back through the examples, the nuts for **K♣ Q♥ J♦ 9♠ K♥** are **KK** unless you're holding one king, in which case the nuts are **KQ** (making a full house). No higher hand is possible.

For **Q♦ 4♦ T♠ J♥ 8♦**, the nuts are an ace of diamonds and any other diamond. The ace creates a **nut flush**, a flush that cannot be beaten.

Betting, Raising, and Folding

You may be familiar with the concept of an **ante**. It's a small bet made by all the players in a hand to start the pot. This puts money in play and it makes additional bets worth the risk.

Seven-card stud and five-card draw use antes, but hold 'em doesn't. Instead, hold 'em uses a rotating system of **blind bets** to start the pot. Each player is designated in turn as **dealer** for one hand. This doesn't mean the person handles the deck, but it does mean a disk called a **button** is put in front of the player.

The two players to the left of the **designated dealer** must make blind bets to start the pot. The first player to the left of the button makes a **small blind bet** that is less than the table minimum. The exact amount varies depending on the game and the casino. The second player makes a **big blind bet**, which is usually the table minimum. Some games have just one blind.

The casino dealer will confirm that the blinds have been **posted** (placed on the table), then she'll shuffle the cards and begin the hand.

Cards are dealt clockwise starting to the left of the button. Each player receives two cards that are face down. Players carefully lift the cards, look at them, then put them back on the table. There are rules for handling cards that we'll cover in later section, but the important thing to remember here is that you'll generally look at the cards once, and they'll remain face down through the rest of the hand.

The first **action** (opportunity to act) begins with the person to the left of the big blind. That player has three options:

Fold: This is an unconditional surrender. The player returns her cards to the dealer and is out of the hand.

Call: Match the previous bet (in this case it's the bet posted by the big blind). This allows the player to stay in the game and continue playing for the pot.

Raise: Match the previous bet and then bet exactly that much more (in a fixed-limit contest). This allows the player to remain in the game and requires everyone else to call the increased amount, raise, or fold.

A fourth option is sometimes used on later rounds.

Check: Neither bet nor fold. The action passes to the next player. This option is available only when a bet has not yet been made. Players who check and subsequently raise a later bet in the same round have performed a **check-raise**. It's an aggressive move that is prohibited in some private games, but is generally allowed in casinos.

Tip

Action in the first round of hold 'em always begins with the first player to the left of the big blind, and it proceeds clockwise until all the players have called or folded to a single player. In later rounds, action always begins with the first active player to the left of the button.

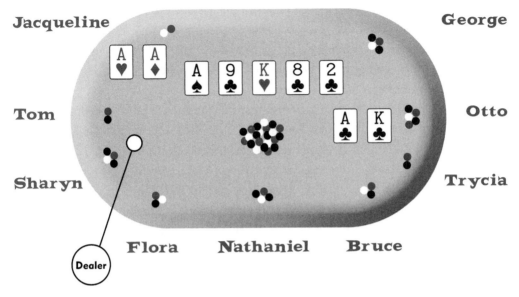

Otto wins with a flush over Jacqueline's three aces. Sharyn was the button for this hand. George was under the gun (first to act before the flop). Jacqueline was the first live player to the left of the dealer after the flop, so she started the action on the flop, turn, and river. Tom will be the button on the next hand.

Anatomy of a Poker Hand

Now let's put it all together. Here's an example of how a hand in a fixed-limit 4-8 game might develop. There are nine players at the table. The blinds are $4 and $2.

Before the Flop

George is **under the gun**; he is sitting to the left of the big blind, and he's the first player to act. George calls the big blind with a bet of $4. Otto is on George's left; he raises $4 for a total wager of $8. Trycia (to the left of Otto) must either call the $8 wager, fold, or raise another $4 to make it $12. Trycia raises. Each of the other players must either put in $12, fold, or raise again.

Four players fold after Trycia and the action moves to Tom, the little blind. He already has $2 in the pot. So he must put in an additional $10, fold, or raise. He folds.

Jacqueline is the big blind. She raises another $4 for a total bet of $16. This particular table has a **cap** of three raises per round so everyone remaining in the hand must either call $16 or fold. No more raises are allowed.

The action moves back to George, the original caller. He decides that his hand was worth $4 but not $16, and he folds. Otto and Trycia call. The pot is now $54.

The Flop

After everyone has either called or folded, the dealer **burns** the top card from the deck (removes that card from play without revealing it). This is a standard security measure to prevent cheating.

The next three cards in the deck are dealt face up on the table. This is known as the **flop**. The board shows:

The first active player to the left of the button starts the betting in this round and in every subsequent round.

That would be Jacqueline in this example. She checks. Otto bets $4. Trycia folds. Jacqueline raises Otto to $8 (a check-raise). Ouch! Otto now wonders if Jacqueline is suckering him or bluffing. Otto is holding:

That gives him two pair (aces and kings). There are only three hands that Jacqueline could be holding to beat Otto at this point. **AA**, **KK**, or **99** would give her three of a kind. Otto calls, "Time." This is a verbal declaration requesting a pause in the action.

Otto thinks it over. Perhaps Jacqueline is holding a combination that he can currently beat or tie (**AK**, **AQ**, etc). He decides to test her hand with a reraise. Otto puts another $8 out (matching Jacqueline's raise and adding an extra $4).

Jacqueline raises again. Yikes! Otto decides she has a **set** (trips made with a pocket pair), or she has nerves of steel. He wants to find out which it is, so he calls. The total in the pot is now $86.

THE FACT IS...

The Turn and the River

The dealer burns another card and a fourth card is revealed. This round is known as the **turn**. Betting levels are double the previous rounds.

The turn card is **8♣**. Otto still has two pairs, but now he has four cards to a club flush. Jacqueline bets $8. Otto calls. The pot swells to $102.

Another burned card, and the last card is revealed. It's **2♣**. This round is called the **river**. The board shows:

Remember that Otto is holding **A♣ K♣**, so his hand has improved to an ace-high club flush. There is no pair on the board, and that means a full house is not possible. Similarly, the cards on the board cannot make a quad, straight flush or royal flush. Otto has the nuts. Jacqueline checks. Otto bets $8. Jacqueline calls. The betting is concluded. The dealer asks both players to reveal their hands for the showdown. Otto flips up his **A♣ K♣**. Jacqueline turns over **A♥ A♦**.

She was winning with trips until the last card. The dealer pushes $118 in chips to Otto, moves the button clockwise to the next player, and the new hand begins.

"You're good, kid, but as long as I'm around you're second best. You might as well learn to live with it."

—Lancey Howard, as played by Edward G. Robinson in *The Cincinnati Kid* (1965)

Otto's profit is $70 ($118 less his contribution of $48). Jacqueline lost $48. Trycia lost $16. George lost $4. Tom lost $2. The other players folded before contributing anything to the pot.

Analysis of the Action

Even though Jacqueline lost, she played her hand well. Otto played well, too. Trycia and George maybe not so well. Here's why.

Keep in mind that you cannot control how the cards will come, so a big part of poker strategy involves hand selection (deciding when to play). We'll get into the intricacies of hand selection in the next chapter, but right now I'll tell you that A♣ K♣ and A♥ A♦ are premium hands. No hand will win every time, but premium hands always earn more than they lose over time.

Another thing to remember is that the pot was built with money from other players besides Otto and Jacqueline. Let's say Otto and Jacqueline get involved in a nearly identical hand on the very next round (**AA** vs. **AK** with a similar board), but this time Jacqueline wins. Both players will still be net winners.

How is this possible?

They are extracting money from the rest of the table. Their long-term profit mostly comes *not from each other*, but from the blinds and from contributions of opponents who call with inferior hands.

If you were to watch Otto and Jacqueline play for a few hours, you'd see that they don't compete in a lot of pots, and they don't win a lot of pots. But they win a lot of money.

The Object of the Game

It is a curious fact that players who win the most pots usually lose the most money.

I'll explain why as we go along, but right now just keep this in mind: The ultimate goal in poker is *not* to win a lot of pots. Rather…

The goal in poker is to win the most money.

A comprehensive strategy to reach this goal will sometimes lead you to actions that seem counter-intuitive, such as folding frequently, raising with weak hands, or just calling (rather than raising) with strong ones.

THE FACT IS…

Poker terms: A player is **loose** when he tends to call or raise a lot. He is **passive** when he calls more than he raises. He is **aggressive** when he raises more than he calls. A player is **tight** when he tends to fold a lot. The most profitable players tend to be aggressive and tight. Players who are loose and passive tend to lose a lot.

Generally, a profitable poker player will win fewer pots than the table average, but those pots will be bigger than the table average.

In the next chapter we'll cover strategies for betting, raising, and folding (to help you avoid hands that are likely to lose and to help you build big pots). But first, let's discuss poker etiquette.

Tip

It's perfectly okay to look at your cards more than once, but handling them too much has some drawbacks. You may inadvertently foul your hand, and frequent glances can sometimes help your opponents guess what you're holding.

How to Handle Cards

It is bad form to lift cards completely off the table, and it's entirely against the rules to remove them from the table or conceal them in any way.

Here's a good way to look at your cards: Square them. Hold your hands over one end of the stack and use one thumb to gently squeeze up the corners showing the indices.

Put a short stack of chips on the cards when you're finished. This prevents a dealer from accidentally **mucking** your hand (retrieving the cards and tossing them into the discard pile). It happens more often than you might think. Unprotected cards are permanently dead when they hit the muck. Even if the dealer made a mistake, there is no way to resuscitate that hand. Remember, it's your responsibility to **protect your hand** and prevent it from being **fouled** (made invalid).

There are other ways that a hand can be fouled: when two hands touch or are otherwise intermingled, when cards fall off the table, and when a player accidentally mucks cards.

Let's say you're in a three-way showdown and an opponent announces that she has a straight. You muck a pair of kings. Another player turns over a pair of queens. The last player proudly turns up a worthless hand that at first glance looks like a straight. The dealer stares at the two hands for a long moment and then announces that the queens win. The owner of the busted straight is surprised, and then realizes that she misread her hand.

Yes, it was an honest mistake, but it's too late. You mucked the kings, and your hand is dead. The pot goes to the pair of queens.

The Cards Speak

The previous scenario is the perfect reason why it's a bad idea to muck a hand in a showdown unless you're absolutely sure it's a loser. If you have any possibility of winning, it's better to expose the cards and allow the dealer to determine the winner (with the table's supervision). The rule is that **the cards speak**. In other words, verbal announcements are invalid and unnecessary; the only thing that matters is what can be seen on the cards.

Some people don't like to reveal losing hands in a showdown. They're embarrassed or they don't want to give away information about the hand they played, so they just muck. That's acceptable if a hand is clearly busted, but I've seen many hands where the supposed winner wasn't. Here's a typical example in hold 'em:

You hold:

Your opponent has:

And the board shows:

At the showdown your opponent triumphantly flips over his hand and exclaims, "I've got the high two pair."

Does that beat a pair of jacks? Yes, it does. Should you muck? No, because your hand isn't a pair. It's two pairs: jacks and fours. You're the winner.

So when the showdown comes, don't be coy, and don't hesitate. Just reveal your cards. Announce the hand if it pleases you, but the cards speak.

THE FACT IS...

Players are not required to reveal their hands if everyone folds to one player before a showdown. But if anyone mucks at a showdown, any player at the table can request to see the mucked hand. The purpose of this rule is to prevent collusion, but it should be invoked sparingly because it may offend some opponents.

Thou Shalt Not

It's somewhat ironic that nearly every dramatic betting maneuver you've seen in the movies is forbidden in real poker.

Throwing Chips into the Pot

Throwing chips into the pot is called **splashing the pot**. This is forbidden because the dealer and other players must be able to verify that a bettor has contributed the correct amount. The dealer must **count down** the chips in the pot if it has been splashed. This is time-consuming and a real drag. The correct way to bet is to place chips in front of your position. The dealer will collect the chips at the end of the betting round and put them in the pot.

String Bets

You probably have seen this on a television drama or in a movie. The hero is playing poker with a bunch of bad hombres. The year is 1880 or maybe 1920. Our hero has an awesome hand, but he's short of money. Nevertheless, he makes a big bet, almost half of his stake. One of the bad guys throws some cash into the pot and says, "I'll see your $1,000 (dramatic pause) and raise you $3,000." Then he tosses another stack of bills onto the pile. The hero must fold or bet his horse.

The bad guy's two-part wager is called a **string bet** or **string raise**, and it's forbidden in real life. When a player says "call," then that's it. No raise is allowed. This rule prevents a bettor from using a call as a psychological ploy to read an opponent's reaction, then morphing the call into a raise when weakness is perceived.

Another form of string bet is to say nothing, put enough chips out for a call, and then return to the stack to raise. Once again, this is forbidden. Some people do it innocently because they're just counting chips, but it's still against the rules. If an opponent objects, the wager will be restricted to a call.

The best way to avoid any confusion is to simply say, "Raise." That's binding, then you can take as much time as is required to get the chips off your stack.

Acting Out of Turn

Consider the hand I described on page 196 when Otto took the pot. Imagine if Jacqueline had announced out of turn, "I love my hand. I'm raising this one, and I'm reraising if anyone raises ahead of me." What effect would that have had on the rest of the players? It is probable that George would have folded rather than called, and maybe Trycia would have folded, too. The betting might not have been capped in the first round. At the very least it would have cost Otto $4, possibly more.

Acting out of turn is unfair, and it disrupts the game. Players should always wait until the action reaches them before tossing cards, checking, raising, or calling.

Sharing Hands and Revealing Cards

This is a taboo related to the previous one. It's against the rules for someone with a live hand to reveal those cards to another active player (unless everyone else has folded). Anyone who does this is cheating.

Some players bend this rule by showing cards to people behind them or to others who have folded at the table. Revealing cards in this manner is borderline bad form, but it's acceptable as long as the other person doesn't comment or offer advice. To do so violates the principle of **one player to a hand**. If the cards are revealed to anyone who has folded, then you have the right to see those cards when the hand is over. That rule is called **show one, show all** and it ensures that everyone has equal access to the same game information.

In some sloppy games (often at lower limits), you'll hear players loudly speculating on other people's hands: "Uh oh! A pair is on the board. Roger has a full house." This is against the rules, and you have the right to stop such comments by appealing to the dealer or a supervisor. Ditto for people who talk about hands that they've folded.

Of course, you may profit more in some situations by saying nothing and allowing minor infractions to pass. It's a judgment call with many variables. Forcing the situation with a strict interpretation of the rules may put an opponent on guard and make him play better. You don't want that.

Tapping the Table While Thinking

There are two ways to check: a player can say "Check," or he can tap the table. A person who unconsciously taps the table while thinking may be restricted to a check if other players subsequently take action. At the very least, idle tapping often causes unpleasant confusion. Other players bet or check, the thinker usually doesn't notice at first, and then he finally complains when it's too late. The whole thing can quickly become a comedy of errors. So be aware that tapping means a check.

THE FACT IS...

Casinos in North America generally require people to speak only English at a poker table. This prevents players from selectively sharing information.

Pulling the Pot

You've seen it in the movies. The winner reaches out and rakes in the dough (sometimes throwing it into his hat just as the cops arrive). In real life you must wait for the dealer to push you the chips. This gives players time to reveal their hands, and it gives the dealer an opportunity to resolve disputes. Once she pushes the pot, the hand is over.

Tip

If you don't have the proper denomination chip for a particular bet or raise, just state your intention and put out a larger chip (or chips). The dealer will make the appropriate change. If you don't make a verbal declaration, a larger chip will be considered a call unless it's exactly the denomination of a raise.

Table Stakes

When I was a youngster I would watch poker movies and think about strategy. Back then it seemed pretty straightforward; the person with the most money simply would bet more than opponents could afford to call. Competitors would be forced to fold their hands while moaning piteously, "Ah cain't call that bet without sellin' the homestead."

I promised myself to always sit down at a poker table with $1 million, and that would ensure my income forever. I never did figure out why anyone other than a millionaire would sit in a game like that, and it never occurred to me that someone with $10 million might wipe me out.

In the real world of poker one cannot be forced out of the pot by running out of money. The game uses a system called **table stakes** to prevent that from happening. The chips sitting in front of a player at the beginning of a hand are the only ones that can be used in the hand. If a player runs out of chips, this is called being **all in**. A **side pot** is created from subsequent bets and raises. The player who is all in can win the main pot, and someone else can win the side pot. Or another player can win both pots. But the all-in player can't win any of the later bets.

That's the negative side of table stakes. You can't buy more chips and raise if you smack a monster hand. So it's always a good idea to have an ample supply of chips sitting in front of you. And that's why I recommend buying in for more than the minimum in a fixed-limit game.

The Casino's Cut

The casino isn't anyone's adversary in poker, so it doesn't earn money when a player loses as it does in most casino games. Instead, the casino charges a fee for providing the venue and the dealer. It collects this fee in one of three ways.

Rake: A portion of the pot is set aside by the dealer before the chips are passed to the winner. It's usually a fixed amount. Three or four dollars is common, so a $50 pot might have the same rake as a pot twice that size. It depends on the game.

Time Charge: The dealer collects a fee from every player on the half hour.

Button Charge: The dealer collects a fee from every player on the button.

One system isn't necessarily "better" but you'll notice that a rake

THE FACT IS...

In frontier days, players often used a buckhorn knife to designate the rotating dealer position in a poker game. The knife was replaced by a silver dollar as the frontier gave way to towns, and so dollars came to be called "bucks." When players passed the responsibility of dealing to someone else they were "passing the buck." President Harry Truman was an avid poker player, so when he said, "The buck stops here," he was using a poker metaphor to indicate that his responsibilities and privileges would not be shifted elsewhere.

favors **tight** (conservative) players who maximize profit on fewer hands. In contrast, a time charge or button charge tends to penalize patience in the short run, and it encourages **loose** players who are willing to gamble on speculative hands.

Then again, loose players are exactly the kind of opponents you want to encourage.

Whatever method the casino uses, it adds up. A typical hour of poker will cost a player $10 to $20 depending on the game. An afternoon or evening of poker can easily put $50 to $100 into the casino's coffers. So you might finish a session ahead by $200 when you actually won $300.

Or you might go home poorer by $75 when you actually won $25.

In other words, being an average player will cost you money. The only way to consistently win at poker and beat the rake/collection is by being much better than average.

THE FACT IS...

Casinos will typically give you up to thirty minutes away from the table for bathroom breaks or meals. Count your chips and leave them, then tell the dealer you're stepping away. It's the dealer's job to hold your seat and protect the chips until you return.

Toking the Dealer

Most people toke (tip) $1 when they win a pot larger than $20, sometimes more for pots over $100. Some people toke when the dealer gives them change. It doesn't require an elaborate ritual; just toss the dealer a chip and say, "This is for you."

Essentially

- Poker is different from most gambling games because the opponent in poker is not a casino; the opponents are other players who have various skill levels.

- Poker hand rankings reflect the probability that a particular hand will appear in a randomly dealt five-card combination. Higher hands occur less frequently.

- The object in poker is to win the most money. Winning the most pots is not necessarily the best way to win the most money.

- Hold 'em players use two personal cards and five shared community cards to build a five-card poker hand. Hold 'em has four rounds, pre-flop, flop, turn, and river.

- If a bet has not yet been made, players have two options when action reaches them: they can check or bet. If a bet has been made, then a player can fold, call, or raise.

- A player who holds an unbeatable hand is said to be holding "the nuts." Recognizing when you have the nuts (or when you don't) is an important part of profitable poker.

- It is your responsibility to protect your hand and prevent it from being fouled. One way to do this is to put a short stack of chips on your cards to prevent them from being accidentally mucked by the dealer.

- Don't muck your hand in a showdown unless you're absolutely certain that it's a loser. The rule is that the cards speak; don't rely on verbal declarations.

- Poker rules prohibit splashing the pot, string bets, and acting out of turn.

- Buying chips during a hand is not allowed. You can only play with table stakes, the chips you have available.

- It is customary to tip $1 when you win a pot, unless the pot is extremely small (less than $20).

Poker: Advanced Hold 'Em Strategies

Welcome to Chapter 13. Anyone who is superstitious, such as someone who believes in the unluckiness of 13, should skip this chapter. In the next few pages we're going to review practical poker tactics that rely entirely on math and psychology rather than superstition. In fact, advantage players (that includes me and hopefully you) respectfully ask superstitious players to ignore the following material. We'd like to keep our edge. Thank you.

Okay... Is it just us advantage players who are left? Great. Let's get on with the strategies.

Dancing With Them That Brung Ya

The title of this section comes from an old Texas saying that is frequently used these days in the world of politics. "Dancing with them that brung ya" means that you're entirely dependent upon whomever or whatever brought you to "the party." You cannot dance with others because your fortune is tied to the fate of your partners or benefactors.

Starting cards are your dance partners in the world of poker.

Low-quality starting cards are bad dancers that will often embarrass you at the shindig. They're unreliable and they frequently fail at the most critical moment.

In contrast, high-quality starting cards generally perform well, and they consistently earn more than they cost.

Choosing good starting hands is the first step to long-term poker success.

THE FACT IS...

Most of the profit in poker does not come from bluffing or other trickery. Profit mainly comes from people who make strategic mistakes. Your goal is to make zero mistakes and to seek out opponents who are unskilled and/or likely to deviate from optimal strategy.

A Good Starting Hand Has...

Starting hands are like everything else in poker, very situational. Your position in relation to the button, the number of active players, the number of bets or raises ahead of you, and the possibility of bets or raises behind you all have an enormous impact on the viability of any particular combination of cards.

So the "good" attributes listed on the next few pages are only the first standards for judging a hand. In other words, a hand with some good qualities is not necessarily always playable. More importantly, any hand that doesn't meet these basic standards can be immediately folded.

A note about notation:

Lowercase "**s**" after a card combination (**AKs**, **T9s**, etc.) indicates the cards are of the same suit.

Lowercase "**n**" after a card combination (**QJn**, **98n**, etc.) indicates the cards are not of the same suit.

Card combinations without "**s**" or "**n**" can be either suited or not suited.

"**T**" stands for 10, and a lowercase "**x**" stands for any card.

First we'll cover desirable hand attributes, and then we'll group the hands into ranks of relative value.

Big Cards

Let's say you hold **AK** and your opponent holds **87** before the flop. It's a curious truth that you both have an exactly equal chance of finishing the hand with a pair, two pairs, trips, a full house, or **quads** (four of a kind). But in a **heads-up** situation (only these two hands in competition) **AK** has a tremendous advantage because it will win if **87** does not improve to at least a pair. And **AK** will win if both hands improve equally. Consider a board showing the following:

"I must complain, the cards are ill shuffled till I have a good hand."

—Jonathan Swift, author of *Gulliver's Travels*

AK was beating **87** before the flop, after the flop, and throughout the rest of the hand. Both players finished with a full house, but **AK** finished with jacks full of aces, while **87** dragged in with jacks full of eights.

So, **big cards** are good. Two cards that are jacks or higher always deserve a second look (though they're not necessarily always playable).

Suited Cards

Two cards of the same suit are more likely to make a flush than two cards of mixed suits. Suited cards flop a four-card flush about 11 percent of the time. When that happens, the

probability of finishing with a flush is better than one-in-three (2:1). **Suited cards** always deserve a second look, but only long enough to determine if they have additional good attributes. Suit alone is not enough to play a starting hand.

Connectors

Cards that are next to each other in rank have a higher probability of making a straight. This probability drops dramatically as the gap between the cards increases. **JT** can make a straight four ways (**AKQ**, **KQ9**, **Q98**, **987**) while **J7** can only make a straight with **T98**. As with suited cards, **connectors** by themselves are not good enough to play a starting hand, but it's an attribute you should consider.

Pairs

A **pocket pair** is generally a good thing. Of course **AA** is worth considerably more than **22**, but any pair should get a second look.

Pairs are typically divided into three groups that reflect their relative power and profitability. Big pairs are **AA** through **JJ**. Medium pairs are **TT** through **77**. Small pairs are **66** and below.

Ranking the Starting Hands

The following ranks are general, and there is a range of value within each rank. Keep in mind that a hand's value can change substantially on the flop. Nevertheless, a premium hand like **AA** will consistently earn more money than a bargain hand like **76s**. Also remember that the suited version of a hand is always *much* stronger than the mixed-suit version.

Hold 'Em Starting Hands

Premium hands	AA, KK, QQ, JJ, AK
Average hands	AQ, AJ, KQ, KJ, QJ, JT, AT, TT, 99, 88
Bargain hands	T9s and suited connectors down to 54s
	77 and pairs below
	Axs (suited hands containing an ace and any small card)
	KTs, QTs, J9s
Trash	Any hand that doesn't appear in the above three groups

Hands without "s" or "n" indicate both suited and non-suited.

Heads-Up Comparisons

Premium hands are the most reliable and profitable combinations. Big pairs frequently can pick up the pot without improvement, and a single ace or king on the board often will put **AK** over the top.

In contrast, average hands are generally less reliable and less profitable. They usually need improvement, and they're frequently beaten by premium hands.

Bargain hands continue the downward trend in quality. They almost always need improvement, and they sometimes lose even when the board gives them a boost. Nevertheless, they're still profitable when played carefully.

Trash hands fall right off the scale of profitability. They always cost money over the long-term regardless of how well they are played. One example would be **76n**. That combination would be buried against premium and average hands like **KK**, **AQ**, and **KJ** if the flop were unexceptional (**QT7** or **JT4**).

Note that some poker authors divide hold 'em starting hands into as many as eight categories plus trash. This is because there is a big difference between a nearly premium combination like **AQs** and something much closer to the bargain end like **ATn**. While this distinction is very important, I decided not to cross your eyes with a list that has more than half a dozen categories and six dozen entries. Clearly, **AJs** is superior to **JTn**, **KQs** is stronger than **QJn**, and **AA** has an advantage over **AKn**. The more you play hold 'em, the more you'll learn the subtle nuances of these combinations, and you'll see that every hand really deserves its own category.

A Warning about Big Pairs

Big pairs usually dominate the game, but they have a fatal weakness. They don't perform as well when there are many players in the pot. It's like a bunch of little guys ganging up on a bully. Each additional competitor increases the probability that someone will hit a long-shot hand and slam the big pair. In contrast, suited hands and connectors tend to play very well against multiple competitors. These hands win less frequently, but when they hit against a full table, it's often for a monster pot.

Tip

Some hands are "borderline trash" like **K9s, Q9s, J8s,** and **T9n.** It's not necessarily always incorrect to play them, and you'll sometimes see an expert throw in borderline hands to mix up opponents, but it's a judgment call. These hands are frequently more trouble than they're worth. Beginners should avoid them.

Tempting Trash

You'll frequently see people winning with **Kx, Qx, 92s, 65n,** and other garbage. If you play hold 'em for any length of time (especially at lower limits), you'll occasionally be beaten silly by these hands. Here's a typical scenario. You hold **A♠ K♠** and your opponent has **6♣ 5♥.** The board shows:

You flopped a four-flush and top pair. The turn improved you to two pairs, but your opponent played trash. She went for a **gutshot straight draw** (needed one specific rank), and she made it on the river. Ouch! It happens.

Losing a pile o' chips can seriously mess with your attitude and put you on tilt. You may be tempted to play loose and crazy like the person who beat you. Don't do it!

Remember, any two cards *can* win. But trash probably won't.

The Power of Position

Remember the example of acting out of turn that I mentioned in the last chapter? If Jacqueline had announced her intentions to raise,

George would have folded his hand and saved himself $4. Information has value.

A similar effect occurs when a player is close to the button. The later you act, the more information you have. Position is power. In fact, all hold 'em strategy varies in direct relation to a player's position.

Early position is generally defined as the first three seats to act. **Middle position** would be the next two (or three) seats, and **late position** would be the final three.

Premium hands can be played in any position, but they're particularly well suited for raising in early position.

Average hands also can be played in any position if the game conditions are right. That's a big "if" that we'll cover later, but average hands are generally best suited to middle position and late position in a pot that hasn't been too aggressively raised.

Bargain hands are best suited for late position in an unraised pot. This insures that a bargain hand will get enough action to be profitable if the flop is a good one.

The Power of Folding

Imagine if you sat in a 4-8 hold 'em game for four hours, and you did nothing but fold. Not counting your seat fees, you'd lose about $18 per hour in blind bets or $72 during the session.

That's roughly comparable to what Otto won on just one pot (in our Chapter 12 example).

Now imagine if you were to play like George and call every hand. That would cost about $120 per hour or $480 during a session, and that's just one call and no raises before the flop. The cost doubles with every raise and every round. George has to win a lot more chips to cover the price of not folding.

Muhammad Ali said, "Float like a butterfly, and sting like a bee."

The poker equivalent of this philosophy is **tight and aggressive**. Your opponents should be swinging at air most of the time. Remember, every player has an equal probability of being dealt the best hand. The only way for you to create an imbalance in your favor is to spend nothing or very little on losing hands, and cause your opponents to contribute a lot when your hand is a winner.

So folding has more power than most people realize. Let's say your opponent has the strongest possible hand, a royal flush. What happens when you fold? Your opponent's royal flush loses some of its worth. If everyone folds, then a royal flush is essentially worthless (winning only the blinds).

Fortunately for us, most players don't fold or they fold later than they should, and thus it is the weaker hands that give the stronger ones value.

Only about 20 percent of hold 'em starting hands are playable, and a win rate of 30 percent to 60 percent is common with even the strongest starters (depending on the game). That means you should be folding about 80 percent of your hands before the flop, and about half of the rest should be folded after the flop or on the turn. Only about 10 percent of your starting hands will generate 100 percent of your winnings in a typical game. Of course, some nights will be better than others, and good hands sometimes come in streaks, but profitable poker involves a lot of waiting and constant trash removal.

You'll find that this approach differs greatly from the way most people play, especially at the lower limits. For many players, calling a blind bet is almost as automatic as an ante. This is good news for you because it puts more money in the pot, and it means your starting hands usually will be the strongest at the table.

Pot Odds and Betting Decisions

Here's a quick quiz. You hold **QJ** in late position and the flop comes **984 rainbow** (mixed suits). That gives you a gutshot draw to the high straight. Should you call a bet on the flop or fold?

The answer is that you don't have enough information to make that decision. I haven't told you how much money is in the pot or the size of the bet. The two figures are used to calculate **pot odds**, a system that helps you decide if a hand is worth pursuing.

The calculation is simple. A player compares the money in the pot to the proposed bet. Say, for example, there is $100 in the pot, and the cost to call is $10.

Sounds great, but what is the chance of actually winning that money? If the odds *against* the hand (essentially the probability of losing) are worse than 100:10 (10:1), the hand should be folded. Why? Because in the long run the hand will not earn enough to justify the cost of the competition.

Let's say the pot odds are 10:1 and the odds against the hand are 22:1. The player will win $100 once and lose $10 twenty-two times (assuming he plays the same hand multiple times). The deficit is $120. Not good.

But if the odds of winning the hand are better, let's say only 5:1 against, the player will win $100 once and lose $10 five times. That's a positive gain of $50. The hand should be played.

Of course, there's no way to predict exactly when that one win will occur, but it doesn't matter. It's a like owning a slot machine. The individual spins aren't as important as the long-term favorable odds.

THE FACT IS...

Poker strategy is much more complicated and situational than strategies for other casino games. For more information about poker strategies, check out *The Smarter Bet Guide to Poker*. And if you want to play poker in a non-casino setting, try *Playboy Guide to Playing Poker at Home*. Both books expand on the basic concepts introduced here.

Pot Odds Made Easy

But how can you know the exact odds against a hand? In most cases you can't know exactly, but you can estimate very easily. Here's a classic example. You hold:

And the board shows:

This is a no-brainer. You have fifteen **outs** (cards in the deck that will complete the hand). Eight cards in the deck will give you a straight, and nine cards will give you a flush. Two of those cards are the same (giving you a straight flush), so the total is fifteen rather than seventeen.

A four-card flush always has nine outs. An open-ended four-card straight (four adjacent ranks) has eight outs. Gutshot straights have four outs. Two pairs to a full house is four outs. Pairs to trips is two outs.

The next two tables give you the probability and odds against improving on the flop and after the flop.

Probability of Improving on the Flop

Hand	Improvement	Probability	Odds Against
Any two cards	Making a pair	32.4%	2:1
Suited	Four-flush	10.9%	8:1
Pocket pair	Trips	11.8%	7.5:1

Probability of Improving After the Flop

Outs	Probability	Odds Against	Outs	Probability	Odds Against
1	4.3%	22.5:1	9	35%	2:1
2	8.4%	11:1	10	38.4%	1.5:1
3	12.5%	7:1	11	41.7%	1.5:1
4	16.5%	5:1	12	45%	1.25:1
5	20.4%	4:1	13	48.1%	1:1
6	24.1%	3:1	14	51.2%	1:1
7	27.8%	2.5:1	15	54.1%	1:1
8	31.5%	2:1	16	57.0%	0.75:1

Odds against are rounded. Probability of improving after the flop is with two cards to come (turn and river).

Okay, let's consider the hand in the most recent example, **Q♦ J♦** with a board of **A♠ T♦ 9♦**. The pot holds $56 and the price of a call is $4. Is this a good bet?

Yes, it is. The pot is offering a hefty 14:1, and odds of making a straight or flush are about 1:1. You have a tremendous edge. This hand is worth a raise.

As a general rule, big pots make it easy for **drawing hands** (hands that

Tip

One easy way to calculate the probability of improving without memorizing the table is to simply multiply the outs by four, and then put a percent sign after it. That will get you close to the correct number.

need improvement) to justify sticking around. Smaller pots aren't worth the risk. Think about how that affects the big pairs vs. bargain hand effect that I previously described. An enormous pot with a cheap price for entry is not what a big pair wants to see.

In fact, some very unlikely hands can become playable if the pot odds are large enough.

Tip

It is tempting to call with a hand that has turned into a probable loser after you have invested a lot of money in the pot. This is a mistake. The only calculation that matters is the total value of the pot compared to the chance of hitting the hand. A bad hand will not be "healed" by remaining "faithful" to lost bets. If pot odds tell you to fold, then fold.

Implied Pot Odds

Let's say you're on the button with **77**. Four players call ahead of you. The pot is offering 5.5:1 (including the blinds). The chance of flopping trips is 7.5:1. This would seem to indicate a fold, but remember that you'll likely win bets in later rounds if you flop a **7**. The value of those extra expected bets should be included when you decide to call or fold before the flop.

In other words, the value of the pot at any given moment should be only part of the calculation. You should also reasonably estimate the value of the bets that will come when you hit a hand. Conversely, if hitting a hand will still leave you vulnerable, or your opponents will fold because the board will be exceptionally scary, then the **implied odds** are considerably less or perhaps even reversed.

Hold 'Em Optimal Strategy

Okay, here is where we put it all together. First a few reminders:

- Premium hands want few opponents, a large pot, and a high price for entry (thus discouraging bargain hands). Premium hands create this condition by raising and limiting the field.

- Bargain hands want to cheaply see the flop, so they limp in without a raise when possible. Conversely, if a bargain hand is in late position with a lot of callers, then it sometimes raises for value (doubles the size of the pot while getting excellent pot odds).

- Average hands sometimes want few opponents and sometimes they want many opponents. It depends on the flop. That's why average hands (particularly the higher suited connectors) tend to play like premium hands in early position, and more like bargain hands in later position.

- Poker strategy is very situational. A raise from a tight and aggressive opponent is different than a raise from a loose and passive player. Your decisions should reflect the actions taken by particular opponents.

- The following strategy is best suited for a fixed-limit table with six or more players (see the sidebar below).

Early Position

Note that the term "raised pot" refers to action from a seat on your right.

EP Premium hands and an unraised pot: Raise with all premium hands in early position.

EP Premium hands and a raised pot: Reraise **AA**, **KK**, and **QQ**. Just call with **AK** and **JJ**. Cap the pot with **AA**, **KK**, or **QQ** if someone raises behind you. Reraise with **AKs** if a raise comes from behind and four or more players are in the hand, but with three or less just call any raise.

Keep in mind that **AKs** is a drawing hand; much of its value comes from the contributions of multiple opponents.

Tip

More hands become playable when a game is shorthanded (five players or less). This is true in all versions of poker. For example, a hand such as **A9** in hold 'em is relatively weak at a full table, but it is generally stronger in a heads-up situation. Thus you should loosen up considerably when a table gets shorthanded. But watch out; your opponents will play looser, too. If you're not willing to mix it up, don't play shorthanded.

EP Average hands and an unraised pot: Raise with **AQ**, **AJ**, **KQs**, and **TT**. Call with the rest of the *suited* average hands, **KQn**, **99**, and **88**. Throw away everything else.

EP Average hands and a raised pot: Call **AQs**, **AJs**, **KQs** and **TT**. Fold everything else *unless* the raiser is loose and tends to raise with substandard hands. If he is, and if you reasonably expect many callers (four or more), then call with all the *suited* average hands, **AQn**, **99**, and **88**. Toss the rest of the unsuited hands.

EP Bargain hands and an unraised pot: Throw them all away unless the game is *extremely* and consistently loose/passive and you are certain to get many callers and no raises. If these perfect conditions exist, you can sometimes limp in. Remember, George was in early position when he tried to limp in, and he was buried by three raisers. So don't say I didn't warn you.

If the game is tight, and your opponents are experienced, you should occasionally raise with a bargain hand in early position just to throw the watchers off. But most of your opponents in low-limit games won't be experienced. They'll be clueless and entirely unresponsive to nuance plays. Don't waste your time or your chips.

EP Bargain hands and a raised pot: Throw them all away.

EP Two raises: If you're in the third seat and facing two raises, fold everything except premium hands. Follow the strategy for premium hands and a raised pot.

Middle Position

MP Premium hands: Same strategy as in early position.

MP Average hands and an unraised pot: Raise everything except **QJ** and **JT**; call with those.

MP Average hands and a raised pot: Call with the suited hands and pairs. If the raiser is loose and tends to overvalue his starting hands, also call with **AQn**, **AJn**, and **KQn**. Throw away the rest of the unsuited combinations.

MP Bargain hands: Same strategy as in early position.

MP Two raises or a capped pot: Play only premium hands and sometimes **TT** if both raisers are loose and reckless. Follow premium strategy with one exception. If it's three bets to you, don't cap the pot every time. Instead, just call about half the time and give the original raiser a chance to cap the pot. This will disguise your hand and give you information about the raiser. If she caps, then she probably has a premium hand. If she only calls, then she's probably holding a higher-quality average hand.

Late Position

LP Premium hands: Same strategy as in early and middle position.

LP Average hands and an unraised pot: Same strategy as in middle position except also raise **QJs** and **JTs** if there are four or more callers ahead of you.

LP Average hands and a raised pot: Same strategy as in middle position.

LP Bargain hands and an unraised pot: Fold all the bargain hands *except* pairs if there are three or fewer callers. Stay in if there are four or more callers. If the game is tight and you're in late position with no callers, raise with a bargain hand in an attempt to **steal the blinds** (see page 232).

LP Bargain hands and a raised pot: Fold everything unless nearly everyone is in the pot, the game is extremely loose, your opponents are weak, and you're on the button. Then call *carefully* with the bargain hands (see the tip on page 220).

LP Two raises or a capped pot: Same strategy as in middle position except if there are many callers (nearly the whole table). Then you can also play **AQs**, **AJs**, and **KQs**.

The Blinds

Remember that the blinds are last to act before the flop and first to act in all the later rounds. Also keep in mind that the big blind has already bet, so the only decision here is to raise or call a raise.

Generally you should play the blinds with a late-position strategy, but occasionally you can play a bit looser if there was an early raiser

and a lot of callers because you might be looking at a huge pile o' chips and a single extra bet as the price for entry. Pot odds might be 10:1 or better.

If that's the case, go ahead and call a raise in the big blind with all the average hands, bargain hands, and even some marginal trash like **Kxs** and **T8s**.

If you have a bargain hand or marginal trash (**Qxs**, **Txs**, **89n**, **Axn**, and similar combinations) in the little blind with a lot of callers and no raises, call for one-half bet or less.

Tip

Calling a raise is safer when your action will end the round. That's not necessarily the same as being on the button. A late raiser to your right and active players to your left expose you to a possible raising war.

If there has been a raise, carefully consider your pot odds before contributing any chips.

The issue of defending the blind against a possible steal is a complex subset of poker strategy. You won't have to face this much in loose games because opportunities to steal are rare. If there are other callers, simply fold when your hand doesn't warrant a call. If you're heads up against a late raiser, fold the first time it happens and reraise the second time with a bargain hand or better.

Exceptions, Exceptions

The more you learn about hold 'em, the more you'll find exceptions to the pre-flop strategy I have outlined. There are situations when it is correct to raise with trash, and there are times when a premium hand clearly does not merit a raise.

There are plenty of experts who would *not* raise **TT** in early position, and some who *would* raise **99**. Other disputed hands include **AT**, **A9**, **JT**, and **88**. In fact, every hand has its exceptions.

The point here is that you shouldn't play like an automaton. Instead, you should consider position, the pot, and your opponents, then choose the best strategy for that particular situation. In most cases you'll find the best strategy is the one outlined on the previous pages.

If you come across a situation that has you completely stumped, follow this advice: When in doubt, throw it out.

The Flop and Beyond

The flop is the pivotal moment in hold 'em. Five of the seven cards (71 percent) have been revealed. The character of the hand is generally set, and three rounds of betting are ahead. The flop is the best time to drop an obvious loser or begin the process of pumping a hopeful winner.

Poker hands generally fall into one of the following categories during the last three rounds of hold 'em.

Strong hand: A combination that is the nuts or unlikely to be beaten.

Vulnerable leading hand: A hand

that is definitely leading, but could easily become a second-best hand in a later round. Trips is a typical example of a vulnerable leading hand.

Weak leading hand: This hand is probably leading but extremely vulnerable. There are a lot of ways it could lose. One example would be **AQ** with a flop of **QJ8**. If **AQ** was the only pre-flop raiser, then it's probably top pair (though it's entirely possible someone else is holding **QJ** for two pairs, or **T9** for a straight). Either way, the hand is vulnerable to anyone holding a nine or ten, especially **JT**, **AT**, **J9**, **QT**, and **Q9**. There might even be an **88** lurking out there.

Second-best hand: Using the previous example, someone holding **AJ** would be second best to **AQ**. **AQ** would be second best to **QJ**. Players who are second best and don't realize it are the primary source of profit in poker.

Drawing hand: This is typically a four-card flush or four-card straight looking for a fifth card, but it also includes any hand that is clearly an underdog and hoping to improve. One example would be two pairs drawing to a full house when the board and pattern of betting indicate that someone has a flush.

Obvious loser: A hand like **T♦ 9♦** against a board like **K♣ K♥ 8♥** with a raise and reraise ahead is an obvious loser. Hands competing with the nuts or in other unwinnable situations are said to be **drawing dead**.

General Goals on the Flop and Afterwards

Strong hands want to extract the maximum amount of money from the table. It's a pleasant job, but not as easy as you might imagine because experienced opponents can often tell when someone is holding a better combination, and they drop.

Drawing hands generally want to continue as cheaply as possible, though they sometimes want to build the pot if the pot odds will exceed the probability of hitting their hand.

Vulnerable and weak leading hands want to make each round as *expensive* as possible so that drawing hands won't stick around and improve.

Obvious losers want to quickly identify their unhappy condition and stop putting money in the pot.

Second-best hands are somewhere between obvious losers and drawing hands. They can improve and win, but they often don't, so they want to see the turn and river very cheaply or for free, otherwise they're looking to fold.

Reading the Flop

Position plays an important role on the flop (as it does in every round of hold 'em). A bet, raise, and reraise tells you a lot, as does a bet and long line of callers. It also helps to remember how an opponent played pre-flop. Here are a few examples:

This is a flop that looks good to **AA**, **KK**, and **QQ** (assuming they're not all simultaneously competing). Of course, this is a strong flop for **JJ**, and it also looks inviting to **AJ**, **KJ**, **QJ**, and **JT**. See how the latter hands can be crushed by the former? How can you tell who has what? Let's say that you're holding **AJ** and you were the only raiser before the flop. It's likely that your pair of jacks with an ace kicker is the best hand. But if you called a pre-flop raise, **AJ** is possibly second best (behind a higher pocket pair). This is nearly certain if the same player raises again.

This is the kind of flop that usually gets a lot of action and breaks a lot of bankrolls. **KK** is probably the best hand here if there was a lot of pre-flop raising. If there wasn't, then someone may have limped in with **AT** or **T9**. Any of these three hands will hurt **AA**, **QQ**, **JJ**, **AK**, **AQ**, **AJ**, **KQ**, **QJ**, or **KJ** unless a ten falls and makes a straight for anyone holding an ace. Another heart may finish a flush. If the board pairs then the straight or flush may be beaten by a full house. One way or another it's going to be a monster pot with a wild finish.

This flop turns **AKn** into semi-trash. It's also bad news for **AJn** and **KJn**, and it could be trouble for **JJ** and **TT**. Anyone holding a queen is in good shape unless another diamond falls to make a flush, or another low card appears to fill in a straight.

Flops like this usually produce small pots because hands without an ace are unlikely to stick around if anyone bets. **AK** is a strong favorite over other hands that have an ace and a lower kicker. **A5** has a full house but may still be beaten by a higher full house if the wrong card comes on the turn or the river. Sometimes it happens. You can be sure that **AK** and **AQ** will call (and sometimes raise) all the way to the end hoping to snap **A5** or **55**.

This is a scary flop for **A♦ A♥**. There are a lot of ways to lose, including to a straight, a flush on the turn or river, or two pairs. Note that high cards next to each other in rank or one-gapped often give opponents two pairs.

This is the kind of flop you'll love when holding **88**, **99**, or **TT** (as well as higher pairs). It's death to big unpaired cards.

There are countless more examples, but these few flops give you a taste of the thought process and the dynamics of hold 'em at this stage. The best way to handle these situations is largely determined by your position and the actions of your opponents.

Bet or Check, Raise or Fold

Strategy on the flop and afterwards is much more complex and situational than pre-flop strategy. That's because there are only 1,326 possible two-card starting hands but over 2.5 million five-card combinations. Nevertheless, hands of a certain type generally can be played similarly.

Two Overcards

If you've got no pair but two strong **overcards** with a non-threatening board (example: **AK** with a flop of **T62** rainbow), it's usually a good idea to come out betting if nobody has yet entered the pot. Everyone may fold to you. If not, then you'll at least thin the field. A raise from behind will alert you to the fact that somebody has a pair or better. Go ahead and call one raise if the pot is large enough. Don't call any reraises. If someone bets ahead of you, evaluate the flop and then fold if the pot is not large enough. Beware of suited cards, straight cards, high connectors, or high pairs on the board. Yes, it's tough to part with **AK** and other big connectors, but calling with no draw and an ace-high is often a waste of money.

Top Pair, Two Pairs, and Trips

If you've got top pair with a strong kicker, two pairs, or trips, then come out betting on the flop. Raise if someone bets ahead of you. Opponents calling behind you rather than raising would generally indicate that you're probably the best hand (unless you're up against a monster combination that is waiting for the next round).

But what if someone raises you?

Let's say you're holding **KJs**. You called a raise before the flop. Now you're looking at a flop of **J72** rainbow. You dutifully bet or raise on the flop (as I recommend) and someone raises behind you. Guess what. You have some valuable information that may save you money on the turn. You're probably up against **AA**, **KK**, **QQ**, or maybe trips or **J7**. A call here would be correct. The turn will either improve your hand and give you a reason to bet or raise, or a blank will give you a reason to fold if someone bets into you. Just drop the hand.

Note that an experienced opponent with a superior hand may not raise you on the flop. If he has a big pocket pair or trips, he simply may call your bets all the way to the river, or he may raise on the turn. This strategy hides the strength of his hand and encourages you to bleed off chips.

Straight or Better

Flopping a nut-straight, nut-flush, or better isn't too common. Hands like this should be **slow-played** on the flop. Checking and calling will lure people into hanging around for the turn and double bets. That's when you should become aggressive. On the other hand, don't slow-play without the nuts. Be especially careful with low cards (example: **87** with **JT9**).

Drawing Hands

Are you drawing to a strong hand? If yes, then check if you're in early position, and call or raise in any position if the pot odds justify it (they usually do in loose games). If you're drawing to a strong hand *and* you've got top pair, just play it aggressively.

Obvious Losers

Check and fold if the flop misses you completely and you don't have two overcards. Fold if you've got middle or bottom pair with a weak kicker (example: **98** and **AQ9**). Fold if you have top pair with a weak kicker, and you're facing a raise (example: **A5** and **AQJ**). Fold when you're clearly second best unless you have a draw to the best hand and favorable pot odds. Generally, if a hand is not worth a bet or raise, then it's not worth a call (except when drawing to the nuts or near-nuts).

Tip

Sometimes you can read the table perfectly and win with middle or bottom pair. Sometimes you can miss the flop completely and finish with trips on the river. Sometimes it is correct to **chase** with a second-best hand. Poker has millions of "sometimes" situations. You should not play like an automaton, but the strategies here are optimal in the majority of circumstances.

The Turn and the River

The noose tightens on the turn. Bets double, and the probability of improving drops dramatically. By this point you should be leading, or bluffing well, or you should have a clear idea of how you will win if someone calls you on the end. If you don't have a plan, then check or get out of the hand. Remember that bankrolls are mostly consumed by too much calling on the flop and turn, not by bad beats on the river.

Raising to Get a Free Card

A **free card** is a powerful multi-layer and multi-round strategy that is generally unknown among casual poker players. Here's an example of how it works.

You're in late position. Four people call ahead of you before the flop and you raise with **A♣ T♣**. All four players and the big blind call your raise. The flop produces:

Four players check and the fifth bets. What should you do?

You should raise. You may have the best hand right now, but even if you don't, a raise will make you look as if you do. You have a 1 in 3 chance of making the nut flush, and your opponents will remember that you also raised before the flop. Why is this memory important?

If the turn fails to help anyone, your opponents may check to you because they'll want to avoid another reraise. They'll expect you to bet, but you won't bet. You'll check and end the round. They'll be relieved, but it's you who has reason to celebrate. You've just given yourself a **free card**. It's an extra opportunity to improve your hand without investing anything in the process.

Conversely, you don't want to give away free cards. There's not much you can do when an expert **semi-bluffs** like this. But most opponents aren't experts. Generally, you should bet the flop *and* the turn when your hand is leading. Make opponents pay to see the cards.

Now let's extend this strategy to a deeper level.

If you take a free card on the turn, an expert player may correctly read your tactic and (if you fail to improve) he may try to bluff you on the end with a bet.

A not-so-expert player may try to bluff you on the end even if you do improve. And when he bets, you'll be able to hit him with a raise.

Betting or Calling on the End

Folding on the end is rarely correct unless you're absolutely certain that a hand is a loser. Pot odds are usually so enormous by this point that any reasonable chance for a win deserves a call. That's why Jacqueline called on the end in the Chapter 12 example. Of course, if a hand is clearly busted, then you should save yourself the bet.

Conversely, it's rarely correct to bet on the end unless the bet is a pure bluff, or your hand is exceptionally strong. That's because (as I explained in the previous paragraph) good players will call you only if they might win. That's not a problem when you're holding the nuts or something close, but it's a big problem when the lead is not so well defined. You might be holding a big pair of aces and find yourself beaten by two pairs. Checking in this situation would save money (that's what Jacqueline did, and she saved herself the cost of a reraise). Remember, betting on the end is pointless if only the losers fold.

Bluffing

Good players bluff occasionally, but not too much. Instead they semi-bluff, raise for value, and make other strategic bets that confuse their opponents.

THE FACT IS...

Even bad players get good hands from time to time. Opponents who raise on the turn are rarely bluffing. Those who bet or raise on the river are (almost) never bluffing.

Pure deception is like pepper. You should use it sparingly. The complexity of your basic game should be the major source of misdirection. Besides, everyone watches television, and they imagine themselves capable of exposing a bluff.

I once had an opponent who decided I was a loose bluffer when he saw me (correctly) fold a number of hands that had originally merited raises. The next time I raised, he reraised, and I crushed him with a full house. So your best opportunity for profit is not in bluffing. Instead, profit comes when you capitalize on the mistakes of others.

Also remember that it's nearly impossible to bluff multiple opponents. Somebody is going to have a hand that is worth a call.

Table Selection

You'll learn a lot about poker if you play only with people who have superior skills. But you'll go broke paying for that education. So you should avoid sitting with more than two or three good players. Ideally, the majority of your opponents should be loose/passive. Practically, you'll also see a fair number of over-the-top loose/aggressive players at the lower limits. You won't regularly run into tight/passive until you get into games above 6-12, but loose/passive players sometimes temporarily morph into conservative players if they have a good run of cards.

Give a table about thirty minutes, and if four or more of your opponents are playing well, cash in and find greener pastures. Remember that winning pots and playing well are not necessarily synonymous. There is lucky, and there is good. Luck eventually turns. Good is forever.

Tells

Tells are behaviors that give you a clue about what an opponent is holding. There are dozens of tells, but they're not always reliable because a player may not correctly value his cards. In any case, here are some of the strongest tells.

Shaking hands: A player with shaking hands believes he is on the verge of winning. He's had a rush of adrenaline. Be careful.

Sighs and rolling eyes: This is usually bad acting to cover a strong hand (unless the player folds).

Looking away: Once again, this is an attempt to conceal sheer glee. Beware.

Looking at you: A player who looks at you (rather than through you) is interested in your reaction because he has a vulnerable hand. Note that this doesn't necessarily mean that your hand is stronger.

Becoming an Expert

For more in-depth information about hold 'em poker, check out *The Smarter Bet Guide to Poker*. And if you want to play poker in a non-casino setting, try *Playboy Guide to Playing Poker at Home*. Both books expand on the basic concepts introduced here.

In the next chapter we'll cover various other versions of poker including seven-card stud and Omaha hi-lo, and we'll talk about strategies for no-limit contests.

Essentially

- The best hold 'em starting hands include big cards, suited cards, connectors, or pairs. Hands that don't have these attributes (trash hands) sometimes may look tempting, but they invariably cost more than they win.

- Position is power in hold 'em. Players who are closer to the button have more information about their opponents. Most hands are unplayable in early position. The range of hands that are playable increases when a seat is closer to the button.

- Folding is a powerful strategy for minimizing losses. Only about 20 percent of hold 'em starting hands are playable, and a win rate of 30 percent to 60 percent is common for even the strongest starters (depending on the game).

- Pot odds is a system of comparing the potential profit of a bet to the possibility of winning a hand. When the profit is higher than the risk, the hand should be played.

- Big pots with a cheap price for entry are good value for drawing hands, and they're dangerous for big pairs.

- Loose and passive players tend to lose money. Players generally become more profitable as they become tighter and more aggressive.

- The flop is the pivotal moment in hold 'em. Five of the seven cards (71 percent) have been revealed. Hands at this stage generally fall into four categories: strong hands, vulnerable hands, drawing hands, and losers.

- Generally, strong hands should be slow-played until the turn. Vulnerable hands should be aggressively played. Drawing hands should be played in ways that maximize their value when they hit. Obvious losers should be dropped.

- When in doubt, throw it out.

CHAPTER 14

Poker: No-Limit, Seven-Card Stud, & Other Versions

New poker versions are easy to learn when you understand the basics of pot odds, the power of folding, the importance of selecting the best starting hands, and the other concepts we covered in the previous two chapters.

Of course, specific strategies change with each version (sometimes dramatically), but remember that the underlying systems remain the same.

No-Limit

No-limit poker is a very different game than its sibling limit poker, even though the two games might seem similar to the casual observer.

In no-limit you can bet any amount at any time. Thus you can lose your entire stake in one hand. That's no small issue. Of course, you also can double your stack with one hand. This extreme volatility has profound implications on pot odds.

Indeed, strategies for no-limit games often involve sizing bets to manipulate pot odds. For example, you can "protect" top pair on the flop by betting enough to make a flush draw unprofitable.

Manipulating Pot Odds

The concept of manipulating pot odds is simple. We'll use no-limit hold 'em as an example. Let's say you're in early position with **Ks Qs** and the board shows:

You have flopped top pair. There is also a flush draw on the board. If you bet an amount that is greater than the size of the pot, your bet skews the pot odds and makes a call unprofitable by anyone holding draw cards (hands that need at least 2:1 odds to continue). Of course, this assumes that nobody else calls or raises your bet before a drawing hand acts.

This is where reading your opponents becomes critical. What else is out there? How likely is it that someone snuck in pre-flop without raising **AA**, **KK**, **QQ**, or **AQ**, or limped in with **88**, or **22**?

If your poker sense tells you that your hand is the best, and the board doesn't look dangerous, then you should make a big bet with top pair. You want to take the pot before more cards come.

If an opponent calls or raises your big bet on the flop in a no-limit game, then you're in trouble. That opponent is probably *not* on a draw.

NL Hold 'Em Before the Flop

On television it looks cool to go all-in with a hand like **A9**. Indeed, that's fine in a tournament when the worst that can happen is you go home, and the best that can happen is that you double up.

But in a cash game, you should be very careful about going all-in. In general, you should be very reluctant to call a large raise pre-flop with anything less than a premium hand. Most players know this, and they know you know it, so no-limit cash games tend to be passive before the flop. A lot of players call the big blind with all sorts of weak combinations, and even big pairs and big cards often will raise only small amounts. Everyone wants to see the flop because pre-flop pots in cash games tend to be very small (and thus hardly worth winning). Anyone who makes a big pre-flop raise tends to fold the field and win only the blinds.

Now you might say to yourself, "That's okay. I'll make big raises frequently before the flop and win the blinds. The money adds up." This tactic is called **stealing the blinds**. It's a valuable tool for an expert who has a good read on his opponents, but it can be dangerous in the hands of a beginner.

If you raise pre-flop with anything less than a premium hand (or perhaps a very strong average hand), then you risk folding most of the field and running into a call or reraise from one opponent with a bigger pair or bigger cards. A heads-up situation with you holding an inferior hand is exactly *not* where you want to be.

Thus in a no-limit cash game where the blinds are $2 and $3, you should raise mostly premium hands for an amount somewhere between $15 and $25. The closer you are to the button, the more you can safely raise.

Call modest raises with premium hands. Call an unraised pot with average hands. Fold everything else.

NL Hold 'Em Strategies for Later Rounds

Once you get to the flop in a no-limit cash game, everything shifts gears. If you have a viable hand that is *not* the nuts, you should protect it with a bet. Your opponents also will be aggressive.

Tip

Stealing blinds with a pre-flop raise is an important tactic in tournament poker because the blinds and antes can be quite large in relation to the size of your stack or an opponent's stack. But in cash games, blinds tend to be relatively small, so stealing blinds in no-limit cash games is only nominally profitable. Do it if you can, but don't overdo it.

Be wary if you're raised. It means your opponent is probably not bluffing. He is trying to protect his hand and take the pot right there. Do you have a better hand? Once again, reading your opponent is critical because you cannot inexpensively call him down to the river as you would in a limit-game. Here's an example.

Let's say you have **A♠ K♠**. You make a $20 pre-flop raise in middle position. Two people call. The flop comes:

You bet $75 (slightly more than the size of the pot). The button raises to $200. Should you call this bet?

Probably not unless you want a nail-biter on the turn and river. Remember, this is a cash game. Your opponent called a pre-flop raise, and is now raising you on the flop. Clearly, he doesn't fear **AK**. He probably has at least **AA** or **KQ** and maybe **KK**, **QQ**, or **88**. So it's likely that you are an underdog right now with only a few outs to win the hand.

Is it possible that the button is trying to bluff you off the hand? Yes, it is. Perhaps he has only **AK** or **JJ**. What are the chances of that compared to the chances he has **AA**, **KQ**, **KK**, **QQ**, or **88**? It will cost you $125 to call, and the pot currently contains $340. So the pot is currently offering 2.7:1. How much more does the button have in his stack? What if he bets again on the turn?

Let's turn it around.

Imagine you're the person on the button. You called a pre-flop raise with **KK**. Now you're looking at a flop where you clearly have the best hand (trips), but there are ways that it can lose on the turn and river. Someone bet into you, probably with **AA**, **AK**, or **QQ**, maybe **KQ**. Now is the time to pop it. If he calls your raise or reraises, then at least you'll be getting the right price for the additional risk of seeing extra cards.

Similar issues affect action on the turn.

On the river all the cards are out, so you're no longer worried about a draw. At this stage it's just an issue of reading your opponent and deciding who has finished with the better hand.

Again, beware of opponents who bet big (on the end or anywhere else). Yes, it's possible they are bluffing, but in most situations big bets represent legitimate hands. Be sure to calculate your pot odds and don't call a big bet with anything mediocre or speculative.

Seven-Card Stud

Seven-card stud doesn't use community cards like hold 'em. Each player builds a poker hand from seven personal cards, four of which are exposed.

The game begins with an ante. Each player receives two cards face down and one face up. The player with the *lowest* exposed card is required to make a small initial bet (less than the table minimum) called a **bring-in**.

The player to the left of the bring-in can call the bet to the table minimum, raise, or fold. Action proceeds clockwise from that position. This round is called **third street**. Subsequent rounds are similarly named for the number of cards in a hand, though **seventh street** is sometimes called the river.

THE FACT IS...

Suit is used to determine the bring-in when cards are of the same rank in seven-card stud. The suits are valued lowest to highest in alphabetical order: clubs, diamonds, hearts, spades.

Action on fourth street and later rounds begins with the player who has the *highest* exposed hand. Fourth street through sixth street are dealt face up and seventh street is dealt face down. In a fixed-limit game, bets double on fifth street.

The Importance of Live Cards

Most of the strategy of seven-card stud revolves around the concept of live cards. Let's say you're dealt a starting hand of:

The **5♦** is the **door card** (exposed card). You look out on the table and see that four of your six opponents are showing diamonds. That means the probability of finishing with a diamond flush has dropped dramatically. If the other two opponents show aces or kings then your starting hand is in trouble.

Conversely, no diamonds and a lot of small cards showing would justify a call if the pot has not been too aggressively raised. If you do choose to proceed, then you must note when a competitor receives a card that you were wanting, and you must remember the cards that are folded. Let's say another jack arrives on fourth street. It's worth less if two jacks have already gone into the muck.

Seven-Card Stud Starting Hands

As you might expect, suited cards, pairs, trips, and connectors make the most powerful starting hands. While I don't want to imply any *exact* parallels with hold 'em starting hands, it's fair to say that the same general patterns apply. You should play big pairs hard and fast. Drawing hands should be played cheaply or raised for value when the pot odds exceed the probability of hitting the hand.

Trips should be slow-played on third street, and then raised on fourth or fifth street depending on how many players are still in the hand and the degree of strength they're showing.

If you don't have any of the above and no big cards, then fold the hand.

Tip

Beware of paired door cards. A paired door card dramatically increases the probability that you're up against trips (or better), particularly when the door card is of a higher rank.

Later Streets

Five of the seven cards (71 percent of the hand) have been revealed by fifth street. This is where bets double, so it's best to fold here if you're not leading or if you don't have a strong draw. Remember that the overall probability of seeing any particular seven-card combination is exactly the same in seven-card stud as in hold 'em, but the extra variable is live cards. So use the charts from Chapter 13 and subtract outs when you see them in other hands.

A Rat-Pack Strategy Example

Here is how Frank Sinatra and Dean Martin played seven-card stud in the 1958 film classic *Some Came Running* (which also starred Shirley MacLaine). This hand brings up some interesting strategy issues.

Six guys are playing no-limit. Frank is dealing. Dino is to his left. The scene begins on fourth street. Frank deals Dino a **2♠** that pairs the door card, which is **2♥**. The rest of the players get **blanks**, including (it seems) Frank. His door card is a **6♠** and his fourth-street card is a **7♣**.

Dino has the high hand (a pair of twos). He bets $2 and gets three callers, including Frank.

The action moves to fifth street. Dino gets **2♣** to make trips on the board. Blanks to everyone else except Frank, who pairs his door card with **6♣**.

Dino bets $25. Two guys fold. Frank raises to $175.

Actually, Frank makes a string raise. He calls $25 and then raises $150. He also writes Dino an IOU (violating the rules of table stakes). But this is a private game, so I won't quibble about the rules.

Dino reraises to $325. Frank "pops" it to $825.

Should Dino call? What is Frank holding?

Think about it for a second. Obviously, Frank has something that can beat trip deuces. Here are the cards.

Dino's hand:

Frank's hand:

Ready for the answer?

Dino tosses his cards and says, "Fellas, I think he's got the third six."

Frank replies, "Now there is a smart poker player." Then he takes the pot.

The scene is fairly realistic, though I think Frank overplayed his hand if he had only another buried **6**. He should have just called Dino's reraise because Dino might have had a buried pair and thus a full house.

On the other hand, Frank might have feared that Dino's hand would improve to a full house on sixth or seventh street, so Frank decided to grab the pot right there.

Another possibility is that Frank had a **6** *and* a **7**, giving him sixes full of sevens. But in this situation, he probably should have slow-played and sucked Dino in for even more.

What about the possibility that Dino might have had a fourth deuce in the hole. It turns out that he didn't, but Frank should have been concerned about that unless he saw the fourth deuce in someone else's hand.

In any case, you can see how the strategy for seven-card stud can be somewhat more complicated than the strategy for hold 'em because you have to keep track of more cards.

Omaha Hi/Lo

The original version of this game is called Omaha. It's hold 'em played with *four cards* in the pocket, and *exactly two* of those four cards must be used to make a hand. So if you have:

And the board shows:

You don't have a straight or a flush. You have a pair of kings. The best five-card Omaha hand from the above cards is K♣ K♠ A♦ Q♦ 7♦ (using two of the four cards in your hand).

These days Omaha usually is played as Omaha hi/lo. The high hand splits the pot with the lowest hand that is **8** or better (which really means **8**-high or worse). The low hand in the previous example is A♦ 2♥ 3♦ 4♦ 7♦. Straights and flushes don't count when competing for the lowest hand, so the best combination is **A** through **5**.

For more on low hands see the razz section on page 234.

Omaha Hi/Lo Starting Hands

Omaha hi/lo is a chaotic contest because so many cards are in play and there are so many ways to win. Pots often become very large because everyone figures they have a shot. A lone pair of jacks or queens can often win an entire pot in hold 'em, but this rarely happens in Omaha hi/lo. If an ace and king hit the board, it's nearly certain that someone is holding at least one of those cards, probably both. High pairs and even two pairs are anemic hands. A typical winner is a straight or better, and remember, half the pot goes to a qualifying low hand.

The best starting hands are combinations that can work for both high and low. Examples would be A♣ A♥ 2♥ 3♣, A♦ K♥ 3♥ 4♦, or A♠ 2♠ K♦ K♥.

A playable, but less flexible hand would be A♣ K♣ Q♦ Q♠ because this could only capture high. Examples of hands to toss include K♦ J♠ 10♥ 9♥ and Q♦ J♥ 7♣ 6♣. Note that these hands could be played as two-card combinations in hold 'em, but they simply won't hold up in Omaha hi/lo.

Tip

It's easy for beginners to be confused about what beats what when ranking low hands. The solution is to determine the highest hand as you would normally, then flip the decision. Thus A-3-4-5-6 would lose to A-2-4-5-7 when playing for high, but it would win when playing for low because **7** is higher than **6**.

Other Poker Games

Pineapple is hold 'em played with three pocket cards. One of the three must be discarded on the flop. The rest of the game plays like hold 'em.

Razz is seven-card stud played for low. The rules are identical to regular seven-card stud except the hand ranks are reversed. Pairs and above are bad (straights and flushes don't count). The best hand is **A** through **5** which is called a wheel or bicycle. The next-best hand is **A-2-3-4-6**, third-best is **A-2-3-5-6**, and so on. A hand like **2-3-4-5-8** is much worse, and anything above **10** is generally unplayable. The way to win at razz is to start with three low cards (**A-2-3** is best), and keep track of how many lows are still alive as the hand develops. Seven-card stud can also be played hi/lo.

Five-card draw is the original poker version. The game uses an ante and a rotating dealer. Five cards are dealt face down. Action begins to the left of the dealer. Players have an opportunity to discard and receive replacement cards after the first round of betting. There is another betting round followed by a showdown.

Lowball is five-card draw played for low. See the razz section for more on ranking low hands.

Poker Tournaments

Gambling-tournaments are covered in Chapter 23, but here I want to address specific strategy issues unique to poker tournaments.

A poker tournament is a great way to see a lot of action and maybe win a big prize. You buy in for a particular amount ($50, $500, $10,000, or whatever), and the money goes into a prize pool. Everyone begins with the same amount of tournament chips, and people leave the tournament as they bust out. Blinds and antes gradually increase as the tournament continues. Prizes go to players who last the longest. Some tournaments pay 10 percent of the field, some pay 20 percent; others award only one prize to the final winner.

Whatever the payout structure, the downside to tournaments is that you may play a long time, hours and sometimes days, and have little or nothing to show for it even if you beat most of your competitors. How often will you reach the money? That depends on your level of skill.

In contrast, cash games allow you to "grind it out." Session winnings of $100 here and $200 there add up over time. You can play as long as you want, and quit when you want.

One format isn't necessarily better than the other; it's a personal choice.

If you decide to play in a poker tournament, remember that early aggression with premium and average hands is the best way to bet. You want to build your stack quickly and dominate the table, or bust out quickly and move on to more profitable games elsewhere. The worst situation in a tournament is to meekly hang on with a small stack, winning just enough to survive, and then get knocked out just before reaching the money.

Don't be reckless; be aggressive.

Essentially

- In no-limit hold 'em you can bet any amount at any time. This volatility has profound implications on pot odds. Players can size their bets to manipulate pot odds and push opponents out of the pot, or encourage them to stay in.

- No-limit cash games tend to be passive before the flop; a big raise usually will cause most players to fold and the raiser will win only the blinds. So it's best to raise only a moderate amount before the flop if you want callers.

- In a no-limit cash game, you should be very careful about calling a big bet. Most opponents are not bluffing in these situations.

- There are no community cards in seven-card stud. A player receives seven personal cards. Three are dealt face down and four are face up. Action begins with the lowest exposed card on the first round. Action on later rounds begins with the highest exposed hand.

- Omaha is similar to hold 'em except it is played with four cards in the pocket. Exactly two of those cards must be used to make a poker hand. In the hi/lo version of Omaha, the pot is split between the player holding the high hand and the player holding the low hand (when the low hand is eight or "better").

- When playing in a poker tournament, early aggression with premium and average hands is the best way to bet. You want to build your stack quickly and dominate the table, or bust out quickly and move on to more profitable games elsewhere. Don't be reckless; be aggressive.

CHAPTER 15

Roulette

A wheel turns. A small white ball spins around the wheel's edge. Gradually the ball slows down, and then it falls. All eyes are on the sphere as it bounces from one numbered slot to another. Finally, it comes to rest. Where?

Roulette is a beguiling drama. The contest draws the eye and stimulates the senses. Once upon a time it was the hottest "salon" game in the world. The Grand Casino in Monte Carlo literally was built on the profits from roulette. It didn't matter that poker, blackjack, and craps ruled in the bars and back rooms. Roulette was queen under the chandeliers.

To this day, roulette still dominates the layout at the Grand Casino. Elsewhere it has been eclipsed by newer games, but the grand dame of gambling still commands a loyal following and remains a fixture in casinos around the world.

Besides the drama of the wheel, players are drawn to roulette's air of refinement and its charming contradiction; it is ordered and precisely mathematical, yet the outcome is thoroughly random. This paradox causes some punters to look endlessly for patterns in the winning and losing. It is not a coincidence that many betting systems focus on roulette. The game's façade of predictability and symmetry is seducing. But in fact, the contest is relentlessly random, and the house has an edge. Roulette is the archetype of a negative-expectation game.

As with most gambling games, there are strategies to lower and erase the house edge, but they're not always as easy to apply as in other casino contests. So should you play roulette? Sure, if you can accept that you're bucking the odds. With a little luck and planning you *can* beat the wheel. And even if you don't, the game can be fun.

A Brief History of Roulette

Roulette is a French word that means "little wheel." The idea of using a wheel for gambling has been around since ancient times, but it was the famed mathematician Blaise Pascal who put a ball on a wheel around 1658. He was doing research on cycloids. Pascal dubbed his scientific device roulette.

The first roulette-like gambling game appeared in England in 1720. It was called roly-poly. The contest had a wheel with forty alternating black and white spaces and a spinning ball. You could bet on black or white. One slot was labeled "bar black." Another was "bar white." That was it, no numbers. Roly-poly was eventually outlawed in 1739. The next version of the game was called even-odd or EO. Same contest, different name. English lawmakers killed that one in 1745.

Meanwhile, in France, punters were playing a game called biribi. It involved choosing numbers. The winning number was drawn from a bag.

It is possible that biribi and EO inspired roulette. There are also stories about a Parisian policeman, Gabriel de Sartine, who supposedly had a hand in developing roulette. We'll probably never know definitively.

What we do know is that the numbered wheel with thirty-eight slots first appeared in Paris around 1796, and roulette with thirty-seven slots debuted in 1842. Both versions came from French sources (see the sidebar on this page), but the former version became popular in the United States. So the thirty-eight-slot game is now called **American roulette** while **European roulette** is the thirty-seven-slot contest.

We'll focus on the American game in the next few sections and discuss the European version later in the chapter.

The Wheel and the Table

An American roulette wheel has thirty-eight slots numbered 1 through 36, zero, and double-zero. The wheel rotates counterclockwise. A dealer spins a marble-like ball clockwise around the wheel's perimeter; centrifugal force keeps the ball on a grooved track as it moves. When the

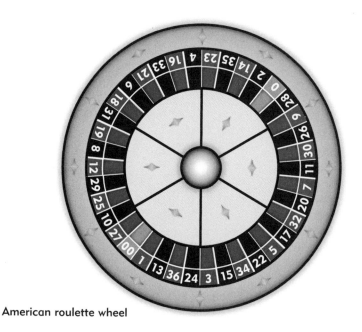

American roulette wheel

ball loses speed it falls into one of the numbered slots, and the various attributes of the number determine winners and losers.

The wheel's numbers are arranged in what seems to be a haphazard fashion, but it's actually a complex system designed for maximum variability. Red and black alternate; pairs of odd and even alternate; pairs of high and low alternate. Every odd number has its even successor directly across the wheel.

The roulette table is equally marvelous. The numbers are arranged sequentially, but the patterns of red, black, high, low, odd, and even create betting options that ensure no bet has an advantage over any other bet. The table can accommodate dozens of unique wagers; all of them have various probabilities of success and yet all of them (with one exception) have an *exactly identical house edge* of 5.26 percent.

The result is a game that is relentlessly systematic yet utterly unpredictable.

Betting and Winning

Roulette uses a unique system of colored chips that distinguish one bettor from another. This allows two or more people to make

Tip

Don't leave the table with your roulette chips. The dealer should not allow it, but if there's a slip-up and you do walk away with some roulette tokens, they will be worthless everywhere else in the casino (including at other roulette tables).

identical bets without confusion, and it creates some interesting contrasts. Your chips may be worth $5 each. The player next to you may be betting $100 per chip. There is no way to know unless you watch a person buy in.

Most roulette tables can accommodate six to eight players. Just walk up and lay your chips or cash on the felt, and the dealer will give you roulette chips. As with every table game, it's a good idea to read the upright plastic card next to the dealer. It will have important information about the game and table limits. Roulette often has different restrictions on amounts that can be wagered "inside" and "outside" the layout.

A standard roulette table is pictured below. Wagers placed directly on single numbers or combinations that pay 5:1 or better are "inside" bets. Wagers on the edges of the layout that pay 1:1 and 2:1 are "outside" bets.

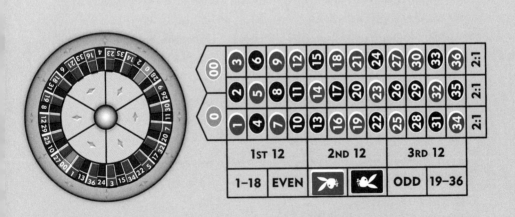

Roulette table

Inside Bets

Inside bets have the highest payoffs and the highest probability of losing.

A **straight bet** is a wager on one number. Just put your chips on the number. The casino pays 35:1 if the ball falls on that number.

A **split bet** is a wager on two numbers. You make the wager by putting your bet on the line between two numbers. The bet wins if the ball falls on either number. The casino pays 17:1 on a split bet.

A **street bet** is made by putting one or more chips at the end of a row of three numbers or at the intersection of three numbers at the top of the layout. The bet pays 11:1.

A **square** or **corner bet** is made at the intersection of four numbers. The bet pays 8:1.

Six-number bets are placed on the intersecting lines at the end of two rows. They pay 5:1.

American roulette has a **five-number bet**. It's made at the end of the row where the one and the zero intersect and it covers zero, double-zero, 1, 2, and 3. It pays 6:1 and it is the only exception to the 5.26 percent rule. A five-number bet has a house edge of 7.89 percent.

Outside Bets

Bets on the outside of the layout cover more numbers and they win more often, but they pay less. The payoff is 2:1 when you win on a group of twelve (1 through 12, 13 through 24, or 25 through 36). You can also bet a column of twelve numbers for the same payoff.

The remaining outside bets are red, black, even, odd, 1 through 18, and 19 through 36. They all pay 1:1.

European Roulette

European roulette (sometimes called French roulette) is similar to the American version, but the European contest has a few distinct differences.

> *"I really do know the secret [of winning at roulette]. It is terribly silly and simple and consists of keeping one's head the whole time, whatever the state of the game, and not getting excited. That is all."*
>
> —Fyoder Dostoevsky, in a letter to his sister-in-law (1863)

The biggest difference is that there is no double-zero on the wheel. This cuts the house edge down to 2.7 percent.

Another difference is a rule called **en prison**; bets on red, black, odd, even, high, or low that lose to zero are not automatically lost. Rather, they are "trapped" on the layout for another spin. If the bet loses a second time, the dealer takes it. If it wins the second spin, the player gets it back (resulting in a push). This cuts the house edge on 1:1 bets down to 1.35 percent.

THE FACT IS...

Some American casinos offer **surrender**, which is a modified version of the European rule en prison. If surrender is allowed, then 1:1 wagers that lose to zero or double-zero are only half-lost. You can leave the bet on the layout and hope for a push or take half back. Casinos in Atlantic City have this option, and it cuts the house edge on 1:1 bets down to 2.63 percent.

Yet another difference is the numbers on a European wheel. They are arranged differently than on an American wheel. Mathematically, this has no significance, but the alternate arrangement of numbers is the basis for a whole other system of betting used in Europe that is known as **call bets**. These are bets that you request verbally. Dealers handle them in a way that is similar to the way dealers handle place bets in craps (if you're playing online, a call bet is simply a combination bet).

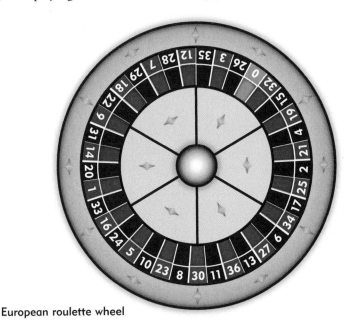

European roulette wheel

Call bets come in various types. As we review them, remember that bets on combined numbers pay the same as if the single numbers have been wagered individually. Also note, these bets originated in France, so they have French names.

Voisins du Zero (Neighbors of Zero): This bet covers seventeen numbers in an arc between 22 and 25. It costs nine chips. The numbers 0-2-3 are covered with two chips, and the remaining fourteen numbers are covered with seven chips. You win fifteen chips net if the ball drops on 0-2-3, and you win nine chips net if it drops on any of your other numbers.

Tiers du Cylindre (One-Third of the Cylinder): This bet covers the twelve numbers in an arc between 27 and 33. It costs six chips and pays 2:1.

The remaining eight numbers on the wheel located in mini-arcs 1–9 and 6–17 are called appropriately **orphelins** (orphans).

Orphelins en Plein: This covers the orphans with one chip on each number. It costs eight chips and pays 7:2.

Orphelins a Cheval: This bet covers the orphans with one chip on 1, one on 17, and the remaining three chips on the other numbers (technically 17 is bet twice with a split, but the practical result is a one-chip bet). You win thirty-one chips net if the ball drops on 1 or 17. You win thirteen chips net if the other numbers win.

Neighbor Bets: This bet covers any number and the slots to the left and the right, either three, five, seven, or nine numbers in all. In a casino you would say "25 and its neighbors," naming whatever number is in the center of the group. The bet costs one chip for each number.

Typically, call bets are placed on a special "race track," which is an elliptical representation of the wheel.

One other major difference between European and American versions of roulette is that the Europeans do not use special roulette chips. Everyone uses standard casino

Tip

If you find a European (single-zero) wheel in an American casino, don't assume that the dealers will know about French call bets or en prison. Be sure to check the upright card for the rules of the game or ask the dealer before making your bets.

chips. This requires attentive dealers (as in craps) to be sure that nobody is cheated.

The Flow of the Game

One dealer can run a roulette table, but very busy tables usually have two dealers. On a crowded night people press around the table and lean across the layout like they're playing a grown-up game of Twister.

Betting continues (and the pace often quickens) as the dealer spins the ball on the perimeter of the wheel. After a few additional seconds of betting, the dealer waves her hand over the layout to indicate that bets are no longer accepted.

All eyes turn to the wheel and the table goes silent. The ball gradually slows down and plummets into the depths of the wheel like an errant satellite plunging into the ocean. Typically, it hops and skips a bit before finally settling into a particular slot.

Players either gasp or sigh. The dealer puts a plastic token (usually a small upright cylinder) on the layout over the winning number. Losing bets are raked in. Winning bets are paid off starting from the outside of the layout and proceeding inward. When the last straight bet has been paid, the process starts again.

Roulette Betting Systems

The casino's entire edge in roulette is a result of two green slots (zero and double-zero) floating in a sea of red and black. Without those slots the game is a no-edge contest. With the extra slots, the house has a considerable advantage.

Betting on zero and double-zero (or including those numbers in a combination bet) doesn't change the situation. There is no system, no method, no pattern for playing roulette that will prevent the game from extracting a house edge of 5.26 percent on a double-zero wheel.

There are only two exceptions to this mathematic tenet, bias and rule changes (such as playing a single-zero

THE FACT IS...

If a number or combination you want is already covered with a bet, you can stack your chips on top of the other player's chips. Roulette is the only game that allows this because (in the American version) each player has different-colored tokens.

wheel). We'll cover both tactics later in this chapter, but right now let's examine why most roulette betting schemes don't work.

Inside Bets vs. Outside Bets

A straight bet obviously has more risk and offers more reward per spin than a bet that pays 1:1, but both bets cost exactly the same over time. That's the roulette paradox.

People who spread chips around the table lose at the same long-term rate as those who bet single numbers or groups. The adjacent table shows why. Betting multiple chips on a combination is identical to dividing the bet on individual numbers. For example, $10 split between 11 and 14 will return the same amount as $5 straight up on 11 and $5 straight up on 14. This is true for all combinations.

"But what is zero?" she inquired. "Just now I heard the flaxen-haired croupier call out 'zero!' And why does he keep raking in all the money that is on the table? To think that he should grab the whole pile for himself! What does zero mean?"

—Fyoder Dostoevsky, from his story *The Gambler*, written in 1866

Multiple Straight Bets vs. Combination Bets

Numbers	11 & 14	4,5,6	19,20,22,23	7–12	19–36
Straight bets	2	3	4	6	18
Win amount	35	35	35	35	35
Losing bets	−1	−2	−3	−5	−17
Net total after win	34	33	32	30	18
Combination Bets	2 chips split	3 chips street	4 chips box	6 chips on two rows	18 chips on high
Win amount	34	33	32	30	18
Losing bets	0	0	0	0	0
Net total after win	34	33	32	30	18

Putting multiple chips on a combination bet returns the same amount as splitting the wager and betting each number individually.

There's nothing wrong with spreading bets around, but there's nothing right about it. In the long run it doesn't make any difference. Similarly, betting $10 on a single number may seem riskier and more expensive than betting $10 on red, but both bets cost the same in the long run. The table labeled "Straight Bets vs. Outside Bets" shows the results from 380 decisions when there is an exactly average outcome.

Straight Bets vs. Outside Bets

Straight bets pay 35:1		$10 wagers
Total Decisions	380	
Wins	10	$3,500
Losses	370	$3,700
Net Result		–$200
Outside bets pay 1:1		$10 wagers
Total decisions	380	
Wins	180	$1,800
Losses	200	$2,000
Net Result		–$200

Straight bets and outside bets have the same long-term cost. These numbers reflect average results after approximately eight hours of play.

Of course, results are rarely exactly average. That's the lure and the heartbreak of roulette. Normal streaks of winning and losing make some people think that particular bets or combinations of bets win more than others. Indeed, some bets do win more frequently, but they're all equal when it comes to the house edge.

Squeezing and Stretching Risk

Take another look at the table above. Both bets cost the same over time, but the total amount won and lost is much higher when betting single numbers. Roulette's house edge is unyielding, but squeezing and stretching risk is quite easy. This is where many people get confused and get into trouble. They imagine that it's possible to bet a certain way and squeeze the risk right out of roulette, or stretch it so thin that it has no effect. But it can't be done. Fortunes have been lost by people who tried.

The following betting systems squeeze and stretch risk. They can be fun to play, but keep in mind that they won't put you ahead in the long run unless you're lucky.

So if you're looking for strategies that actually lower or eliminate the house edge, skip ahead to page 254.

Betting two groups of twelve. This is a well-known system that is popular among people who like to see the dealer frequently pushing them money. The player bets an identical amount on two groups of twelve. For example, $10 on 1–12 and $10 on 13–24. If the ball lands on 1 through 24, the bettor wins net $10 ($20 on the winning dozen less $10 on the losing dozen). A bet on two dozen wins 63 percent of the time. The wins and losses together add up to a predictable 5.26 percent average loss, but it's certainly fun to "win" more than six out of ten times.

Betting one group of twelve and 1:1. A system that "wins" even more frequently is betting two units on a group of twelve and three units on a totally opposite 1:1 contest. An example would be $10 on 1–12 and $15 on 19–36. This combined wager pushes the risk into only eight numbers, 13–18, zero, and double-zero. A win either way pays an aggregate of $5. A loss costs the bettor $25. Losses occur 21 percent of the time, about one in five spins. Wins occur the other four times, so five spins usually will cost $5.

Of course you might win ten consecutive times and be ahead $50. Or you could lose three times in a row. That would cost you $75. One way or another, the wins and losses eventually will add up to a 5.26 percent loss on all your action.

A Roulette Progression

We cover progressive betting systems in Chapter 25, but here we're going to review a **progression** specifically designed for roulette.

It is a **closed-end negative progression**. The entire amount of the progression is your price to play. In other words, you're risking the entire amount in various increments on the proposition that you'll win at least one straight-up bet in thirty-eight attempts. Overall, you have about a 64 percent chance of winning this multiple-spins bet.

The columns on the left side of the table on the next page show the progression. The shaded area on the right side shows a person betting a flat $20 per spin on the same number.

Notice that the flat bettor's net gain gradually drops while the progressive bettor's gain goes up. At no time does the progressive bettor risk more of the total session bankroll than the flat bettor.

But remember, the house edge doesn't change. We're just pushing the risk and reward around a bit. Flat betting costs more, but it also returns more if the bettor wins in the first fifteen spins.

Strategies for Beating the Wheel

The various systems that we covered in the previous sections may be fun to play, but they don't do anything to change the casino's advantage. If you play roulette using one of those systems, or another betting scheme, or you just make random wagers, your bankroll will begin to shrink sooner or later. The only way to slow this process (or prevent it altogether) is to lower or eliminate the house edge.

Play like the French

One way to squeeze the casino is to play a European-style single-zero wheel. This cuts the house edge from 5.26 percent down to 2.7 percent. That's a considerable chunk.

Happily, you don't have to visit Monte Carlo to play a European wheel. Many American casinos and gambling websites have them. But sometimes it's with a catch. The European wheel will have a higher table minimum than a double-zero version at the same casino. No problem if you were planning to risk the extra money, but don't play for higher stakes just to get a lower house edge.

Surrender and En Prison

Some American casinos (primarily those in Atlantic City) offer a modified version of the European rule en prison; it's called **surrender**. When surrender is allowed, a 1:1 bet that loses to zero or double-zero is only half-lost. You can leave the bet on the layout and hope for a

A Roulette Progression

	Closed-End Progression				Flat $20 Bets			
	38 Spins Risks $751				38 Spins Risks $760			
Bet Number	Bet	Prior Losses	Single Win	Net Gain	Bet	Prior Losses	Single Win	Net Gain
1	5	0	175	175	20	0	700	700
2	5	5	175	170	20	20	700	680
3	5	10	175	165	20	40	700	660
4	5	15	175	160	20	60	700	640
5	5	20	175	155	20	80	700	620
6	6	25	210	185	20	100	700	600
7	7	31	245	214	20	120	700	580
8	8	38	280	242	20	140	700	560
9	9	46	315	269	20	160	700	540
10	10	55	350	295	20	180	700	520
11	11	65	385	320	20	200	700	500
12	12	76	420	344	20	220	700	480
13	13	88	455	367	20	240	700	460
14	14	101	490	389	20	260	700	440
15	15	115	525	410	20	280	700	420
16	16	130	560	430	20	300	700	400
17	17	146	595	449	20	320	700	380
18	18	163	630	467	20	340	700	360
19	19	181	665	484	20	360	700	340
20	20	200	700	500	20	380	700	320
21	21	220	735	515	20	400	700	300
22	22	241	770	529	20	420	700	280
23	23	263	805	542	20	440	700	260
24	24	286	840	554	20	460	700	240
25	25	310	875	565	20	480	700	220
26	26	335	910	575	20	500	700	200
27	27	361	945	584	20	520	700	180
28	28	388	980	592	20	540	700	160
29	29	416	1015	599	20	560	700	140
30	30	445	1050	605	20	580	700	120
31	31	475	1085	610	20	600	700	100
32	32	506	1120	614	20	620	700	80
33	33	538	1155	617	20	640	700	60
34	34	571	1190	619	20	660	700	40
35	35	605	1225	620	20	680	700	20
36	36	640	1260	620	20	700	700	0
37	37	676	1295	619	20	720	700	−20
38	38	713	1330	617	20	740	700	−40
Net after 38 losses				−751				−760

push or take half back. Surrender cuts the house edge on 1:1 bets down to 2.63 percent.

As I mentioned previously, en prison on a European wheel drops the house edge on 1:1 bets down to 1.35 percent. The extra spin is mandatory in Europe, which is why they say "en prison."

THE FACT IS...

In the 1942 movie *Casablanca*, Rick (Humphrey Bogart) suggests to a desperate roulette player that he bet on 22. The man is trying to win money to buy exit visas for himself and his wife. The player follows Rick's advice (not knowing the wheel is rigged). Rick signals the croupier, and the couple wins enough money to escape from the city.

Avoid the Five-Number Bet

A five-number bet (zero, double-zero, 1, 2, and 3) is available only on American wheels. The house edge is a hefty 7.89 percent. It's a bad bet; don't make it. If you truly have a vision that one of those numbers will win, then bet it straight up or make a street or split bet. That will cut the house edge by more than 2 percent and will return between two to six times more than a five-number bet.

Bias

Obviously, roulette cannot deliver impartial results if the wheel is unbalanced. An unbalanced wheel would create a **bias** toward certain numbers, and this would be a condition that players could exploit.

Roulette wheels are built with extreme precision, and they're checked frequently for balance and wear. But nothing in life is perfect, and biased wheels occasionally slip through. Since these wheels don't have big signs announcing their condition, you must find them yourself.

If a particular number comes up two or three times in a row, this is not necessarily an indication of bias. A number must hit consistently more than once in thirty-six trials (thirty-eight minus the house edge) over an extended period, usually at least 1,000 games. The process of recording spins is called **clocking a wheel**, and professional gamblers usually do it in shifts. It's a twenty-four-hour operation because any breaks during or after clocking give the casino an opportunity to move the wheel to another table. When a gambling team finds a biased wheel, they want to get in quickly and earn a profit.

Good for them, but you don't have a full-time crew. How can you find a biased wheel? In most cases you can't. But if you're playing roulette anyway, here's a system that at least will give you a chance.

Clock a wheel for 50 spins while betting normally. After 50 spins, bet on any numbers that have won three or more times. Straight-up bets or combinations are fine. Meanwhile, expand your sample to 100 spins and bet on any numbers that win at least six times (drop numbers when they turn cold and include numbers that heat up). Expand the sample by increments of 50 spins and three occurrences. Any numbers that consistently reach these criteria will be appearing much more frequently than normal.

Just remember, most wheels aren't biased. You might clock dozens of wheels before you find one that is out of balance, and the next day it might be gone. It's a lot of work, and usually not worth the effort unless you really love roulette (or you're a professional gambler).

Dealer Signature

Dealing can be a monotonous job. Certain actions become automatic, including the release of the ball. When an experienced dealer is on mental autopilot, the ball's speed and trajectory are amazingly consistent from spin to spin. The big variable becomes the release point. Of course, there are metal stops on the wheel that are designed to deflect the ball as it comes off the track. But even with deflection, it's possible to predict the winning zone.

First you need to find a consistent dealer. Do this by carefully watching where the ball is released and where it lands. Once you have determined that a particular dealer has a signature spin, you'll have just a few seconds after the spin to calculate where the ball will stop and to make a wager. Becoming familiar with the wheel layout will help you bet zones quickly.

Tip

Most roulette tables have an electronic display that shows the results of the last few spins. It's a handy tool to use when clocking a wheel. Another handy tool is a pen and some paper. Nevada regulations allow players to use writing devices at roulette tables. Ditto for baccarat. But don't try this at a blackjack table.

Most dealers don't have predictable signatures, but it doesn't hurt to check. The nice part about roulette is that even when a system doesn't work, the result is never worse in the long run than the alternative, a wild guess.

Tip

Don't Lose Your Head

It is a testament to the genius of roulette's anonymous inventor that the game survives and thrives more than two centuries after its introduction with essentially no rule modifications. The double-zero game you play on the Strip, the Boardwalk, or wherever is identical to the contest Parisians played when the French Revolution was in its guillotine-crazed heyday.

Indeed, it not entirely a coincidence that roulette was invented at about the same time as the guillotine.

Both machines reflect an eighteenth-century sensibility. They embody the Newtonian ideals of order and mechanical balance applied to the messy business of real-world results.

Of course, the guillotine is an awful thing, and roulette is (hopefully) a source of pleasure. Nevertheless, when playing roulette it pays to remember the basic lesson of the French revolution. Don't get carried away and lose your head.

Essentially

- There are two versions of roulette. The thirty-eight-slot game is called **American roulette** while **European roulette** is the thirty-seven-slot contest.

- An American roulette wheel has thirty-eight slots numbered 1 through 36, zero, and double-zero. The wheel rotates counterclockwise. A dealer spins a marble-like ball clockwise around the wheel's perimeter. When the ball loses speed it falls into one of the numbered slots, and the various attributes of the number determine winners and losers.

- The casino's entire edge in roulette is based on two green slots (zero and double-zero). Without those slots the game is a no-edge contest. With the extra slots, the house has a 5.26 percent advantage.

- There is no system, no method, no pattern for playing roulette that will prevent the game from extracting a 5.26 percent house edge on a double-zero wheel (7.89 percent on the five-number bet). There are only two exceptions to this mathematic tenet: bias and rule changes (such as playing on a single-zero wheel).

- Playing roulette on a single-zero wheel lowers the house edge to 2.7 percent.

- Other tactics for lowering the house edge include taking advantage of "surrender" on an American wheel (lowers the house edge to 2.63 percent) or "en prison" on a European wheel (lowers the house edge to 1.35 percent).

- An unbalanced roulette wheel will be biased toward certain numbers. The best way to determine if a wheel is biased is to "clock" the wheel while you're playing. If a particular number or section of the wheel consistently wins more than three times in fifty spins, then this indicates that a wheel is biased.

- Some dealers spin the roulette ball in such a consistent way that it makes the results of the spin somewhat predictable. This is called a "dealer signature." The best way to take advantage of a dealer signature is to watch the dealer's spin and then bet zones of the wheel where you think the ball will fall.

- When playing roulette it pays to remember the basic lesson of the French revolution. Don't get carried away and lose your head.

Roulette

CHAPTER 16

Baccarat

Movie scene…

The year is 1962. The place is a casino in London. Sylvia Trench is a beautiful and wealthy woman, but this night she is very unlucky. Sylvia is losing at some sort of French card game. We cannot see her opponent's face, but we see the cards. Her opponent wins, then he wins again.

Sylvia pulls out a checkbook and increases the stakes. She is gunning for the stranger. The camera has not yet revealed his face, but we hear his voice. He has a melodious English accent mixed with a faint Scottish brogue, and he is perfectly calm.

The stranger opens his cigarette case and says, "I admire your courage, Miss…"

"Trench, Sylvia Trench. I admire your luck, Mr…"

Cut to a close-up of the stranger as he lights a cigarette. The sterling-silver lighter closes with a click. "Bond, James Bond."

Those were the very first on-screen words uttered by Agent 007. The movie was *Dr. No.* The game was chemin de fer (the European version of baccarat).

Classy game, classy guy… That's what the filmmakers were implying when they chose to introduce Bond with baccarat.

But like James Bond, baccarat is very much a result of a carefully crafted romantic myth.

The Mystery and Myth of Baccarat

Most stories about baccarat's origins go like this… The game was invented around 1490 B.C.E. Usually, it is said that baccarat came from Italy, but sometimes the supposed birthplace is France or England. Either way (according to the stories), baccarat was a favorite of the European aristocracy for many centuries before it became a casino contest.

The storytellers also say that baccarat means zero in Italian or French. Indeed, 31 percent of baccarat cards are valued at zero. Occasionally, a connection to tarot is mixed into the legend.

It's a romantic tale that has gained enormous traction in popular culture. Versions of the story can be found even in encyclopedias, and it's nearly impossible to read a history of baccarat that doesn't include some reference to its supposed Renaissance origins.

THE FACT IS...

Baccarat does not have Renaissance roots, at least not directly, but it may have that pedigree indirectly if it was developed from blackjack. The forerunner of blackjack was a game called one-and-thirty, and that contest was popular in the fifteenth century. We know this because Catholic priest Bernadine de Sienne preached against one-and-thirty in a sermon he gave in Italy in 1440.

Are the stories true? Probably not. Research on the subject has progressed considerably over the past few years, and so far, there is no hard evidence to support any of the popular tales. There are no contemporary accounts of baccarat prior to the late nineteenth century. Chroniclers from centuries past are universally silent about the game. And the Italian word for zero is *zero*. Ditto for the French word *zero*.

Baccarat's origin remains a genuine mystery. But perhaps we can uncover at least a portion of the real story.

There is some evidence (from a firsthand account) that baccarat came to the United States in 1959 by way of Cuba. The game was popular at the Capri Casino in Havana during the 1950s. When Castro marched into the capital on New Year's Day 1959, he reportedly surprised wealthy players who were celebrating the holiday. They fled to the U.S. (many still wearing tuxedos and evening dresses from the revelry), and they brought their gambling game with them.

Before Havana, the game may have made a pit stop in Argentina. Previous to that, we know definitively that baccarat had slightly different rules, and it was called chemin de fer. The French phrase literally means "path of iron" or colloquially "railroad." This refers to the way the shoe is passed around from player to player. Chemin de fer was popular in France in the early twentieth century, and it was also played in other places, including Las Vegas (there are eyewitness reports that it was offered at the Flamingo in 1946).

Who invented chemin de fer? Nobody knows. When was it invented? Probably in the late nineteenth century, surely after railroads became common. How did it become such an upper-crust game? Perhaps a smart casino entrepreneur invented chemin de fer at his kitchen table. He concocted all that stuff about Renaissance aristocracy, and then advertised it to the willing nouveau-riche of the Industrial Age. Whatever the source of the myth, the tale surely appealed to Victorian sensibilities.

Tip

Baccarat is pronounced bah-kah-rah; the "t" at the end is silent. But if you've been saying "back-a-rat" for years, don't worry, you're in good company. The latter pronunciation was popular in Las Vegas during the 1960s. Wiseguys, entertainers, dealers, players, and everyone else in the Neon Oasis used to say "back-a-rat."

As a result, baccarat and chemin de fer have become games that are legitimately associated with wealth, prestige, and James Bond. You don't have to be rich or a secret agent to play them, but as you'll see, they are not the sort of contests that lend themselves to low-stakes action.

We'll focus on baccarat right now and explain chemin de fer in a later section.

Playing the Game

Full-scale baccarat typically is played on a special table in a high-limit section behind velvet ropes and under crystal chandeliers. The limits for "big" baccarat usually start at $100 per hand and stretch into the stratosphere.

There is also a mini version of baccarat played on a standard-sized casino table. Mini-baccarat has betting limits comparable to other casino games, and it can be found in the table-games section on most casino floors.

The procedures for playing each version are somewhat different, but the basic game is the same.

The contest uses six or eight standard fifty-two-card decks shuffled together and held in a shoe (called a **bank**).

Dealing and Drawing

Only two hands are dealt regardless of how many people are sitting at the table. One hand is called **banker** and the other is called **player**.

Bettors wager on either player, banker, or a tie (more on payoffs in a later section).

Each hand initially receives two cards. The suits of the cards mean nothing; their rank is of sole importance. Two through nine are counted at their number value. Tens, jacks, queens, and kings are counted as *zero*. Aces are counted as one. Hands that total more than nine are reduced by ten. This is done by dropping the first digit; fourteen becomes four, twelve becomes two, seventeen becomes seven.

The highest possible hand is a nine. It's called a **natural**, or more formally "le grande natural." An eight is "le petit natural."

If neither hand is a natural, then each hand receives exactly one additional card as specified by the rules. Player draws first. After the draw, the hand with the highest point total is the winner. The table on page 265 shows the rules for drawing cards. They're interesting to read, but bettors have no control over how the cards are drawn. So the rules for drawing are about as relevant as the rules for shuffling. The procedure is necessary, but it's the dealer's job to do it. Just be sure he is doing it correctly.

Betting and Winning

As mentioned previously, bettors can wager on either player, banker, or a tie. A win on player pays 1:1.

A win on banker also pays 1:1 technically, but the casino collects a 5 percent vig (commission) on each banker bet that wins. The resulting payoff for banker is 0.95:1. Some casinos charge only 4 percent when the bank wins. There are a few casinos that don't charge a vig, but they pay only 1:2 when the banker wins with a six.

A tie is a push for player and banker; no money changes hands.

A winning wager on tie pays 8:1. Some casinos pay 9:1 (the true odds for a tie are about 9.5:1).

The mathematics for winning at baccarat somewhat resemble blackjack, so banker has an advantage in win frequency, but the casino's vig ensures that the house has an edge. The adjacent table shows the resulting house edge for each bet.

Baccarat Rules for Drawing

1. Naturals automatically win or are tied (nine beats an eight). No cards are drawn.

2. If neither side has a natural, then the following applies:

If Player's Hand is	Player Must	
0–5	draw	
6–7	stand	

If Player Does Not Draw and Banker's Hand is	Banker Must	
0–5	draw	
6–7	stand	

If Player Draws and Banker's Hand is	Banker Will Draw if Player's Third Card is	Banker Will Stand if Player's Third Card is
0–2	banker always draws	banker always draws
3	1–7, 9 or 0	8
4	2–7	1, 8, 9, or 0
5	4–7	1–3, 8, 9, or 0
6	6 or 7	1–5, 8, 9, or 0
7	banker always stands	banker always stands

Two hands are dealt in baccarat, one for player and one for banker. Each hand initially has two cards. Player and banker may receive one additional card according to these rules. Player always draws first. The highest point total wins.

Baccarat's House Edge

Player	1.24%
Banker 5% vig	1.06%
Banker 4% vig	0.60%
Banker no vig with 1:2 payoff on a winning hand of 6	1.46%
Tie Pays 8:1	14.36%
Tie Pays 9:1	4.84%

Big Baccarat

The big version of baccarat is played at a table like the one on page 266. Games like these are found only in high-limit areas. Look for velvet ropes, dealers in tuxedos, and people wearing serious bling.

If you have the money to wager, then this is the place to do it.

Choose a seat as you would at any casino table and make yourself comfortable.

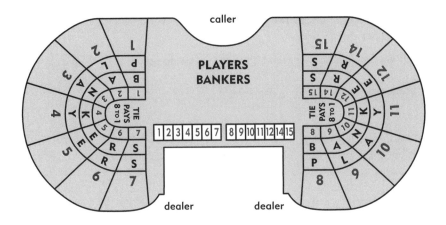

This is a baccarat table. Each number around the edge is a player seat.

Some casinos use special baccarat chips (referred to as cheques or plaques) that are larger than normal. This is one of the many amenities that casinos provide in baccarat to enhance the VIP feeling. Obviously, you don't have to shout "change" here as you would when playing craps. Put your money down and ask for cheques. A crew of three dealers and a server or two will attend to your every need.

The Shuffle and the Deal

The shuffle for big baccarat is like everything else, it's fancy. Six or eight decks are elegantly mixed. One player is offered the cut. The decks are then placed into a shoe (called the bank). The first card is turned over and its number indicates how many additional cards will be burned (discarded).

One dealer, known as the caller, runs the game. Two additional dealers across the table handle the financial matters. At the beginning of the game (assuming all the players have just arrived) the first player to the caller's right is offered the bank and an opportunity to deal the cards as banker. It sounds important, but the procedure is simple and it is done completely at the direction of the caller.

Players (including the banker) can bet player, banker, or tie by placing chips in the appropriate space on the layout in front of them. When the wagering is finished, the caller instructs the banker to deal four cards face down into two hands: "Card for the player. Card for the banker." It's easy to follow. The banker pushes the first and third card (player's hand) to the center of the table and tucks the second and fourth card (banker's hand) slightly under the edge of the shoe.

The Showdown

The caller picks up the player's hand and delivers it to the person who made the highest wager on player. That person looks at the cards and then turns them over with an appropriate expression of either satisfaction or disappointment. The caller retrieves the hand, and the two cards are placed at the center of the table.

The banker then reveals his hand. Additional cards are drawn at the caller's direction, and the contest is finished. If banker wins, the shoe stays with the person who is dealing. A win for player moves the shoe counterclockwise to the next person. Banking is not mandatory and you (like James Bond) may offer your regrets and pass the shoe to André.

Note that some casinos require the banker-dealer to bet on banker. And in some games the bank (shoe) stays with the player who is betting the most on banker, regardless of who wins.

Of course, none of this elaborate ritual has any effect on the outcome of the game. Frankly, players don't need to handle the cards, and one dealer can do everything. That is exactly how the low-stakes version of baccarat works.

Mini-Baccarat

Mini-baccarat is played at a standard card table like the one on page 268. Players buy in as they would for any table game. The dealer shuffles six or eight decks in a standard fashion, and

THE FACT IS...

One of the many perks of playing "big" baccarat is that you can fold, puncture, tear, or do whatever else you want to the cards in your hand. The casino will gladly sacrifice decks to keep you betting at $100 or more per game. So if you have a sudden inclination to make an origami swan from a red nine while playing big baccarat, go ahead, indulge yourself.

one player cuts them with a plastic stop. The dealer puts the decks in a shoe, reveals the value of the first card and then burns that number of additional cards.

Bettors wager on player, banker, or tie by placing chips on the various marked areas of the table. The dealer then draws cards according to baccarat rules and pays or collects bets. Players never touch the cards.

Mini-baccarat is not as fancy as the big version, but the minimum-bet limits are much lower, typically $10 per hand ($25 on busy nights).

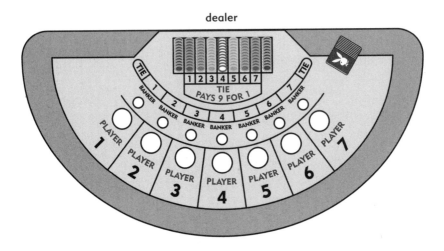

Mini-baccarat is played at a regular-size card table with only one dealer. Players don't touch the cards in this version.

Chemin de Fer

Chemin de fer (sometimes called "shimmy") is similar to big baccarat, but in this version of the game the banker actually banks the action. Everyone else plays against the banker. The **punter** (bettor) who risks the most on player handles the player's cards. There is no tie bet.

Also, the starting hands are revealed *after* the draw, and the drawing rules are not so rigid. Player must draw on totals of four or less, and stand on six or more, but he has the option of standing or drawing on a two-card hand that totals five.

The banker can draw or stand as he wishes, but in most situations, the traditional draw strategy is the best. Of course, that strategy is disrupted when the player stands on a five. Thus chemin de fer has an element of bluff and variable tactics that are missing from baccarat.

Baccarat Optimal Strategy

The strategy for baccarat is simple. Never put money on tie; it's a sucker bet. Always bet on banker or player; both are about evenly matched. Banker wins 50.7 percent of the hands (not including ties), and player wins 49.3 percent of the hands. Ties occur about 9.5 percent of the time.

Even after the 5 percent vig, banker has a slightly lower house edge than player, but just by a smidge (1.24 percent vs. 1.06 percent).

If you're playing chemin de fer, the best mathematic strategy is to always follow baccarat rules for drawing. However, you may gain an advantage occasionally by deviating from basic strategy and standing on five if you're the player, but only if it causes the banker to draw incorrectly.

If you're the banker, there is not much you can do if a player stands on five (representing a six or seven). Unless you have a good read on the player, assume he has a six or seven and draw or stand accordingly.

Following Trends and Counting Cards

Some people try to predict baccarat results by analyzing previous wins and losses. In fact, you often will see players diligently scribbling notes hoping to forecast the outcome of the next hand. Casinos have special

Tip

In some European casinos, you occasionally will see chemin de fer offered as baccarat, and baccarat is called punto banco. The best way to avoid confusion is to check the rules before playing. Also, if you see players revealing their hands before the draw, then the game is standard American-style baccarat. Likewise, mini-baccarat is always American-style.

rules that allow this, and they even supply paper and writing instruments. When your opponent (the casino) encourages you to use a particular system, then you can be sure that it's worthless. This certainly applies to the alchemy of analyzing win-lose trends.

Similarly, counting cards is not an effective strategy in baccarat. Strictly speaking, the edge *can* be shifted somewhat as penetration increases (for more about penetration, see Chapter 9), but the positive effect is so small, counting has no practical consequence.

THE FACT IS...

The Elegant Choice

So which will it be, banker or player? Your guess is as good as any other. Either way, the house edge is slightly more than one percent. That is much lower than slots, and it beats most table games. Nice. But people play baccarat for more than just a low house edge. Baccarat attracts players mostly because of its trappings and its rhythm. The contest has an inscrutable cadence that is enticing.

Baccarat's roots are mythic and manufactured, like James Bond, but the myth delivers a real experience of elegance and style. It's fun in a fancy way.

Essentially

- In baccarat only two hands are dealt regardless of how many people are sitting at the table. One hand is called banker and the other is called player.

- Each hand initially receives two cards. Cards ranked two through nine are counted at their number value. Tens, jacks, queens, and kings are counted as zero. Aces are counted as one. Hands that total more than nine are reduced by ten. The highest possible hand is a nine.

- Additional cards are drawn according to a specific set of drawing rules. Bettors have no control over the draw. At the conclusion of the deal, the highest-ranked hand (banker or player) wins the round.

- Bettors wager on either player, banker, or a tie. A win on player or banker pays 1:1; a tie is a push for these bets and no money changes hands. A winning wager on tie usually pays 8:1.

- Typically, the casino charges a 5 percent vig on banker bets that win. Some casinos charge only 4 percent. Others charge no vig but pay only 1:2 when the bank wins with a six.

- Full-scale baccarat typically is played on a special-size table in a high-limit section. There is also a mini version of baccarat played on a standard-size casino table on the main casino floor.

- Chemin de fer is a European version of baccarat in which bettors actually bank the game. The drawing rules for chemin de fer are slightly more flexible than the drawing rules for baccarat. Player has the option of standing or drawing to a five.

- The strategy for baccarat is simple. Never put money on tie; always bet banker or player. This strategy will give the house a slender edge of just above one percent.

CHAPTER 17

Other Table Games

 Imagine if you were a casino executive and you were surveying the tables at your casino. Blackjack can be beaten when a player counts cards. Poker has no house edge; it earns only a flat rake for the casino. Craps has an edge of less than one percent when a player uses optimal strategy. Roulette's edge can be pushed down 1.35 percent. Baccarat can be pushed down to 1.04 percent.

Of course, *any* casino edge is profitable for the house, but the above numbers are paltry compared to the typical edge for most slots. Usually, slots hold between 5 to 12 percent of their action.

What can a casino executive do to remedy the low edge at the tables?

One option is to replace table games with slot machines. That trend has been happening for decades. Slots dominate the casino floor these days. But there is a limit to how far that trend can continue. Some players prefer tables, and they won't switch to slots under any circumstances.

Another strategy is to offer players free alcoholic drinks in the hopes that they will get tipsy and play poorly (see page 31 for more on avoiding alcohol when playing). Casino executives will never tell you that this is an actual policy, but practically speaking, it is an unspoken truth. Alcohol is expensive and casinos wouldn't give it away if it didn't produce positive results.

And finally, there is the tactic of offering card games with a house edge that cannot be pushed close to zero.

That's the philosophy behind the newest table games.

Keep in mind that "new" is a relative term. Most of the contests we cover in this chapter have been around for many years, but they're newborns when you compare them to the classic contests. Craps has been around for about 1,000 years. Blackjack and poker have roots that stretch back to the Renaissance. Roulette was invented in the eighteenth century, and baccarat was invented in the nineteenth century.

In fact, the reason why most classic games *are* so beatable is because they are very old. Originally, they were designed to be played in private or semi-public settings, such as private clubs (roulette is the only exception to this). In the old days, nobody had an advantage, or maybe the "bank" had a small advantage; this was an incentive for one player to fund the action. For example, blackjack used to have a rotating dealer, much like poker.

THE FACT IS...

Classic gambling games such as blackjack, poker, craps, and chemin de fer were developed originally with a "bank" or dealer that rotates around the table. This was ideal for private contests because it allowed everyone to be evenly matched. The first widely popular gambling game that was designed specifically with a house edge was roulette. Newer casino table games such as Caribbean Stud Poker have an edge comparable to roulette.

The worst casino bets, such as hardways in craps, or the tie bet in baccarat, are relatively recent inventions. They were added to the old games by casino entrepreneurs in the last century. But if you strip away the newfangled high-edge bets, the basic games underneath still reflect the old balance. Each has a low edge or no edge when a player uses optimal strategy.

And thus the newest table games were developed to "fix" these shortcomings (from the casino's standpoint).

Most new table games share these common elements:

- They're based on poker or other classic card games.

- They're easy to learn, but somewhat resistant to strategy.

- Generally, they have a house edge between 2.5 percent and about 5 percent. That is better for you than slots, but not as good as the classic games.

Overall, the newer games are fun to play. They can be an enjoyable alternative to the classics, and sometimes they deliver big wins. But if you're nursing a bankroll, these games can be expensive. Caveat ludio (let the player beware).

Caribbean Stud Poker

Like most of the newer table games, Caribbean Stud Poker is a trademarked product. It is licensed to casinos by a company called

Progressive Gaming. While the idea of licensing a table game may seem odd, think of it like a 3D slot game. Anyone can develop a contest based on poker, but specific rules combined with artwork and a particular presentation can be patented, trademarked, and otherwise sold as intellectual property.

In any case, Caribbean Stud is essentially a heads-up showdown version of poker with a progressive jackpot tacked on for some added excitement.

The dealer is your only opponent. She has specific rules to follow, so it's really just you against the odds. Unfortunately, they're stacked against you. But hey, you're paying for the convenience of not having to compete against a table full of players.

Regular poker can be vexing when you get a dream hand and the pot holds only a few paltry dollars. You bet, everyone folds, and your straight flush or whatever is nearly worthless. Or you pump a lot of money into the pot, and your dream hand gets beaten by an even better hand.

Caribbean Stud Poker solves that problem. It guarantees a fat pay-out when the perfect once-in-a-lifetime combination of cards comes your way. Of course, it may take a lifetime before you see that combination, but before we get to the bad news let's see how the game is played.

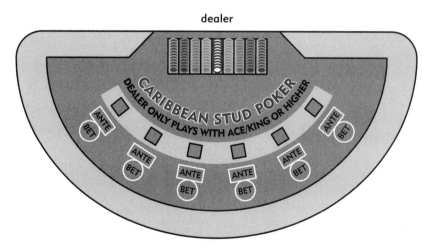

Rules for Holding and Folding

Caribbean Stud Poker is played at a standard-size card table. The hand begins with a player ante (a bet equal to at least the table minimum) and an optional $1 side bet on a progressive contest. We'll review the side bet in a later section. The dealer gives each player five cards face down and deals herself four cards face down and one face up.

Players look at their cards without revealing them to others at the table. Each person can either fold and lose the ante or call. A call requires an additional bet of twice the ante amount, so a $10 ante would require a $20 call for a total bet of $30. The call bet really functions more like a poker raise as you'll see. When the folding and calling is completed, the dealer reveals her cards. If her hand contains anything less than one pair and it does not contain at least an ace *and* king then she does not **qualify**; the dealer folds. The ante bets are paid 1:1 and the call bets are returned (as raises would be in a regular game of poker).

If the dealer qualifies, she turns over all the hands that have called and compares them to her hand. Winners are determined by standard poker-hand rankings (see the section in Chapter 12 that explains how poker hands are ranked). If the dealer's hand beats the player's hand, the ante and call bets are collected. Players who beat the dealer are paid 1:1 for their ante bets and a graduated amount for the call portion of the wager. The scale is listed in the table below. Note that some casinos have slightly different pay schedules.

Caribbean Stud Poker Payouts

Ante Wager Payout		
All Hands	1:1	
Hand	Call Wager Payout	$1 Progressive Bet Payout
Royal flush	100:1	100% of Jackpot
Straight flush	50:1	10% of Jackpot
Four of a kind	20:1	$100
Full house	7:1	$75
Flush	5:1	$50
Straight	4:1	$0
Three of a kind	3:1	$0
Two pair	2:1	$0
Pair or less	1:1	$0

The ante is always paid 1:1. For example, if the hand is a straight and the ante bet is $10, the payoff would be $80 for the $20 call bet and $10 for the ante, a total of $90. Some casinos pay more for a straight, flush, full house, or four of a kind.

Caribbean Stud Poker also offers the chance to win a progressive jackpot for a $1 side bet. The jackpot amount is displayed on a meter mounted over the table. Drop a coin in the slot, draw a flush or better, and you'll win the jackpot or a bonus. The progressive bet is valid even if the dealer does not qualify. It's valid even if the dealer beats your hand. In spite of this, the progressive bet is usually a bad bet. I'll tell you why in the next section.

Tip

If you decide to make the $1 progressive bet when playing Caribbean Stud Poker, be sure the light on the slot is illuminated after you insert the coin. This indicates that the system has received your wager. If there is no light, you cannot win the jackpot.

Caribbean Stud Poker: Strategies for Winning

You and the dealer have an exactly equal probability of receiving any particular hand. And yet the dealer has an advantage. How can this be?

It's simple. The dealer acts last. Just as in regular poker, the player who is last to act has an advantage. In the case of Caribbean Stud Poker, the casino wins if it beats you, but it also wins if you fold and the dealer fails to qualify. Considering this imbalance, you might be tempted to call every hand, but that would be an expensive mistake. To see why, check out the table below. It shows the various probabilities of receiving a particular hand.

Frequency of Caribbean Stud Poker Hands

Hand	Percent Probability
Royal flush	0.00015%
Straight flush	0.0014%
Four of a kind	0.02%
Full house	0.14%
Flush	0.20%
Straight	0.39%
Three of a kind	2.11%
Two pair	4.75%
One pair	42.26%
A/K as per strategy	2.37%
Total Calls as per Optimal Strategy	**52.23%**
Everything Else	**47.77%**

One look at the numbers tells you that calling with anything less than **AK** is a bad idea. The dealer will beat you for three bets more than half the time. But you win only 1:1 when you call with an inferior hand and the dealer fails to qualify. That's not a good ratio. The house edge on an "always-call" strategy is a painful 16.6 percent.

A better strategy is to call only with a pair or better. This lowers the house edge to 5.5 percent.

If you want to squeeze the house even further and play a few more hands, then you should raise on any hand of **AKJ83** or better and any **AK** hand in which one of your cards matches the dealer's exposed card. That lowers the house edge to about 5.3 percent.

Unfortunately, it doesn't get much better than this. Perfect optimal strategy covers about 900 different **AK** decisions and lowers the house edge by only another 0.1 percent. Clearly, it's not worth the trouble.

So the best you can get is a house edge of about 5.3 percent. That's a bit higher than double-zero roulette, and about five to ten times higher than blackjack.

The Progressive Bet

Caribbean Stud Poker's $1 progressive bet is not a very good wager. First, it's highly volatile. If the pay schedule begins with a flush, you will win 0.37 percent of your bets, or about one in 273 times. And of course, the vast majority of those wins will be either a flush or full house. So you will lose a buck 272 times, and you will win $50 or $75 once. Not a good deal.

On the other hand, you always have one chance in 649,740 of smacking a royal flush and winning the amount on the meter. That ain't a bad payday if the meter is in the six figures.

The actual house edge (or player edge) on the progressive bet constantly changes as the amount on the meter increases; a portion of every bet feeds the jackpot. The break-even point for the pay table listed on page 276 is $263,205. In other words, the player has a mathematic edge when the meter is *above* this amount; the total payout exceeds the total expected risk over time. When that happens, the progressive bet is (at least technically) a profitable wager.

Some casinos offer bigger payments at the lower end, and this lowers the break-even point. For example, $50 for a flush, $100 for a full house, and $500 for a quad pushes the break-even point down to $218,047. And $100 for a flush, $150 for a full house, and $500 for a quad lowers the break-even point to $159,810.

Remember that this calculation assumes one person is wagering every dollar. But in fact, thousands of people are wagering, and each bet is bucking odds of 1 in 649,740 for the big jackpot. If you play one hand per minute for ten hours a day every day of every year, you can expect to see a royal flush in about three years. And when that happens, who knows what amount will be on the meter? Someone may have won the jackpot ten minutes earlier, so the meter may be only $10,000. Overall, the side bet usually has an edge in the neighborhood of about 30 percent.

Nevertheless, it's a bit of fun for a buck. If you play for a couple of hours, you'll probably blow an extra $80 or so on the side bet. If that's okay with you, then make the progressive bet.

Let It Ride

If you spend time around card tables in any casino you'll eventually see a Shuffle Master. It's a handy machine that shuffles cards (actually it's a whole line of machines). A few years ago the company that makes the machines introduced Let It Ride, a table game that (not surprisingly) uses a Shuffle Master. The contest is based on poker and plays like an ersatz hand of Texas hold 'em.

Tip

You are sixteen times more likely to draw to a royal flush (as in video poker) than be dealt one without a draw. The probability of drawing to full house in video poker is about 1 in 87. The chances of receiving a full house in Caribbean Stud Poker are about 1 in 694. Think about that before you bet the extra dollar in Caribbean Stud Poker. It's a long shot bet.

Let It Ride is popular because it gives people an opportunity to take back a portion of their wager if the hand develops unfavorably. What a concept! Unfortunately, this feature doesn't quite erase the house edge.

How to "Let It Ride"

The object of Let It Ride is to use three personal cards and two community cards to build a poker hand that includes a pair of **10**s or better. There is no opponent. The game is played at a standard-size card table like the one below.

Each player's section of the layout has three circles labeled 1, 2, and $. A bet equal to the table minimum must be placed in each circle, so if the table minimum is $10 the total bet will be at least $30. A player can withdraw two of the bets during the course of the hand. Here is how it works.

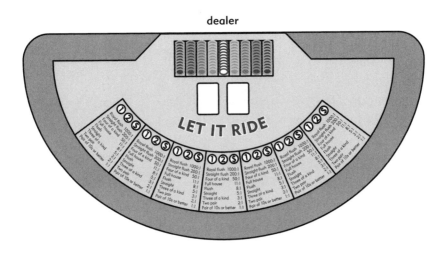

dealer

The Shuffle Master does its thing and the dealer delivers three cards face down to each player and two cards face down in the center of the table. Players should wait until cards are placed directly in front of them before reaching out to review the prospects. Remember, the object of the game is to get a poker hand with a pair of **10**s or better.

Let's say we have player named Omar. His first three cards are two jacks and a king.

Omar's hand is already a winner, and it may improve as the community cards are revealed.

Bonnie is sitting next to Omar. Her first two cards are an unsuited **10**, **6**, and **6**.

Bonnie has nothing.

Tom is sitting next to Bonnie, and he has a pair of **2**s, and a **4**. He also has nothing.

Everyone has a moment to review cards, and then the dealer offers everyone a chance to withdraw the bet in circle 1 or to "let it ride." Obviously, Omar should let his bet ride. He does this by slipping the edge of his cards slightly under the chips in the first circle or simply saying, "Let it ride." Bonnie (unless she is an optimist) should signal the dealer to return her bet. She does this by scratching the edge of her cards on the table in a motion towards herself; it's similar to calling for a hit in blackjack. A verbal direction is also fine: "Push it back." The dealer will push chips toward players who request them. For security reasons the dealer should do the pushing. Don't do it yourself.

Tom also scratches the felt, and the dealer returns his first bet.

Everyone else at the table makes a decision about their first bet, then the dealer reveals the first community card.

It's a **10**. The dealer gives everyone an option to withdraw the second bet. Omar is winning with a pair of jacks. He says, "Let it ride." Bonnie has a pair of **10**s. She tucks her cards under the second bet. She's riding the second bet to the end. Tom still has nothing, so he scratches the felt, and the dealer returns his bet.

The other players make their choices, and the dealer reveals the last card.

It's an ace. Tom doesn't have a pair of **10**s or better, so he loses one base bet (he pulled back two others). Omar wins and he is paid for three bets. Bonnie pulled back one bet, so she is paid for two. Payments are made on a graduated scale listed in the table below.

Let It Ride Payouts

Hand	Payout
Royal flush	1000:1
Straight flush	200:1
Four of a kind	50:1
Full house	11:1
Flush	8:1
Straight	5:1
Three of a kind	3:1
Two pair	2:1
Pair of 10s or better	1:1

The payout is based on the total amount remaining in all three circles when the last card is revealed.

Let It Ride: Strategies for Winning

The table on page 283 shows the probability of drawing **10**s or better. Alas, 76 percent of Let It Ride hands are losers. About 16 percent pay 1:1, and only 8 percent pay 2:1 or more. These horrible percentages are somewhat improved by the fact that the first three or four cards occasionally show a clear winner; this allows players to bet the maximum. But Let It Ride is somewhat like its poker cousin hold 'em. Winning requires patience. The best strategy is to wait and lose and lose and lose and lose and lose some

THE FACT IS...

Let It Ride tables have a maximum payout limit. So be sure you're not betting more than the table can pay if you win the top prize. For example, a $75,000 limit would mean that $25 would be the maximum you should bet per circle on Let It Ride. A $50,000 limit lowers that amount to about $15.

more until the right hand comes along. Then you bet the max, and hopefully smack a big payoff.

Frequency Of Let It Ride Poker Hands

Hand	Number of Occurrences	Percent Probability
Royal flush	4	0.0002%
Straight flush	36	0.0014%
Four of a kind	624	0.02%
Full house	3,744	0.14%
Flush	5,108	0.20%
Straight	10,200	0.39%
Three of a kind	54,912	2.11%
Two pair	123,552	4.75%
Pair of 10s or better	422,400	16.25%
Pair of 9s or worse	675,840	26.00%
Everything else	1,302,540	50.12%
Total	2,598,960	

Players will lose 76 percent of Let It Ride hands. About 16 percent of the hands will pay 1:1. About 8 percent of the hands will pay 2:1 or better.

What is the right hand? The first bet should ride in the following situations:

● A pair of 10s or better

● Three consecutive cards to an open-ended straight flush

● Three almost consecutive cards to a straight flush with at least two high cards (Example: 8♥ 10♥ J♥ or 9♠ J♠ Q♠)

If you don't have one of the above hands, pull back the first bet. The strategy for the second bet is as follows:

● A pair of 10s or better

● Four cards to a flush (including straight flush and royal flush)

● Four cards to an outside straight

If you don't have one of the above hands, pull back the second bet.

Tip

Let's say your first three cards in Let It Ride are K♦, 4♣, and 2♥. What is the probability that the dealer will pair your king? It's 12 percent or about one in eight. Those are poor odds considering the payoff will be 1:1. If you have less than a pair and no draw to a straight flush, you should withdraw your first bet.

This strategy will push the casino's edge down to about 3.5 percent. But remember that a big part of the total payback is in the higher hands, and about three out of four hands are losers. Let It Ride is extremely volatile (tends to cause big swings in a bankroll), and few people will play the more than half-million hands normally required to see a royal flush.

By the way, some Let It Ride tables offer an additional $1 side bet for a bonus payout. Payoffs usually start at 6:1 for two pair, and the top prize for a royal flush typically is $20,000. It's tempting, but the side bet is not a good wager. The house edge varies (depending on the pay table) from about 14 percent to nearly 37 percent. Generally, you're better off putting your money into a Megabucks machine.

Three Card Poker

Three Card Poker is another branded product from Shuffle Master. It's a heads-up poker contest somewhat like Caribbean Stud Poker, but it uses three-card hands.

Like the other games covered in this chapter, Three Card Poker is played at a standard-size card table. The hand begins with a player ante (a bet equal to at least the table minimum) and an optional side bet called **Pair Plus**. We'll review the side bet in a later section.

The dealer gives each player three cards face down and deals herself three cards face down.

Players look at their cards without revealing them to others at the table. Each person can either fold and lose the ante or play. A play requires an additional bet equal to the size of the ante, so a $10 ante would require an additional $10 bet for a total bet of $20. When the folding and betting is completed, the dealer reveals her cards. If her hand contains anything less than a queen high she does not qualify; the dealer folds. The ante bets are paid 1:1 and the play bets are returned.

If the dealer qualifies, she turns over all the hands that have played and compares them to her hand. If the dealer's hand beats the player's hand, the ante and play bets are collected. Winners are determined by the rankings in the adjacent table (note that a straight beats a flush, and three of a kind beats a straight).

Players who beat the dealer are paid 1:1 for their play bets and a graduated amount for the ante portion of the wager (which is the opposite of the way it is done in Caribbean Stud Poker). The scale is listed in the table below. Note that some casinos have slightly different pay schedules.

Three Card Poker Hand Ranks

Hand	Percent Probability
Straight flush	0.22%
Three of a kind	0.24%
Straight	3.26%
Flush	4.95%
Pair	16.94%
Ace, king, or queen high	43.98%
Jack high or lower	30.41%
Dealer must have a queen-high or better to qualify.	

Three Card Poker Payouts

	Play Wager Payout	
All Hands	1:1	
	Ante Wager Payout	
All Hands	1:1	
Hand	Ante Wager Bonus	Pair Plus
Straight flush	5:1	40:1
Three of a kind	4:1	30:1
Straight	1:1	5:1
Flush	–	4:1
Pair	–	1:1

The play bet is always paid 1:1. For example, if the hand is a straight and the ante bet is $10, the payoff would be $10 for the play bet, $10 for the ante, $10 for the ante bonus, and $60 for the pair plus, a total of $100. Some casinos pay less for a flush, straight, three of a kind, or straight flush.

Pair Plus

Pair Plus is a separate and optional wager. Unlike the base contest, you don't have to beat the dealer. You simply have to get a hand of a pair or better. Payouts are listed in the table above. Note that some casinos have different pay schedules.

There is not much to this bet. You make it. You get your cards, and you either win or lose.

You can bet Pair Plus by itself without betting on the base contest. And you can wager any amount within the table limits. The ante bet and the Pair Plus bet do not have to be the same size.

Three Card Poker: Strategies for Winning

As with Caribbean Stud Poker, in Three Card Poker you and the dealer have an exactly equal probability of receiving any particular hand. The dealer has an advantage because she acts last.

The optimal strategy is simple. Play any hand that is **Q64** or better. This lowers the house edge to 3.4 percent. Some casinos pay only 3:1 on the ante bonus for a straight flush and 2:1 for three of a kind. This bumps up the house edge to 4.3 percent, but it doesn't change the strategy.

The Pair Plus pay table on page 285 gives the casino an edge of 5.6 percent. Some casinos pay 6:1 for a Pair Plus straight, and that lowers the house edge to 2.3 percent. But beware of casinos that pay 6:1 for the straight, and then lower the payment on the flush to 3:1. Tricky, huh? That gives the house a 7.3 percent advantage.

Also note that Pair Plus is a volatile game. You'll only win about one in four hands, and only about one in eleven hands pays better than 1:1. So you probably will lose a lot before you win a lot with pair plus.

The base game is less volatile. You'll fold and lose one bet about 30 percent of the time, and you'll have about a 50/50 chance of winning two bets by risking two bets the rest of the time. You'll win an ante bonus approximately once in every twenty-seven hands, and that bonus will be 4:1 or 5:1 about once in every 221 hands.

Should you play Three Card Poker? Sure. Why not? It can be fun. Can you find a casino game that is easier to beat? Absolutely.

THE FACT IS...

You should always check the pay schedule of a game before you sit down to play. Some payouts are standard, such as 1:1 for a winning pair in Three Card Poker, but sometimes casinos jigger pay tables in the middle payouts or on the bonuses. This gives the casino a bigger edge and costs you money in the long run.

Pai Gow Poker

Pai gow (pronounced "pie gow") is an Asian dominos game. A version of the contest that uses cards instead of dominos has become quite popular in the West and is known as pai gow poker (unlike the other contests covered in this chapter, pai gow poker is not a branded product).

The game has many charms, two of which are that it moves quite slowly and often ends in a push (tie). Smaller bankrolls can last quite a bit longer than they would with a game like Caribbean Stud Poker or Let It Ride. Also, pai gow poker has no hidden house edge. Casinos and card rooms charge a 5 percent vig (commission) on winnings or sometimes a flat per-hand fee for each player.

Rules for Dealing and Setting Hands

Pai gow poker uses a standard deck of cards and one joker. Two to seven people can play simultaneously. The table layout is shown in the illustration below. The object of the game is to beat the banker. Or if you're the banker, the object is to beat the players at the table. We'll cover special rules for banking in a later section.

Each player receives seven cards and must arrange those seven cards into two poker hands. Five cards are in a **back hand**; two cards are in a **front hand**. Both player's hands must beat the banker's hands (front must beat front, back must beat back) for a win. If one hand wins and the other loses then it's a tie. Hands with equal rank are called **copies**; the banker wins all copies.

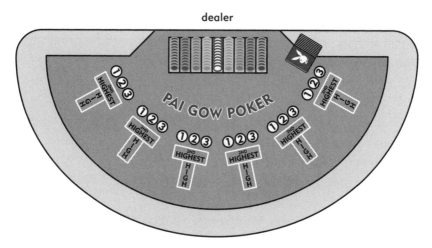

Pai gow poker table layout. The two-card hand is called the front hand because it is placed closer to the center of the layout.

Tip

Standard poker rankings are used, but there are a few exceptions. **A-2-3-4-5** is the second-highest straight. The joker can be used as an ace, or to complete a flush or a straight. **A-A-A-A-A** (four aces and a joker) beats a royal flush.

There are no straights or flushes in the two-card hand. The highest rank is **A-A**, and the lowest rank is **3-2**.

The game begins with bets and a shuffle. The dealer makes seven stacks of seven cards each. Then the banker shakes a device called a teacup or dice cup that holds three dice (loudly slamming the dice cup on the table is a time-honored tradition). Some casinos use an RNG. Whatever the method, the resulting number determines who gets which stack first at the table. As you know, from a probability point of view it doesn't matter who gets which stack. From a tradition point of view it's critical. The rules for stack distribution are numbingly arcane. The dealer will handle it.

Players look at their cards first and set their hands. The rule is that the five-card back hand must have a higher value than the two-card front hand.

If the two-card hand is set higher in value than the five-card hand, both are foul and automatically lose. We'll cover how hands should be set in the next section.

After setting their cards, players lay them face down in the appropriate spaces. The dealer turns the banker's cards over and arranges them into two hands following a strategy called the **house way**. When she's finished, the players' cards are revealed, and the dealer compares them to the banker's cards. Winning combinations are paid 1:1 (minus a 5 percent vig). Losing bets are collected and the hand is over.

Pai Gow Poker: Strategies for Winning

Pai gow poker odds are nearly even. The bank has a slight edge because it wins copies (two hands of identical rank). The downside to banking is the requirement of risking up to six times a normal bet on one hand. Nevertheless, players have a mathematic advantage when they frequently bank. Casinos discourage people from hogging the bank with rules that require the bank to rotate among the players. If nobody wants to bank (which is often the case), the house does the job.

Tip

Does pai gow poker strategy make your eyes cross? No sweat. You can ask the dealer to set your hand. She will follow rules called the "house way" which are similar to the strategies printed here. Getting help from the dealer is a charming custom that distinguishes pai gow poker from other table games where help from a dealer is prohibited.

Another thing that affects the edge is the strategy for setting hands. A pai gow poker player can win significantly more by using optimal hand selection. It's not as easy as it seems. For example, four jacks shouldn't necessarily be loaded in the back hand. The other cards determine if the quad should be split. Two jacks might go in the front hand and the other two might be combined with the remaining cards in the back hand. Remember, both hands must win for the player to win the bet.

As you can see, pai gow poker strategy can become quite complex. The table on page 290 contains a near-optimal strategy. To make it easy to learn, some of the more arcane nuances have been dropped (such as not splitting a full house if the lower pair are deuces and there is an ace and king in the hand).

Here are a few examples of how the strategy works.

A♦ 9♦ 7♥ T♣ 5♣ 9♠ 6♠	would be	A♦ T♣ / 9♦ 9♠ 7♥ 6♠ 5♣
2♠ 4♥ J♠ K♣ J♥ 7♣ J♣	would be	K♣ 7♣ / J♣ J♥ J♠ 4♥ 2♠
A♣ A♠ Q♦ Q♥ 6♣ 2♦ 7♥	would be	Q♦ Q♥ / A♠ A♠ 7♥ 6♣ 2♦
K♠ T♠ T♥ 4♠ 9♠ A♥ J♠	would be	A♥ T♥ / K♠ J♠ T♠ 9♠ 4♠
Q♥ J♦ T♦ 9♥ 8♣ 8♦ Q♣	would be	8♣ 8♦ / Q♥ Q♣ J♦ T♦ 9♥
5♠ 5♣ 5♦ K♣ K♥ A♦ 6♦	would be	K♣ K♥ / 5♠ 5♣ 5♦ A♦ 6♦
A♠ A♣ 4♠ 4♦ 7♥ 7♣ Q♦	would be	A♠ A♣ / 7♥ 7♣ 4♠ 4♦ Q♦

The casino's commission on a winning pai gow hand is 5 percent, and the probability of winning a non-tied decision hovers near 50 percent (depending on how often you bank). So the house edge on pai gow poker is approximately 2.5 percent.

Pai Gow Poker Strategy

Pairs	Back Hand (Five Cards)	Front Hand (Two Cards)
No pair (or other higher combination)	Highest card	Second and third highest card
One pair	Pair	Two highest singleton cards
Two pair no ace singleton	High pair	Low pair
Two pair with an ace singleton	Both pairs	Ace and next highest card
Three pair	Second and third highest pair	Highest pair
Three of a Kind		
Aces	Two aces	One ace and the next highest card
Kings through deuces	Three of a kind	Two highest singleton cards
Two sets of three	Lower three	Two from the higher set
Straights and Flushes (Including Straight/Royal Flushes)		
With no pair	Lowest straight/flush to free up the highest ranked cards	Two highest cards
With one pair	Lowest straight/flush to free up the highest ranked cards	Pair if possible, if not then two highest cards
With two pair	Follow the two pair rule	Follow the two pair rule
With three of a kind	Straight or flush	Pair
Full House		
Without an extra pair	Three of a kind	Pair
With an extra pair	Full house	Highest Pair
Four of a Kind		
With a pair or trips	Four of a kind	Pair
Aces, no pair or trips	Two aces	Two aces
King through 7 without a pair, trips, or ace singleton	Two of the four	Two of the four
King through 7 without an extra pair or trips, with an ace singleton	Four of a kind	Ace and next highest card
6, 5, 4, 3, or 2 with or without a pair	Four of a kind	Two highest cards or pair
Five aces (one joker) no pair of kings	Three aces	Two aces
Five aces (one joker) and a pair of kings	Five aces	Pair of kings

Such a Nice Game!

The nice thing about pai gow poker is that it has extremely low volatility. Hands tie about 42 percent of the time, and it takes a while to complete a hand. Pai gow poker is not the sort of game where you can quickly toast $1,000 in five minutes (unless you're betting $500 or $1,000 per hand).

When you do lose, it won't be multiple bets per hand. And pai gow poker players tend to win more decisions than players betting at Caribbean Stud Poker, Let It Ride, and Three Card Poker.

In fact, a typical player's win frequency in pai gow poker (not including ties) is higher than many classic casino game. That includes blackjack, many craps bets, and roulette.

Of course, win frequency isn't everything, but the point here is that low volatility makes pai gow poker an easier ride than many table games.

THE FACT IS...

Pai gow poker is as much a ritual as it is a game. Dedicated players will sometimes bet the minimum on empty seats so that the cards will be distributed as they would be at a full table. This ensures that the order predetermined by fate and the universe is not disturbed.

Even More Games

Casinos offer a cornucopia of other table games begging for your dollars. Here are a few:

War: Yes, the contest you played as a kid is now available in a casino. Tommy didn't take your money as frequently as the casino will. There is no strategy to war, but there is a house edge. Depending on the rules, it's usually about 3 percent. Stay away from the tie bet.

Four Card Poker: It is like Three Card Poker except you get five cards and the dealer gets six cards. Then each of you makes the best four-card hand. Hmmmm… Six cards versus five cards. I won't go into great detail about this one except to say you should fold a pair of deuces and below. Raise one bet on a pair of **3**s through **9**s. Raise the max with a pair of **10**s or higher. This will push the casino's edge down to about 4 percent.

Red Dog: Yet another game from your childhood (you may know it as acey-deucey). The strategy is simple. Raise on a spread of seven or more.

Sic Bo: It's an Asian dice game. Bet only "small" or "big." Stay away from all the other bets.

Keep in mind what I mentioned at the beginning of the chapter. These games can be fun to play, but they are resistant to strategy. You can push down the house edge just so far, usually to a range between 2.5 percent and 5 percent, and no farther.

That is better than most slot games, but it's not better than video poker, blackjack, craps, baccarat, traditional poker, and single-zero roulette.

Essentially

- The newest casino table games are designed to be easy to learn and resistant to strategy. Generally, they have a house edge between 2.5 percent and about 5 percent. That is better than slots, but not as good as classic games such as blackjack.

- Caribbean Stud Poker is essentially a heads-up showdown version of no-draw poker with a progressive jackpot tacked on for some added excitement. The dealer is your only opponent.

- The basic strategy for Caribbean Stud Poker is to call with a pair or better, and fold everything else. This lowers the house edge to about 5.5 percent. A more aggressive strategy is to call with some combinations of AK or better.

- Generally, Caribbean Stud Poker's $1 progressive bet is not a good wager. You should avoid it unless you're feeling lucky.

- The object of Let It Ride is to use three personal cards and two community cards to build a poker hand that includes a pair of 10s or better. A player can withdraw two of three bets during the course of a hand.

- The house edge on Let It Ride is about 3.5 percent when a player uses optimal strategy. But a lot of the game's payback is in the royal flush. On average, three out of four Let It Ride hands are losers.

- Three Card Poker is a head-up poker contest somewhat like Caribbean Stud Poker, but it uses three-card hands.

- The optimal strategy for the base game in Three Card Poker is to call with Q64 and above. This lowers the house edge to 3.4 percent.

- Typically, the Pair Plus bet in Three Card Poker gives the casino an edge of 5.6 percent. There is no strategy for playing this bet.

- In pai gow poker, players compete with a banker to simultaneously win two poker hands. A player's five-card back hand must always outrank the two-card front hand. The banker wins all copies.

- Pai gow poker winners are charged a 5 percent vig (commission) on their wins. This works out to a house edge of approximately 2.5 percent. Players who frequently bank the game can lower this edge substantially.

PART FOUR

The Keno Lounge and the Sports Book

CHAPTER 18

Keno, Bingo, and Other Lottery Games

 Twenty years ago, keno and bingo were minor blips on the casino scene. They were venerable and fading. Casinos offered the games to please a few die-hard customers.

But these days, bingo is at the center of a slot revolution known as **Class II Machines,** and keno has found new life on multi-game platforms.

Meanwhile, state lotteries are still rolling along, servicing more customers than the entire casino industry (though lotteries earn less money than casinos).

Obviously, lottery-style games are a big part of gambling. So how do they work? And more importantly, how do we beat them?

Let's begin with…

Keno

Like all lottery games, keno is about choosing numbers. The cool thing about keno, compared to a typical state lottery, is that you can choose more than five or six numbers. And you don't have to wait three days to play the game. If you want, you can play it every five seconds. Another great thing about keno, compared to state lotteries, is the payback. Most state lotteries have an overall payback of about 50 percent to 60 percent. In contrast, keno's *worst* payback is usually 70 percent, and on many machines it's about 90 percent. Of course, keno's payback is awful compared to video poker or blackjack. But hey, it's better than the lotto game down at the convenience store.

There are two types of keno: live keno and video keno.

Video Keno

Video keno is offered usually on a multi-game slot platform, but there are some stand-alone keno machines.

The contest is simple. A screen shows you a field of numbers labeled one through eighty. You can select up to twenty numbers (some games allow only ten or fifteen selections). Then the machine randomly selects twenty numbers from the field of eighty. If the player's numbers **catch** (player's selections match the machine's selections), the player wins. The match doesn't have to be exact, but a closer match wins more.

Bets are paid in direct proportion to the amount wagered. Thus a $2 bet wins twice as much as a $1 bet, and so forth.

The chart below shows a portion of a typical keno pay table.

THE FACT IS...

Keno, bingo, and modern lotteries are all derived from lotto, a lottery game developed in Italy in the sixteenth century. The word *keno* comes from the Italian word *quinto*, which means one-fifth. There were five winning numbers in the first Italian lottery.

I've included payouts for one, four, five, six, seven, eight, nine, and ten numbers. A full pay table would include all the winning possibilities up to the casino limit (sometimes fifteen or twenty catches). But it would never include the information in the shaded area. Those are the true odds of catching the numbers.

A Typical Keno Pay Table

	1 credit pays	Odds of Catching (1 in N)	Frequency	Return
Mark 1				
Catch 0	0	1.3	75.0%	0.0%
Catch 1	3	4	25.0%	75.0%
			Total Payback	75.0%
Mark 4				
Catch 0–1	0	1.4	74.1%	0.0%
Catch 2	1	5	21.3%	21.3%
Catch 3	3	23	4.3%	12.9%
Catch 4	125	326	0.3%	38.3%
			Total Payback	72.5%
Mark 5				
Catch 0–2	0	1.1	90.3%	0.0%
Catch 3	1	12	8.4%	8.4%
Catch 4	15	83	1.2%	18.1%
Catch 5	700	1,551	0.06%	45.1%
			Total Payback	71.6%

	1 credit pays	Odds of Catching (1 in N)	Frequency	Return
Mark 6				
Catch 0–2	0	1.2	83.8%	0.0%
Catch 3	1	8	13.0%	13.0%
Catch 4	4	35	2.9%	11.4%
Catch 5	88	323	0.3%	27.2%
Catch 6	1,500	7,752	0.01%	19.3%
			Total Payback	70.9%
Mark 7				
Catch 0–3	0	1.1	93.8%	0.0%
Catch 4	1	19	5.2%	5.2%
Catch 5	20	116	0.9%	17.3%
Catch 6	400	1,366	0.07%	29.3%
Catch 7	8,000	40,979	0.002%	19.5%
			Total Payback	71.3%
Mark 8				
Catch 0–4	0	1.02	97.9%	0.0%
Catch 5	1	54	1.8%	7.3%
Catch 6	100	423	0.2%	23.7%
Catch 7	1,800	6,232	0.02%	28.9%
Catch 8	25,000	230,114	0.0004%	10.8%
			Total Payback	70.7%
Mark 9				
Catch 0–4	0	1.04	96.1%	0.0%
Catch 5	5	31	3.2%	16.3%
Catch 6	30	175	0.57%	17.2%
Catch 7	300	1690	0.06%	17.7%
Catch 8	5,000	30,682	0.003%	16.3%
Catch 9	50,000	1,380,688	0.00007%	3.6%
			Total Payback	71.1%
Mark 10				
Catch 0–4	0	1.07	93.5%	0.0%
Catch 5	1	19	5.1%	5.1%
Catch 6	20	87	1.1%	23.0%
Catch 7	150	621	0.2%	24.2%
Catch 8	1,000	7,384	0.01%	13.5%
Catch 9	8,000	163,381	0.0006%	4.9%
Catch 10	50,000	8,911,711	0.00001%	0.6%
			Total Payback	71.3%

These are typical payouts for a live keno game. Video keno usually pays back somewhat more, typically 75 percent to 92 percent of total action. Actual amounts vary from casino to casino. Percentages are rounded.

Clearly, keno is a highly volatile game. You win nothing or very little after most trials, but every so often the game dumps some big bucks on you. One dollar can win you $25,000, $100,000, or even more. The total payback is usually worse than a typical progressive slot game, but the bets can be so small that an hour or two of keno will hardly dent your bankroll if you use some good money management.

Tip

Sometimes keno turns $1 into thousands of dollars. But most times the contest swallows money with little or no payback. Typically, keno players win between 2 percent and 25 percent of trials (compare this to blackjack where players win about 48 percent of trials). Thus the best way to wager at keno is to stretch your bankroll waiting for the big wins. Play conservatively with small bets.

Live Keno

The live version of keno is played in an area known as a **keno lounge** (similar to a bingo hall, but smaller). It's a bucolic place set apart from the ringing bells, snapping cards, and clattering balls of the main casino. People unfamiliar with keno often find it by accident. They stumble in with hurting feet, tired of wandering the mega-maze of tables and machines. Pretty soon they're ordering free drinks and playing keno specials.

The lounge has tables and chairs or desks. In some casinos the desks look very much like the kind of desks you used in high school. Other places have plush couches and squishy-comfortable chairs. Either way, the seats are arranged in rows facing a large electronic board. The display shows eighty numbers, and it highlights numbers that have been selected.

Some casinos still use an old-fashioned keno machine that blows numbered Ping-Pong balls randomly into a tube, but many keno lounges use an RNG machine to determine the numbers.

Below the display board is an area where wagers are made, winnings are claimed, and the game is conducted.

Players write their selections on slips of paper called **keno tickets**. Forms like the one on page 301 are everywhere in the lounge. You'll also find a glossy brochure with the various payouts. Read the brochure and decide how many numbers you want to play. The basic bet is a **straight ticket** (one set of numbers). Let's say you want seven numbers. The minimum bet on a straight ticket is usually $1.

Use a crayon (provided by the casino) to mark an × over each of the seven numbers. Write the amount wagered, the number of games, and the number of spots in the designated spaces above or to the right of the grid. Then take the ticket to the desk. A **keno writer** will take your money, process the ticket, and return a printed copy.

Check to make sure that the printed ticket matches the one you marked. If a mistake is not corrected before the game begins, the printed ticket stands as the wager.

Straight Keno Ticket

This is a straight keno ticket written for one game. Seven numbers have been marked, and the wager is $1.

If everything checks out, just grab a seat, order a drink, and relax. A new keno game begins every few minutes. The drawing takes approximately thirty seconds.

It's similar to a bingo-hall drawing. The keno writer calls out the numbers as they are selected.

Check your ticket after the numbers are displayed on the big board. If you have a winner, then cash it in. And don't dawdle. Once upon a time, all casinos required that keno tickets had to be redeemed before the next game or they would be invalid. Usually, this is *not* the case today. Nevertheless, all tickets expire after a certain period of time, and you might be in that one casino that still has a next-game cutoff. So it pays to know the time limit.

Also note that live keno and the video version work the same way as slot games in that they keep your original bet. So a $1 win on a $1 ticket is actually a push. And if you bet $1 on a one-spot ticket, you'll win $3 but net only $2.

Betting the Easy Way

Here's why live keno is so cool. Let's say that you want to bet two different sets of numbers in one game, perhaps six numbers and then

Combination Ticket

The line separates two simultaneous bets on one keno game.

four numbers. Do you have to write two separate tickets? Nope. You can put it all on one **combination ticket** (see the example at left). The line separates two straight bets. Try doing *that* on a video keno machine!

And it gets better. Let's say you bet the combination ticket and three numbers catch on one side while two numbers catch on the other side. Nice, but wouldn't it be cool if you could also get credit for winning five catches out of ten?

You can do this in live keno by writing a **way ticket.**

The illustration below shows how it's done. In this case, four sets of three numbers have been selected. The sets are circled and the notation on the right indicates how many bets have been placed. The top figure above each slash is the number of bets; the bottom figure is the number of spots. Thus three spots bet four ways is 4/3. Six spots bet

Way Ticket

This is a way ticket for one game. Twelve spots have been marked in four groups of three. Fifteen bets have been placed. The total amount wagered is $15.

six ways is 6/6. Nine spots bet four ways is 4/9, and twelve spots bet one way is 1/12. It's one ticket with fifteen bets (6 + 4 + 4 + 1) for $15 total. Fifteen straight tickets could be written for the same wagers, but a way ticket saves time and helps you efficiently cover every number combination.

This particular ticket pays for as few as two spots, depending on which numbers are drawn. A straight ticket with twelve numbers wouldn't pay for anything less than six spots.

Cool, huh?

Now look at the ticket on the next page. Eight spots are marked and they're separated into groups of two. The bets are 4/2, 6/4, 4/6, and 1/8. The total wager is $7.50, and the price for each bet is only $0.50. Casinos often allow the minimum wager per way to be less than what would be required for the same bet on a straight ticket. The more ways you bet, the lower the price for each way. Some tickets are only $0.10 per way. The keno brochure will tell you the minimum that you can bet per way on a ticket.

Of course, the payout on each winning combination is reduced proportionately when the base bet is reduced. If all eight numbers were to catch for this ticket, according to the pay table on pages 298–299, the top

THE FACT IS...

A way ticket is a good way to spend less per bet and simultaneously increase the overall chance of a win. But a way ticket doesn't change the odds, the payout ratio, or the house edge. The probability of winning a particular bet (one way) is always the same no matter how many ways you bet.

prize would be $12,500, not $25,000. The other fourteen wagers would win too, but those totals would be paid on the basis of $0.50 bets.

And remember that the straight ticket costs only $1. This particular way ticket costs $7.50.

On the other hand, if four numbers were to catch, the way ticket could pay up to $80.50, while the straight ticket would pay nothing.

Keno Specials

If a casino has a keno lounge, chances are it has keno specials. You can pick extra numbers, or specific numbers, for a fixed amount, and the payoff is made on a scale established just for that special. Patterns are popular specials. Page 304 shows some common examples; page 305 shows the corresponding pay tables.

Betting the edge is common. Another favorite combination is top and bottom.

Way Ticket

Eight spots have been marked on this way ticket. There are fifteen bets and the wager is $0.50 per way, or $7.50 total.

PLAYBOY CASINO

TOTAL PRICE **5.00**

PRICE PER GAME **5.00**

1	2	3	4	5	6	7	8	9	10
11	12	13	14	15	16	17	18	19	20
21	22	23	24	25	26	27	28	29	30
31	32	33	34	35	36	37	38	39	40

Keno Limit $100,000 Aggregate Players per Game

41	42	43	44	45	46	47	48	49	50
51	52	53	54	55	56	57	58	59	60
61	62	63	64	65	66	67	68	69	70
71	72	73	74	75	76	77	78	79	80

GAMES **1**

Ways/Spots Rate **Top/Bottom**

ACCT #

Special Keno Bets

These are common casino specials. The E in the center of the ticket indicates an edge bet. T/B means top and bottom. Both tickets cost $5.

Keno on the Go

The cool thing about live keno is that you don't have to be in the keno lounge to play the game. You can play it just about anywhere on the casino property—in the restaurants, at the pool, wherever. Casino employees (called **keno runners**) will take your tickets to the lounge, place your bets, and return with your winnings.

And if you want to skip the constant back-and-forth, you can simply write a **multi-game** or **multi-race ticket**. It is one ticket repeated for as many games as you choose. You can play dozens, even hundreds of games. Your keno numbers will be catching (or not) as you golf, dine with friends, play blackjack, or relax by the pool.

Tip

Do you have a question about how to write a particular ticket? Ask the keno writer for help. That's her job. She will show you how to mark the more complicated combinations, and she'll explain any shorthand that is unique to the casino.

Indeed, you can be asleep in your room and still be playing keno. Some people go directly to the keno lounge at the beginning of their casino visit, write a multi-game ticket, and don't return until hours or days later.

As I mentioned before, the rules for when you must redeem a ticket vary by property. Check before playing. Here is the strictest version of the rules. Follow them unless you read something different in the keno brochure.

- Redeem single-game tickets before the next game begins.

- Redeem multi-game tickets written for twenty games or fewer after the last game is called and before the next one begins (many properties extend this deadline to twenty-four hours).

- Redeem multi-game tickets written for more than twenty games up to one year after the last game is called.

Edge Bet and Top/Bottom Pay Tables

$5 Edge Catch		$5 Top and Bottom Catch		
		Top	Bottom	
0	25,000	0	20	250,000
1	1,500	1	19	50,000
2	300	2	18	3,000
3	30	3	17	1,000
4	10	4	16	200
5	3	5	15	40
6	1	6	14	10
7	1	7	13	3
8	1	8	12	1
9	1	9	11	1
10	1	10	10	1
11	3	11	9	1
12	10	12	8	1
13	50	13	7	3
14	200	14	6	10
15	1,000	15	5	40
16	5,000	16	4	200
17	25,000	17	3	1,000
18	60,000	18	2	3,000
19	100,000	19	1	50,000
20	250,000	20	0	250,000

These are sample pay tables for a keno edge bet and a top/bottom bet.

Keno Strategies

Frankly, there is no strategy for choosing keno numbers. They all have an equal probability of catching. You may see patterns develop as the games progress, but those patterns are in the past. There is no way to predict how the numbers will come in the future.

However, there is a strategy for choosing keno games and keno bets. For example, video keno generally pays back about 90 percent while live keno is much stingier, paying back about 70 percent. So if you prefer betting straight tickets, then video keno is the way to go.

Another thing to consider is the pay table. The odds for a particular catch can be in the millions, but keno payouts usually are not. All regular keno games have a limit. It may be $100,000, $250,000, or something else, but there is always an amount per game beyond which the casino will not pay.

Thus if you want to hit the top payout, it's a bad idea to bet more than eight spots on a straight ticket. The odds of catching eight of eight are 1 in 230,114. Nine spots increases the odds to more than 1 in 1.3 million, and ten spots bumps it to over 1 in 8.9 million. But the top prize *does not* increase accordingly. In some cases, payments are increased farther down the pay table. In other cases, if your base bet is too big, you simply bump into the game's payout limit. In other words, eight of eight wins you $100,000, and ten of ten wins you the same amount. Bummer!

The only exception to this is when the keno game has a large progressive jackpot. When that happens, there is no upper limit to the payout. So you can shoot for the moon. In fact, a keno progressive jackpot can become

Tip

One number grouped by itself on a way ticket is called a king. Writing a ticket with seven or eight kings makes it highly likely that the ticket will pay something (even if the total bet is not profitable). The probability of catching one, two, or three out of seven or eight is actually greater than the probability of catching zero.

Tip

If you're scratching your head about which numbers to pick, try keno's quick pick. The numbers are chosen randomly, so you have a slightly better chance of winning a large amount. Why? People tend to pick numbers from 1 to 31 (birthdays, anniversaries, and such). You're more likely to split a large jackpot if you bet only lower numbers. Quick pick usually will give you many numbers over 31.

(technically) a positive-expectation contest if the top prize goes high enough. Unfortunately, the odds of winning are still extremely long.

If you want to give yourself a shot at the top prize and also win with more frequency, a good strategy is to bet multiple ways. If the keno gods smile on you, you'll hit the big one, but you'll also win with other combinations that are hundreds and thousands of times more likely to appear.

Here are some other suggestions to stretch your money:

THE FACT IS...

It is customary to tip keno runners, especially when they return with wins. A tip of $1 or $2 is appropriate for wins between $10 and $40. Five percent is common for amounts up to $500. Use your judgment for wins above that.

- Don't bet more than $5 on a straight ticket.

- Keep the total cost for a single-game way ticket at $20 or less.

- Always bet the minimum per way.

- Don't bet more than $20 on a special ticket.

A Volatile Game

I mentioned this before, but it bears repeating. Keno is a highly volatile game. Occasionally, you will smack a big prize or break even, but it is more likely that you will lose some or all of the money that you bet.

So why should you play keno? Well, you shouldn't if you prefer only low-edge games. But keno actually can save you money depending on how you bet. For example, if you bet $10 per hand at blackjack and you hit an unlucky patch, it's pretty easy to lose $50 in about three minutes.

The same $50 easily can last an hour when you're playing live keno.

Now think about this. How much

THE FACT IS...

If you smack a big keno win, Uncle Sam shares in your good fortune. You must pay the tax man. The casino is required by law to file a form W-2G any time a player wins $1,500 or more ($1,200 for video keno). That means you need ID and a Social Security number to collect your winnings. Without the number, the casino is required to withhold at least 28 percent, and in some jurisdictions you get nothing without proper ID.

can you win risking $50 at blackjack? Compare that to keno. It's easy to see why some people consider keno to be a positive-expectation experience, even if it's not a positive-expectation game. Keno's house edge is enormous, but the actual cost of playing it can be minuscule.

Besides, there is something very relaxing about hangin' in the keno lounge.

State Lotteries

State lotteries are keno-style contests. But unlike keno, the selection is limited. For example, a player might be allowed exactly six choices from a range of numbers, and lottery officials randomly draw exactly six numbers from the same range. If the player's numbers catch (player's selection matches the lottery's selection), the player wins. The match doesn't have to be exact, but a closer match wins more.

The range of numbers and the exact methods of drawing vary from state to state. Lottery jackpots are usually progressive.

"I won! I won! All the years I waited for this. Years! I've been coming here for years. Never won. Never won once and now... I won! The money is mine! I have the money. The money is mine. I got it. For the first time I have the... Aaaargggg!"
(He dies of a heart attack.)

—Sid Caesar, as keno player Mr. Ellis in *National Lampoon's Vegas Vacation*

Most Americans have played the lottery (probably you, too), so I won't go into great detail about the mechanics of placing a bet or claiming a prize. The gaming procedures at 7-11 in California are pretty much the same at Piggly Wiggly in Florida, or Circle K in Texas. So let's just jump straight into the mathematic analysis.

What are the odds of winning the various prizes in a local state lottery? There are dozens of lotteries in the United States, so let's focus on two states with fairly typical games, California and New York. The adjacent tables show the odds and sample payouts for three contests offered in 2006.

California SuperLotto Plus

Catch	Odds 1:N	Sample Payout
5 of 5 and Mega	41,416,353	$11,000,000
5 of 5 no Mega	1,592,937	$21,778
4 of 5 and Mega	197,221	$1,814
4 of 5	7,585	$10
3 of 5 and Mega	4,810	$58
3 of 5	185	$1
2 of 5 and Mega	361	$1
1 of 5 and Mega	74	$2
0 of 5 and Mega	49	$1
Overall Odds of Winning	23	

Players choose five numbers from a field of forty-seven and one "mega" number from a field of twenty-seven.

California Fantasy Five—New York Take Five

Catch	Odds 1:N	Sample CA Payout
5 of 5	575,757	$52,868
4 of 5	3,387	$382
3 of 5	103	$16
2 of 5	10	Free Replay
Overall Odds of Winning	9	

California Fantasy Five and New York Take Five are two separate games, but the odds of winning are the same in both states. Players choose five numbers from a field of thirty-nine.

California Mega Millions and New York Mega Millions

Catch	Odds 1:N	Sample Payout
5 of 5 and Mega	175,711,536	$88,000,000
5 of 5 no Mega	3,904,701	$226,840
4 of 5 and Mega	689,065	$12,373
4 of 5	15,313	$152
3 of 5 and Mega	13,781	$159
3 of 5	306	$7
2 of 5 and Mega	844	$11
1 of 5 and Mega	141	$3
0 of 5 and Mega	75	$2
Overall Odds of Winning	40	

Mega Millions is a multi-state lottery. Players choose five numbers from a field of fifty-six and one "mega" number from a field of forty-six.

Note the odds for the top prizes. As a point of comparison, the probability of drawing a royal flush in 9/6 jacks-or-better video poker is 1 in 40,388. The probability of being dealt a "natural" royal flush without a draw is 1 in 649,740. Thus your chances of hitting the Mega Millions top prize are about the same as drawing 270 natural royal flushes. How many natural royal flushes have you seen in your life?

Tip

If you play the lottery, be sure to check your tickets soon after the draw. All lottery tickets have an expiration date. Winning tickets become invalid after that time. For example, in California the time limit is 180 days. The limit varies by state, but when the deadline passes, the money is gone.

And what about the "easy-to-hit" Fantasy Five? If you play it five days a week, every week, you can expect to win the top prize once in about 2,214 years. In other words, Julius Caesar had a reasonable chance of winning the top jackpot (if he somehow could have managed to survive his assassination and then lived an extra two millennia), but you likely will be long gone before you hit the big one in Fantasy Five.

Nevertheless, these lotteries are not bad bets because of long odds. They're bad bets (essentially sucker bets) because of the low payouts at the bottom of the scale.

Low Lottery Payouts are the Killer

Typically, almost half of every dollar collected by a state lottery goes to the state rather than back into prizes. That is *much* worse than any typical casino game, even keno. Combine that with a top-heavy prize structure, and you get a game that quickly bleeds you dry. For example, the probability of catching *anything* in Super Lotto is 1 in 23, and that prize usually pays only $1 or $2 (really $1 or a push since the game keeps your initial bet). The other twenty-two times you win nothing. Compare that to video poker or blackjack where you win or push nearly 1 in 2 times, regularly replenishing your bankroll.

It's simple arithmetic. A typical lottery doesn't give you enough payouts at the low end to keep you in the money so you can reach the big wins, and the big wins aren't even that big when you consider the overall risk. Frankly, compared to a lottery, you're better off playing anything in a casino. That includes Megabucks, keno, even the big wheel! The worst craps sucker bet has about a 30 percent higher overall payback than a typical state lottery. Yup. Sad, but true.

Essentially, there is only one reason to play the lottery; it's a cheap thrill. It's fun to buy a ticket and say, "Hey, I might be a gazillionaire tomorrow." Occasionally, this entertainment is worth a buck. And who knows? You might catch lightning in a bottle and hit the big one.

But if your goal is to turn $100 into $200, skip the lottery. Go play blackjack, poker, or video poker.

Bingo and Class II Machines

Bingo is a church-hall staple in communities across the United States. It is also the foundation upon which the *multi-billion dollar* Indian gaming industry has been built.

You haven't heard?

Yes, bingo is big in ways you may not realize. But first, let's learn a bit about the game in its purest form.

Classic Bingo

Bingo is a lottery-style game that uses a field of seventy-five numbers. Players compete with each other using bingo cards (which usually are not cards at all but rather slips of paper). Each card has twenty-four randomly-generated pre-selected numbers. The goal is to complete a particular pattern on a card. The simplest pattern is a single row or column (see the adjacent illustration). Other patterns include letters such as T or X, or the corners of the card.

A casino employee known as a **bingo caller** randomly selects numbers from the field of seventy-five. Players match the numbers (or not) as they are called, and the first player to complete the required pattern shouts "Bingo!"

B	I	N	G	O
7	26	35	51	73
14	23	44	55	63
6	19	FREE 14733	48	64
12	22	32	54	70
11	16	33	47	69

Bingo Card

This is a typical bingo card. Note the free space in the middle. Patterns that run through the middle require fewer numbers to win.

The odds of winning the contest are determined by the number of people who compete and the number of cards each person purchases. If 1,200 cards are in play, then the odds of winning are 1 in 1,200 for each card. If you have six cards in that game, then your odds of winning are 6 in 1,200 (or 1 in 200). The exact edge is determined by these odds and the size of the prize. It varies from game to game. But bingo is often a low-edge or no-edge contest. Sometimes jackpots are progressive. Theoretically, a diligent player could play bingo for a living, but the average size of the prizes compared with the total time invested usually sends professional players looking elsewhere.

THE FACT IS...

The laws and regulations of the United States use the terms "Indian nations," "Indian country," "Indian gaming" and so forth. The phrase "Native American" is commonly used in media reporting, and it is politically correct, but it is *not* an actual legal term or standard. Since many Native Americans refer to themselves as Indians, and U.S. law calls them Indians, we use the formal legal terms in this chapter.

Bingo is played in a super-sized version of a keno lounge called a **bingo hall** or **bingo parlor**. Not every casino has a bingo hall. In fact, most of the larger casinos in Las Vegas do not offer bingo, but it's a staple at many Indian casinos.

Moreover, bingo is largely responsible for the unprecedented expansion of Indian gaming in the past few years. But ironically, it is not bingo played in a bingo hall that has driven this expansion. Rather, it is the legal definition of bingo that has turned the gaming industry on its ear.

Indians, Bingo, and Slots

As you probably know, Indians in the United States experienced many hardships in centuries past. By the late 1980s, as a result of unfortunate U.S. policies, tribal societies were usually in remote places, and their citizens were underemployed, undereducated, and impoverished compared to the general population. Alcoholism and suicide rates were sky high. Per-capita income in Indian country (see the sidebar re this phrase) in 1990 was $4,478, compared to a national average of $14,420.

And then came bingo.

In the 1980s the Seminoles in Florida, and later the Cabazon and Morongo Bands of Mission Indians in California, offered bingo games with prizes that were larger than those allowed by state laws. In both cases the states shut them down. The tribes then sued in federal courts and won (based on Supreme Court decisions from the previous century). Tribal leaders across the U.S. experienced a universal "Aha!" moment. They realized that this could be something profitable, something that could revitalize the Indian nations and help lift Indians out of poverty.

Meanwhile, state lawmakers were outraged that they could not control gaming within their borders. Congress wanted to avert a political battle, so in 1987 it stepped in and created the Indian Gaming Regulatory Act. This law governs gaming on tribal lands, and it defines three classes of contests that tribes can offer:

Class I: Social games for prizes of minimal value (penny-ante stuff).

Class II: Lotto, bingo, and card games that are not banked by the house (such as poker).

Class III: All other gambling games, including traditional slots, roulette, blackjack, and so forth.

And of course, the gambling has to be on tribal land.

In deference to the states, a tribe can offer a Class II or Class III gambling game only if that game is already legal in the state. Also, Class III games require a "compact" with the state. The two parties supposedly decide together exactly what games will be offered, who will be allowed to play, and so forth. The whole system is regulated by the National Indian Gaming Commission (NIGC), a federal agency.

It sounds very reasonable, yes? But as you'll see, reasonable people have a way of disagreeing when billions of dollars and thousands of jobs are at stake.

Tip

If you're visiting a particular Indian casino for the first time, be aware that you may not be able to play your favorite games. At least not in the usual ways. Some Indian casinos (such as Foxwoods and Mohegan Sun in Connecticut) have all the standard casino games, but this is not uniformly the case across the country. For example, dice games are illegal in California, so craps is played with cards.

Is it Bingo or a Slot Machine?

In 1988, tribal gaming earned a meager $288 million. By 2005 that figure was about $20 billion. Much of the growth has involved bingo. But not in ways you might imagine.

Specifically, what happens when a state doesn't want slot games within its borders? Theoretically, a tribe cannot offer slots without a state compact. But bingo does not require a compact. So some tribes squeeze around a slots prohibition by offering bingo games that play like slot machines.

Literally, these are slot terminals that sell electronic bingo cards. The terminal plays the bingo games over a linked network. You can watch the cards, or you can watch video reels that deliver the same win/lose results as the cards.

Some of the buttons on these machines may be slightly different from the controls of standard slot games, but the overall experience is nearly identical to a typical slot contest.

Also, there are ersatz slot machines called video-lottery terminals or VLTs. They sell virtual scratch-off tickets. For the sake of convenience, I will refer to all of these devices, virtual scratch-off contests *and* electronic bingo games, as VLTs.

Setting politics aside, here's the critical question for players: Is the strategy for finding loose VLTs the same as the standard strategy for finding loose slot machines?

The ironic answer is: Yes, but in the case of VLTs, they are rarely loose.

Chapter 3 has a comprehensive review of how slots work, but in brief, it doesn't really matter how a contest "spins the reels" as long as the process is sufficiently random.

The mathematic methods of supplying the decisions in VLTs are radically different than traditional RNG methods. But in the end, 1 in 10 is still 1 in 10, and 1 in 5,000 is still 1 in 5,000.

THE FACT IS...

Many Indian tribes have successfully negotiated compacts for Class III games, though most have not. Of the 562 Indian tribes officially recognized by the United States, only 224 have casinos—and some of those casinos offer only Class II games.

Alas, VLTs tend to be tight simply because they are offered in markets where there is little competition. Generally, the payback on these machines is somewhere between 85 percent and 92 percent. Looser games are rare.

If you're playing in a casino that offers VLTs and traditional slots, you probably will be better off choosing the traditional slots.

If the casino has only VLTs, play as your prefer but remember that the machines are likely to be extremely tight compared to games in jurisdictions such as Las Vegas.

Essentially

- Keno is a lottery-style game played with a field of eighty numbers. A player can select up to twenty numbers, and a keno machine randomly selects twenty numbers. If the player's selection matches the machine's selection, the player wins. As with a lottery, the match doesn't have to be exact, but a closer match wins more.

- Keno is a highly volatile game. A player will win nothing or very little after most trials, but on rare occasions the game delivers a major windfall. One dollar can win $25,000, $100,000, or even more.

- There are two types of keno, a video version and a live version. Video keno generally pays back about 90 percent, while live keno is much stingier, paying back about 70 percent. However, live keno is a slower game, and thus it can cost less over time.

- Betting a keno way ticket is a good way to spend less per bet and simultaneously increase your overall chance of a win. But a way ticket doesn't change the odds, the payout ratio, or the house edge. The probability of winning a particular bet (one way) is always the same no matter how many ways you bet.

- The payback in a typical state lottery is much worse than any regular casino game, even keno.

- Bingo is a lottery-style game that uses a field of seventy-five numbers. Players compete with each other using bingo cards; each card has twenty-four randomly generated pre-selected numbers. The goal is to complete a particular pattern on a card.

- The odds of winning bingo are determined by the number of people who compete and the number of cards each person purchases.

- Some Indian casinos offer video lottery terminals that play like slot machines. VLTs tend to be tighter than regular slot machines.

CHAPTER 19

Sports Betting

 Of all the various forms of gambling, sports betting is probably the most popular. Football, basketball, baseball, and other sports generate billions of dollars in wagers. News outlets offer statistics and the latest "lines." The Super Bowl, March Madness, and the World Series keep gamblers riveted to their televisions, radios, and computers. By some estimates, sports betting accounts for about 15 percent of all gambling expenditures in the United States. But ironically, these numbers are impossible to verify with any precision because sports betting is illegal in 48 out of 50 states.

Yup. Illegal. Lotta action, and most of it takes place in the shadows. Some of it happens in the "office pool" or a handshake between friends, but the big dollars go through illegal bookmakers or to offshore Internet books (which are also illegal from the perspective of U.S. law enforcement).

It's a shame, and a political hot potato that is unlikely to cool in the near future.

You can play blackjack in New Jersey, but you can't bet legally on sports. You can play craps in Mississippi, but no sports betting is allowed in the Magnolia State. Slots in California, yes; sports betting, no.

This is the rule everywhere in the U.S. with the following exceptions:

- **Horse racing, dog racing, and jai-alai are available in various states (and we cover those in the pari-mutuel section later in this chapter).**

- **Sports betting is legal in Oregon on a limited basis via the state lottery.**

- **Sports betting is legal in Nevada. People in the Silver State bet on contests via licensed sports books.**

That's it. Two states and some pari-mutuel contests.

So if you're in Tunica, San Diego, Atlantic City, and so forth, keep in mind that you won't find the sports book conveniently located between the keno lounge and the coffee shop. You'll have to go to Las Vegas, Reno, somewhere else in Nevada, Oregon, or somewhere outside the U.S. to bet legally on New England over Miami.

What's My Line?

A sports book performs a function similar to a stock broker. The stock broker's goal is to provide a market for buyers and sellers of stock. In the case of a sports book, the market is a particular contest, and the goal is to match bets from both sides. Strictly speaking, the book doesn't play against a bettor as in blackjack or slots. Rather it charges a vig (commission) on the wager and hopes to find someone on the other side to cover the bet.

Since there is usually an underdog, there must be a **line** established to handicap the favorite and make the contest equal. Without a line, the bettors on one side would outnumber the bettors on the other side and create an inefficient market (and a lot of unpleasant exposure for the sports book). Everyone would bet on the favorite and nobody would bet on the underdog. A line makes a bet on an underdog potentially profitable.

The Spread

A spread is one way to designate a line. Let's say the Denver Broncos are playing the Oakland Raiders. Experts will analyze the two teams and then set the line as a **point spread**. If Denver is favored to win, and the experts think that a handicap of ten points will divide the betting public evenly, then the line is Denver Broncos –10. The spread would be displayed in a sports book this way:

509	Oakland Raiders	21 o/u
510	DENVER BRONCOS	–10

The home team is always at the bottom. The negative number indicates the spread and is next to the favored team. The larger number is the total points expected in the game. The designation o/u means over or under; it's the basis for a bet that I'll explain later. The number preceding each team's name is a reference for placing the bet. Sometimes the display is different, but not much. A full display would include the time of the contest, the money line (covered in the next section), and other pertinent information.

Let's say you bet Denver. They must win *and* beat the spread (win by more than ten points) for you to win. What if you bet Oakland? The Raiders can win or lose, but a loss must be by *less* than ten points for you to win the bet. If you bet the Raiders, you lose if the Broncos spank them by twenty points. If the game ends with Broncos ahead exactly ten points then it's a push and your money is returned.

Where's the vig? This ain't baccarat; the sports books stick it to the losers. You risk $11 to win $21 (your original $11 plus $10). So if you bet correctly, you net $10. Back a loser and you'll be out $11. The sports book earns $1 on the transaction. You're not required to bet in multiples of $11, but it makes payments easier and that's how experienced players do it.

THE FACT IS...

Some sports books display a plus amount next to the underdog that mirrors the spread (such as +10 when the line is −10). Don't let this confuse you. The minus number is the spread, and it always appears next to the team favored to win. When you see the letters PK in the line, that means "pick"; the two teams are even. A name next to a baseball team indicates who is pitching for that game.

The Money Line

Contests like baseball often are decided by one run, so a spread isn't an effective way of establishing a line. In baseball and in most sports you can also bet the **money line**. It's similar to taking or laying odds in craps (see Chapter 10). Here's a typical money line. Los Angeles is the visiting team and they're favored:

959	LA Dodgers	−135
960	OAKLAND ATHLETICS	+115

A $100 bet on the A's will earn $115. The bettor is **taking odds** that the A's will win. Someone who prefers the Dodgers would **lay odds** and risk $135 to win $100. The profit to the sports book is the twenty-point difference in the two numbers. The wider the difference, the bigger the profit.

Other Sports Bets

If **straight bets** on the spread and the money line aren't enough to excite you, many other sports wagers are available. They include the following:

Over/Under. This is a bet on the total points scored by both teams. Will the total be over or under the o/u amount? As with betting the spread, the wager is usually offered with a payoff of 10:11, but sometimes it is offered as a money line.

Propositions. Almost any question can be the subject of a proposition. Who will score the first touchdown? Who will kick the first field goal? Who will make it to the World Series? Will Elvis be found alive? Odds vary depending on the question.

Parlays. The bettor is making a wager on the outcome of a combination of contests. All of the bettor's choices must win for the parlay to win. Parlays can be cheap to bet, and they offer big payouts, but they have a high house edge, and they're tough to win.

Teasers. This is a parlay with the point spread shifted in the bettor's favor. The downside is a corresponding drop in the payout.

Making a Sports Bet

A typical sports book looks like a cross between mission control in Houston and your Uncle Al's TV den. It's usually designed in dark colors with giant video monitors on the walls. Placing a bet is easy. Simply walk to the desk and hand money to the writer with instructions on what to bet. Remember that multiples of $11 are preferred for bets on the spread. The writer will give you a printed ticket. It is your only proof that you made a bet, so treat it like money until it is paid or the contest is decided against you. Winning tickets are paid at the cashier's cage in the sports book or at the cage in the main casino.

Sports Betting Strategies

A common misconception is that the line represents what the experts think will be the outcome of the contest. This is not exactly true.

Let's say you're making odds on a football game between the Maulers and the Smashers. The Maulers are huge favorites even though their starting quarterback injured his thumb last week. The team says he is expected to play this Sunday. Your brother happens to be an orthopedic surgeon, and he tells you that the injury (as reported in the press) probably is far more debilitating than the reports suggest.

Tip

Don't wait too long to redeem your winning tickets. Most tickets are good for a limited period of time, usually sixty days. Read the back of the ticket to know exactly how much time you have. Also, before leaving the window, be sure to check the front of the ticket to be sure that the bet has been recorded correctly.

Normally the line would be Maulers –7 (Maulers to win by seven), but you think the Smashers will stun their opponents by ten points.

Remember, you're the oddsmaker. How will the public react if you set the line at Smashers –10? You certainly will be swamped with bets on the Maulers. Fans of the Maulers will double and triple their usual bets. Great, but nobody will bet on the Smashers. Not even Smashers fans will make such a (they think) stupid bet because the Maulers are expected to win. The sports book will have to cover all the wagers on the Maulers without any offsetting Smashers wagers.

The line is accurate (you think), but you have a lot of financial exposure.

Now what happens if the Maulers fall behind by seventeen points (even more than you predicted) and the coach pulls the starting quarterback? The backup does an admirable job and the Maulers score two unanswered touchdowns, but it's no use. The Smashers win by three points. That's not what the public expected, but the Smashers *did not make your spread of –10*. Your sports book has to pay all those bets on the Maulers.

Wouldn't it have been smarter to set the line where the public expected it to be set at Maulers –7? Is it the sports book's job to publicize and promote what might (or might not) be the "real" odds?

Or is a sports book's job simply to make a market for betting? Maulers −7 would have worked for everyone. On game day there would have been a lot of surprised winners and losers, and your sports book would have been one of the winners.

THE FACT IS...

Sometimes the oddsmakers are too good and they get the spread exactly correct. If the final score matches the spread exactly, then it's a disaster for the sports books. Everyone gets their money back. This is one of the reasons why point spreads are often set in half numbers (3.5, 7.5, and so forth).

So the line is a combination of the actual factors affecting the game and the psychological effect of those factors on the betting public. The purpose of having the line is *not* to predict the game, but to divide the bettors evenly. The public isn't stupid, so the line is usually close to the likely outcome, but sometimes it's off. Your goal as a bettor is to know when the line does not reflect the actual odds. The public can be swayed by a flamboyant personality, wishful thinking, or simply a lack of information. The line will shift as the public (including the oddsmakers) change their perceptions. Is the new information revealing or misleading? Is the public misinformed or are you? That's the critical question.

Beating the Vig at a Sports Book

Betting on sports can be a very profitable activity, but only if you consistently pick winners. Average luck won't do it. If you win half of your bets, you'll lose 4.5 percent of your total action when betting the spread. You must win at least 52.4 percent of your bets overall to beat the vig.

Unfortunately, there is no basic strategy as in blackjack or video poker to direct your decisions when betting on sports contests. The only way to win consistently is to know the sport and know the personalities who are playing it. You have to be smarter and have more information than most of the general public. Anything less and you'll be guessing. Speculation is certainly okay, and it can be profitable when you're blessed with some good luck. But it can be expensive when luck turns against you.

So remember the lessons you learned in Chapter 2. Manage your bankroll. Don't sink too many dollars into one contest. Limit your volatility, and expect a cost of at least 4.5 percent of your action, unless you have knowledge of the game that gives you a predictable edge.

Pari-Mutuel Contests

Tip

One potentially valuable betting strategy is to favor underdogs, especially underdogs at home. They tend to beat the spread. For example, from 1983 to 2004, home underdogs in the NFL beat the spread approximately 52 percent of the time. They lost 45 percent of the time, and hit the spread exactly about 3 percent of the time. In contrast, home favorites tend to underperform (even when they win the game).

In a pari-mutuel contest (typically horse racing, dog racing, or jai-alai) all the bets are pooled together into one big sum called a purse. Expenses for the event are extracted from that purse, and the remaining funds are distributed to the winners on a basis that is in proportion to the original wagers.

Here's an example. Let's say there is a three-horse race (quite unusual, but useful for our purposes). If a total of $1,000 is bet on horse A, $750 is bet on horse B, $500 is bet on horse C, and the commission is 15 percent, then the purse after commission is $1,912.

- If horse A wins, the payout is $1,912/$1,000 or $1.91 for every dollar that was wagered on horse A.

- If horse B wins, the payout is $1,912/$750 or $2.55 for every dollar that was wagered on horse B.

- If horse C wins, the payout is $1,912/$500 or $3.82 for every dollar that is wagered on horse C.

More wagers on a particular contestant mean a bigger purse, and thus the payout odds on a bet are never locked in until the betting has ended.

There are more types of pari-mutuel bets than just wagers on who will win. Various bets are explained in the table on the next page.

Types of Pari-Mutuel Bets

Bet	Result
Win	Contestant will finish first.
Place	Contestant will finish first or second.
Show	Contestant will finish in the top three.
Exacta	Contestant A will finish first and contestant B will finish second.
Trifecta	Contestant A will finish first, contestant B will finish second, and contestant C will finish third.
Quinella	Contestants A and B will finish first or second in any order.
Exacta Box	A combination bet that is similar to a quinella, but can include three or more contestants. Any of the chosen contestants can come in first or second, and the payoff for that particular combination is paid at the exacta rate.
Trifecta Box	Same as an exacta box but covers first, second, and third in any order.

As with other types of sports betting, knowledge is valuable when you're betting at the track or the jai-alai fronton. Of course, it may take some time for your knowledge to translate into a measurable edge. Favored horses often lose. Dogs underperform. Players miss the ball. The variables are so much more complex and harder to quantify than the easy-to-calculate advantages in games such as blackjack. Unless you study the contestants diligently, the best way to approach pari-mutuel contests is to make your best choice and simply hope that good luck is with you.

Essentially

- Sports betting is legal only in Nevada and Oregon; it is illegal in the other 48 states. The only exceptions to this rule are horse racing, dog racing, and jai-alai contests, which are available in various states.

- A sports book provides a market for bettors. The book's goal is to match bets from both sides of a contest. Since there is usually an underdog, oddsmakers handicap the favorite to divide the bettors evenly.

- The two most common types of sports bets are bets on the point spread and money-line bets.

- When you bet that a team will beat the spread, you risk $11 for every $10 you hope to win.

- When betting the money line, you take or lay odds similar to the system of odds in craps. You take odds when you bet on the underdog, winning more than the amount risked. You lay odds when you bet on the favorite, winning less than the amount risked.

- If you win half of your bets, you'll lose 4.5 percent of your total action when betting the spread. You must win at least 52.4 percent of your bets overall to beat the vig.

- In a pari-mutuel contest (typically horse racing, dog racing, or jai-alai) all the bets are pooled together into one big sum called a purse. Thus payout odds on a bet are never locked in until the betting has ended.

Sports Betting

PART FIVE

Practical Stuff

CHAPTER 20

Cash, Credit, Safety, and Casino Rules

 Gambling games are fun. Indeed, they can be quite beguiling. But let's be frank. Gambling isn't just about games. It's about the thrill of risk and reward. That means money.

Money plays a role in our lives (unless we move to a monastery, ashram, mountain, or wherever). For those of us living in the material world, money has worth, and games are exciting when wealth is at risk.

Thus casinos are intoxicating places because money is everywhere. Piles of chips litter the tables. Slot machines dispense payoffs with noisy abandon. Signs, banners, boards, and meters promise big rewards. People thumb through thick wads of cash. Dealers "drop" countless greenbacks.

Very exciting. But this super-charged atmosphere can cloud a person's judgment, not just during one game but during an entire session.

The purpose of this chapter is to give you strategies for handling financial decisions in and around a casino. These tactics can save you money and help you keep more of your winnings. As with all strategies, it's best to learn the nuances now so you'll be prepared for situations that arise in the heat of the game.

Let's begin with the basics.

Casino Chips

Casinos use chips rather than cash at their tables. There are various reasons for this. Chips are easier to count and handle than paper. Chips are bulky in large quantities; that makes them difficult to conceal and steal. And of course, chips are a debt. The "real money" is stored in locked drop-boxes and at the **cage** (the bank-like area of the casino).

Generally, chips come in denominations that range from fifty cents to thousands of dollars, and sometimes they are referred to as checks (or cheques) because that's the way they function. They're a promise of payment.

Each casino has custom chips. Colors that signify a particular denomination are somewhat standard in the gaming industry. Denominations usually are as follows:

Tip

Do you have too many small chips? Ask the dealer to "color up." It's a casino term that means exchanging chips of a lower denomination for fewer chips with a higher value. Just push the chips forward and say, "Color these up."

$1	White/Light Blue
$5	Red
$25	Green
$100	Black
$500	Purple
$1,000	Orange or Yellow
$5,000	Gray or Chocolate

But there are variations. For instance, in some California casinos, chip colors are $0.50 peach, $1 white/blue, $5 yellow, $25 purple, and $100 white with trim.

Whatever the color, remember that chips represent money, but they're only pieces of clay and plastic. Ideally, you should cash out at the end of each session. If you want to take a few chips home with you as souvenirs, that's okay, but there is no guarantee that the tokens will have value when you return. Chips aren't currency and the casino can change the design at any time. When that happens, the old chips become worthless (except to collectors).

Cash and Credit

The easiest and cheapest way to gamble in a casino is with cash. It's uncomplicated, fee free, universally recognized, and accounting is effortless. When it's gone, it's gone.

Most people have a personal limit for how much cash is comfortable to carry. Don't press your comfort level, but if you can carry your session bankroll as cash, then do it.

The next step down in convenience from folding money is an ATM/debit card. Some people will tell you to leave your ATM/debit cards in the hotel safe or at home so you won't gamble extra money on impulse. That tactic is okay, but if you have the willpower and don't feel like carrying cash, then the ATM is a convenient alternative.

The only drawback is the fee the casino machine will charge per withdrawal. Expect about double the cost that you would pay anywhere else.

A credit card is absolutely the worst way to bankroll your session. The fees are exorbitant, usually about 3 percent to 10 percent of the amount advanced. The exact fee depends on the credit system and how much you request. Of course, you must pay interest on the money, and the credit card company may charge a cash advance fee, too. The only advantage to using a credit card is having access to more dollars. Many ATMs top out at $300 per day. Credit cards can be tapped for amounts stretching into the thousands. But having access to that much money isn't such an advantage when you consider the astounding cost.

THE FACT IS...

Debit cards are a somewhat better alternative than credit cards when you're funding a session bankroll. The advantage of debit cards is that there are no interest charges and you can get an amount up to your daily purchase limit. But the fees for getting non-ATM cash from a debit card are still steep, typically 3 percent to 10 percent of the amount advanced.

Thus it is best to avoid using credit cards to fund your bankroll.

Casino Credit

Casino credit is a much better alternative to getting an advance on your credit/debit card. That's because there is no charge for casino credit. That's right. No charge!

You apply for casino credit as you would for credit at a store or a bank. The casino will check your regular credit history and will also review your gambling history through a company that specializes in gambling credit information. If you already have a big credit line at another casino, that may help or hurt. It depends on your income and your history of action. With good credit and money in the bank you'll get at least $1,000 and often $5,000 or more on a casino line.

The process takes a few minutes or a few hours, depending on your specific requests and circumstances, so you may want to send an application before your next visit. When the credit is approved, and you sign the appropriate forms, then simply sit down at a table and ask for a **marker** drawn for a particular amount. A floor person will give you a

piece of paper that will look very much like a check. That is because it is a check, and it is written on your bank account (more about this in the next section).

Sign the marker and a floor person will bring you chips. The casino will hold the marker until the end of your visit, and usually for a few days after that. You can buy the marker back with cash, chips, or a regular check. Markers that aren't redeemed are eventually deposited, but most casinos prefer that you settle up before you leave the casino because the money is *interest-free*. A floor person may ask you to buy the marker if you're winning. The cashier will probably ask you to settle the marker when you cash chips at the cage. Some casinos require you to sign an agreement that you won't leave with cash or chips when you owe them on a marker. The exact arrangement between you and the casino regarding how the marker will be repaid can vary, but the basic system is designed to make playing convenient, and at the same time make it difficult to move the borrowed money out of the house. Casino A doesn't want to finance action at Casino B.

Tip

You can bypass time-consuming credit applications and the issue of settling markers by depositing "front money" directly at the cage via cash, check, or a bank transfer. Your markers are drawn from the debit account, and everything is automatically settled. The cage is also a good place to hold money when you have too much to carry safely.

When is a Loan not a Loan?

When you get a "loan" from a casino it's not really a loan. As I mentioned in the previous section, the marker you sign is actually a check. It can be deposited against your checking account. This has tremendous legal significance.

In the United States, if a person doesn't pay a loan, the non-payment is usually a civil matter rather than a criminal one, unless the non-payment involves fraud.

Furthermore, gambling debts are not legally enforceable in most jurisdictions. This is a well-established precedent in English common law (and therefore the laws of most states).

In other words, if you and your neighbor bet against each other (let's say $1,000 on the Super Bowl), and you win but he welshes, your claim is unenforceable in most circumstances.

However a marker is not a gambling debt. It is a check, and if it bounces…well… Writing a bad check is a felony.

Once upon a time, guys with names like Guido and Pauly collected on bad casino debts, but these days bad markers are turned over to the local district attorney. The D.A. issues an arrest warrant that can be served anywhere in the world. Errant players have been pursued across North America, and to other countries for their bad markers. When a lawbreaker is found, he is handcuffed and unceremoniously taken to jail in the jurisdiction where the offence took place.

And it gets worse. Let's say a player declares bankruptcy. He can wipe away his debts, but not his markers. Bankruptcy cannot shield a person from criminal prosecution or court-ordered restitution when a crime has been committed.

Of course, these drastic legal measures are the last option for casinos. They would prefer to deal with customers rather than defendants. Indeed, a casino often will discount a large debt to encourage a quick settlement. The casino simply lops off a portion of the total amount, usually 5 to 10 percent, occasionally 15 percent (more about this in Chapter 22). So if you're a responsible player who happens to have a bad session, casino credit can save you some money.

Just be aware that a casino has a lot of legal clout if you have a disagreement over a marker.

> *"A marker is not just a piece of paper saying, 'I owe you one thousand signed Nathan Detroit.' A marker is the one pledge that a guy cannot welsh on. Never. It's like not saluting the flag."*
>
> **Nathan Detroit, as played by Frank Sinatra in *Guys and Dolls* (1955)**

Staying Safe

"Hey, you dropped something."

That's how the scam starts. The player sees a well-dressed man or woman pointing to the floor beneath the seat. The scammer smiles and the player bends over. Sure enough, a dollar is under the seat. The player grabs it. When she comes back up her purse is gone. So is the crook.

It's unfortunate, but the mixture of money, confusing noises, tourists in "fun mode," and the constant push of the crowd in a casino creates a prime environment for larceny. Purses, wallets, bags, chips, and anything not nailed down or attached to one's body are in danger of disappearing into a mass of pulsing humanity. Here are some tips to help you avoid becoming a statistic:

- Don't carry a purse or bag. If you must carry a bag, place it securely between your legs or in your lap when sitting.

- Thieves often use a loud noise or a nearby disturbance to distract attention while they grab unattended items. If you hear a loud noise or you see a disturbance, look down and secure your belongings before you look up to see what is happening. Craps players should be especially diligent because a hot table usually involves a lot of shouting and a throng of people who are elbow to elbow. It's a good idea to keep an eye (or a hand) on your chips.

- If someone bumps into you hard enough to knock you off balance, don't worry about who will apologize to whom. Immediately prepare yourself for a possible robbery. Hold your belongings tightly because in the next millisecond someone may try to force something from your hand, arm, or pocket. Also, beware when you're "accidentally" doused with a spilled drink. The loud drunk who is frenetically dabbing your gin-soaked crotch may be covering for a confederate who is lifting your wallet.

- Don't toddle upstairs with a stack of black and purple chips stuffed in your pocket. Cash out and leave most of it on deposit at the cage.

- If you decide to carry a large amount of cash, ask the casino for a security escort. Do it even if you're a tough guy. Anyone can be robbed.

On the other hand, there are actually places in a casino where you safely can leave your chips just laying around. More about that in the next section.

Casino Rules and Customs

Some of the following items I covered briefly in other chapters. But I'm collecting them here in one place and expanding the information so you can see how it all fits together.

It is important to remember that the purpose of casino rules is to protect the integrity of games, safeguard financial transactions, and promote basic safety. Therefore...

Tip

When you buy in to a game, ask for "change" in a specific denomination such as, "Change please, and make them greens." And be sure to keep the bills away from a betting circle or space. If you just plop money onto the felt in a space meant for bets, the dealer may think you're making a cash wager, and he may ask, "Money plays?" If you hear that, tell him no, or your entire bankroll will be wagered for the next hand.

The Game Must Be Observable

Everything you do should be easily viewable by the cameras in the ceiling. When you buy in to a table game, lay money flat on the table. Don't hand money to a dealer. Make clear motions when hitting or standing in blackjack, or when taking action in other games. Don't touch chips that are in play, and don't touch anyone's stack but your own.

Even if your spouse or friend is sitting at the chair next to you, don't touch that person's chips unless you are placing chips in a rack, or both of you are changing seats. If you break this rule, you may have to explain to security officers that you are not stealing chips. Why put yourself through the hassle?

Follow the Rules

You must always follow the rules of the game and the directions of the dealers and the floorpeople.

If a dealer asks you to do something, then either do it or call a floorperson to handle the dispute. If a dealer plays the game in a way that you think is incorrect, you *definitely* should call a floorperson. Explain the problem succinctly and without hyperbole. If a floorperson rules against you, your highest appeal in most circumstances is to a pit supervisor (some highly unusual problems might involve a shift supervisor). If you're still not satisfied, then leave the game and register a formal complaint with the casino.

Resist the temptation to be loud or belligerent. A casino will eject you without hesitation if a supervisor decides that you need a "time out." Getting walked out of casino by big burly security guards is not fun, so don't give anyone a reason to see you as a security threat.

Mechanical Assistance is Forbidden

I mentioned this in Chapter 9, but it bears repeating.

According to Nevada statute 465.075, "It is unlawful for any person at a licensed gaming establishment to use, or possess with the intent to use, any device to assist: 1. In projecting the outcome of the game; 2. In keeping track of the cards played; 3. In analyzing the probability of the occurrence of an event relating to the game; 4. In analyzing the strategy for playing or betting to be used in the game, except as permitted by the commission."

The statute goes on to say, "A person who violates any provision of NRS 465.070 to 465.085, inclusive, is guilty of a category B felony..."

Other states have similar laws. Generally, you can use a pen and paper when playing baccarat and roulette, and that's it. No computers, no calculators, no other mechanical assistance when playing table games. Ditto for anything that would affect the outcome of a slot machine game. Casinos and law enforcement take infractions very seriously.

THE FACT IS...

Writing and referring to handwritten notes is specifically allowed when playing roulette and baccarat. It is technically *not* allowed during games such as poker, Caribbean Stud Poker, and pai gow poker. But generally, writing or reading is tolerated if a player does it between hands. Blackjack is the only game in which taking notes is absolutely forbidden at all times.

The "Eye in the Sky" and Your Game

Every portion of the casino floor is under periodic surveillance by video cameras twenty-four hours a day.

Yes, periodic.

Areas such as the cage, tables, and some machines are under constant surveillance. But some machines and some non-gaming areas are *not* constantly monitored. Television documentaries and movies would have you think that surveillance is everywhere at all times with multiple cameras, but the truth is that even the most sophisticated systems do not capture everything.

Of course, if surveillance notices suspicious activity in a general sweep of the casino floor, then multiple cameras *will* cover the suspicious action. And supervisors, dealers, and security personnel are constantly observing the games.

So be aware that everything and everyone is being scrutinized, but don't assume that the cameras see everything, or that video necessarily will help you in a dispute. There have been countless instances of disagreements involving machines or table games (and occasionally customer-on-customer theft) where the video was nonexistent or not conclusive.

In other words, don't rely only on the casino's security and surveillance to protect the integrity of *your* game. You have a responsibility to protect yourself. As I mentioned previously, if a dealer makes a mistake that costs you money or puts you at a disadvantage then you should speak up. Notify the dealer, and if the problem is not resolved, then call a floorperson. Do not make further play actions until your concerns have been addressed. Delay the game (without being belligerent). You'll get some attention very quickly.

Conversely, if another player is having a problem, it is generally best to stay out of it.

Tokes

We first discussed **tokes** (the casino term for tips) in Chapter 9. Here's a quick recap for all the games.

Toke more when you're winning. Toke less or not at all when you're losing.

Tip

The surest way to get immediate attention for a pressing problem is to hold up the game. Casinos want to keep games moving because action earns them money. If you refuse to make a play action during a dispute (let's say refusing to call or fold in poker) this freezes the game. A floorperson will be at that table pronto. But use this tactic rarely and sensibly. Do it only when you have a legitimate and serious complaint.

At tables such as blackjack, roulette, craps, and baccarat, toke about 10 percent of one average bet per hour. That would be $1 to $5 per hour for a player betting $10 to $50 per hand. If you have a particularly good run of luck, then double or triple your toke.

When you're playing poker, the minimum toke should be $1 for each pot that you win when the pot is larger than $20. Generous players toke $2 or $3 on pots larger than $100.

Toke keno runners $1 per run, and at least $1 or $2 for wins between $10 and $40. Five percent is common for amounts up to $500. Use your judgment for wins above that.

Toke chip runners $1 per run if they actually make a special trip to get your chips. If they're just standing there with a full rack of chips waiting for your money, then a tip is not necessary.

When servers bring you free drinks, toke based on the value of the drinks if you had paid for them. Ditto for tipping servers after comped meals (see Chapter 22 for more on comps).

Toke slot attendants and other casino personnel (but not supervisors or hosts) depending on the services they perform.

Special Extras

When you're playing at a table, you're allowed to leave that table for periodic breaks and still keep your seat. The exact amount of time you're given for a break depends on the number of customers in the casino. Ten minutes is usually the minimum, and the maximum is typically thirty minutes.

Ask the dealer how much time is allowed, then simply tell the dealer you're taking a break. Count your chips and leave them at the table.

Yes. *Leave them.* The dealer will reserve your seat and protect your chips until you return.

A similar system applies if you're playing at a machine. You can have it **locked down** (made unavailable for other players) by a slot attendant while

THE FACT IS...

Tokes should not affect how a dealer runs the game. But regular tokes can influence a dealer to make less damaging calls in borderline situations. This is especially true if you're counting cards in blackjack. Don't blow your profits trying to buy goodwill, but a few well-placed tokes may give you better penetration. And if the dealer is earning money, he may be less likely to turn you in as a counter.

you take a break or have a meal. As with tables, the time limits for a lockdown can vary. Generally, you will be given up to an hour.

Essentially

- The easiest and cheapest way to fund your session bankroll is with cash. If you can carry cash comfortably, then do it.

- ATM/debit cards and credit cards are convenient, but using them can be expensive. Casino credit is a better and cheaper alternative to using credit/debit cards. The casino charges you nothing when it loans you money.

- A marker is a check, not a loan. If you don't redeem a marker, it will be deposited to your checking account.

- Some casinos discount large debts to encourage quick settlements. Discounts are usually in the range of 5 to 15 percent.

- Be wary when carrying valuables in a casino. Thieves often use loud noises and confusion to distract victims while robbing them. Always be mindful of your belongings.

- Always follow the rules in a casino. Many areas are under surveillance, but don't assume that cameras see everything. You have a responsibility to monitor your game and protect yourself.

- Toke your dealers, keno runners, and chip runners. Most of their income comes from tokes.

CHAPTER 21

Jackpots and Taxes

 Here's something that you won't see in a typical book about casino gambling. It's an entire chapter devoted to what happens when you win. This isn't just cheerful optimism; it's a practical truth. If you aim at big payoffs, and you play long enough, you *will* smack a big win. It's mathematically inevitable.

For example, let's say that your favorite game is video poker. You can expect to see a royal flush jackpot (typically 4,000 credits) about once in every 110 hours of single-hand video poker, or once in every 22 hours when you play five hands per game. You may play that much in a few weeks, or it may take months or years, but if you continue playing then it *will* happen. Maybe it won't happen in exactly 110 hours, 22 hours, or whatever. It may happen sooner, or maybe later, but it's coming. Ditto for a slots jackpot. Ditto for any gambling game with a large payout.

Granted, you'll never hit a big win playing blackjack or baccarat at a flat $25 per hand, but it can happen if you parlay. In roulette, $10 wagered straight up and parlayed only once turns into $12,960. The probability of that happening is 1 in 1,444. Compared to some other games, those are pretty easy odds. In fact, if you parlay regularly, you'll hit the big one about once every 28 hours. It's true! You may lose $14,440 on the way to the big win, but that won't stop your windfall from coming. Indeed, it might happen five minutes after you sit down.

So one way or another, if you aim for big numbers at machines or tables, sooner or later a big win *will* happen. It might be a giant profit or an amount that simply erases a fraction of your aggregate losses, but either way, you want to keep the money. You don't want it delayed, disallowed, or stolen. It's coming, and you've earned it. So don't stick your head in the sand. Prepare now.

What Could Go Wrong?

Let's begins with slots. We'll cover tables in a later section.

Minor jackpots are no big deal. A bunch of credits appear on the meter, you cash out and buy something nice. Yay! But things change considerably when a jackpot is large enough to require a **hand-pay** (a cash or check payment from a casino employee). In the United States, hand-pays occur when the win from a single slot spin or video poker game exceeds a tax reporting threshold of $1,200 or more.

Winners must provide identification and a social security number or 31 percent of the jackpot will be withheld for federal taxes. No exceptions. Ever.

In many U.S. jurisdictions the casino will withhold the entire amount if you are unable to provide identification. That's right. No ID? No money. Nevada is marginally more flexible. You might get the remaining 69 percent without identification in some casinos, or you might not.

The most accepted form of identification is a driver's license with your picture. Military IDs and the like are also suitable, but voter registration cards, credit cards, a hunting license, or your grocery card won't cut the mustard.

People without identification are photographed, and the casino holds the money until they return with the necessary documents (additional withholding applies in various circumstances). No amount of pleading, tears, or threats will influence casino managers to bend these rules. Managers must uphold these policies because they have been decreed by the U.S. Treasury and local regulators.

THE FACT IS...

Casinos in the United States use IRS form W2G to report jackpots of $1,200 and over. One copy goes to you, and the other goes to the government. Amounts under $5,000 are reported, but they're not subject to federal withholding when the player provides a social security number. Amounts above $5,000 require 28 percent withholding when the payoff is more than 300 times greater than the wager.

Minor Problems

Dolores Banyai was thrilled when she pressed the button and hit a $220,200 jackpot on a Wheel of Fortune machine at the Hilton in Atlantic City. Unfortunately, she was only nineteen years old and the minimum legal age for gambling in a casino in New Jersey is twenty-one. A slot attendant appeared and requested identification. Banyai realized that this would be a problem, so she got sneaky. She said her ID was in a hotel room. Banyai then pressed her twenty-one-year-old boyfriend, David Baum, into service, and he returned later to claim the jackpot. This happened over a matter of hours, and there was a shift change, so the casino paid the prize. But what these youngsters didn't count on is that every large jackpot is video-taped, and the tape is checked for verification. In this case, it took longer than it should have to catch the mistake, but the result was inevitable. The casino realized what happened, and they immediately contacted New Jersey Division of Gaming Enforcement.

The state filed criminal charges. Banyai lost the jackpot and she was fined. Her boyfriend was indicted on one count of theft by deception (prosecutors later dismissed the charge). The casino was fined $10,000.

The minimum gambling age varies by jurisdiction and by game types (casinos, lotteries, pari-mutuel, bingo), so some gamblers are not even aware that they cannot wager legally in a casino in Nevada, New Jersey, Mississippi, and many other places until they're twenty-one. But they inevitably become very aware moments after hitting the $1,200 threshold. Underage players are not paid jackpots. There are no exceptions. No amount of legal wrangling has ever changed that anywhere in the U.S. Just ask Russell Erickson. His son Kirk was nineteen when he hit for $1 million at Caesars Palace in 1987. Russell sued, but the jackpot was disallowed.

Switching with an older person is a common ploy that consistently fails. Sometimes the winner just walks away. But the end result is always the same, a heartbreaking loss. Underage gamblers can't win.

Tip

The minimum age for casino gambling is twenty-one in Nevada, New Jersey, New Mexico, North Dakota, South Dakota, Mississippi, Missouri, Maryland, Indiana, Iowa, Louisiana, Delaware, Connecticut, Colorado, and Arizona. Players sometimes are unaware of these age limits because many states (such as New Jersey) have a minimum age of eighteen for lottery purchases. And some Indian casinos have a minimum age of eighteen. So anyone under twenty-one should check before playing in a casino.

Friends Don't Let Friends Share Jackpots

"This one's for you, Puddin'." That's what Mary Iacono remembers Carolyn Lyons saying just before Carolyn pushed the button. Seconds later the slot machine delivered a jackpot of $1.9 million. Mary was ecstatic because she thought half the money was hers, but that's not how it worked out.

The two women were vacationing together in Las Vegas, and (according to Mary) they made an agreement to split their winnings. Mary says Carolyn even paid for the trip because she thought her friend would be "lucky" for both of them.

They were down $47 and late for a show when Mary (who uses a wheelchair) begged her friend to stop on the way out and play once more. Carolyn resisted but eventually gave in. The big one came on the second spin.

The person who pushes the button and initiates the game is the winner. That's the rule, and everybody in the casino business follows it. A winner can certainly share a jackpot, but only one person is the winner.

In this case the winner was Carolyn, and she didn't share. Mary claimed they had an oral contract. She sued. Headaches and heartache for everyone.

The lesson here is that you should play your own game. It might seem romantic for one person to push in the money and another to press the button, but unless you have a written agreement of some sort (or you're married) then you're playing with fire while you're playing with slots.

Pay No Attention to the RAM Behind the Curtain

One of the surest ways to "lose" a jackpot is to psych yourself into thinking that you've won a big prize when in fact the machine has simply malfunctioned. Too many people spend years of their lives litigating such "stolen" prizes, and they often come up short. Here's how it happens.

You're playing a progressive. The symbols line up, lights flash, bells ring, but something is wrong. The progressive meter hasn't reset.

People may already be congratulating you on your good fortune, but a slot technician checks the machine and eventually the bad news arrives. The machine malfunctioned. "But the symbols lined up," you sputter. "That's a jackpot. Who cares if some electrical doodad didn't send a signal? The reels told me I had a jackpot! I won $10 million!"

That "electrical doodad" is the RNG. It is the computer chip that plays the game. Think of the reels like the scoreboard at the Super Bowl, and the RNG is like the teams and the field. The stadium display helps you understand who is winning, but it has no bearing on the actual game (for more about RNGs check out Chapter 3).

What could cause a slot machine to malfunction? Designers and regulators go to extreme lengths to ensure that slots operate properly, but in spite of that they sometimes break. Problems include corrupted RAM (random access memory), power interruptions, reel malfunctions, or just a bug in the program. The latter happened to Nhung Housekeeper. She was playing a progressive at Spirit Mountain Casino in Oregon and hit a $2.9 million jackpot. Unfortunately, it was a nickel machine with a top payout that should have been only $10,000. The casino refused to pay. Here come the lawyers!

When is a Jackpot a Jackpot?

There is more to a jackpot than reels and ringing bells. A genuine win includes a combination of external indicators that you can see immediately, and there are some internal items that can be checked only by the casino. Remember, the following are all indicators, but the RNG is what matters.

Of course, it starts with the reels or display. You should see a winning combination. Next, the machine must lock up. If it doesn't, then you don't have a hand-pay jackpot. The lock-up feature ensures that you won't accidentally "play away" your big win. The tower light should be on and in many cases it should *not* be flashing (it depends on the game). Bells or music should be sounding continuously. If the contest is progressive and you hit

THE FACT IS...

Look closely, and you'll see that slot machines are labeled with the phrase, "Malfunctions void all pays and plays." It's like buying a soda. Let's say the machine breaks and fifty sodas come out. You're entitled to one soda, not fifty.

the big prize, then the progressive meter should reset. If any of the above indicators are missing then you probably have a malfunction. If everything appears correct then get ready to be excited, but don't celebrate just yet.

Verifying a Jackpot

A casino representative should approach you within a few minutes after you hit (though it may seem like an eternity). Some casinos are slower than others, especially on weekends. Once someone arrives you do the ID thing. Jackpots under $10,000 are paid with little fanfare. Amounts above that receive a higher level of scrutiny. The casino will check surveillance cameras to be sure that you were the person playing the machine. They'll also run the video back to see if the machine was rigged before it paid off. Don't feel insulted; scams are a problem.

If the win was on a wide-area progressive then an additional inspection occurs. Casinos don't pay progressive slot wins when games are linked to multiple properties (as in Megabucks). The slot manufacturer handles those payments. The casino notifies the manufacturer when a jackpot hits, and company representatives come out to examine the machine and cut a check.

How is a machine examined? A technician looks for normal functions of the type described earlier. Then the machine is inspected for signs of forced entry. Chip seals are observed to ensure that they are unbroken. EPROM chips are unsealed and tested to verify that the correct program was running. The whole process can take a couple of hours, depending on the machine. Some casinos use this opportunity to run a background check on the player (to confirm that he/she doesn't have a history of defrauding casinos). In some jurisdictions a state inspector must also scrutinize the win. For example, Mississippi gaming officials review all jackpots above $100,000.

If your jackpot makes it through this gauntlet, then the prize is yours. Time to celebrate!

Tip

Are you wondering what the current jackpot is on Quartermania or Megabucks? You can call toll-free and get the latest totals on those and all the wide-area progressives made by IGT. The number is (888) 448-2WIN.

When the Sky Falls

What should you do if your jackpot is disputed? First, you should set aside any notion that the casino, the state, or the machine manufacturer is trying to "steal" the money by not paying you. Progressive jackpots are held in special accounts and legally are considered players' money waiting to be won. Regular jackpots come off the casino's bottom line, but they're an amortized cost of doing business. Jackpots make great press. Everyone loves them. Everyone wants to pay, but they also want to follow the rules and avoid running afoul of the law. Remember Dolores Banyai? Imagine the hands that were spanked at the Hilton over that one.

Okay, you're thinking clearly. Now what? Consider the win. Was it clean? People have gone to court and litigated for years over symbols that almost lined up, machines that didn't lock up, and lights that didn't flash (or did). In most of these cases the RNG indicated no win or the machine had some other malfunction. Results of litigation have been mixed. Here are a few examples:

- Cengiz "Gene" Sengel thought he had won $1.8 million at Silver Legacy in Reno in 1996 when the reels stopped on a winning combination. But an inspection determined that the RNG didn't deliver a win. The bill receptacle in his machine malfunctioned; that froze the reels. Sengel went to court. Four years later Nevada's Supreme Court ruled against him.

- Sylvia Gutierrez thought she hit a $112,600 jackpot on a Betty Boop Thrillions machine in 1999 at the Sands Regency in Reno. The reels certainly said so. Bally disagreed. The machine did not lock up. There were no lights, bells, or an RNG win. One year later Bally caved in and cut a check. They had lost in court and decided not to appeal.

- Herminia Rodriquez nailed a $330,000 winning combination in 1997 as Harrah's Ak-Chin Casino in Arizona. The machine apparently malfunctioned, but Rodriquez didn't see it that way. She went to the media; sixty-four-year-old grandmother vs. casino. Harrah's quickly paid up to end the bad publicity.

- Effie Freeman allegedly lined up the symbols for a $1.7 million win at Splash Casino in Tunica in 1995. Casino Data Systems said it was a hopper jam. The machine did not lock up. Four years later the Mississippi Supreme Court ruled against Freeman.

- Mark Cowsert thought he won a slot jackpot of $13.7 million at Greektown Casino in Detroit in 2005. Greektown says the machine malfunctioned. The casino subsequently delivered the machine to the Michigan Gaming Control Board. Cowsert filed a complaint with the MGCB and then sued. An appeals court dismissed his lawsuit saying the "plaintiff was required to first exhaust his administrative remedies before the MGCB."

And the list goes on and on. Losers outnumber winners, but every case is unique.

For every dispute settled by a judge or jury there are thousands more that are resolved by the casino or regulators before reaching the courts.

And of course, some situations are clearly not wins. One obvious example is the catastrophe that occurs when a player smacks the top combination with less than max credits. That's a $3,750 mistake when playing $1 video poker, and it can mean millions on a progressive. There's no legal maneuvering that can change that ugly reality. You must wager maximum credits to receive the top prize.

Table Games

Similar caveats apply to table games. If you want to win the progressive jackpot in Caribbean Stud Poker, Let It Ride, or some other table game, then you must bet the extra dollar. And if you hit the top prize, your win will be scrutinized in the same way a slot jackpot is scrutinized. You will need ID, the cameras will be checked, the deck will be checked for tampering, and so forth.

Consider the case of Let Nguyen, and a $50,000 jackpot he missed.

THE FACT IS...

Wide-area progressives (progressive games linked across multiple properties) typically are owned by a slot manufacturer. For example, Megabucks is owned by IGT. The manufacturer leases the machines to the casinos, shares in the revenue, and is responsible for paying the top prize.

On December 10, 1996, Nguyen was playing pai gow poker at the Grand Casino in Biloxi. During his session, he made a play-partnership agreement with another person who was sitting at the table, Tung Phan. Nguyen supplied the bankroll and Phan made the bets and set the hands. Phan was fortunate enough to hit a royal flush. This normally would have earned Phan and Nguyen a $50,000 jackpot, but Phan was under twenty-one.

At first Nguyen tried to claim the jackpot, but surveillance revealed that Phan was the actual winner. When Phan finally produced his ID, it was discovered that he was under the legal age for betting in a casino. Phan was arrested and removed. The jackpot wasn't paid. Nguyen brought his case to the Mississippi Gaming Commission. The claim was denied. No jackpot.

And then there are table limits to consider. Lorena Higginbotham was playing Let It Ride at Circus Circus in Reno a few years ago. She hit a hand with a payout of $35,000 based on her bets, but the table limit was $25,000. A pit supervisor approved the payout (apparently in error), and the casino subsequently tried to get its money back. Call the lawyers!

Will That Be Cash or Check?

When the gambling gods smile and the RNG or pit boss concurs, then you have some important choices to make. Cash is a reasonable option if the win is under $2,000, but anything substantially over that is probably best taken as a check. Remember, hundreds and maybe thousands of people just saw you jumping up and down screaming, "I'm rich! I'm rich!" Bells were ringing and lights were flashing. It was hard to miss. A few of the spectators might have been crooks, so a wad of cash will make you a walking target. Request a

Tip

At some table games, a bettor who is *not* receiving cards is allowed to place wagers on a player who *is* receiving cards, as long as the player receiving cards does not object. Special betting circles are provided in these circumstances. Wagers such as these are acceptable, but you should avoid any partnership wagers that do not include a clear separation of bets or a formal written agreement.

check or put the money on hold at the casino's cage. Many casinos also offer direct deposit to a checking account. If you must carry cash then request a casino security escort to the car. Don't be shy about asking. That is their job.

But hey, you're not going to the car. That's because the casino is offering you a free room, meals, and by the way, could you sign this promotional release? They want to use your name and image for publicity. Some folks think it's a kick. Others prefer to remain anonymous. Do you want crazy Uncle Elmer to know that you're suddenly wealthy? It's a personal decision. Choose wisely.

Everybody Loves A Winner

Smaller cash jackpots will be delivered as Ben Franklins with a few Andy Jacksons sprinkled on top. Do you suppose someone was expecting a tip?

A casino isn't a restaurant, so don't feel obliged to give away a big chunk. Some people tip the extra twenties. Others give one percent of the win ($100 for $10,000). One school of thought says that tipping is absurd if the jackpot doesn't negate losses for the trip.

On the other hand, remember that you're tipping for service. How long did you wait for payment? How were you treated? It's certainly appropriate to reward those who helped the process along. But you should definitely not tip if you waited a long time, more that thirty minutes for a standard jackpot. Wide-area progressives should take two to three hours to process, occasionally longer.

Keep the Good Times Going

While you're waiting some "new friends" may appear and keep you company. They'll be very entertaining and they'll like you very much. You'll be invited to dinner, drinks, or maybe a party. Scrutinize these agreeable instant companions carefully. Not everyone is a con artist, but don't let a giddy glow muddle your judgment. It's really a drag to win $4,000, foolishly take cash, go out with a new friend, and find the money and the friend missing when the bill comes (for more on personal safety and handling money, see Chapter 20).

Remember, a certain amount of winning is inevitable when you play regularly, but some losing is inevitable, too. Gambling lore is filled with stories of people who hit big and blew it all. Plan ahead, and you won't be one of them. If the win is substantial then consult an investment advisor. Buy something that generates income. Don't plow everything back into the games (unless you're purchasing gambling stocks). The glow lasts a lot longer when the cash stays in your pocket.

Gambling and Taxes

It's simple. You win money; you owe Uncle Sam. You lose money, that's your problem.

Gambling losses *can* be deducted from your taxable income, but only up to the amount of your gambling profits. So let's say you lost $10,000 this year. Well, that's just too bad. Better luck next time.

> "One of these days in your travels, a guy is going to show you a brand-new deck of cards on which the seal is not yet broken. Then this guy is going to offer to bet you that he can make the jack of spades jump out of this brand-new deck of cards and squirt cider in your ear. But, son, do not accept this bet, because as sure as you stand there, you're going to wind up with an ear full of cider."
>
> **Sky Masterson, as played by Marlon Brando in *Guys and Dolls* (1955)**

On the other hand, maybe you won $15,000 playing poker this year, but you got burned for $5,000 at the slots. You must declare the entire $15,000 you won. And if you want to deduct the slot loss, the IRS expects you to keep records including the date and time of the session, the game, the place you were gambling, the amount you won or lost, the machine or table number, and similar info.

But let's say you won $6,000 at 11 p.m. and lost $2,000 just four hours later at 3 a.m. Do you have to declare the full $6,000 as income? Yes, if you received a W2G tax form for $6,000 from a casino, and then subsequently lost $2,000. But if the loss was during a single session, you were up and then you were down four hours later, then simply declare the net $4,000 profit. The IRS doesn't expect you to report every hourly bounce in a bankroll. But you must keep records.

As with all things involving taxes and government, there are a bazillion nuances to the law. Talk to a tax professional if you have questions about deductions or income.

The important thing to remember is that the IRS *will* ask questions about your sources of money if you are audited. So always declare your income.

Currency Transaction Reports

The U.S. government has an intricate system to prevent money laundering at casinos. Law-abiding gamblers (as well as nefarious ones) inevitably come into contact with this system when *cash* transactions reach $10,000 per day or above. When a player hits the magic number, a casino is required to fill out a **currency transaction report** (CTR), which is a U.S. Treasury form. This will *necessarily involve the player* because a floorperson will ask for identification including a social security number. Failure to provide this information doesn't prevent the report from being filed, but in some circumstances it does cause the casino to file a separate U.S. Treasury report regarding suspicious activity.

The threshold for reporting includes multiple transactions that reach the $10,000 limit, and it covers various cash in and cash out circumstances, including purchasing and redeeming tokens, cash payments at the cage, and redeeming markers with cash.

Doing anything to circumvent the limit such as dividing transactions into smaller amounts, using surrogates, and so forth is strictly forbidden (this is called "structuring"). Law-abiding players must *never* do this.

If you find yourself in the happy circumstance of handling cash in excess of $10,000 and getting questions about it from a casino employee, don't put up a fuss. Simply give the casino supervisor or cage person the information that he/she requests.

THE FACT IS...

Casinos report a player's gambling winnings to the Internal Revenue Service using form W2G (the player gets a copy of this form). But your gambling income is taxable even if it is *not* acquired in a casino or reported on a W2G. Federal law requires that you declare *all* your income.

Also note that casino personnel informally track cash transactions starting at $1,000 to $3,000, so they're aware when a player reaches the $10,000 threshold.

And keep in mind that these reports are about *cash* transactions. Non-cash transactions involving chips, checks, and wire transfers are recorded as they are made and thus do not require a CTR.

Essentially

- In the United States, all slot machine jackpots of $1,200 or more are reported by the casino to the IRS. The form used for this is a W2G. Withholding is mandatory for amounts above $5,000 or for any amount when the player doesn't provide identification.

- Casinos in most states require that a player provide identification before receiving a large jackpot. The most accepted form of identification is a state- or province-issued driver's license or identification card.

- Underage gamblers are not paid jackpots. There are no exceptions to this rule.

- The person who pushes the button is the jackpot winner. Keep this in mind if you're playing one machine with another person.

- A regular jackpot should be paid within thirty minutes. Wide-area progressives often take two or three hours before a check is cut.

- Always play maximum credits if you want to be eligible for the top prize.

- Casinos report cash transactions of $10,000 and above to the U.S. Treasury. If a casino employee asks you for identification to fill out a cash transaction report, you should always cooperate.

CHAPTER 22

Comps

 Most players fit somewhere on a spectrum between the following extremes.

The Wanderer: This person likes to visit many different casinos. It's Bellagio in the morning, Venetian in the afternoon, and Caesars Palace at night. Lots of walking; very little playing.

The Regular: Bettors of this variety sit down at a table or machine in one casino and don't move for hours.

For obvious reasons, casinos prefer customers who are regulars. Casino-marketing systems are designed to find and cultivate these players (who are described in the industry as being **casino-oriented**). Loyal customers get **comps** (complimentary rooms, meals, shows, gifts, tournaments, special-event invitations, and other incentives). Wandering players get a friendly smile and the bill for dinner. All customers are held to this standard. Strictly speaking, comps are *not* an enticement. They are a compensation for allowing the casino a shot at your money.

Should you pursue this relationship? It depends. First let's explore how the comp system works, and then we'll examine its potential value for you.

The Players Club

Every major casino has a card system that electronically tracks and rates wagers. Getting into the rating system is easy. You go to a players club desk, fill out a form, and the casino gives you a personalized card (it takes about a minute). Insert your card into a slot machine and your action will be recorded; give the card to a dealer or floorperson and your play will be monitored. Points accrue for dollars wagered. The casino offers comps and cash back for points. It also offers promotions and discounts for simply being a players club member.

Of course, this is a casino, so everything isn't always entirely straightforward. The first mystery is how many dollars equal a point.

Some club brochures clearly tell you. Some have fuzzy information, so you have to ask a host. Occasionally you'll find a club that treats the question as a company secret. When you ask, the host will say (with a straight face), "We just don't know."

The second mystery is what you can get for the points. Most club brochures state clearly how many points it takes to get a comp room, a comp meal, or comp dollars, but they usually don't mention that a **casino host**, **pit boss**, or **slots supervisor** has the option to give you more.

Tip

Got a players club question? Ask a casino host (one of the well-dressed perpetually sociable people you'll find hanging around the players club desk). That person will tell you how much action is required for a restaurant comp, free room, or whatever other comps the casino is offering. It never hurts to ask.

Theoretical Win and Free Stuff

Whatever you get and however the casino calculates points, the total value of comps is based primarily on a casino's **theoretical win**; that's the average amount the casino expects to earn from you. The casino anticipates fluctuations so they don't look too much at actual net wins and losses (unless the actual numbers deviate from the theoretical numbers for an extended period of time). In other words, you may be lucky and another person may be unlucky; the casino wants to reward you for your action, not your luck.

A casino typically will "reinvest" between 10 percent to 50 percent of theoretical win (comps are called "reinvestment" in casino industry parlance). A reinvestment of 20 percent to 35 percent is most common.

The tables on page 357 show you how it works. House edge is the inverse of game payback; 92 percent payback = 8 percent house edge. Keep in mind that these amounts are average. Some comp programs are more liberal than others. Also, sixteen levels are provided here as examples, but most comp programs don't have so many levels. Some have only one tier for slots, one tier for video poker, and three or four tiers for table games. And even when a system has additional levels, the casino can only guess how well you're playing the game.

Consider what this means. A casino's estimate of the house edge *does not* necessarily reflect the actual house edge.

For example, most casinos assume that an average blackjack player loses 2 percent of his action, so anyone playing with a near-zero edge usually gets comped at a higher level. But a blackjack player who is identified as an expert is judged to be giving the house nothing, even if he is in fact *not* playing at an expert level.

Intriguing, yes? We'll return to this subject in a bit, but let's continue examining the charts.

Theoretical Casino Win and Typical Daily Comps for Slots

House Edge	$0.50 Bets	$0.50 Comps	$1 Bets	$1 Comps	$5 Bets	$5 Comps
10%	$100	$30	$200	$60	$1,000	$300
9%	$90	$27	$180	$54	$900	$270
8%	$80	$24	$160	$48	$800	$240
7%	$70	$21	$140	$42	$700	$210
6%	$60	$18	$120	$36	$600	$180
5%	$50	$15	$100	$30	$500	$150
4%	$40	$12	$80	$24	$400	$120
3%	$30	$9	$60	$18	$300	$90
2%	$20	–	$40	$12	$200	$60
1%	$10	–	$20	–	$100	$30

A casino's theoretical win is the average amount per day per customer that the casino expects to earn on a particular game. These figures are calculated on the basis of 500 decisions per hour, a four-hour session, and 30 percent reinvestment. Machine payback is the inverse of house edge (92 percent payback = 8 percent house edge). Actual casino comps will vary by property.

Theoretical Casino Win and Typical Daily Comps for Tables

House Edge	$10 Bets	$10 Comps	$25 Bets	$25 Comps	$100 Bets	$100 Comps
6%	$144	$43	$360	$108	$1,440	$432
5%	$120	$36	$300	$90	$1,200	$360
4%	$96	$29	$240	$72	$960	$288
3%	$72	$22	$180	$54	$720	$216
2%	$48	$14	$120	$36	$480	$144
1%	$24	$7	$60	$18	$240	$72

A casino's theoretical win is the average amount per day per customer that the casino expects to earn on a particular game. These figures are calculated on the basis of 60 decisions per hour, a four-hour session, and 30 percent reinvestment. Actual casino comps will vary by property.

You'll notice that playing $0.50 per spin on a slot machine that has an 8 percent edge garners about $24 of comps during a four-hour session. Typically, this translates into a buffet comp or maybe a coffee-shop meal. On the other hand, playing $5 per spin at 8 percent for four hours is theoretically worth $800 to the casino and will probably get you about $240 back in comps. That's usually good for free **RFB** (room, food, and beverages) at a modest level. A player who bets $100 per hand on a table game such as Three Card Poker would get a similar rating.

Typical House-Edge Estimates for Theoretical Win

Game	Standard House Edge	Expert House Edge
Blackjack	2%	0%
Craps	5%	1%
Baccarat	5%	1%
Other Table Games	5%	2% to 5%
Video Poker	2% to 4%	1% to 2%
Slots ($1 and higher)	6% to 8%	6%
Slots ($0.50 and lower)	7% to 10%	7%

A casino's estimate of the house edge does not necessarily reflect the actual house edge. This is because the casino is averaging multiple bets and estimating each player's ability. These percentages vary by property.

Now some people might ask, "Very interesting, but so what? The players club computer will track my play, and a casino host will simply tell me what I am entitled to receive. Right?"

Yes, or maybe no. There's no rule that says a casino host has to give you the maximum goodies allowed. Asking will sometimes get you something more. And wouldn't it be nice to know in advance how much your business is actually worth?

THE FACT IS...

Back in the "old days" of Las Vegas, comps were available only for players at tables. The comp formula was simple; it was one average bet per hour. So if you bet $100 per hand for four hours, you got $400 in comps. That's a 33 percent comp rate for a game with a 5 percent edge. The old-style formula is still useful as a shortcut if you don't have a calculator handy.

How do you compare the players club at casino A versus casino B when they have entirely different point systems? The best way to do it is with theoretical win.

Another advantage of these calculations is that they help you to see how much "free" comps actually cost. It's not bad luck that empties your pockets. Rather, it's average luck over time.

But all of the above advantages pale in comparison to the major reason why you should sharpen your pencil to figure theoretical win. It's all about…

Double-Dipping for Freebies!

What happens if you receive comps for playing a 96 percent game, but you actually play a 99 percent game? Let's say you wager $5 per hand on video poker. You "theoretically" lose $400 per day, but you actually lose only $100 (on average). The casino comps you $120, and that puts you ahead by $20 in real value.

It might seem too good to be true, but it happens every day for anyone who is willing to make an effort to use optimal strategies on the right games.

As I explained in Chapter 1, most people don't use optimal strategies. So they lose. The casino is counting on it.

Isn't that wild?

But before we continue with the magic numbers, think about this…

Comp Caveats

You can see how the entire subject of comps automatically leads players to ask, "What do I have to do to earn comps? How much should I bet?"

That's what casinos want. It's one of their biggest marketing ploys. They want you to focus on getting comps and forget about how much it costs to get them. Don't fall for the hype.

An average player on a typical slot machine or table usually receives only about $100 in comps for every $340 he *loses!*

Spending $3.40 to get $1 is a horrible investment.

Yes, there are situations when you can double-dip, get your comps, and beat the house, but these situations involve specific games and particular tactics. Professional players diligently calculate comps and payback numbers, and they refuse to play when the conditions aren't right. You may not want to be so zealous. That's okay. Just be aware that comp systems are as varied as gambling games, and not every one is beatable.

Tip

The next level up from RFB (room, food, and beverages) includes limousine service, paid travel expenses, and discounts on markers. Don't hesitate to ask for these perks if your play warrants it.

The general rule is… Don't bet more or play longer to get more comps.

But do realize that comps *are* a valuable part of your payback. You should get every comp that you deserve for the action you give.

Basic Comp Programs

When you sign up for a players card, the casino will ask for your e-mail and street address. This is a good thing because they want to send you offers for free stuff.

A typical offer includes a free or discounted hotel room with a cash-back coupon or another valuable promotion. It might be a free spa visit, a free tournament entry, a free show, $50 of free slot play, or something like that. The advantage of these offers is that (usually) you are under no obligation to give the casino any particular level of action. Of course, subsequent offers will take into account your past action, but the current offer is ironclad.

Many comp systems also have cash-back promotions; you get cash or checks based on your level of play. Payments vary, but cash back is usually about 0.25 percent to 1 percent of your action.

Most comp systems also have **comp dollars**. These are dollars you accumulate that can be spent (via your players club card) almost any-where on the property.

As you might expect, savvy players use the free-room offers and other promotions and save the comp dollars for merchandise, meals, and amenities that aren't included in a particular comp package. The casinos know this, and it's okay with them.

Getting More Comps for Less Action

As I mentioned previously, some comp tactics may be too much effort for your taste. That's okay, but you should know how they work.

First, you must join the players club and you must use your card.

This might seem obvious, but some people forget to insert their club cards when playing slots, or they don't tell the dealers when playing at tables. The casino will not comp you if it doesn't record your action.

Second, you must play with optimal strategies and avoid any games that pay back less than 97 percent (3 percent house edge). This eliminates nearly all slot machines and it limits your choice of games mostly to video poker, blackjack, craps, and baccarat.

Third, you must present yourself as an "average" player, and you must protect that image. A casino will *not* rate you as an expert player unless you tip them off in some way (see the sidebar on this page).

Ratholing

A key component of maintaining the perception of you as an average player is a strategy known as **ratholing**. It's a nasty name for a valuable tactic used when playing table games. Casinos initially rate you with their standard "plain vanilla" calculations for theoretical win. But if they see that you are consistently beating them, or losing less than they anticipated, then they lower your rating.

Ratholing is a technique of stealthily slipping chips off the table and into your pockets to make you look like a loser. As with counting cards, ratholing is legal (see the sidebar on the next page for exceptions), but it's not appreciated in a casino. If you're caught ratholing, the pit supervisor will know instantly that you are an experienced player and your rating may go to zero.

Tip

There are various techniques for ratholing. The easiest is to simply palm a chip (press one chip into your palm) as you aimlessly fiddle with a stack. Keep the chip hidden until you're sure the dealer or the pit hasn't noticed. Wait a minute, then reach for something in your pocket while leaving the chip. Do this two or three times per hour and you can finish a session looking like a loser even when you're a winner.

THE FACT IS...

Ratholing is *not allowed* in poker or *any* gambling tournament. Also, ratholing is illegal when it is used to circumvent U.S. Treasury cash transaction reporting requirements. Excepting the above, ratholing is allowed in most jurisdictions, though it is unwelcome in casinos. A player who is caught ratholing may see his comp rating dramatically lowered.

Note these precautions. These are suggested guidelines to keep you from attracting a pit supervisor's attention, and to insure compliance with game rules and with currency transaction reporting requirements (see Chapter 21).

A dealer and pit boss will track black chips much more carefully than greens and reds. Never rathole more than one black chip per hour or five black chips per session. Never rathole any chip in a denomination for which you have less than fifteen chips sitting on the table. Never rathole purple chips or higher denominations. Never rathole if you're the only player at the table.

Do not rathole black chips if you are the only black-chip player at the table.

Do not rathole more than $500 in a session.

Do not rathole anything if you buy in for more than $4,000 or expect to cash out for more than $4,000. The reason is that a run of good luck could easily tip you over $10,000, and you must never (never, never, never) hide your winnings or cash transactions from a CTR.

Rathole only in standard table games. Never rathole in a tournament. Never rathole in *any* pot-style poker game.

Ideally, you should rathole mostly greens and sometimes reds at a rate of about 3 percent of your action. Thus bets of $25 per hand would be about two green chips per hour.

If you have chips in your pocket, and you hit a losing streak and need to rebuy, don't use the concealed chips. Use cash or a marker.

One final caveat… Chips embedded with RFID (radio frequency identification) tags may someday make ratholing obsolete. Essentially, each chip can be uniquely identified and (theoretically) tied to a particular player. An actual system for tracking this info is years down the road, but it is on the way. RFID is already being used at a few properties, primarily to find counterfeit chips.

RFID systems are expensive, so most casinos don't have them now, and probably won't have them for a while.

Tip

But if you find yourself at a casino that uses RFID (or some other chip-tracking technology), you'll know because the table will look high-tech with an oversized chip tray and a club card reader embedded or connected to the table. The dealer will be very particular about how you position your chips on the circles. Everything will scream RFID. If you're feeling the RFID vibe (maybe it's radio waves), then rathole carefully, or not at all.

Other Comp Tactics

Obviously, ratholing is not possible when you're playing video poker or slots. But there are other tactics that you can use to pump up your ratings on the machines.

- Restrict your play on video poker machines to games paying 99 percent and better. Many casinos will continue to comp you as if you are playing 96 percent or 97 percent payback.

- Shift your action away from the weekends and play on days or at times when the casino is offering bonus points and extra promotions.

- Play video poker games that have built up large progressive meters. An example would be a progressive 8/5 jacks-or-better game that has the equivalent of 8,000 credits on the meter. The base game technically pays about 97.3 percent, but the jackpot increases the payout to above 99 percent (for more on this see page 77)

- Play dollar machines or higher denominations. A $3 bet on a dollar machine often will garner *better* comps than an equivalent bet on a nickel or penny machine, even though the lower-denomination game has a higher hold. The reason for this seemingly backward policy is that the casino assumes you have a larger bankroll if you are betting in dollar chunks rather than in nickel or penny chunks.

Perhaps the most effective tactic of all is to shift the bulk of your action from multiple casinos to one property (or two properties that are owned by the same company). Granted, this is exactly what casinos want you to do, but in this case you will be rewarded for your loyalty.

Let's say you normally spread your gaming dollars around to four casinos that are owned by different companies, 25 percent to each property. If you change that to 70 percent at one property and 10 percent at the other three, you'll get significantly more comps for the same dollars risked.

Poker Comps

Comps are calculated differently for pot-style poker compared to other casino games. This is because poker has a rake (or fee) rather than a house edge.

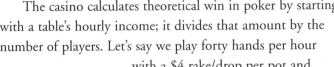

The casino calculates theoretical win in poker by starting with a table's hourly income; it divides that amount by the number of players. Let's say we play forty hands per hour with a $4 rake/drop per pot and there are nine players. That is:

$40 \times \$4 \div 9 = \$17.70$ per hour theoretical win per player.

Alas, most poker rooms will not comp back anywhere near 30 percent of that. You're lucky if you get $1 per hour in cash back or comp dollars, a free meal every twenty-four hours, and (maybe) a discount room.

THE FACT IS...

The comp clock is still ticking at the table when you take a break, so it's a good idea to step away at least once an hour. Usually, you'll be allowed at least ten minutes. Comps will continue to accumulate even while you're stretching your legs, washing your hands, or window shopping.

Why are casinos so stingy when it comes to poker? Sadly, they figure that an average poker player is worth about the same as a $15-per-hand blackjack player. But the blackjack player may eventually move up to bigger bets, while the poker player will never be worth more than $17.70 (or whatever the rake generates) regardless of how much he bets. There is no such thing as a $50-per-pot rake in poker.

So poker is treated as a promotional contest, sort of like bingo. Strictly speaking, it is offered as an attraction for other games.

It can be argued that this logic is flawed, that a customer who spends $17.70 per hour should be encouraged and comped. But despite these arguments, the casino industry has largely held to the conventional paradigm.

Perhaps a casino entrepreneur will come along someday and knock the gambling world on its ear with substantial poker comps.

Comps for Mid-Limit and High-Limit Action

About the time you sign your first marker, or maybe the first time you buy in for $3,000, a friendly gentleman or lady in a stylish suit will come to say hello. This gregarious person will be a **casino host**. Hosts work in a department called "player development." They're looking for casino-oriented players, particularly those betting at the higher limits.

A casino host can handle your reservations for rooms, shows, and dinners. He can get you the best seats, the best suite, the most expensive meal. The host can comp the entire package and top it off with a limousine ride from the airport and a basket of fruit

"May I have five thousand dollars? No, make it ten thousand. Two thousand dollar limit... I'll take the full odds on the ten, two hundred on the hardway, the limit on all the numbers, two-hundred-fifty on the eleven. Thank you very much."

—James Bond, as played by Sean Connery in *Diamonds are Forever* (1971)

or champagne when you arrive. The only thing you must do is play at a certain level for a specific length of time; $500 per hand, six hours per day would be nice.

If you play for lower stakes, let's say $100 per hand and only four hours per day, well... You've seen the charts. The comps will have less value, and the host will be less accommodating. If you slide down to $20 per hand, the host probably will disappear. If you call his cell phone, you'll get voice-mail. When you leave a message, someone from the players club desk will return the call.

Awkward.

It's simply economics. Every property has unique criteria for who gets a host and what that host will offer. A **whale** (casino slang for an ultra-high-limit player) is defined differently in Las Vegas compared to Laughlin. And a player who is classified as a mid-limit customer in Atlantic City may be considered a high roller in Louisiana.

Keeping this in mind, here is how the comp system works when you have a host.

Working with a Casino Host

If you're risking at least $100 per hand at the tables or $5 per spin at slots, then probably you'll be dealing with a host at least some of the time.

The host will be (as you require) a sort of concierge, making sure you're comfortable at the casino. Other casino staff may handle your particular requests, but the host will act as a maestro. He will smooth the way so you'll have a good stay. Part of the smooth-the-way process is awarding comps.

When the time comes to give you comps, the host will rate your play by using a formula that begins with your expected theoretical loss. It also takes into account how much you actually won/lost during your last few sessions. Other factors include your style of play, how often you visit the property, and your credit history.

The host puts it all together and then makes a decision that is within particular parameters that have been established by the casino's marketing wizards. Occasionally the host will be swayed by some horse trading on your part (give me this instead of that). Thus if the numbers indicate a $900 reinvestment, you may be able to push that amount up to $1,100, but you won't get much more.

Remember, the host doesn't owe you a thing. If it seems as if you are shopping for comps and aren't particularly casino-oriented, you'll get a free buffet, maybe.

By the way, a lot of this usually happens at the end of a visit. At the beginning of a visit the host frequently will tell you, "Charge it all to your room, and when you leave we'll see what we can give you."

If bazaar-style bargaining leaves you feeling queasy, you can see why the latest cutting-edge comp systems have been gradually weaning players from host-approved comps. People don't want to go "hat in hand" to receive favors from a casino host; casino managers understand this. So at many properties, even high-limit players now use club cards and receive some comp packages up front.

THE FACT IS...

One of the advantages of being a players club member is that the casino will give you (upon request) an annual statement of your "estimated" wins and losses. While it's not necessarily a complete record of your gaming, it can be a valuable tool in tax planning and record keeping.

On the other hand, there is something *very* alluring about having a personal casino host, someone who will book your entire trip when you make just one phone call.

And there is no direct-mail piece in the world that can woo a customer like a host who smiles and says, "Hey, do you like Elton John? I have a couple of front-row tickets to his show that you might enjoy. The price? Forget the price. I just want you to have a good time."

Yes! Oh, yes!

Clearly, casino hosts will never disappear. And the tradition of host-approved comps will continue forever for high-limit players.

So here are some things that you can do to put a host in a more generous mood.

- Buy in big. Let's say your trip bankroll is $3,000, and each session bankroll is $1,500. Buy in for the full $3,000, and then exercise some self-control. Wager only the $1,500 per session you intended to risk. Piling up the chips gives the casino a better idea of the total amount you will eventually risk. Perception is everything when it comes to comps.

- Use markers and front money. This is another tactic to give the casino a clear picture of the total amount you are risking.

- Comps of all types are easier to get during the middle of the week and off-season. Busy periods, especially conventions, are the worst times to ask for freebies.

- If you want more attention for your action, play at a smaller casino. Your $50 bets will look bigger when the table limit is $10.

Remember, the more stuff that you can get comped free and clear at the beginning of the trip or during the trip, the less you'll need to negotiate at the end of the trip. When you're asking for comps at the beginning of your visit or during your stay, here are some tactics that can help.

- Generally, a room comp is easier to get than an upper-tier restaurant meal. That's because the room is charged at a fixed rate but the meal is (in some cases) open-ended. And who knows how much you'll spend on the wine? Also, if the host (or someone else) writes a fixed-limit comp for a restaurant but you don't spend that much, your comp account may be charged for the full value of the comp. For all these reasons it is easier to get a room comp. Once you have the room nailed down, then definitely go for the restaurants.

- Be flexible and phrase your requests so that it's tough to say no. For example, "My spouse and I are celebrating our twenty-fifth wedding anniversary. Can you get us a good table at Le Riche? Is there anything else you would suggest?" If the host can't deliver Le Riche, you'll surely get a good alternative.

- Pit supervisors and slots supervisors can authorize comps just as a host can. However, their willingness to do so has diminished somewhat as the newest comp systems have come online. But it never hurts to ask. Just be prepared for the supervisor to say, "Pardon me, Mr. Z, but I don't need to write you a comp. I checked your comp account and you have plenty of comp dollars to get whatever you want for free."

Whatever you do, don't let a supervisor or host get away with a flat "no." Begin a negotiation. You never know what might come up in the conversation.

Discounts on Markers

Obviously, you can't ask for a discount on a marker if you have a winning session. But you *can* expect a discount when all the following conditions occur together.

- You lose substantially more than the expected theoretical amount.

- The value of comps that you have received is less than 30 percent of the net amount you lost.

- Your net losses for a trip are over $2,000.

For example, if your "theo" is $1,000, you were comped $350, and you lost $3,000 on a marker, that's an amount that may be discounted.

But nobody is going to discount a $3,000 loss if you received $1,200 in comps.

When the time comes to settle up, say something like this to your host, "You guys really clobbered me on this last trip. I appreciate the basic comps, but can I get some sort of discount on the debt?"

A discount of 10 percent to 15 percent would be reasonable. If you're a good customer, you may get a bit more than that. At the very least you should get 5 percent off. If the host gives you nothing, then go somewhere else to play.

The Philosophy of Comps

The casino understands probability, so don't feel bad about asking for comps when you're winning. It's not your fault that luck is temporarily against the house. The casino should be happy to comp you because they want another shot at your money.

Conversely, losing is not necessarily a reason for you to deserve more comps than anyone else who has risked the same amount of money. So you lost. So what? It's gambling. Burning through a $5,000 bankroll on an unlucky streak may get you some nice meals and a free room, but don't expect to be treated like a sultan unless the casino expects that you'll come back and spend the same amount next time.

The type of gambler most likely to be disappointed is the one who loses $300 and expects to get $250 of it back in comps. It simply doesn't work that way.

And, of course, be realistic. Use the comp formulas in this chapter and ask for what is reasonable. Hosts and supervisors want to say yes. Make it easy for them.

Essentially

- Every major casino has a card system that electronically tracks and rates wagers. The system is used to calculate the casino's theoretical win; that's the average amount the house expects to earn from each player. Comps are awarded to players based primarily on theoretical win.

- A casino usually will "reinvest" about 20 percent to 35 percent of theoretical win (comps are called "reinvestment" in casino industry parlance).

- An average player on a slot machine or table usually will receive only about $100 in comps for every $340 he loses. So it is not a good idea to bet more or play longer to get more comps. But comps *are* a valuable part of your payback. So you should get the most for your action.

- There are various tactics for getting more comps. These tactics include favoring one casino over multiple casinos, shifting action away from weekends, taking advantage of promotions, playing higher-denomination slot games, and ratholing.

- If you're a mid-limit and high-limit player, comps will come more easily if you buy in big, use markers and front money, and play at smaller casinos. You also can get discounts on markers when your losses have substantially exceeded theoretical expectations.

- When asking for comps, be realistic. Hosts and supervisors want to say yes. Make it easy for them.

CHAPTER 23

Tournaments

 When people think of gambling tournaments, the first thing that usually comes to mind is the World Series of Poker or maybe World Poker Tour. But there are "worlds" of gambling tournaments beyond poker.

Just about every casino game can be played in a tournament format. Slot tournaments are huge! Ditto for video poker and blackjack. Some of these are million-dollar competitions. And best of all, they are often free.

Yes. F R E E !!!

Gambling tournaments serve a dual purpose in the casino industry; they are used as comps to reward customers, and they also are used as promotions to get new customers onto the property. Even the venerable World Series of Poker serves this double role. It was invented to promote Binion's Horseshoe Casino (now it promotes Harrah's properties), and some entries are comped. But before we get into the specifics of the WSOP, let's cover gambling tournaments in general.

The best tournaments (from a player's point of view) are invitational contests with big prizes and no buy-in fees. Ideally, they are multiple-day events with food and rooms comped, sometimes even airfare.

Does that sound good? Yes, it does. Here are some tips to help you get the most from these most excellent comps. We'll begin with slots and video poker, then continue with table games.

Slot Tournaments

All slot tournaments have the same basic components.

Contestants: There may be eight, eighty, or even 800 players. It varies, but the size of the field is an important factor in calculating the value of the event.

Rounds: Contestants compete in sessions, typically called "rounds." The goal is to accumulate game credits (more about the games a bit later). Rounds usually last between five minutes to thirty minutes; ten or fifteen minutes is standard. Some tournaments have only one round. Others have two or three rounds, and the credits are combined to produce a final score. Sometimes there are semifinals, and top players go to a final round.

Prizes: Every tournament pays a grand prize for the top score and smaller prizes for lower scores. Some casinos pay the top tenth of the field. Some pay the top one-fifth. Some pay half the field, or even the full field. Tournament prizes vary dramatically; amounts between $100 and $100,000 are typical. Some tournaments have top prizes of $1 million.

Buy-in vs. Free: Tournaments with smaller prize pools often require a buy-in, anywhere from $10 to $200. Most buy-in contests are open to the general public. Ironically, tournaments with bigger prizes usually have no entry fees, but only invited guests are allowed to play.

Tournament Groups: Contestants compete at different times in sub groups, usually anywhere from eight people to eighty. So let's say a tournament has 320 contestants. The casino might have four sessions of eight players for each round, and three ten-minute rounds over two days.

The Slot Tournament Experience

A slot tournament is a festive event held in a ballroom or other meeting space; usually, there is an MC and music. Family members and friends are welcome.

The machines are arranged so that competitors can see each other. Generally, the games are popular favorites such as Double Diamond or Blazing 7's. Some properties have casino-branded machines. Whatever the game, everyone plays the same version and pay table, so nobody has a built-in advantage. The machines are configured in a "tournament package," which means they pay around 1,800 percent; that's twenty times more than standard casino machines.

Tip

Want to spin your way to a million? Harrah's Millionaire Maker comes in two varieties, one for video poker and the other for slots. Every Harrah's property has quarterly semi-final contests; two or three winners advance to the big show to compete for a top prize of $1 million.

When a round begins, you simply press the spin button as often as is necessary to get the reels to spin continually. The credits you earn are tournament points, not real money (darn it). But if you keep those reels spinning, and luck is with you, you'll outscore the competition and win a prize.

Even if you don't win, the casino will reward you with goodies. Some tournaments give everyone a gift when they register. Other properties have cocktail receptions and banquets with awards and entertainers. And of course, the entire package comes with a room and regular comp rewards.

Small Tournaments

If you're not already receiving tournament invitations, it's a good idea to begin your "tournament training" by playing in a small contest. This gives you a taste of a slots competition so you can see if you enjoy the experience. It also brings you to the attention of the casino's marketing department (which may get you invited to bigger tournaments).

Most casinos have weekly competitions that are free or require a small buy-in. They are open to anyone. Typically, these are contests with a top prize of less than $5,000, and a total prize pool of less than $15,000. In some cases the top prize may be only $100.

Besides being good practice for the bigger events, a small tournament also gives you an opportunity to practice an important strategic calculation.

Calculating the Value of a Tournament

Like every gambling game, a tournament has a positive or negative long-term value. You should know the value of a contest before investing your time. The calculation is easy.

Divide the total prize pool by the number of players in the competition. The result is the "average value" of competing. There is no guarantee that you'll actually get this much after one tournament, but like any edge, it's an average value over time.

Add to this the value of what you are guaranteed to receive (gifts, food, rooms, or whatever). Then subtract any entry fee. If the final number is negative, you're paying more than you're receiving.

If it's positive, you're getting a good value. Here's a hypothetical tournament as an example:

Prize pool = $5,000

Contestants = 100

Gift to Every Player = $25

Hotel = $100

Entry Fee = –$75

$5,000 ÷ 100 = $50—This is the average value of being a contestant.

$50 + $100 + 25 = $175—This is the total value of everything you receive (including the average value of being a contestant).

$175 – $75 = $100—This is the value of the contest after paying the entry fee.

Note that this contest would have a negative value of –$25 without the gift and the free hotel room.

To see the result expressed as a percent advantage, divide the net profit or loss by the action (the entry fee). For example, $100 ÷ $75 = 133 percent edge for the player.

A tournament with a positive edge is always best, but even a tournament with a negative value may be worth the price if you really want the experience. It comes down to a personal choice.

Getting into Bigger Slot Tournaments

Of course, you don't want to play only in small or entry-fee tournaments. You want the free ones with the big prizes, cocktail receptions, hors d'œuvres, banquets, hotel suites, and so forth. Here's how you get into those.

First, you need to play regularly at a property. As with comps, this is best done without increasing your overall level of action. Follow the tips from Chapter 22 regarding shifting your action from multiple casinos to one or two.

Second, you need to read your mail. If you're a regular slots player, it is inevitable that eventually you will receive an invitation to a free slot tournament. The size of the tournament and the prizes will vary depending on the level of action you're giving the casino.

It's that simple.

If you're already a regular slots player, but you haven't yet received an invitation, it never hurts to ask your host or someone at the players club. Just say you want to be included in the next tournament. If your action warrants an invitation, then surely you will get one.

Video Poker Tournaments

Most of what we've covered up to now also applies to video poker, but there are some differences.

When playing in a video poker tournament, be sure to play quickly enough to complete as many hands as possible. Accuracy is important, but don't lose time fretting over obscure strategy nuances. Remember, each hand costs nothing, so the more hands you play, the greater your possible score.

Also, you may need to make dramatic strategy adjustments if you're falling behind, or to preserve a lead.

For example, when playing jacks or better, **A♦ K♦ Q♦ J♦ 7♦** normally would be a draw to a royal flush (drop the **7♦**) in a non-tournament situation. But if you're leading by a small margin, you may want to take the pat flush and move on to the next hand. If you draw, you'll lose value about 83 percent of the time. Or to put it another way, four times out of five you'll draw and get less or nothing. You'll improve only one out of forty-seven times, and then you'll get way more than you need.

"Generally the way it works is that somewhere in the organization a decision is made that we want to get a group of customers that fit a certain criteria in for a tournament. There are several different criteria that we may pull on. One would be the person's average daily play. Another...would be their cumulative play over a certain period of time... We may have a Diamond-only tournament, or a Platinum-only tournament."

—**Northscott Grounsell, director of slots at Harrah's North Kansas City**

On the other hand, if you're trailing by a wide margin, then you may need to shoot for a royal in situations that normally would not be royal draws. Consider A♦ A♠ A♥ K♥ Q♥. Usually, you would hold the three aces and hope for a quad. But if trips or a quad won't keep you in the money, then they are worthless. You must hold the suited cards and hope for a royal.

Blackjack Tournaments

Blackjack tournaments are similar in structure to slots and video poker tournaments in that there are groups of contestants, rounds, and so forth. Standard blackjack rules apply with the following variations:

- You get a finite amount of tournament chips.

- Some tournaments have a time limit; others play a specific number of hands.

- In blackjack tournaments, as in poker, the "first action" position (first person to act) moves clockwise around the table. Thus everyone gets an opportunity to be last.

- Blackjack tournaments often have special rules that are more favorable than standard cash games; common variations include 2:1 payouts on naturals, and double down on any two cards.

- Winners are determined by chip count at the conclusion of the action.

Money management is the key. You can win a blackjack tournament by winning the most, but you also can win in some circumstances by losing the least. And this may require variations from basic strategy.

For example, you may find yourself in a double-down situation where an opponent can beat you only if you risk extra dollars. Thus a double down will jeopardize your lead. So in this situation, you should hit instead of double.

Or turning the example around, suppose your opponent doubles when he shouldn't, and he loses. You may

THE FACT IS...

The formula used to calculate the average value of a blackjack or poker tournaments is the same one used for slots and video poker (see page 376).

need a double-down to beat him. In this case, you *must* double down, even on a stiff hand.

Poker Tournaments

Poker tournaments are played like standard poker games, but with the following differences:

- Everyone begins with the same amount of tournament chips.

- The game continues until there is one winner and all the other players have lost all their chips. There is no time limit or limit to the number of hands dealt.

Tip

Some poker and blackjack tournaments allow rebuys. If you go broke, you can buy back into the contest for the price of another entry fee. However, many tournaments (including most World Series of Poker events) do not allow rebuys. So if you go broke, then it's over for that event.

- A player goes out of the tournament only when his chips are gone (there have been occasions when a player with just one remaining chip has come back and won a tournament).

- Forced bets, antes, and betting limits escalate over time, so players cannot stay out of the action too long without losing chips.

- Tournaments usually award prizes to players who go out toward the end of the competition, even when they don't win. In other words, a second-place finish means you lost all your chips, but you still win a prize in most tournaments.

As I mentioned in Chapter 22, poker has a peculiar status in the gambling world. It doesn't generate as many comps as other gambling games. The same is true for poker tournaments. Casinos subsidize and sponsor poker competitions, and occasionally you'll see an invitational or a "freeroll." But overall, poker tournaments aren't comped as much as other gambling tournaments. Nevertheless, there are plenty of entries that are given away as promotions (including entries to the WSOP). And if you're a high-limit player at another game, then the casino will gladly comp you an entry to almost any poker tournament (except maybe a tournament at a competing property).

Poker Tournament Strategies

As with video poker and blackjack, poker strategy in tournament situations sometimes varies dramatically from the strategy in standard cash games. One of the most notable variations is the option of going all in. You can do it in a no-limit cash game, but if you lose the hand, you lose actual money (perhaps a lot). Then again, you can reach into your pocket, buy in, and continue playing the next hand.

In contrast, if you go all in during a tournament, the most you can lose is the value of your entry fee. But once you're knocked out, then you can't continue in the tournament unless rebuys are allowed.

As a result, some players use an "all-in strategy" when playing in tournaments. They frequently go all in and bully their opponents off pots. The opponents say to themselves, "He's probably bluffing, but I don't want to risk my tournament life on any hand except a sure winner." So the opponents fold and the all-in player steadily builds his stack.

The drawback to this super-aggressive strategy is that it occasionally requires some super-good luck. Sooner or later someone with a monster hand will call, and the all-in player must win those showdowns to stay alive.

Another problem with the all-in strategy is that it works only when your stack rivals or covers (is greater than) your opponent's stack. If you are short-stacked, then your opponents are not threatened by your all-in moves. In fact, they may be *more* likely to call because they can afford the risk and they want to eliminate you from the tournament.

Here are some additional tips to help you reach the final table.

- Be aggressive early. You want to double and triple your stack quickly (or bust out early and spend your time productively elsewhere). The worst strategy is to hang on meekly as the clock ticks away and the blinds wear you down; in the end, you're forced to play aggressively anyway, but with a diminished stack. Don't be reckless, but push the envelope early, and then you can be selective with a big stack.

- If an all-in strategy is too aggressive for your taste, bet the size of the pot or just slightly more. This tactic will weed out long-shot hands and you'll get mostly legitimate calls to your bets. These calls will be hands that probably would *not* have folded even if you had bet substantially more.

- If a tournament is worth a buy-in, then it's worth a rebuy. So you should re-buy and add-in for the maximum, to whatever limit you can comfortably afford.

- Don't be discouraged when you're running low on chips. The temptation is to play anything that comes along. But if you can wait a round or two, then a better hand might appear. For instance, Q9 offsuit begins to look very attractive when you're three blinds away from elimination in a hold 'em tournament. And it might be the right hand to play…but probably not. Be patient, and play your hands correctly.

"One of the biggest mistakes that I see a lot of these guys make who are inexperienced in no-limit tournaments is that they bet way too much or way too little… Most of the time you should be betting the pot. If there is $1,000 in chips [in the pot], and I check to you, and you decide to bet…bet $1,000… Don't bet the minimum…and don't bet $3,000. [If you bet too much] yes, you're going to get me to fold most of the time, but every time I don't fold, I'll have [your] top pair beat badly."

—Greg "Fossilman" Raymer, winner of the 2004 World Series of Poker.

If you're lucky enough to reach the final table in a poker tournament, many more hands become playable as opponents are eliminated. For example, a hand like A8 suited often is weak against nine opponents in hold 'em (pre-flop), but it may be quite strong when there are only three opponents.

Tournaments vs. Cash Games

If a tournament is free, then go for it. It's a shot at money for nothing. But what if it costs money? Should you pay to play, or should you stick to standard cash games?

That depends on your value calculations. What is the value of the tournament compared to your return (or cost) when playing for cash?

Another consideration is volatility. Tournaments are highly volatile; sometimes you'll win a lot, but most times you'll win nothing. Cash games are less volatile; you can play a few hands and walk away with a small win or small loss.

And then you should consider the time it takes to play a tournament. Slot tournaments can go pretty quickly, but blackjack and poker tournaments can take a while. That can be a good thing if you want a lot of action for a finite amount of money, or it can be a time-swallowing hole.

Most tournaments are a good value for the money (primarily because they are promotions), but as I mentioned before, it comes down to a personal choice. It is always best to play the game you prefer.

Essentially

- All of the most popular casino games are played in tournament formats. These include slots, video poker, blackjack, and poker.

- Like every gambling game, a gambling tournament has a positive or negative long-term value. You should calculate the value of a tournament before investing your time.

- The best tournaments (from a player's point of view) are free. Ideally, they are multiple-day events with food and rooms comped, sometimes even airfare.

- The surest way to be invited to a free tournament is to give one casino a lot of action. This is best done by shifting your action from other casinos rather than playing more overall.

- There is little skill involved in winning a slot tournament (other than quickly pressing a button), but tournaments for video poker, blackjack, and poker require an understanding of basic strategies and also money-management tactics. Choices that would be optimal in cash games might be incorrect in tournament situations.

- Poker tournaments are not comped as frequently as other gambling tournaments, but entries are often given away as promotions.

- It's best to be aggressive early in a poker tournament. The worst strategy is to hang on meekly as the clock ticks away and the blinds wear you down. Don't be reckless, but push the envelope early, and then you can be selective with a big stack.

- If a tournament is free, then go for it. But if it costs money, then you should compare the long-term value of the tournament vs. the long-term value of playing for cash. In many cases, the tournament will be a better value. But ultimately, you should play the game that you prefer.

CHAPTER 24

The Casino Business

 When you bet money on a hand of blackjack, push a bill into a slot machine, or buy into a game of poker, you're not just trying to beat the game. You're also making a judgment about the venue.

Essentially you're saying, "This is a place I trust. I understand and accept the rules of this casino."

This decision should not be made lightly. Many people think gambling is like buying milk at the convenience store. They expect the product is safe and the same on every corner. But in fact, milk in Pittsburgh is different from milk in Paducah, and the difference is even greater in Panama or Pakistan. Likewise, gambling is *not* a uniform product in the United States. And the diversity increases internationally and on the Internet.

The games may *seem* to be the same, but the product "in the carton" may be an unexpected surprise.

So this chapter is about the casino business. How it works in your state, in the United States, on Indian reservations, on the Internet, on the high seas, and in other places.

The States are the Bosses

The government of the United States regulates casinos in the following areas:

- The federal government plays a role in the negotiations between Indian casinos and the states, and it is the final authority on what is allowed to occur on an Indian reservation.

- The United States does not allow Internet casinos to operate within its borders (more on this later in the chapter).

- The U.S. Treasury Department monitors and establishes monetary regulations for businesses that handle large amounts of cash. This includes casinos.

But when it comes to actual operational regulations (games to be offered, and so forth), the U.S. government mostly defers to the individual states.

Thus the most important aspects of a casino's character are dictated by the state in which it operates. Casinos and the corporations that own them may seem powerful, but it is politicians who have the ultimate say about what games are offered and how they are presented. Why can't you find a dice game in California? Ask the legislature. Why can't video poker machines in Atlantic City pay back more than 99.9 percent? Ask the legislature. Why are all Tunica casinos on barges? Ask the legislature. Every state has its own ideas about how casinos should operate. The state makes the rules and the casinos follow them. End of discussion.

THE FACT IS...

Any new game or change in an existing game, no matter how minor, must be approved by state regulators. Nevada slots are tested in a lab and then go through field tests of at least 180 days. Slot machines in New Jersey are tested in high-speed simulations to assure their payback percentages will be consistent over a period of at least six years.

What happens if a casino breaks the rules? Penalties start with fines and can escalate into a total closure. It happens, but not very often because casino owners are even more concerned about following the rules than the regulators. They want to continue earning money.

So if you want to play craps in California, don't ask the casino. Write a letter to your local legislator.

What Happened to the Mob?

Once upon a time, organized crime dominated the casino industry. Notorious mobsters such a Ben "Bugsy" Siegel and Meyer Lansky were the sort of people who owned or ran most of the gambling operations in the United States. That was then. These days the casino business is squeaky clean. The turnaround is due to a number of factors which can't be easily described in a few paragraphs without oversimplification (entire books have been written on the subject), but with that caveat here is what happened.

Before 1900, casinos in the U.S. were relatively small operations. Basically they were clubs that were loosely regulated or unregulated, much like bars and other small businesses at that time. Gambling was legal in some places, illegal in others, and enforcement was fairly lax. Generally, you could find a game just about anywhere.

Sometimes the game was honest; sometimes it wasn't. Back then, you didn't ask too many questions because everyone was packing heat. You either played your hand, or you found a better game.

Then in the early twentieth century, a spirit of prohibition swept the land. Alcohol prohibition was inserted into the U.S. Constitution. Gambling prohibition came at about the same time. Casinos didn't get the federal treatment, but nonetheless, almost all forms of gambling were outlawed throughout the U.S. (including Nevada) via state prohibitions.

As history has taught us so many times, prohibition stimulates organized crime. In this case, mobsters got into the casino business about the same time they got into the liquor business.

By the time Nevada legalized gambling in 1931, all the best and brightest casino-industry "experts" were mob-connected criminals. Some of these people were absolutely awful human beings, but many of them were otherwise upstanding people who wanted to work in the gambling business, and they didn't want to earn a living doing anything else. Thus they made a choice (for better or worse) to live on the wrong side of the law.

In the following decades these "entrepreneurs" (the good ones and the bad ones) left their legal hassles in other states and moved to Las Vegas where they could operate openly. Ben Siegel and the Flamingo are examples of this period in gambling history.

The Mob owners often skimmed profits to avoid income taxes, but otherwise, the operations were generally law-abiding. Las Vegas was officially neutral territory, so there were no gang

> *"They were great bosses. I miss that loyalty, that respect. I don't say I respect how they got the money. It's none of my business anyway. That was for Elliot Ness to handle. [pauses] No one ever got killed that wasn't supposed to."*
>
> **Debbie Reynolds, in the documentary *The Real Las Vegas* (1996)**

Tip

wars or bloody killings. If someone had a vendetta, he would wait until his victim left town and then "whack" him elsewhere.

This situation persisted until the 1960s, when a change in Nevada law allowed corporations to buy casinos.

Organized crime sold out, mostly to Howard Hughes, because they couldn't compete with the infinitely larger bank accounts of organized business. Mobsters and crime syndicates apparently aren't as rich as Hilton and Harrah's.

Improved state regulations encouraged the Mob exodus.

Doing business with suitcases full of cash gradually gave way to shareholders meetings and annual reports.

So in the end it was a combination of a lack of capital and an inhospitable legal environment that drove organized crime out of Las Vegas. These days the regulations are tougher than ever.

New Jersey learned a lesson from Nevada's struggles. The regulatory system that the New Jersey legislature established for Atlantic City has produced an industry that can only be characterized as super-squeaky clean. Extensive background checks are required for anyone who works in a casino from a janitor to the president. Gambling regulators are on site at every casino at all times, and New Jersey's game-approval process is certainly the nation's toughest. That's why you won't see the big six and big eight on Atlantic City craps tables.

Other states have followed Nevada's and New Jersey's examples. Corporations run the casinos, and the states supervise them. Organized crime has no room to operate. Disorganized crime is another issue. Graft and cheating happen, though they are not widespread (see page 401).

A Casino's Corporate Structure

A casino is created by a person who has a vision. Sometimes it's an individual with a high profile like Steve Wynn or Donald Trump, but just as often it's someone like Bob Stupak, Ed Fishman, or Jack Binion. Who are they? Lesser known casino entrepreneurs, but visionaries nonetheless.

Famous or otherwise, the person sees slots and tables where there is currently asphalt or an empty field. These individuals become the proverbial bee in the bonnet. Bankers and boards eventually throw up their hands and shout, "Okay! Okay! You can have the money!" And so the casino is built.

Casino Executives

The visionary sees a giant tower or a gleaming building of gold, but it is casino executives who make these visions function on a practical level.

A casino's upper hierarchy is pretty standard. It starts with a president who supervises vice-presidents. Each VP is in charge of operations, marketing, finance, or another vital area. The VP of casino operations will be over a casino manager who in turn will supervise shift managers. The highest person you will likely encounter in normal dealings will be a **pit boss** (the newfangled term is "pit supervisor") or a **slot supervisor** who reports to a shift manager.

Pit Boss and Floorpeople

A **pit** is a collection of tables arranged in a loop, and though there may be many people who seem to have authority in the pit there is only one pit boss. That person's responsibility is to ensure that the games are conducted according to casino procedures and that transactions such as refilling a table with chips or providing a marker are properly handled.

THE FACT IS...

The term pit boss is a holdover from the early days of casinos when owners actually worked the floor. The person running the pit really was a boss, a Mob boss. As the casinos expanded and the big bosses moved upstairs, the new person in the pit was designated the "pit boss."

Floorpeople assist the pit boss. They monitor the change and chip requests, handle markers, rate players for comps, and generally supervise the games.

Dealers

Dealers make the games go. They handle the cards, spin the balls, and move the chips. They are trained in security procedures and usually spend weeks (sometimes months) learning how to properly deal each game.

Nevertheless, they generally know little or nothing about the inner workings of the games from a strategic point of view.

For example, the average blackjack dealer knows basic strategy and how to spot a card counter, but he generally doesn't know strategy variations for **H17** versus **S17**. He knows that a 3:2 natural in blackjack is better for a player than a 6:5 natural, but the dealer probably cannot tell you the value of the extra payoff (1.37 percent).

Dealers aren't stupid, but they often are not particularly involved in the game. They watch people win and lose all day long, so your contest is nothing special. If they do care, they usually are rooting for you to win because you might give them a tip. Besides getting tips, the dealer's main concern is following procedures to avoid a rebuke from the pit.

Tip

Dealers don't control the games in any way that allows them to determine the outcome (unless they're cheating). So if a game is properly dealt, and you lose, it is not the dealer's fault. On the other hand, you shouldn't stay at a table if a game is poorly dealt. Mistakes and misunderstandings can cost you money. If you have a bad dealer, find another table or go to another casino.

Slot Supervisors, Attendants, and Technicians

Slots have their own hierarchy. A slot attendant is the first person you'll encounter if you have a question or problem with a machine. Slot supervisors (the slot equivalent of a pit boss) are over the attendants. The machines are repaired by slot technicians. None of these people has any control over how often a slot pays. Most attendants don't even know how a slot works. The average slot attendant thinks RNG is the minimum level of vitamins you should have every day.

Their biggest concern is security and hospitality. They rarely have a clue as to where the loose slots are, but they'll be happy to direct you to the last few machines that have hit big jackpots.

Gambling Jurisdictions

Nevada held the casino monopoly in the United States for nearly half a century until Atlantic City came along in 1978. For another decade it was only Nevada or Atlantic City, but a boom in legalized gambling swept the nation in the 1990s and now almost every state either has casinos or is adjacent to a state that does. You can choose a riverboat, a barge, an Indian reservation, a cruise ship, the Boardwalk, the Strip, and so forth. If you're connected to the Internet you can gamble in a virtual casino and never leave home.

Where is the best place to play? Every jurisdiction has obvious advantages and most have some not-so-obvious disadvantages.

Las Vegas

It's the big enchilada, the granddaddy, the city where gambling was defined. People come from all over the world to take their shot in this desert town.

Clark County (where Las Vegas is located) has some of the loosest slots on the planet. Ditto for high-payback video poker, blackjack, and just about any other gambling game.

But you must choose carefully. Las Vegas is also filled with a lot of bad deals and unfavorable rules. For example, some games on the Strip rival eastern casinos in their overall tightness. The best games usually can be found at properties that are on the north end of the Strip, downtown, on the Boulder Strip, or in North Las Vegas.

On your way to those games you will be distracted by castles, palaces, a pyramid, a pirate ship, a replica of the Eiffel Tower, strip shows, miles of neon, wacky museums, chic clubs, and so much more. It's all a beguiling plan to draw you in and get you to bet money on less favorable games. Being seduced was never so much fun!

Las Vegas is mythic and beautiful, wild and crazy, and deservedly the standard by which all other gambling venues are judged. It ain't perfect, but it is certainly the best.

Atlantic City

Atlantic City is not wild and crazy. Rather, it is charming and inviting. It is a town with incredible pedigree.

People were vacationing in Atlantic City long before Las Vegas had indoor plumbing. Back in the nineteenth century Atlantic City attracted famous visitors such as President Ulysses S. Grant, H. J. Heinz (of ketchup and pickle fame), millionaire Diamond Jim Brady, and inventor Thomas A. Edison.

This is the town that inspired the board game Monopoly. All those names you remember from childhood, like Baltic Avenue and St. James Place, are real streets in Atlantic City.

It is the place that invented words such as "boardwalk" and "postcard."

The rolling chairs are romantic. The White House subs are delicious. The taffy is legendary.

The gambling is just okay. The slots are tight compared to those in Nevada. There are no 100 percent-plus video poker machines. Most blackjack games are six- or eight-deck behemoths. Ironically, roulette and craps are slightly easier to beat because of rules imposed by the state (surrender in roulette, and no big 6/8 in craps).

Speaking of rules, Atlantic City is probably the most regulated gambling jurisdiction in the world. So it takes a while for the newest slot games from Nevada to make it through the gauntlet and onto the floors in New Jersey.

Another thing to remember about Atlantic City is it attracts a somewhat older crowd. The town hosts a steady stream of day-tripping retirees who arrive in an endless line of buses.

Of course, there are young people who visit Atlantic City, too. The ultra-hip Borgata opened in 2003,

THE FACT IS...

Nearly 40 million people visit Las Vegas every year. The average stay is four days. The average bankroll is $627. About 60 percent of LV visitors play slots; 18 percent play blackjack; 10 percent play video poker. Most people play two to three hours per day.

and that has spawned a vigorous competition among the other casinos to draw younger customers.

Nevertheless, in 2005, the *average* age of a visitor in Atlantic City was fifty-two; in Las Vegas it was forty-seven.

AC ain't wild and crazy. But it is classy and delightful. Monikers like Caesars, Hilton, and Trump announce to the world that Atlantic City knows how to entertain visitors.

Connecticut

Foxwoods and Mohegan Sun are the largest and second-largest casinos in

Tip

Here are some fun local-style things to do in Atlantic City when you're not gambling. **1.** Take a ride on the Boardwalk in a rolling chair. **2.** Walk barefoot on the beach. **3.** Buy some taffy from James' Candy Company or Fralinger's. Mmmmmm! **4.** Visit Steel Pier. **5.** Get a sandwich from White House Sub Shop.

the world, respectively. The phrase "in a class by themselves" certainly applies to these properties.

Both are located in the southeast corner of Connecticut, so they're roughly the same distance from New York as Atlantic City (but in the opposite direction), and they compete to some degree with the New Jersey casinos. But where Atlantic City casinos charm and impress visitors, Foxwoods and Mohegan Sun astound them.

Where to begin? Besides the sheer size (each is two to three times the size of most Strip casinos in Las Vegas), both properties excel in services and amenities. The finest suits, the finest restaurants, you name it, and they have it.

Foxwoods is a bit more traditional in presentations and architecture while Mohegan Sun is an explosion of art and design. In fact, when the super-stylish Borgata was built in Atlantic City, one Mohegan Sun executive sniffed, "Clearly, they copied us."

Unfortunately, the games in Connecticut aren't quite as amazing as the venues. Both casinos have the full complement of contests that you would expect at world-class properties, but they're comparable in tightness to Atlantic City, perhaps just a tad looser.

Both properties are on Indian reservations. More about that in the next section.

Indian Casinos

We first touched on the subject of Indian casinos in Chapter 18. Essentially, Indian casinos are located on sovereign lands mostly beyond state control. But U.S. law gives states some oversight regarding the games that Indian casinos can offer (see page 313 for a complete description of this arrangement).

What this means for you is that some Indian casinos have all the games you can find in Las Vegas or Atlantic City, but other Indian casinos are restricted by their states to offering only particular games. For example:

- Traditional roulette is not allowed in California, neither is craps, but all card games and slots *are* allowed.

- In Minnesota, reel-spinning slots, roulette, craps, and baccarat are not allowed. But video slots and blackjack *are* permitted.

- Arizona prohibits roulette, craps, and baccarat, but it permits all forms of slots and blackjack.

Another thing to consider is that Indian casinos are often in faraway places. This is the unfortunate result of politics from past generations. Getting to an Indian casino sometimes requires a long trip via car or bus.

And these remote locations add yet another unfortunate element to the mix. Games at Indian casinos tend to be tight. Who can blame the casino managers? They have a captive audience. Things would be different if the competition was across the street.

Nevertheless, when an Indian casino is the only game within 300 miles, most players are not inclined to complain. They're just happy to be playing.

Besides Foxwoods and Mohegan Sun, there are plenty of top-rated Indian casinos in America. Some of the better properties are listed in the adjacent table. All of these casinos placed first, second, or third in two

THE FACT IS...

Indian casinos are regulated at three levels. Each casino is regulated internally by a tribal gaming commission. There is also a state gaming commission, and all tribes are regulated nationally by the National Indian Gaming Commission (NIGC), a federal agency.

or more categories in the 2006 Best of Gaming survey conducted by *Casino Player* magazine.

Best Indian Casinos 2006

Barona Valley Ranch	California
Foxwoods	Connecticut
Golden Moon	Mississippi
Grand Casino Hinckley	Minnesota
Harrah's Prairie Band	Kansas
Harrah's Rincon	California
Ho-Chunk	Wisconsin
Mohegan Sun	Connecticut
Mystic Lake	Minnesota
Oneida	Wisconsin
Pala	California
Paragon	Louisiana
Pechanga	California
Seminole Hard Rock—Hollywood	Florida
Seminole Hard Rock—Tampa	Florida
Seneca Niagra	New York
Silver Star	Mississippi
Soaring Eagle	Michigan

Indian casinos that were ranked highly in more than one category in the 2006 Best of Gaming survey conducted by *Casino Player* magazine.

Lake Tahoe

If there's a place on earth that qualifies as being nearly heaven, it's probably the area around Lake Tahoe. The lake sits on the border of Nevada and California where the state line takes a sharp turn to the southeast. Lake Tahoe is a natural draw for players who want time at the tables interspersed with visions of beautiful vistas and recreations such as skiing and hiking.

Properties with familiar names like Harrah's and Hyatt can be found on the shores of the lake, but the jewel

Tip

Reno and Lake Tahoe are close to each other (about forty-five minutes by car), so if you visit one you really should try to see the other. Both places are a charming counterpoint to their louder and gaudier cousin to the south.

of Lake Tahoe for many people is the Cal-Neva Resort and Casino on Crystal Bay. Frank Sinatra once owned Cal-Neva, and Marilyn Monroe frequently stayed there. Some people say she and John F. Kennedy used Cal-Neva as a rendezvous, but that's probably not true. What is true is that mobster Sam Giancana stayed at the resort once, and it cost Frank Sinatra his gaming license. Giancana was on Nevada's "List of Excluded Persons" (popularly called the Black Book), thus Frank was a bad boy for hosting him. The punishment was that Nevada regulators forced Sinatra to sell out.

In any case, the Rat Pack worked and played in Las Vegas, and Lake Tahoe was where they went to really get away.

Reno

The great thing about Reno is that the games are essentially identical to what you can get in Las Vegas (including sportsbooks), but the rooms tend to be less expensive and the paybacks are sometimes higher because…well…it ain't Las Vegas.

Reno is wonderful and delightful in its own unique way. Of course, there is the legendary Peppermill (a must-see if you go to Reno). There is a "gambling mall," which covers six city blocksand contains the casinos Eldorado, Silver Legacy, and Circus Circus. And the city has many other fine properties, including Reno Hilton and Harrah's.

Besides gambling, Reno is great if you like outdoor activities. It is northeast of Lake Tahoe (about forty-five minutes by car) and the area offers plenty of golfing, camping, hiking, biking, skiing, and other outdoor diversions.

Laughlin

In 1966, at about the time Caesars Palace was opening in Las Vegas, Don Laughlin opened the Riverside Resort Hotel and Casino in… well the place didn't have a name yet, but people generally called the area South Pointe because it was at the southern tip of Nevada, about a hundred miles south of Las Vegas. Laughlin's new "resort" had eight rooms (four of which were occupied by Laughlin's family), twelve slot machines, and two gaming tables. The U.S. Postal Service needed to give the location a name so that Don could get his mail. The casino entrepreneur suggested they name the place Riverside because his "resort" was on the Colorado River just north of the Arizona border. The postal inspector chose the name Laughlin instead.

These days Laughlin (the mail location) has ten casinos, 11,000 hotel rooms, and it hosts about 4 millions visitors every year. Of course, that's a drop in the bucket compared to Las Vegas, but the town prides itself on being a relaxed and inexpensive alternative to the Neon Oasis. Laughlin offers things that visitors can't get in Las Vegas such as the Colorado River, Katherine Mine, and of course, Don Laughlin's Riverside Resort. It now has 1,400 rooms and 800 RV spaces.

No togas or Roman columns, but Laughlin, Nevada can be a fun place to play.

The Heartland

Besides the jurisdictions mentioned previously, casinos can be found in many other places.

Some of these gambling markets are quite popular. For example, the casinos near Chicago (in Illinois and Indiana) are riverboat operations, but their combined income makes Chicago the third most profitable casino market in the U.S. after Las Vegas and Atlantic City.

Likewise, Mississippi has some excellent casinos in Tunica, Vicksburg, and the Gulf Coast. You can gamble in Detroit, Kansas City, Council Bluffs, and dozens of other burgs.

Great towns, all of 'em, but each state imposes its own quirky restrictions on gambling.

Sometimes the incoveniences are minor (from a player's perspective). For example, the casino area may be restricted to a riverboat or a barge. Or the casino may not have a hotel. Other times, the restrictions can be a hassle.

THE FACT IS...

Wild Bill Hickok was shot and killed while playing poker in Deadwood, South Dakota. His hand was two pairs, aces and eights (now popularly known at the "Dead Man's Hand"). The place where Bill played his last hand is Old Style Saloon #10, and it is still in business. The saloon offers poker, blackjack, and slots. And it sells souvenirs. What would Bill have thought about T-shirts and baby clothing emblazoned with #10 logos?

- In Missouri, you're not allowed to lose more than $500 in two hours, and there is an elaborate system in place to enforce this rule. The system is kind of endearing (in an irritating way). The legislators of the Show-Me state must have been saying to themselves, "Who in his right mind would want to lose more than $500 in two hours?"

- Colorado casinos limit bets to $5, and they don't offer games such as roulette and craps. Perhaps those legislators were talking to the ones in Missouri.

- Slots in West Virginia are prohibited from paying back more than 95 percent (most WV slots pay back around 92 percent).

- In Louisiana, a casino cannot be larger than 30,000 square feet.

And so on in casinos, racinos, and on riverboats across the nation.

Generally, the games fall somewhere on a spectrum between Nevada-loose and New Jersey-tight (see page 52 for information about slot paybacks in particular jurisdictions). As I mentioned before, local competition plays a big role. Some properties that are in very competitive markets have extremely high paybacks.

The good thing about all of these places is that they're regulated to standards which are comparable to those governing Nevada and New Jersey. In other words, the games are honest and there is a legal system established for settling disputes between customers and casinos. This is absolutely the case in every regulated casino in the United States.

Unfortunately, things change when you cross international borders.

Cruise Ships

Cruise ships are not riverboats. The games are not regulated by individual states or the United States. They're conducted in international waters and the only authority is the cruise ship company. The rules and payouts are whatever the company decides they will be. You can't double down except on 10 or 11? Too bad. Craps only has 2× odds? Too bad. The slots are tight? Too bad.

Not all cruise ships have unfavorable games. Players are savvier these days than they were twenty years ago, and the cruise companies know this. Nevertheless, a lack of competition and a captive audience are hardly incentives to offer contests with a low house edge. Many people who cruise are just thrilled to be gambling.

If your choice is no gambling at all, or gambling on a cruise, then go ahead and try the cruise. You might be lucky and find a loose game or soft table. If not, limit your bets to the minimum, or skip the casino and enjoy the buffet and the fresh sea breezes.

Don't blow your bankroll on the high seas.

Tip

Don't expect to gamble immediately once you're onboard a cruise ship. The boat must cruise to international waters before the games can begin.

The Internet

Gambling on the Internet embodies a classic yin-yang gambling choice.

On the upside, gambling on the Internet is the perfect gambling convenience. No need to get dressed up and drive a gazillion miles. You can be online in less than a minute and play in your pajamas.

Wait! It gets better! Low overhead on the Internet allows casinos to offer player-favorable rules that are rarely found in traditional brick-and-mortar operations. Generally, the games in the virtual world are far superior to what you find in the physical world.

And the choices! Oh, the choices! If Casino Z doesn't suit your taste, you can switch action to Casino Y with a click of the mouse. If Casino Y doesn't suit your taste, you have hundreds of other choices instantly available.

It's all so wonderful!

But unfortunately, it's illegal in the United States.

Very illegal.

Various federal and state statutes prohibit gambling online. Most of these laws are aimed at casino operators, so that's why you haven't seen stories about FBI teams arresting people who are playing blackjack in their underwear. Placing a bet online is a "gray-area" activity, not necessarily illegal in some states, but definitely against the law in others. Ditto for Internet casino advertising. Confusing? Yup, it's clear as fog.

Should you gamble online? That's a personal decision. First you should check the laws of your state.

Then you must find a reputable casino.

Online gaming is a multi-billion dollar industry, and about half of that money comes from the Unites States.

So clearly, most Internet casinos play and pay fairly. But you can't expect an honest game everywhere. It takes some research to separate trustworthy operators from scammers.

Think of it like buying a DVD player from a stranger at a yard sale in another city. Will you be cheated? Probably not, but there are no guarantees. "You pays yer money, and you takes yer chances."

Most Internet casinos *are* licensed and regulated in the countries where they physically reside, but that is cold comfort if you have a dispute about a payment. Your state's attorney general doesn't have much influence in Costa Rica.

Ideally, Internet gambling should be regulated. But so far, the U.S. Congress has been adamantly opposed to anything except prohibition (and we know where prohibition gets us).

Will Internet gambling ever be legal in the United States? Surely, someday. When? Nobody knows. It took fourteen years for alcohol prohibition to be repealed.

In the meantime, play carefully and don't break any laws.

THE FACT IS...

At least nine states have laws that specifically prohibit Internet gambling or financial transactions related to Internet gambling. These include Illinois, Indiana, Louisiana, Massachusetts, Nevada, Oregon, South Dakota, Utah, and Washington. Other states that have issued legal opinions saying that their laws prohibit Internet gambling include Texas, Florida, Oklahoma, Minnesota, Kansas, New Jersey, and Wisconsin.

International Gambling

Gambling rules and regulation in the Caribbean, the United Kingdom, Europe, and the rest of the world can vary considerably. Some places are fair and friendly, some aren't. And let's face it; if you suspect cheating or you disagree with a particular decision, you're probably not going to complain to the local constabulary.

So you should treat casinos outside the U.S. as you would casinos on a cruise ship. Use the strategies we covered in previous chapters to evaluate the games, and stay away from contests that are unfamiliar or too tough.

Casino Cheating

You'll recall in Chapter 20 I mentioned that the lure of money is everywhere in a casino. In that chapter we covered surveillance, safety, and casino rules. We touched on various aspects of cheating in Chapters 9 and 11. But here we're going to jump right into the dark side of the subject.

First, a few questions about your favorite casino:

Is it unregulated? To get into this casino, do you knock at a door and give a secret password? Do large muscular men pat you down for weapons before you're allowed to play? If you answer yes to the above questions, then it's possible you may be cheated at this casino.

On the other hand, if you're playing in a public casino in Las Vegas, Atlantic City, in another U.S. municipality, or in a country that has a well-regulated casino industry (such as the United Kingdom or Monaco), then the chances of you being cheated are slim.

Regulated casinos have little incentive to cheat their customers. The casinos have a built-in advantage, so they would rather follow the rules and not kill the golden goose by running afoul of the law.

As a result, most casino cheating involves scams *against* the house. These are schemes perpetrated by players or dealers. A casino is a big, rich target, much more attractive to cheaters than an individual player.

Dealer Scams

When dealers leave a table they clap their hands and then turn them palms up. The fingers are spread to show the cameras that no chips are concealed.

That is just one example of the how casinos are fanatical about preventing theft. Here is what they fear:

Palming Chips: Crooked dealers will hide chips in shoes, in shirts, under belts, in the mouth. It might be uncomfortable but at $100 a pop it's a lucrative scam.

Relay: The dealer conceals a chip and a confederate in the pit moves it out. The dealer appears clean.

Overpaying: This is done with one or a series of player confederates at an otherwise empty table. The player bets four chips and gets paid five when he wins.

Stacking the Deck: This is done with a player confederate. The dealer shuffles the deck, and the player just happens to have a hot run. Wow! What luck!

Player Cheats

Here are some examples of why a seemingly innocent move (such as touching chips that are in play or dropping a card) may create a furor in the pit.

Past Posting: Cheaters have a variety of techniques for increasing a bet after the contest is decided. Five chips can suddenly become six. That is why dealers and pit people will become very unpleasant if you have any contact with your bet after a decision has been rendered.

Switching dice or cards: It takes less than a second to switch out a pair of dice. Cards are a bit more complicated; that takes about two seconds. So dealers want the implements of the game in clear sight at all times.

Marking cards: One popular trick is to "peg" cards with a ring that has a tiny sharp stud on it. It leaves a little hole on the back of the card that can only be seen if you're really looking for it. That's why many blackjack games are dealt face up and players are not allowed to touch the cards.

Bet Claiming: This is a craps scam that occurs at a busy table. The thief claims a bet placed by a

THE FACT IS...

Slot claim-jumping is one particularly nasty player scam that has become obsolete because of the advent of video cameras. Two or three confederates would wait for someone to win a large jackpot. One of the scammers would push the player aside and claim the pot. The others would corroborate the thief's lie.

player who has six or seven bets out. The sucker probably won't miss that one wager. If the thief is challenged, a confederate backs the false claim.

The Consequences of Cheating

Do the casinos ever take cheaters "for a ride?"

Bodily harm inflicted upon casino thieves is a thing of the past, but these days casinos do something almost as damaging. First, they call law enforcement, and the person is arrested and prosecuted.

During this process, the casino takes the thief's picture, collects as much identifying information as it can about that person, and then shares the information with other casinos via various databases. A person listed in these databases can never again work in a casino or gamble in a normal way. That person can never again check into a casino hotel, join a slot club, or receive a comp using his or her real name.

Tough stuff, but it's done to ensure the integrity of the game.

State regulators, casino staff, surveillance, security, and outside companies are all working together (and watching each other) so that everyone stays honest.

Essentially

- The individual states and the federal government are the ultimate authorities about what games are allowed in a casino and how those games will be presented.

- Once upon a time, organized crime dominated the casino industry. This is no longer the case. Modern regulations insure that organized crime cannot operate in the casino business.

- Dealers don't control the game in any way that allows them to determine the outcome. So if a game is properly dealt, and you lose, it is not the dealer's fault.

- Every gambling jurisdiction has advantages and disadvantages. You should consider these differences when you choose where to play.

- Various federal and state statutes prohibit gambling online. If you decide to gamble online, you should check the laws of your state to be sure the activity is legal. Also, you should research casinos where you may play to be sure the businesses are reputable.

- Regulated casinos have no incentive to cheat their customers. Most cheating in casinos is by players or dealers at the expense of the house. Dealers or players who are caught cheating in casinos are arrested and prosecuted. Happily, most games are honest.

CHAPTER 25

Gambling Systems

 You'll love this. It's one of the cool tricks of the universe.

In any series of bets that pay 1:1, if you double up after losing a bet (1, 2, 4, 8, and so forth), then one win anywhere in the series wipes out all previous losses. Plus it nets one unit, the value of the base bet.

For instance, consider this sequence: lose-lose-win. The results are −1, −2, and +4. The net profit is 1. Pretty nifty, huh? It works with *any* pattern of losses and wins. Any pattern!

The system is called the **martingale**. But before you rush out to try it in a casino, you should read the rest of this chapter because the martingale can be very dangerous. Ditto for other gambling systems when they are used improperly.

What is a gambling system?

Strictly speaking, a system is synonymous with a strategy. But in the jargon of the casino world, the word "system" implies a strategy that doesn't work.

This is somewhat unfair because (as you can see) the martingale *does* work. It just doesn't work as everyone might hope that it would. I'll explain why in the next section.

In any case, the martingale is a type of system called a **progression**. It is method of systematically raising and lowering bets based on previous results.

Positive progressions raise bets after wins, and **negative progressions** raise bets after losses. In the next few pages we'll explore various progressions.

The Martingale

Nobody knows who invented the martingale. The first person to write about it was Giacomo Girolamo Casanova. He was a famous lothario who gambled and slept his way across Europe in the eighteenth century. We know about his exploits because he

> *"For four hours we gave ourselves up to every kind of pleasure... After the last assault she asked me, in return for her kindness, to spend three more days at Aix. 'I promise you,' I said, 'to stay here as long as you continue giving me such marks of your love as you have given me this morning.'"*
>
> **Giacomo Girolamo Casanova (1725–1798), from his autobiography *The Story of My Life***

meticulously recorded everything for his autobiography, *The Story of My Life*.

Casanova used the martingale in 1754 to win (and later lose) a small fortune. He wrote…

"M.M. [my lover] asked me to take some money, go to her casino, and play in financial partnership with her. I did so. I took all the gold I found and played the martingale, doubling my stakes continuously, and I won every day during the remainder of the Carnival. I was fortunate enough never to lose the sixth card. If I had lost it, I should have been without money to play, for I had two thousand sequins on that card."

Casanova was playing faro, a game with a very low house edge. Of course, the martingale doesn't erase the house edge. It only squeezes the risk into a tiny but powerful possibility. So Casanova's fall was inevitable. It took a few months, but eventually he reported…

"I still played on the martingale, but with such bad luck that I was soon left without a sequin. As I shared my property with M.M., I was obliged to tell her of my losses, and it was at her request that I sold all her diamonds, losing what I got for them; she had now only five hundred sequins by her. There was no more talk of her escaping from the convent, for we had nothing to live on! I still gamed, but for small stakes, waiting for the slow return of good luck."

Don't feel too bad for Casanova. A few years later he helped establish France's state lottery. That made him quite wealthy, but of course, he lost it all again a couple years after that.

So why can't the martingale beat the house edge? Let's find out.

Deconstructing the Martingale

The martingale is a negative-progression gambling system (it raises bets after losses), and it is typically used when bets pay 1:1, as in roulette, baccarat, or craps. As Casanova reports, the player wagers one unit after every win, and doubles the wager after every loss until a win. The result is always a one-unit profit, assuming the series ends with a win. And that's the problem; there is no guarantee that consecutive losses won't bunch up. Consider the progression in the adjacent table.

The Martingale

Bet #1	Wager = 10	Net If Win = 10	Net If Loss = −10
Bet #2	Wager = 20	Net If Win = 10	Net If Loss = −30
Bet #3	Wager = 40	Net If Win = 10	Net If Loss = −70
Bet #4	Wager = 80	Net If Win = 10	Net If Loss = −150
Bet #5	Wager = 160	Net If Win = 10	Net If Loss = −310
Bet #6	Wager = 320	Net If Win = 10	Net If Loss = −630
Bet #7	Wager = 640	Net If Win = 10	Net If Loss = −1,270

When playing the martingale, the bettor wagers one unit after every win, and doubles the wager after every loss until a win.

What is the probability of seeing seven consecutive losses? It's 1 in 128 on a coin-flip-style 50/50 proposition. The true odds are worse when playing casino games that pay 1:1 (roulette, baccarat, craps, blackjack). For example, the odds of seven consecutive craps or baccarat losses are about 1 in 116. Roulette is about 1 in 89. That happens about once every couple of hours.

The probability of "hitting the wall" and losing $1,270 is always greater than the probability of winning $1,270 in the interim to cover the loss.

Thus the martingale is always a long-term loser against a negative-expectation game. It's unavoidable.

Tip

If you want to experiment with the martingale, be sure to use a closed-end progression (drop back to the minimum after five or six levels even if you lose). Let's say your session bankroll is $315. Your base bet should be $5. That will work to six levels. If the first bet is $1, you can go to six levels with only $63. You will win somewhere in six levels about **98 percent** of the time.

But What If...?

But what if you extend the martingale to eight steps or ten or twenty? At some point, you surely will get a win. Right? Nobody loses twenty consecutive times.

Alas, yes. Some people do. The odds of losing twenty consecutive roulette bets are 1 in 393,560. It seems unlikely, but eventually it happens. Or more accurately, it would happen if a casino were to allow you to make that bet. In the real world, table limits prevent large progressions. Most games have limits such as $10 to $2,000, $5 to $5,000, $25 to $10,000, or something like that.

And even without table limits, the martingale cannot consistently beat a negative-expectation game. Why? It's simple...

Progressions are NOT predictive.

Bets go up and down for no particular reason. The "decisions" in a progression are random because they are following a random pattern. These random decisions are *not* tied to the probability of winning.

Let's use blackjack as an example. The count might be –5 (very unfavorable), and a progression still might have you pressing the limit.

You'll recall the Gambler's Fallacy that we covered in Chapter 1. Past results do not necessarily predict the future. In most gambling games, losing five times in a row tells you nothing about what will happen on the sixth trial.

As a result, there is no long-term advantage to using a progression.

On the other hand, there is no long-term disadvantage either. Aside from putting more money on the table, the net effect is zero. Ironically, that means the martingale is an absolute winner when used on a positive-expectation game.

Either way, a progression simply magnifies good luck at the expense of mediocre luck. How lucky will you be? Flip a coin.

A Closed-End Progression

In all fairness, there is nothing "wrong" with using the martingale. Essentially, it's a **contract bet**. In a seven-step martingale, the gambler risks $1,270 against the casino's $10 that seven consecutive losses *won't* occur.

The bet will win $10 about 99 percent of the time when the game is blackjack, roulette, baccarat, or craps.

The danger in using the negative progression is that the bettor won't be prepared for that one-percent catastrophe of losing $1,270. But if he chooses to play it as a **closed-end progression**, and he sets an absolute limit to the number of steps he will risk, then the martingale loses most of its menace.

Labouchere

This is also called the "cancellation system." The bettor begins with an arbitrary set of numbers (example: 1–2–3–4–5), the sum of which is the win-goal. The first bet is the sum of the outside numbers (5 + 1). If that bet wins, the 5 and 1 are crossed off and the next bet is 4 + 2. Losing bets are added to the end of the sequence, so if 4 + 2 loses, the 6 goes to the end of the list and the next bet is 6 + 2. Labouchere works wonderfully if the ratio of losses to wins does not exceed 2:1. But of course, anything can happen in the short term. Four losses, a win, and then four more losses aren't at all remarkable, but that would cost a bettor seventy-two units!

The system is named after Henry Labouchere, who was a member of Britain's House of Commons in the nineteenth century. Even though the gambling system bears his name, Labouchere credited it to Marquis de Condorcet, an eighteenth-century French mathematician who was also a politician and social scientist (see the sidebar on this page).

D'Alembert

This is a nifty little system in which the gambler increases the bet by one unit after every loss and decreases by one unit after every win. It works well on a **choppy table** (alternating wins and losses), and it's mathematically guaranteed to produce a winning session when the wins and losses are

THE FACT IS...

Condorcet discovered a statistical "paradox" that is still studied and discussed in political circles to this day. Condorcet proved that when a majority of voters prefers option A over option B, and a majority prefers option B over option C, it is still possible (indeed likely) for option C to win over option A. How many times have you scratched your head and wondered, "Who the heck voted for this imbecile?" Well, now you can thank Condorcet for providing the answer.

nearly equal. Unfortunately, there's no mathematic rule that says losing streaks must eventually be cancelled by winning streaks.

This is especially true when casino games pay 1:1 or better because the house must have an advantage in win-frequency to earn a profit. In other words, there are some losses that will never be cancelled by wins, and the absolute number of those losses increases as the number of trials increases. As Homer Simpson would say, "Doh!"

THE FACT IS...

Jean Le Rond d'Alembert was an eighteenth-century French mathematician who was good at math, but bad at making accurate physical observations. For example, d'Alembert correctly understood that when flipping a coin twice, the frequency of seeing heads is 0, 1, or 2. But he incorrectly assigned an equal probability to each outcome (33.3 percent). Of course, there is actually a 50 percent chance of seeing heads once, and a 50 percent chance of seeing heads twice or zero times.

Fibonacci

In 1202, a mathematician named Leonardo Pisano (nicknamed Fibonacci) wrote, "A man put a pair of rabbits in a place surrounded on all sides by a wall. How many pairs of rabbits can be produced from that pair in a year if it is supposed that every month each pair begets a new pair which from the second month on becomes productive?"

The resulting sequence revolutionized mathematics and has challenged gamers ever since. It is 1–1–2–3–5–8–13–21–34... Every number is the sum of the previous two. It's a bit like d'Alembert crossed with martingale. The bettor steps up to the next level with every loss and drops down one level after a win. The series ends with two consecutive wins. The bettor will always finish at least one unit ahead, unless of course a long and nasty string of losses nukes the bankroll.

In fairness to Fibonacci, he never said his series would shift the house edge when playing gambling games. His influence on the world of gaming (and mathematics in general) was much more profound. Fibonacci was instrumental in introducing Arabic numerals to the Western world. Without him, blackjack dealers would stand on XVIII, and roulette's top number would be XXXVI. Very cumbersome for the felt.

Positive Progressions

The idea behind positive progressions is that you should bet more when you're winning and less when you're losing. It sounds logical. Unfortunately, it's difficult to say when someone is "winning." We can only accurately say when someone "has won." Thus positive progressions work well in some situations, but not so well in others.

The chart below shows a side-by-side example of flat-betting compared to a positive progression. In this example we have two players, Sid System and Fred Flatbet. Sid uses a 1–2–3–4–5 positive progression; he increases the bet by one unit after every win, and then falls back to a single unit (the first level of the progression) after a loss.

The system does very well on streaks, but notice how it loses money on a choppy table. Fred Flatbet doesn't do nearly as well during the hot streak, but he doesn't lose when the cards go choppy. Keep in mind that this particular sequence has a streak at the beginning that happens to favor Sid, but it's just as likely for the table to produce a long choppy sequence more favorable to Fred.

Positive Progression vs. Flat Betting

Decision	Flat Bet	Flat Bet Net Win	System Bet	System Net Win
W	1	1	1	1
W	1	2	2	3
W	1	3	3	6
W	1	4	4	10
W	1	5	5	15
L	1	4	6	9
W	1	5	1	10
L	1	4	2	8
W	1	5	1	9
L	1	4	2	7
W	1	5	1	8
L	1	4	2	6
L	1	3	1	5
L	1	2	1	4
L	1	1	1	3

Fred is flat-betting single units. Sid is using a 1–2–3–4–5 positive progression, increasing the bet by one unit after every win, and then falling back to a single unit (the first level of the progression) after a loss.

Tip

Here are some other popular positive progressions: 1–1–2–3–4–5, 2–1–2–3–5–8, 2–1–1–2–3–4, 2–1–2–3–4–5, 2–2–3–3–4–5.

All of the above progressions solve the problem of an extremely choppy table, and in fact, the sequences that begin with 2–1 actually *win* one unit after every two decisions when the table goes choppy. Unfortunately, they're all vulnerable to other patterns such as two wins and two losses. There is no such thing as a perfect progression. Every progression has a weakness somewhere.

Of course, the problem with all of these systems (and with all progressions, both negative and positive) is those darned losses. They're entirely unanticipated because progressive-betting systems are completely disconnected from the actual probability of winning or losing. Bets are going up and down for reasons that have nothing to with a change in the odds. In contrast, systems like blackjack basic strategy, blackjack card counting, hold 'em poker strategy, Caribbean Stud strategy, and so forth raise bets when the probability of winning goes up, and they lower bets (or stop them) when winning becomes unlikely. What a concept!

So if you choose to experiment with progressions, remember that there is only one system that really works. It's called BWAE (betting with an edge), also known as the Miracle Bet. More about that in the next chapter.

Essentially

- A progression is a method of systematically raising and lowering bets based on previous results. Positive progressions raise bets after wins, and negative progressions raise bets after losses.

- Progressions can be fun to use, but they don't change the house edge. Progressions are not predictive; bets go up and down without any connection to the probability of winning.

- Positive progressions are generally safer to use than negative progressions because it is safer to raise bets after wins. Also, positive progressions tend to be less stressful on the bettor. It is psychologically tough to keep pushing out bigger amounts after losses.

- If you decide to use a negative progression it should have a closed-end. You should set an absolute limit to the number of steps you will risk, and think of the progression as a contract bet.

- The best betting system is betting with an edge.

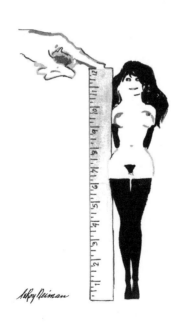

CHAPTER 26

The Miracle Bet

Is there a perfect gambling strategy? Yes. I call it the Miracle Bet.

It applies to all gambling games, poker, blackjack, slots, roulette, golf, bowling, curling, any contest.

Here is a story that demonstrates the strategy (and explains the name).

A few years ago I went to a music performance and afterwards attended a party at a Hollywood landmark called Cat & Fiddle.

At some point during the evening I was standing in a packedroom behind a woman whose throaty laugh was intoxicating. She turned to retrieve a drink on the bar behind me and, well…I fell in love immediately. Imagine Cyndi Lauper at twenty-five (with blonde hair and fewer bracelets). As she reached for the drink, she wrapped her arms around me and gently bit my ear. Yikes! I was a total stranger!

Two seconds later I learned that her name was Miracle. She was a bartender by profession, and a free spirit by nature. She made the most wonderful key lime martinis. After the party we drove around Hollywood. It was like I had been sucked into a Bob Seger song.

This should have been a clue that heartache was ahead. I'll tell you about that later, but first let me tell you about the Miracle bet.

The Gambler Learns New Odds

One night Miracle and I were sitting in Denny's. It's the only restaurant open in Hermosa Beach at 3 a.m. Miracle loved eggs, hash browns, and other breakfast stuff at odd hours. Me, too.

So there we were. I was besotted with affection, and also in a good mood because I had just returned from a splendid poker session at the Bicycle Casino.

Behind the booth where we were sitting, there was an arcade game, the kind with the hanging claw and the stuffed toys. Miracle gave me a devilish grin and asked for a dollar. I rolled my eyes. The game was a sucker bet. I'd seen someone win something with the claw maybe once in my life, after having spent like $50.

But Miracle insisted, so I gave her $3. Each attempt cost $0.50.

To my surprise, she pulled a stuffed animal out of the machine in four tries. The toy was a Cookie Monster. Without taking her eyes off the machine (she was still manipulating the claw) she motioned for more dollars. I handed her five. Two more stuffed toys came out, Bert and Ernie. Another $4 brought a Big Bird. She finally stopped when our food came. I'd spent about $12, and we had about $25 worth of stuffed toys.

Miracle had beaten the machine. Wow! She had an edge on a game that I thought was a sucker bet. She was a gambling goddess! If there had been a notary in Denny's that night, I would have married Miracle on the spot.

Sadly, that was not in the cards. We were like a straight-flush draw that goes bust, or a double down that brings a deuce. We sort of clicked at the beginning, and then everything faded. Maybe I gave up too easily. I dunno. I sure do miss her.

She made an awesome key lime martini.

The Bet You Can Win

Miracle demonstrated the most fundamental and important gambling strategy of all. It is the ultimate betting system, and it works!

What's the best bet in a casino? It's the bet you can win. That might be poker, craps, slots, roulette, or something else. It depends on the game, and on you. The key to winning in gambling games (and also in life) is to find your unique edge and then use it. Everything is situational. People who think that one particular system or strategy is always absolutely "better" than another have never seen a Miracle bet.

So I'm sitting here writing these last few words. I just got back from a poker session where I won an enormous pot with **Q4** offsuit because nobody bothered to raise my big blind. The flop brought me two pairs, and a full house came on the river. That was my edge and I used it.

While I was racking my chips, I was thinking of Miracle. We've entirely lost touch. She's moved, and I don't have her new contact info. There's no way for me to find her (short of using one of those creepy Internet background search services). Maybe I'll see her at Cat & Fiddle some night. If I do, then I'll tell her thank you, from the bottom of my heart.

Additional Tools for Winning

As the saying goes, practice makes perfect. Part of your gambling skill will develop from simply playing. But there is another important part that gambling professionals refer to as "thinking about the game when you're away from the game." The thinking process involves reading books such as this, and it also involves staying up to date on the latest developments in the world of gambling.

Here is a web resource that you'll find helpful: www.SmarterBet.com

This site has supplemental information for *Playboy Guide to Casino Gambling, Playboy Guide to Playing Poker at Home,* and all the *Smarter Bet Guides.* You'll find essays here about gambling strategies for blackjack, poker, video poker, slots, and other gambling games. The site also has links so you can ask me questions.

Now you have all the tools that you need to be a winner.

Enjoy the game!

Essentially

- The best bet in a casino is the bet you can win. Always look for situations where you can have an edge.

- Thinking about the game when you're away from the game is the best way to stay sharp and improve your strategies.

- Enjoy the game!

Glossary

action (1) Dollars wagered; more dollars is synonymous with more action. (2) A player's turn to act.

advantage player A person who uses strategy to gain a mathematic advantage over an opponent.

all in Betting all of one's chips.

ante In poker, a minimum bet placed into the pot that allows a player to be dealt into the hand. In Caribbean Stud Poker and Three Card Poker, the initial bet that allows a player to receive cards.

back hand A player's five-card hand in a game of pai gow poker.

back off Used as a verb. These are casino actions that discourage a blackjack card counter. They include frequent shuffling, no table service, and no comps.

backroom Used as a verb. This is a casino tactic to humiliate and frighten people who count cards. Casino security personnel take the player to a behind-the-scenes security area and treat the person like a suspected criminal (taking photographs, asking for identification, and so forth).

bad beat An improbable loss.

bank (1) A person or entity who provides financial backing for a gambling game. Most gambling games are banked by a casino, but some games (such as poker) are banked by players. (2) The shoe in a baccarat game.

banking game *See* **progressive**.

bankroll An amount of money set aside specifically for gambling.

bar the 12 A craps term that indicates which number is a push for a don't bettor on a come-out roll. Some casinos bar the 2 instead of the 12.

base unit or **base bet** The amount of the lowest bet in a betting system. For example, if a betting system begins at $1 and progresses to $5, the base bet is $1.

basic strategy A set of optimal choices for various playing situations. The term is most commonly used in blackjack, but any game strategy that is optimal and has been reduced to a series of if-then decisions can be considered a basic strategy.

betting progression *See* **progression.**

bias An imbalance or flaw in a roulette wheel or other gambling instrument.

big cards Face cards and aces.

big red Craps slang for seven.

big six/big eight Two sucker bets in craps that are identical in risk to place six or place eight, but only pay even money. Big six and big eight are not allowed in Atlantic City casinos.

blank A card that has no effect on a hand; it does not help or hurt.

blind bet A mandatory bet in Texas hold 'em and other poker flop games. The two players to the left of the designated dealer post blind bets before receiving cards.

board (1) The poker table. (2) Community cards that are dealt face-up in the center of a poker table.

bonus multiplier A game that adds a bonus to the top prize when a player wagers maximum credits.

box cars Craps slang for double sixes.

boxperson The person who supervises a craps game.

bring-in A mandatory first-round opening bet in seven-card stud. The bring-in is made by the player with the lowest exposed card.

buffalo A combination bet in craps that includes the four hardways and seven (or sometimes eleven).

burn To remove a card from the top of the deck without putting it into play. Burning one or more cards is a procedure to discourage cheating.

bust An automatic loss in blackjack that occurs when the value of a player's hand goes over twenty-one.

button Also known as a puck or a buck. A button is a marker that identifies the designated dealer (not the casino dealer) in a flop game. The button moves one player to the left after each hand. *See* **designated dealer.**

buy bet A craps bet on a particular number. The buy bet wins if the number is rolled before seven. Buy bets are paid at true odds but the casino charges a 5 percent vig on the amount wagered.

buy-a-pay A slot game that allows a player to buy an opportunity to hit additional winning combinations. In other words, three bars are worth 50 credits and three sevens are worth nothing if you wager $1, but $2 will "activate" the sevens, and they are worth 100 credits if they hit.

buy-in To exchange money for chips or credits.

C&E Craps slang for craps and eleven.

cage The bank-like area of the casino where money transactions are conducted.

call bet (1) To match a previous bet in poker. (2) A verbal bet in any gambling game. (3) A combination bet in roulette. The player verbally requests the bet and provides the chips; the placement of the chips is handled by the dealer. (4) A required bet in Caribbean Stud Poker when a player decides to not fold.

calling station A player who calls too much in poker.

cap A limit to the number of raises in a round of poker.

card counting *See* **counting cards.**

cards speak A poker rule that requires winners be determined by the cards and not by verbal declarations.

cash out To exchange chips or credits for cash.

casino host A casino employee who administers the casino's frequent-players program. The host issues complimentary rewards.

casino-oriented A term used in the gaming industry to describe a person who plays regularly and strongly prefers one property. Casinos seek customers who are casino-oriented.

catch To select a winning keno number.

center bets *See* **proposition.**

chase To call with a second-best hand in poker.

chasing losses Betting an increased amount in an attempt to recoup a previous loss.

check (1) To offer no bet in a poker round when no player has bet previously in that round. A player who checks must call, raise, or fold if another player bets. (2) A casino chip.

check-raise In poker, to check and later raise an opponent's wager in the same round.

chip A money token used in a casino in lieu of cash.

chip tray The tray that sits in front of a dealer and holds the chips that are used by the dealer to pay bets.

choppy table A game that is producing alternating wins and losses with almost no net positive or negative results.

class II machines Gaming machines with video reels that play versions of bingo or lottery contests. Also called VLTs (video lottery terminals)

clocking a wheel A method of discovering bias in a roulette wheel.

color up Exchanging chips of a lower denomination for fewer chips with a higher value.

combination ticket A single keno ticket written for more than one wager.

come A craps wager that wins with a natural or a point, and loses with craps or a seven-out.

come out The first roll for a do or don't bet in craps.

community cards Cards that are dealt face-up and shared by all the players in a poker hand.

comp dollars Comps valued in dollar units that can be spent at a player's discretion.

comps Complimentary rewards such as free meals, free rooms, free shows, and travel reimbursements. A casino gives comps to players who are perceived to be casino-oriented.

connectors Two cards of adjacent rank.

continuous-shuffling machine or **CSM** A shuffling machine that immediately shuffles used cards back into the deck. Typically used in blackjack, a CSM reduces penetration to nearly zero, and it makes counting cards impossible.

contract bet A bet that requires multiple decisions or multiple trials to win.

copy A player hand that is identical to a banker hand in pai gow poker.

count down The process of counting the money in a poker pot to determine if everyone has contributed the proper amount.

countermeasures Casino tactics used to blunt the effects of various blackjack strategies. Countermeasures include using multiple decks, hitting soft seventeen, and CSMs.

counting cards Observing the cards that have been played in blackjack and using that information to predict what cards will subsequently be played. Card counting is legal but very unwelcome in most casinos. People who count cards sometimes are ejected or barred from further play.

craps (1) The name of a dice game. (2) A dice roll of 2, 3, or 12.

craps virgin A woman who is playing craps for the first time.

currency transaction report or **CTR** A U.S. Treasury Department form that a casino completes and files when a player's cash transactions exceed $10,000 in one twenty-four-hour period.

dead cards *See* **live cards.**

dealer (1) A casino employee who runs a gambling game.
(2) A designated position in poker that indicates the order of action.
See **designated dealer.**

dealer signature An unconscious habit exhibited by some roulette dealers of spinning the ball in a predictably consistent way.

designated dealer A rotating designation used to determine blind bets and the order of betting in Texas hold 'em and other poker flop games.

dice mechanic A cheat who manipulates dice in an unlawful way.

discard tray A tray holding cards that have been burned, mucked, or otherwise taken out of play.

do Any craps bet that wins with a natural or when a point is rolled.

don't Any craps bet that loses with a natural or when a point is rolled.

don't pass/don't come A craps wager that loses with a natural or a point, and wins with craps or a seven-out.

door card A player's first exposed card in a seven-card stud hand.

double down An additional bet during a hand of blackjack, usually an amount equal to a player's original wager. The dealer gives the player exactly one more card and that completes the hand. No additional hits are allowed. Doubling is usually restricted to first action on an original hand.

draw A poker term commonly used in video poker. To "draw" is to throw away cards and receive replacements in the hopes of improving a hand.

drawing dead Playing a poker hand that cannot win.

drawing hand A poker hand that is hoping to improve.

drop A casino industry term for the amount of money invested in the game when a player buys in. Typically, the bills are "dropped" into a locked box at the table.

drop box A fortified box placed under a table that is connected to a slot in the table surface. Dealers put cash (and sometimes chips) into the drop box. The box is periodically replaced and moved to the cage where the contents are removed.

en prison A roulette rule option offered in some casinos. In the U.S. (where the rule is known as surrender), 1:1 wagers that lose to zero or double-zero are only half-lost. In Europe, an even money wager that loses to zero or double-zero must remain on the table for an additional spin of the wheel. After the second spin, losing wagers are taken and winning wagers are returned.

envy bonus A bonus paid all the players at a table when one particular player wins a major jackpot.

eye in the sky Slang for casino surveillance systems.

field bet A craps bet that the next number rolled will NOT be 5, 6, 7 or 8.

first base The player seat to the blackjack dealer's far left. This position receives cards first and is first to hit or stand.

fixed-limit A poker game in which the bet limits are fixed at specific levels.

flat top A slot machine with a top prize that is fixed at a particular amount. *See* **progressive.**

floorperson A casino employee who assists a pit boss in managing a pit. A floorperson handles markers, rates players for comps, and generally supervises the games.

flop (1) The second round of betting in Texas hold 'em and other poker flop games. (2) The point at which three cards are revealed simultaneously during a flop game.

flop games Poker versions with five community cards and four rounds of betting.

fold In poker, declining to call and giving up any claim to the pot. In Caribbean Stud Poker and Three Card Poker, declining to call and forfeiting the ante.

foul To cause a poker hand to be invalid.

free card A card that comes "free" in a poker game because there was no betting in the previous round.

front hand A player's two-card hand in a game of pai gow poker.

gambler's fallacy Refers to the myth that past results affect the current contest.

game theory A scientific system for making decisions in competitive situations.

grind To play conservatively, the opposite of press.

gutshot straight draw To draw to an inside straight (a poker hand needing exactly one rank rather than one of two).

handle The total amount of money that is wagered in a game over a particular amount of time.

hand-pay A jackpot that is paid by a casino employee.

hard hand A blackjack hand of 12 or more that does not contain an ace, or it has an ace counted as one. Hard hands between 12 and 16 are also sometimes called stiff hands.

hard number or **hardway** A 4, 6, 8 or 10 rolled with both dice showing identical numbers. It is more difficult to roll 4, 6, 8 or 10 the hard way than the easy way (with two different numbers).

heads up A contest with only two players.

heat Scrutiny by casino personnel. Heat is directed toward blackjack card counters and it often results in a player being barred from the game, ejected, or backroomed.

heel To offset a stack of chips so that the bottom chip is off center and the stack slants to one side.

hit To request a card in blackjack.

hole card (1) The dealer's face-down card in blackjack. (2) Any face-down card.

hole cards The first two cards that are dealt face down in Texas hold 'em or seven-card stud.

hop bet Any craps bet determined by the next roll of the dice. *See* **proposition**.

horn A combined bet on 2, 3, 11, and 12 in craps.

house edge The financial advantage a casino has in a wager. House edge is usually expressed as a percentage. The term is loosely synonymous with vig. House edge is the inverse of payback.

house odds The amount a casino will pay for a winning bet. Not to be confused with true odds.

house way A casino's basic strategy for setting hands in pai gow poker.

implied odds The size of an expected payoff in poker compared to the size of the proposed bet. This measurement includes the supposed value of the hand if a draw is successful.

inside bets Roulette bets placed on the inside of the layout on a particular number or group of numbers.

inside numbers Points 5, 6, 8, and 9 in craps.

insurance A blackjack bet (typically one-half the value of an original bet) that is allowed when the dealer is showing an ace. The bet wins when the dealer's hand is a natural. Insurance pays 2:1.

jackpot A large prize.

jackpot reserve Money set aside by a casino to insure that jackpots can always be paid.

Kelly Criterion A mathematic system used to determine optimum bet size and/or bankroll size.

keno board A large electronic display posted in the keno lounge and duplicated on video screens throughout the casino. The keno board shows the numbers that catch for each game.

keno lounge The physical location of a casino's keno game.

keno runner A casino employee who picks up keno bets from players throughout the casino, shuttles the bets to the keno lounge, and (hopefully) returns with winning tickets.

kicker The highest unpaired card in a poker hand when that hand is not a straight or flush.

lay bet A craps bet *against* a particular number. The lay bet wins if seven is rolled before the number. Lay bets are paid at true odds but the casino charges a 5 percent vig on the winning amount.

lay odds (laying odds) (1) A side bet on a don't-pass or don't-come wager made after a point has been established. Odds bets are paid at true odds and have no house edge. (2) A money line sports bet on the team favored to win. Having the advantage requires the bettor to risk more to win less. Also known as giving odds.

layout The surface of a craps table where bets are placed.

limp in To call rather than raise the big blind in a poker game.

line (1) A sports betting handicap (often a point spread) used by a sports book to divide bettors into two equal groups. (1) The pass line in craps.

live cards Any cards that have not yet been exposed in seven-card stud.

live one A weak player.

locked down The status of a slot machine that has been taken out of service or otherwise reserved for a player who is taking a break.

loose (1) A game with a low house edge. (2) A player who is likely to bet or call in poker rather than fold.

loss-limit A fixed amount of allowable loss. A disciplined player stops gambling when losses reach the loss-limit. *See* **bankroll.**

marker A promise of payment to a casino. A marker is the legal equivalent of a check. It can be drawn against a player's checking account.

martingale A negative progression in which bets are doubled after each loss.

mini-baccarat A less ostentatious lower-limit version of American baccarat.

money line A sports book's line expressed as an amount required to lay odds or a payout for taking odds. A bet on the favored team requires the bettor to lay odds (risk more to win less). A bet on the underdog allows bettors to take odds (risk less to win more).

money management A system of sizing bets to maximize profits while minimizing risk. *See* **Kelly Criterion.**

muck (1) To throw away cards. (2) The area where cards are discarded.

multiplier A slot game that pays exact multiples of whatever amount is wagered.

natural (1) A perfect hand. (2) A two-card hand of a ten and an ace in blackjack, twenty-one. A blackjack natural will either win or be tied, but it cannot lose. (3) A dice roll of seven or eleven on the come-out in craps. (4) A hand that totals 8 or 9 in baccarat.

negative expectation Refers to a game that retains more money in the long run than it pays. Negative-expectation games have a house edge.

negative progression A system of increasing bets after losses.

no roll An invalid dice roll in craps, also sometimes referred to as "no dice."

no-limit A poker game in which there are no restrictions on the amount that can be bet.

nudge A slot game in which a winning symbol sometimes hits just above or below the payline, then clicks into position to create a paying combination.

nuts Cards that make an unbeatable hand.

odds (1) *See* **true odds.** (2) A side bet in craps made after a point has been established. Odds bets are paid at true odds and have no house edge.

off (1) A craps bet that is on the table but is not working. The dealers and player understand that the money is not at risk. (2) A puck position indicating the craps shooter is coming out.

off and on Being paid for one come bet in craps just as another has established a point.

on (1) A craps bet that is working. Refers to a wager on the table that is in play. (2) A puck position that indicates a craps shooter is trying to roll a point.

on tilt Playing badly or erratically. A bad mood that adversely affects judgment.

once-through A stop-loss system in which each dollar in a bankroll is risked exactly once.

one player to a hand A poker rule that requires each player to make decisions alone and without consultation.

optimal strategy A system of play that lowers or eliminates a casino's advantage.

outs Cards that will improve a poker hand.

outside bet Roulette bets made on groups of numbers on the outside of the layout.

outside numbers Points 4 and 10 in craps, sometimes including 5 and 9.

over/under A sports bet that the combined total of points scored by both teams will be over (or under) a specific total.

overcard In poker flop games, a personal card that has a higher rank than the cards on the board.

parlay (1) A sports bet on the outcome of a combination of games. All the chosen teams must win for the parlay bet to win. (2) To increasing winnings by making multiple winning bets.

pass To roll a natural in craps, or to roll a point before rolling seven.

past-posting Adding or removing chips from a bet after seeing a hand (this is cheating).

pat When a blackjack hand totals hard 17 or more. Pat hands should never be hit.

pay table The schedule posted on a slot machine that shows how much is paid for each winning combination.

payback The long-term financial return from a game, usually expressed as a ratio of action. Payback is the inverse of the house edge.

payline The line on a slot machine where the symbols must appear to indicate a win. Some slot machines have multiple paylines.

payoff The money returned on a winning bet.

payoff odds *See* **house odds.**

penetration The percentage of a deck dealt before a shuffle. In blackjack, penetration of less than 60 percent reduces the chance of profiting from counting cards.

pit The inside section formed by a circle of gaming tables. Casino personnel who work in the pit are supervised by a pit boss.

place bet Similar to a buy bet in craps, except that the casino takes the vig by lowering the payout rather than charging a percent of the wager.

players club A comp system that uses a card to track wagers. The casino rewards players on a scale according to their level of action.

pocket cards *See* **hole cards.**

pocket rockets Two aces in the pocket.

point In craps *after* a come-out, a number that must be rolled for a player to pass. Rolling the point causes pass-line bets to win and causes don't-pass bets to lose.

point-spread One form of a betting line (a sports betting handicap) used by a sports book to divide bettors into two equal groups.

position A player's seat in relation to the button in a poker game. Players in early positions act before those in later positions.

positive expectation Refers to a game that pays more in the long run than it takes. Positive expectation games have a player edge.

positive progression A system of pressing (increasing bets) after wins.

post To place a bet (typically refers to a blind bet in poker).

pot The combined bets of all the players in a poker game.

pot odds The size of a pot (or payoff) in poker compared to the size of the proposed bet. This is expressed as a ratio.

pot-limit A poker game in which any amount can be bet up to the amount in the pot.

press To increase bets after a win.

probability The likelihood of an event happening. Probability is expressed as a number between 0 and 1. An impossible event is 0 and an event that is certain to occur would be 1.

progression A system of raising and lowering bets. Positive progressions raise bets after wins, and negative progressions raise bets after losses.

progressive A slot machine jackpot (or other jackpot system) that gradually increases in value every time the game is played.

proposition (1) Any craps wager that can be decided with a single roll of the dice. One-roll bets in the center of the table are typically referred to as propositions. (2) Any single decision with two possible outcomes that is the subject of a wager.

protect your hand To handle cards in way that reduces the possibility of the hand being fouled.

puck A disk (white on one side and black on the other) that is used to indicate the current point in craps.

push A tie, the player doesn't win or lose.

put an opponent on a hand An accurate guess of what an opponent is holding.

put bet A pass-line bet made after the come-out.

quad Poker slang for four-of-a-kind.

qualify A dealer's hand that is playable in Caribbean Stud Poker or Three Card Poker.

rags A worthless poker hand. A combination of cards that are unlikely to improve.

rail (1) The top edge of a craps table. (1) The spectator's area in a poker game.

rainbow Three or four cards that are not of the same suit.

raise Matching a previous bet and then betting more in a poker game. A raise requires all the other players in the hand to either call, raise, or fold.

rake The money taken by a casino or card room for providing services to a poker game. A rake is usually collected as a percentage of the pot or as a flat fee.

random number generator (RNG) The heart of a slot machine. An RNG is a computer chip that randomly generates numbers to determine the exact reel position or specific cards that appear during a slot game.

rathole To stealthily slip chips off the table and into one's pockets. Players do this to make themselves look like losers and thereby pump up their comps ratings. Ratholing is not allowed in poker or in tournaments.

reel One of three or more wheels inside a slot machine that are visible through a window at the front of the device. The various winning symbols are printed on each reel.

reel-spinners Slot machine games that use physical reels (as opposed to video reels).

RFB A casino-industry abbreviation for "room, food, and beverages."

right Slang for betting the "do" or come in a craps game.

risk of ruin A measurement of the probability that a player's bankroll will be entirely lost, usually expressed as a ratio or a percent.

river The final round of betting in Texas hold 'em or seven-card stud.

rock An extremely conservative player.

rolling stop-loss A combination of a stop-loss and a win-limit that prevents a player from risking winnings beyond a particular dollar amount.

running count The exact number of extra tens and aces or extra small cards remaining in the deck during a blackjack game.

scared money Money needed for living expenses that is being used instead for gambling.

semi-bluff Betting or raising in poker with a weak hand when there is a good possibility that it can improve.

session A period of time designated for gambling.

set In poker, three-of-a-kind made with a pocket pair.

seven-out Rolling a seven while attempting to roll a point in craps. A seven-out causes pass-line bets to lose and don't-pass bets to win.

seventh street The final round of betting in seven-card stud.

shoe A container that holds one or more shuffled decks. Cards are dealt from a shoe when they are not dealt from a deck that is hand-held.

shooter The player who is throwing the dice in craps.

show one, show all A poker rule that allows everyone at the table to see a player's hand if one opponent sees that hand.

showdown The end of the last round of betting in a poker hand when all remaining players reveal their cards.

side pot An extra pot that is created from bets made after a player goes all in to the main pot.

slow-play To play a strong hand passively, representing it as weak in order to draw players into the pot.

snake eyes Craps slang for a dice-roll of 2.

soft hand Any blackjack hand that contains an ace counted as 11.

splashing the pot To throw chips into the center of the table rather than putting them in front of one's position.

split A blackjack move in which the player has an original hand with cards of equal rank (two eights, two aces, two nines, and so on), and the player creates two hands by making an additional wager. A second card is dealt to each hand, and the player can hit, double, split, or stand as necessary.

spot One number on a keno ticket.

spread-limit A poker game in which there is a fixed minimum and maximum bet, but a player can wager any amount between those two figures.

stand To refuse additional cards in blackjack. Stand is the opposite of hit.

steal the blinds Raising before the flop with a substandard poker hand in an attempt to get the blinds to fold.

stickperson The craps dealer who supervises the dice.

stiff A blackjack hand greater than 11 and less than 17 that doesn't contain an ace valued as 11.

stop A section of a slot machine's reel that is covered with a symbol, or in some cases intentionally left blank.

stop-loss A plan for exiting a game when a particular amount of money has been lost.

straight ticket A keno ticket written for one bet and one combination of numbers.

straight up A roulette bet on one number.

street bet A roulette bet on three adjacent numbers. The wager is placed at the end of the row.

string bet or **string raise** To call a bet in poker, and then raise after assessing an opponent's reaction. Not allowed in most poker games.

surrender (1) A blackjack rule that allows a player to retrieve half of the current bet and forfeit the rest. (2) A roulette rule that applies to bets that pay 1:1. If the bet loses to zero or double zero, then the player loses only half his bet. *See* **en prison.**

table limits The betting limits established by a casino for a particular table game. Table limits include the minimum and maximum amounts that can be wagered on one bet. They also include the maximum payout allowed for one hand.

table stakes A poker rule that requires all players to wager with only the chips that are on the table at the beginning of the hand.

take a bet down Remove a bet from the layout.

take odds or **taking odds** (1) A side bet on a craps pass-line or come wager made after a point has been established. Odds bets are paid at true odds and have no house edge. (2) A money-line sports bet on the team expected to lose. Wagering on the underdog allows the bettor to risk less and possibly win more.

teaser A sports parlay with a point spread adjusted to be more favorable to the player. This results in a lower potential payoff.

tell A player's unconscious movement or body position that (when properly analyzed) can reveal what he is holding. Tells are used primarily in poker.

theoretical win The average amount the casino expects to earn from a customer. Theoretical win is calculated by multiplying the total action (total amount wagered) by the house edge.

third base The player seat to a blackjack dealer's far right. This position receives cards last and is last to hit or stand.

tight (1) A player who is averse to taking risks. (2) A game that pays back very little.

time A verbal request for a pause in the game.

toke Casino industry jargon for a tip (gratuity).

tower light A light on the top of a slot machine that indicates when the machine has malfunctioned or has registered a jackpot.

trips Poker slang for three-of-a-kind.

true count When counting cards in blackjack, the running count is divided by the number of decks that have not yet been played. The resulting number is the true count, a standard measure of overall advantage.

true odds The true probability of winning or losing a contest. Not to be confused with house odds.

turn The third round of betting (fourth community card) in a poker game.

under the gun The first player to act in a flop game.

upcard (1) A blackjack dealer's exposed card. (2) Any exposed card.

vigorish or **vig** A casino's edge. The word is used mostly in situations that involve a betting fee or commission charged by the casino.

virtual reels The theoretical reels that spin conceptually in a random number generator.

volatility The natural ebb and flow of the game, winning and losing that occurs irrespective of the edge.

way ticket A keno ticket that combines groups of numbers into multiple bets.

whale A high-limit player.

whirl A one-roll craps proposition bet that combines a horn bet with any seven.

wild card A card that can be used to represent any rank or suit.

win-limit A plan for exiting a game when a particular win goal has been reached. *See* **loss-limit.**

working bet In craps, a bet that is active or on. A wager that can win with a roll of the dice. *See* **on.**

wrong Craps slang for betting the don't.

yo Craps slang for eleven.

Index

casino loans, 332–333
for chips, 329–330
front money, 332
markers and, 331, 332, 333
Five-card draw poker. *See* Poker,
five-card draw
Four card poker. *See* Poker, four
card

G

Gamblers Anonymous, 32
Gambler's fallacy, 16–18
Gambling
advantage players in, 112
advising other players, 133
alcohol and, 31, 34
in Atlantic City, 392–393
card cutting, 134
in Chicago, 397
in Colorado, 398
coloring up, 130
for comps, 31–32
in Connecticut, 393
continuous-shuffling
machine, 134
on cruise ships, 398–399
dangerous, 30–32
dealer mistakes, 132
Indians and, 312–314, 393,
394–395
international, 400–401
Internet, 399–400
jurisdictions, 391–401
in Lake Tahoe, 395–396
in Las Vegas, 391–392
in Laughlin, 396–397

legal age for, 342, 343
legalization of, 387
limits, 31
in Louisiana, 398
in Mississippi, 397
in Missouri, 398
organized crime and,
386–388
past-posting, 131
in private casinos, 388
problem of points in, 11
prohibition, 387
in Reno, 396
riverboat, 397
with scared money, 31
shuffling procedures, 134
on sports, 317–325
state control over, 385–386
staying safe from scams,
333–334
strategy, 9, 12
systems, 405–413
taking a break in, 338, 339
taxes and, 307, 342,
351–353
on tilt, 30, 31
in West Virginia, 398
Game theory, 11, 12, 19
poker and, 184
Giancana, Sam, 396
Golden shooters, 174
Gombaud, Antoine, 9, 10

H

Hazard, 145, 146
Hickok, Wild Bill, 397

Q

Quartermania, 346

R

Random number generator, 42,
    43, 44, 45, 49, 62, 344,
    391
Ratholing, 361–363
Razz poker, 188. *See* Poker, razz
Red Dog, 291
Rhythmic rollers, 174
Roly-poly, 244
Roulette, 243–259, 273
    American, 244
    bankroll for, 258
    betting, 245–257
    bias in, 256
    Biribi, 244
    call bets, 248, 249
    clocking the wheel in,
        256–257
    closed-end progression,
        253–255
    combination bets, 251
    corner Bets, 247
    dealer signature in, 257–
    en prison, 248, 249, 254,
        256
    EO (even-odd), 244
    European, 244, 247–250
    game flow, 250
    game theory and, 12
    history of, 243–244
    house edge, 15, 243, 248,
        250, 254
    inside bets, 247, 250–251

    in Monte Carlo, 243, 244
    neighbor bets, 249–250
    Neighbors of Zero, 249
    number bets, 247
    One-Third of the Cylinder,
        249
    Orphelins a Cheval, 249
    Orphelins en Plein, 249
    outside bets, 247, 250–251
    parlay bets, 253
    payouts, 25
    randomness in, 243
    roly-poly, 244
    split bets, 247
    square bets, 247
    straight bets, 247, 251,
        252
    strategy for beating the
        wheel, 254–257
    street bets, 247
    surrender, 248, 254, 256
    table, 244, 245
    table limits in, 246
    Tiers du Cylindre, 249
    Voisins du Zero, 249
    wheel, 244, 245

S

Sartine, Gabriel de, 244
Scams, 333–334
Scared money, 31
Seven-card stud poker. *See* Poker,
    seven-card stud
Shimmy. *See* Chemin de fer
Shuffle Master, 279, 280
Sic Bo, 291

Notes

Notes